Contemporary Challenges for the Indian Banking Sector

Contemporary Challenges for the Indian Banking Sector

Editors

R.K. Mishra
S. Sreenivasa Murthy
J. Kiranmai

BLOOMSBURY
LONDON • NEW DELHI • NEW YORK • SYDNEY

First Published, 2013
First Reprint, 2013

BLOOMSBURY PUBLISHING INDIA PVT. LTD.
London New Delhi New York Sydney

ISBN: 978-93-82563-30-3

Published by Bloomsbury Publishing India Pvt. Ltd.
VISHRUT Building, DDA Complex, Building No. 3, Pocket C-6 & 7
Vasant Kunj, New Delhi 110 070

Laser Typeset by SHINU
A-5/56, Moti Nagar, New Delhi 110 015

Printed at Anvi Composers
1 DDA Market, Block A-1B, Pachim Vihar, New Delhi 110 063

Contents

Preface

The Indian Banking Sector has made commendable progress in the last decade which is evident from several parameters such as annual credit growth, profitability, reduction in gross Non-Performing Assets (NPAs) etc. Besides the overall favourable economic climate, banks have benefited from various measures and initiatives such as implementation of SARFAESI, establishment of credit information bureaus, improvements in technology and infrastructure, effective appraisal and monitoring systems, robust financial payment systems, suitable risk management framework etc. However, the Indian banking sector continues to face several challenges on account of deregulation of interest rates on saving deposits, tight monetary policy, enhanced stress in some sectors, such as state utilities, micro finance etc., increasing government deficits, restructured loan accounts, implementation of Basel III, down grading of banks by international credit rating agencies etc.

This book contains research articles on the various challenges faced by banks both in the public and private sectors, the need and ways of converting these challenges into opportunities. The contents of the book have been divided into three parts. Part I deals with challenges relating to credit, governance and performance. Part II deals with challenges relating to competition, technology and CRM. Part III deals with challenges relating to financial inclusion, HR and other issues.

Part I consisting of **Chapters 1 to 8** while discussing current practices, also deals with challenges faced by the Indian banking sector in terms of various issues such as asset-liability management, increasing role of foreign banks, fee-based income opportunities, foreign direct investment, performance analysis parameters etc. It also covers corporate governance reforms in public sector banks in India and regulatory compliance issues in Indian banking in the context of anti money laundering regulation.

Part II consisting of **Chapters 9 to 15** tries to focus on customer orientation in the Indian banking sector and the challenges relating to competition, technology and CRM. The important research contributions in this section includes an analytical study of banks' performance using the S-C-P approach, evaluation of quality of service of Indian banks, comparison of relationship marketing in public and private sector banks member satisfaction in urban co-operative banks, increasing role of CRM, utility of CRM index etc.

Part III consisting of **Chapters 16 to 24** highlight the growing importance of financial inclusion initiatives and micro finance. It covers strategies and challenges pertaining to it and other issues such as HR, forex reserves etc. This section includes research articles on financial inclusion strategies, an inter-state analysis of credit and deposit penetration in India, financial inclusion under NREGA, role of micro finance institutions as extended arms of banks, comparison of Indian public and private sector banks based on the banking service quality model. Impact of exchange rate on foreign exchange reserves of the Indian banking industry, need for a more positive HR orientation in public sector banks etc.

The book covers a broad spectrum of contemporary challenges and opportunities for the Indian banking sector and hence would certainly be an enriching source for banking and finance professionals, researchers, academicians and management students.

We take this opportunity to thank all the authors and acknowledge the help of the publication division and Review Committee in bringing out this section. We are thankful to all the members of Advisory Committee and Organising Committee for their valuable suggestions and guidance.

Ram Kumar Mishra
S. Sreenivasa Murthy
J. Kiranmai

PART–I

Challenges Relating to Credit, Governance and Performance

A Comparison of Asset-Liability Management in Public and Private Sector Banks in India

Mihir Dash, K.A. Venkatesh and B.D. Bhargav[1]

Quantitative Techniques School of Business, Alliance University, Bangalore

[1]Banking and Finance School of Business, Alliance University, Bangalore

ABSTRACT: *Asset-Liability Management (ALM) is concerned with strategic management of assets (uses of funds) and liabilities (sources of funds) of banks, against risks caused by changes in the liquidity position of the bank, interest rates, and exchange rates, and against credit risk and contingency risk. ALM has gained significance in the financial services sector in recent years due to the dramatic changes that have occurred in the post-liberalization period. There has been a vast shift in the borrowers' profile, the industry profile and the exposure limits for the same, interest rate structure for deposits and advances, and so on. This has been accompanied by increased volatility of markets, diversification of bank product profiles, and intensified competition between banks on a global scale, all adding to the risk exposure of banks. Thus, banks increasingly need to match the maturities of the assets and liabilities, balancing the objectives of profitability, liquidity, and risk. To this end, the Bank of International Settlements (BIS) has suggested a framework for the banks to tackle the market risks that may arise due to rate fluctuations and excessive credit risk. The Reserve Bank of India (RBI) has implemented the Basel II norms for the regulation of Indian banks, providing a framework for banks to develop ALM policies, and is in the process of implementing Basel III.*

The present study analyses asset-liability management in banks operating in India by determining the liquidity position of banks in India through maturity profiling. The primary objective of the study was to compare the maturity gaps in public and private banks in the Indian banking industry. The study was conducted on a sample of twenty-six public sector banks and twenty private sector banks operating in India. The data used for the study included the major financial details of the sample banks, collected from secondary sources of data, viz. the Capitaline database and the RBI website.

The findings of the study indicate that overall the public sector banks were very conservative in their liquidity risk management, and the private sector banks also had a comfortable short-term liquidity position. In particular, the private sector banks have managed their short-term liquidity better than the public sector banks, contributing to their higher overall profitability.

Keywords: Asset-Liability Management, Basel II, Basel III, Maturity Profiling, Public and Private Sector Banks.

INTRODUCTION

Asset-Liability Management (ALM) is concerned with strategic management of assets (uses of funds) and liabilities (sources of funds) of banks, against risks caused by changes in the liquidity position of the bank, interest rates, and exchange rates, and against credit risk and contingency risk.

ALM has gained significance in the financial services sector in recent years due to the dramatic changes that have occurred in the post-liberalization period. There has been a vast shift in the borrowers' profile, the industry profile and the exposure limits for the same, interest rate structure for deposits and advances, and so on. This has been accompanied by increased volatility of markets, diversification of bank product profiles, and intensified competition between banks on a global scale, all adding to the risk exposure of banks. Thus, banks increasingly need to match the maturities of the assets and liabilities, balancing the objectives of profitability, liquidity, and risk. To this end, the Bank of International Settlements (BIS) has suggested a framework for the banks to tackle the market risks that may arise due to rate fluctuations and excessive credit risk. The Reserve Bank of India (RBI) has implemented the Basel II norms for the regulation of Indian banks, providing a framework for banks to develop ALM policies.

At the macro-level, ALM leads to the formulation of critical business policies, efficient allocation of capital, and designing of products with appropriate pricing strategies, while at the micro-level, the objective of the ALM is two-fold: it aims at profitability through price matching while ensuring liquidity by means of maturity matching.

Price matching basically aims to maintain spreads by ensuring that the deployment of liabilities will be at a rate higher than the costs. Working towards this end, banks generally maintain profitability/spreads by borrowing short (lower costs) and lending long (higher yields). Though price matching can be done well within the risk/exposure levels set for rate fluctuations, it may, however, place the bank in a potentially illiquid position. Liquidity is ensured by grouping the assets/liabilities based on their maturing profiles. The gap is then assessed to identify the future financing requirements to ensure liquidity. The inter-linkage between the interest rate risk and the liquidity of the firm highlights the need for maturity matching. The underlying threat of this inter-linkage is that rate fluctuations may lead to defaults severely affecting the asset-liability position, and, in a highly volatile situation, it may lead to a liquidity crisis forcing the closure of the bank.

Thus, price matching should be coupled with proper maturity matching. However, maintaining profitability by matching prices and ensuring liquidity by matching the maturity levels is not an easy task; in fact they contradict each other to some extent because a spread is possible when a mismatch of maturity is taken up. Thus, a trade-off has to be maintained between profitability and liquidity. Banks generally aim to eliminate liquidity risk while managing interest rate risk. The differential approach is primarily based on the fact that elimination of interest rate risk is not profitable, while elimination of liquidity risk does result in long-term sustenance.

An effective ALM technique aims to manage the volume, mix, maturity, rate sensitivity, quality and liquidity of the assets and liabilities as a whole so as to attain a predetermined acceptable risk/reward ratio. The purpose of ALM is to enhance the asset quality, quantify the risks associated with the assets and liabilities and further manage them, in order to stabilize the short-term profits, the long-term earnings and the long-run sustenance of the bank.

LITERATURE REVIEW

There is a considerable literature addressing asset-liability management in banks. One of the key motivators of asset-liability management worldwide was the Basel Committee. The Basel Committee on Banking Supervision (2001) formulated broad supervisory standards and guidelines and recommended statements of best practice in banking supervision. The purpose of the committee was to encourage global convergence toward common approaches and standards. In particular, the Basel II norms (2004) were proposed as an international standard for the amount of capital that banks need to set aside to guard against the types financial and operational risks they face. Basel II proposed setting up rigorous risk and capital management requirements designed to ensure that a bank holds capital reserves appropriate to the risk the bank exposes itself to through its lending and investment practices. Generally speaking, these rules mean that the greater risk to which the bank is exposed, the greater the amount of capital the bank needs to hold to safeguard its solvency and overall economic stability. This would ultimately help protect the international financial system from the types of problems that might arise should a major bank or a series of banks collapse.

Gardner and Mills (1991) discussed the principles of asset-liability management as a part of banks' strategic planning and as a response to the changing environment in prudential supervision, e-commerce and new taxation treaties. Their text provided the foundation of subsequent discussion on asset-liability management.

Haslem *et al.* (1999) used canonical analysis and the interpretive framework of asset/liability management in order to identify and interpret the foreign and domestic balance sheet strategies of large U.S. banks in the context of the "crisis in lending to LDCs." Their study found that the least profitable very large banks have the largest proportions of foreign loans, yet they emphasize domestic balance sheet (asset/liability) matching strategies.

Conversely, the most profitable very large banks have the smallest proportions of foreign loans, but, nonetheless, they emphasize foreign balance sheet matching strategies.

Vaidyanathan (1999) discussed issues in asset-liability management and elaborates on various categories of risk that require to be managed in the Indian context. In the past Indian banks were primarily concerned about adhering to statutory liquidity ratio norms; but in the changed situation, namely moving away from administered interest rate structure to market determined rates, it became important for banks to equip themselves with some of these techniques, in order to immunize themselves against interest rate risk. Vaidyanathan argues that the problem gets accentuated in the context of change in the main liability structure of the banks, namely the maturity period for term deposits. For instance, in 1986, nearly 50% of term deposits had a maturity period of more than five years and only 20%, less than two years for all commercial banks, while in 1992, only 17% of term deposits were more than five years whereas 38% were less than two years (Vaidyanathan, 1995). He found that several banks had inadequate and inefficient management systems. Also, he argued that Indian banks were more exposed to international markets, especially with respect to FOREX transactions, so that asset-liability management was essential, as it would enable the bank to maintain its exposure to foreign currency fluctuations given the level of risk it can handle. He also found that an increasing proportion of investments by banks was being recorded on a marked-to-market basis, thus being exposed to market risks. He also suggested that, as bank profitability focus has increased over the years, there is an increasing possibility that the risk arising out of exposure to interest rate volatility would be built into the capital adequacy norms specified by the regulatory authorities, thus in turn requiring efficient asset-liability management practices.

Vaidya and Shahi (2001) studied asset-liability management in Indian banks. They suggested in particular that interest rate risk and liquidity risk are two key inputs in business planning process of banks.

Ranjan and Nallari (2004) used canonical analysis to examine asset-liability management in Indian banks in the period 1992–2004. They found that SBI and associates had the best asset-liability management in the period 1992–2004. They also found that, other than foreign banks, all other banks could be said to be liability-managed; i.e. they all borrowed from the money market to meet their maturing obligations. Private sector banks were found to be aggressive in profit generation, while nationalized banks were found to be excessively concerned about liquidity.

Dash and Pathak (2011) proposed a linear model for asset-liability assessment. They found that public sector banks have best asset-liability management positions, maintaining profitability, satisfying the liquidity constraints, and reducing interest rate risk exposure.

The present study analyses asset-liability management in banks operating in India using the asset-liability guidelines provided by the Reserve Bank of India.

DATA AND METHODOLOGY

The present study analyses asset-liability management in banks operating in India by determining the liquidity position of banks in India through maturity profiling. The study covered all scheduled commercial banks except regional rural banks (RRBs), for the year 2008–09. The banks were grouped on the basis of ownership structure: viz. public sector banks (including SBI and associates), private sector banks, and foreign banks. The primary objective of the study was to compare the maturity gaps in public, private and foreign banks in the Indian banking industry.

The study was conducted on a sample of twenty-six public sector banks, twenty private sector banks, and ten foreign banks operating in India. The data used for the study included the major financial details of the sample banks, collected from secondary sources of data, viz. the Capitaline database and the RBI website.

The study was conducted on the basis of the Asset-Liability Guidelines issued by RBI to individual banks. All the balance sheet items have to be distributed into time buckets as follows: 1–14 days; 15–28 days; 1–3 months; 3–6 months; 6–12 months; 1–2 years; 2–5 years; and 5+ years. Bank assets and liabilities were allocated into various maturity periods as per the guidelines issued by Reserve Bank of India. Key items like deposits and advances have been distributed into actual maturity period as per the details submitted by individual banks to RBI, where available. Other items have been distributed into different time frames in a fixed proportion, as suggested by RBI guidelines and demand profiles. The guidelines are reproduced below.

A. Outflows

Heads of Accounts	Classification into time buckets
1. Capital, Reserves and Surplus	Over 5 years bucket.
2. Demand Deposits (Current and Savings Bank Deposits)	Demand Deposits may be classified into volatile and core portions. 25% of deposits are generally withdrawable on demand. This portion may be treated as volatile. While volatile portion can be placed in the first time bucket i.e., 1-14 days, the core portion may be placed in 1 - 2 years bucket.
3. Term Deposits	Respective maturity buckets.
4. Certificates of Deposit, Borrowings and Bonds (including Sub-Ordinated Debt)	Respective maturity buckets.
5. Other Liabilities and Provisions	
(i) Bills Payable	(i) 1-14 days bucket.
(ii) Inter-office Adjustment	(ii) As per trend analysis. Items not representing cash payables, may be placed in over 5 years bucket.
(iii) Provisions for NPAs a) Sub-standard b) Doubtful and Loss	(iii) a) 2-5 years bucket. b) Over 5 years bucket.
(iv) Provisions for depreciation in investments	(iv) Over 5 years bucket.
(v) Provisions for NPAs in investments a) Sub-standard b) Doubtful and Loss	(v) a) 2-5 years bucket. b) Over 5 years bucket.
(vi) Provisions for other purposes	(vi) Respective buckets depending on the purpose.
(vii) Other Liabilities	(vii) Respective maturity buckets. Items not representing cash payables (i.e. income received in advances etc.) may be placed in over 5 years bucket.

B. Inflows

Heads of Accounts	Classification into time buckets
1. Cash	1-14 days bucket
2. Balances with RBI	While the excess balance over the required CRR/SLR may be shown under 1-14 days bucket, the Statutory Balances may be distributed amongst various time buckets corresponding to the maturity profile of DTL with a time-lag of 14 days.
3. Balances with other Banks	
(i) Current Account	(i) Non-withdrawable portion on account of stipulations of minimum balances may be shown under 1-2 years bucket and the remaining balances may be shown under 1-14 days bucket.
(ii) Money at Call and Short Notice, Term Deposits and other placements	(ii) Respective maturity buckets.
4. Investments	
(i) Approved securities	(i) Respective maturity buckets excluding the amount required to be reinvested to maintain SLR corresponding to the DTL profile in various time buckets.
(ii) Corporate debentures and bonds, PSU bonds, CDs and CPs, Redeemable preference Shares, Units of Mutual Funds (close ended), etc.	(ii) Respective maturity buckets. Investments classified as NPAs should be shown under 2-5 years bucket (sub-standard) or over 5 years bucket (doubtful and loss).
(iii) Shares / Units of Mutual Funds (open ended)	(iii) Over 5 years bucket.
(iv) Investments in Subsidiaries/Joint Ventures	(iv) Over 5 years bucket.
5. Advances (Performing)	
(i) Bills Purchased and Discounted (including bills under DUPN)	(i) Respective maturity buckets.
(ii) Cash Credit/Overdraft (including TOD) and Demand Loan component of Working Capital.	(ii) Banks should undertake a study of behavioural and seasonal pattern of availments based on outstandings and the core and volatile portion should be identified. While the volatile portion could be shown in the respective maturity buckets, the core portion may be shown under 1-2 years bucket.
(iii) Term Loans	(iii) Interim cash flows may be shown under respective maturity buckets.
6. NPAs	
(i) Sub-standard	(i) 2-5 years bucket.
(ii) Doubtful and Loss	(ii) Over 5 years bucket.
7. Fixed Assets	Over 5 years bucket
8. Other Assets	
(i) Inter-office Adjustment	(i) As per trend analysis. Intangible items or items not representing cash receivables may be shown in over 5 years bucket.
(ii) Others	(ii) Respective maturity buckets. Intangible assets and assets not representing cash receivables may be shown in over 5 years bucket.

From the maturity profile, the maturity gap was computed by subtracting total outflows from total inflows, giving the mismatch in the outflow and inflow in the particular time bucket. A positive maturity gap means that in the particular time bucket, the inflows are more than outflows, while a negative maturity gap means that in the particular time bucket, the inflows are lesser than outflows.

The maturity gap was expressed as a percentage of outflows to identify the severity of the gap. Also, the cumulative maturity gap was computed on the basis of maturity gap of the bank to give the position of the bank during the future period. The cumulative maturity gap is of immense help for any bank to identify the gaps for the next five years and arrange funds to manage it.

In particular, the time buckets 1–14 days and 15–28 days are indicators of short term liquidity position of the bank. As per the guidelines of Reserve Bank of India, the banks should take care that the maturity gap of the short term liquidity indicator does not cross 20% of the outflow of the respective buckets.

FINDINGS

The Table 1 shows the maturity gap position of the sample public sector banks in the different time buckets.

Table 1

(Rs. In crores)

Maturity Gap of Public Banks								
Bank	1 - 14 days	15 - 28 days	29 days to 3 months	3 - 6 months	6 -12 months	1 - 2 years	2 - 5 years	Over 5 years
Allahabad Bank	9,985.83	346.31	92.44	-3,623.67	-9,003.88	-14,854.28	4,178.80	12,878.45
Andhra Bank	3,783.96	-1,063.86	-398.32	-6,572.15	-9,137.71	-3,706.63	6,447.78	10,646.95
Bank of Baroda	8,818.69	-2,797.51	-442.46	-9,072.81	-22,833.88	9,346.54	17,318.73	-337.31
Bank of India	14,895.95	-5,854.14	5,236.13	-15,074.09	-13,018.22	2,600.87	6,303.82	4,909.70
Bank of Maharashtra	6,331.62	-124.87	-3,777.45	-3,172.16	-6,520.61	-6,775.29	5,112.78	8,925.98
Canara Bank	11,434.45	561.69	7,751.16	-10,841.94	-18,370.40	10,480.77	-12,184.63	11,168.92
Central Bank of India	14,969.79	-1,924.52	-3,492.42	5,104.69	-15,136.43	-15,643.48	2,805.95	13,369.06
Corporation Bank	9,416.78	386.84	5,361.79	-3,385.79	-5,270.28	7,337.42	-5,537.52	-8,309.24
Dena Bank	4,101.11	286.20	-1,853.57	-1,120.41	-3,125.58	-11,581.89	4,253.61	9,040.54
Indian Overseas Bank	8,068.14	-2,769.44	-1,481.33	-7,384.39	-7,247.30	-14,572.07	10,311.52	16,337.34
IDBI Bank Ltd.	5,195.85	-5,408.43	-13,559.41	-10,839.04	-38,320.17	8,924.54	15,053.00	39,189.25
Indian Bank	5,345.26	517.36	1,062.96	-4,021.31	-6,541.83	-360.23	7,359.70	-3,293.18
Oriental Bank of Commerce	12,393.18	356.35	-1,962.09	-12,338.21	-24,836.49	954.27	11,067.89	14,929.13
Punjab and Sind Bank	187.85	-341.77	-464.40	-83.33	-6,066.78	885.17	2,499.13	3,384.12
Punjab National Bank	16,928.84	374.16	-3,024.17	-9,326.45	-6,636.60	-12,544.22	29,294.78	-14,690.88
State Bank of Travancore	2,141.48	3,857.66	548.95	-146.75	-1,328.66	-4,635.12	3,508.29	9,123.08
State Bank of Bikaner and Jaipur	2,760.64	-124.42	-3,103.95	-1,044.87	-4,936.29	5,874.92	-156.94	730.90
State Bank of Hyderabad	12,431.56	-1,280.70	-1,638.01	-2,810.30	-5,541.18	3,222.71	8,210.92	-12,799.37
State Bank of India	85,876.77	-13,151.45	-9,865.03	-19,487.67	-81,564.35	96,671.73	12,007.00	-70,487.01
State Bank of Indore	2,143.08	-540.12	-798.03	-2,085.66	-2,141.74	2,667.85	3,529.89	-2,775.01
State Bank of Mysore	1,665.72	-429.62	-1,622.85	-830.04	-1,609.33	4,916.77	-903.41	-1,187.24
State Bank of Patiala	5,728.63	-899.34	-1,509.15	-6,954.63	-4,776.28	-9,055.44	7,965.94	9,426.02
Syndicate Bank	10,683.31	439.84	-5,731.63	-8,894.33	-18,375.58	-1,150.17	10,045.79	12,982.75
UCO Bank	7,426.45	-1,540.21	-1,703.83	-4,591.87	-17,391.75	920.51	10,949.97	5,930.72
Union Bank of India	10,616.70	1,599.23	-2,590.31	-635.96	-11,681.74	12,464.78	8,021.75	-17,525.25
Vijaya Bank	4,808.05	-667.79	-3,134.15	-6,324.35	-13,913.37	2,678.28	5,650.98	10,902.81

It was found that all the sample public sector banks had excess liquidity in the 1–14 days time bucket, especially so for the State Bank of India, which had an excess liquidity of ₹ 85,876.77 crores in the 1–14 days time bucket. Further, ten of the sample public sector banks had excess liquidity in the 15–28 days time bucket, and six of the sample public sector banks had excess liquidity in the 1–3 months time bucket. It was also found that all the sample public sector banks had liquidity deficiency in the 6–12 months time bucket, especially so for the State Bank of India, which had a liquidity deficiency of ₹ 81,564.35 crores in the 6–12 months time bucket. Further, it was found that nine of the sample public sector banks had liquidity deficiency in the 5+ years time bucket.

The Table 2 shows the maturity gap position of the sample private sector banks in the different time buckets.

Table 2

(Rs. In crores)

Maturity Gap of Private Banks								
Bank	1 - 14 days	15 - 28 days	29 days to 3 months	3 - 6 months	6 -12 months	1 - 2 years	2 - 5 years	Over 5 years
Axis Bank	7,578.02	730.36	-9,958.96	-6,352.60	-12,757.94	4,121.18	14,510.61	2,129.32
Bank of Rajasthan	1,190.27	314.06	-1,003.36	-835.35	-1,192.70	89.12	1,471.14	-33.18
Catholic Syrian Bank	585.54	85.84	-447.57	-382.17	-536.08	40.90	642.85	10.69
City Union Bank	497.56	38.99	-626.68	-454.03	-675.02	151.45	963.76	103.97
Development Credit Bank	351.68	28.54	-388.49	-218.42	-480.44	124.99	613.27	-31.13
Dhanalakshmi Bank	415.91	41.72	-368.58	-285.45	-413.41	81.93	550.30	-22.41
Federal Bank	1,969.67	377.50	-2,287.13	-1,660.87	-2,537.93	1,087.50	3,851.64	-800.38
HDFC Bank	9,300.85	639.19	-12,581.18	-6,621.46	-12,995.12	5,653.51	18,447.69	-1,843.46
ICICI Bank	11,065.40	-2,276.90	-27,020.41	-4,031.10	-29,699.12	19,254.74	43,930.09	-11,222.70
IndusInd Bank	725.06	22.46	-2,005.62	-993.47	-2,185.99	618.15	2,979.54	839.86
ING Vysya Bank	938.60	38.16	-2,348.24	-839.94	-2,433.06	767.42	3,528.07	348.99
Jammu & Kashmir Bank	3,168.16	379.96	-2,381.84	-2,122.16	-3,000.37	551.61	3,434.22	-29.57
Karnataka Bank	795.23	320.00	-1,367.63	-929.00	-1,486.60	476.99	2,260.28	-69.27
Karur Vysya Bank	723.51	103.25	-1,108.13	-818.79	-1,204.75	332.85	1,772.42	199.64
Kotak Mahindra Bank	19.39	-133.74	-1,965.47	-178.77	-2,170.48	1,727.32	3,335.26	-633.52
Lakshmi Vilas Bank	463.92	-6.17	-616.79	-439.94	-641.70	144.75	869.73	226.20
Ratnakar Bank	331.02	39.10	-69.60	-85.87	-112.37	12.31	130.85	-245.43
South Indian Bank	1,123.58	191.16	-1,296.07	-1,108.70	-1,551.00	335.32	1,946.83	358.86
Tamilnad Mercantile Bank	507.40	84.51	-681.41	-539.49	-743.24	277.40	1,089.73	5.08
Yes Bank	691.71	-25.04	-1,672.42	-532.13	-2,083.29	843.25	2,554.19	223.73

It was found that all the sample private sector banks had excess liquidity in the 1–14 days time bucket, and that all except for four of the sample private sector banks had excess liquidity in the 15–28 days time bucket. Further, it was also found that all the sample private sector banks had liquidity deficiency in the 1–3 months time bucket, especially so for ICICI bank, the largest private sector bank, which had a liquidity deficiency of ₹ 27,020.41 crores in the 1–3 months time bucket. Further, it was found that ten of the sample private sector banks had liquidity deficiency in the 5+ years time bucket.

The Table 3 shows the maturity gap position of the sample public sector banks in the different time buckets as a percentage of outflows.

Table 3

Maturity Gap as a % of Total Outflow of Public Banks								
Bank	1 - 14 days	15 - 28 days	29 days to 3 months	3 - 6 months	6 -12 months	1 - 2 years	2 - 5 years	Over 5 years
Allahabad Bank	186.99%	15.96%	1.74%	-33.79%	-63.36%	-40.34%	61.35%	79.18%
Andhra Bank	164.03%	-50.11%	-6.20%	-58.54%	-63.01%	-14.80%	550.56%	185.94%
Bank of Baroda	48.95%	-34.48%	-1.67%	-29.16%	-49.85%	24.43%	231.71%	-0.65%
Bank of India	63.66%	-46.87%	24.93%	-44.35%	-50.61%	9.77%	37.35%	7.46%
Bank of Maharashtra	272.58%	-9.16%	-61.72%	-50.21%	-66.24%	-26.27%	225.91%	177.71%
Canara Bank	62.56%	12.72%	61.95%	-45.51%	-43.52%	36.66%	-33.28%	20.99%
Central Bank of India	161.98%	-37.28%	-33.34%	91.83%	-67.11%	-27.17%	19.37%	60.14%
Corporation Bank	155.77%	17.58%	94.73%	-24.54%	-30.41%	86.64%	-35.71%	-46.38%
Dena Bank	196.67%	26.64%	-44.76%	-28.83%	-40.84%	-47.37%	342.21%	229.89%
Indian Overseas Bank	86.76%	-61.81%	-13.43%	-52.88%	-46.81%	-29.11%	407.72%	114.84%
IDBI Bank Ltd.	31.54%	-77.16%	-63.24%	-50.35%	-73.19%	31.72%	305.62%	191.63%
Indian Bank	130.44%	22.21%	16.54%	-39.20%	-39.13%	-1.39%	709.10%	-19.10%
Oriental Bank of Commerce	193.39%	8.59%	-21.04%	-59.54%	-73.51%	4.91%	349.15%	95.84%
Punjab and Sind Bank	5.14%	-22.53%	-7.82%	-2.13%	-68.98%	13.39%	116.62%	38.41%
Punjab National Bank	140.24%	5.93%	-20.58%	-40.20%	-22.95%	-14.24%	900.12%	-20.87%
State Bank of Travancore	239.13%	184.11%	14.87%	-2.04%	-14.55%	-47.92%	31.85%	213.15%
State Bank of Bikaner and Jaipur	141.05%	-11.06%	-68.28%	-24.89%	-62.40%	44.30%	-3.16%	8.60%
State Bank of Hyderabad	368.75%	-62.19%	-36.18%	-37.15%	-69.37%	15.01%	933.39%	-44.69%
State Bank of India	84.87%	-43.04%	-14.14%	-26.65%	-75.67%	51.13%	10.94%	-24.84%
State Bank of Indore	187.56%	-67.86%	-28.79%	-58.24%	-48.99%	26.79%	1245.57%	-27.29%
State Bank of Mysore	92.15%	-50.81%	-36.70%	-24.23%	-26.96%	54.63%	-16.34%	-12.48%
State Bank of Patiala	166.98%	-45.73%	-22.15%	-42.57%	-33.97%	-43.36%	1101.34%	192.33%
Syndicate Bank	100.60%	13.30%	-49.61%	-53.32%	-63.15%	-3.24%	279.73%	65.11%
UCO Bank	116.56%	-40.92%	-17.33%	-32.37%	-53.59%	7.11%	334.65%	20.34%
Union Bank of India	120.07%	56.71%	-20.51%	-4.40%	-37.94%	50.11%	108.79%	-29.43%
Vijaya Bank	137.60%	-30.93%	-46.95%	-66.14%	-78.84%	15.51%	585.91%	236.68%

It was found that all the sample public sector banks had excess liquidity in the 1–14 days time bucket. It was also found that fourteen of the sample public sector banks had liquidity deficiency in excess of 20% of total outflows in the 15–28 days time bucket. As per the RBI guidelines, the mismatch during the 1–14 days and 15–28 days time buckets should not in any case exceed 20% of the cash outflows in each time bucket. However, as they had a huge surplus (in excess of 100% of total outflows for eighteen of the sample public sector banks) in the previous time bucket, they may have a higher tolerance level in the 15–28 days time bucket.

Further, it was found that fourteen of the sample public sector banks had liquidity deficiency in excess of 20% of total outflows in the 1–3 months time bucket, and that all except for four of the sample public sector banks had liquidity deficiency in excess of 20% of total outflows in the 3–6 months time bucket.

The Table 4 shows the maturity gap position of the sample private sector banks in the different time buckets as a percentage of outflows.

Table 4

Maturity Gap as a % of Total Outflow of Private Banks								
Bank	1 - 14 days	15 - 28 days	29 days to 3 months	3 - 6 months	6 -12 months	1 - 2 years	2 - 5 years	Over 5 years
Axis Bank	61.89%	11.14%	-49.41%	-32.37%	-51.36%	21.16%	488.89%	5.08%
Bank of Rajasthan	91.89%	44.38%	-43.12%	-35.12%	-45.31%	3.59%	415.78%	-0.66%
Catholic Syrian Bank	109.93%	30.04%	-47.03%	-38.90%	-49.05%	3.97%	449.86%	0.53%
City Union Bank	72.40%	10.64%	-51.13%	-35.77%	-47.73%	11.37%	525.78%	3.75%
Development Credit Bank	75.73%	11.30%	-49.54%	-28.43%	-51.28%	16.23%	522.29%	-1.67%
Dhanalakshmi Bank	99.62%	18.65%	-49.44%	-37.06%	-48.23%	10.15%	491.95%	-1.31%
Federal Bank	69.55%	24.74%	-45.90%	-32.73%	-43.88%	20.68%	515.02%	-6.27%
HDFC Bank	65.22%	7.79%	-50.36%	-27.58%	-46.47%	23.60%	471.58%	-3.29%
ICICI Bank	34.82%	-11.84%	-52.42%	-9.18%	-49.89%	49.16%	531.53%	-8.88%
IndusInd Bank	32.53%	1.79%	-52.26%	-26.81%	-49.48%	16.73%	504.51%	10.58%
ING Vysya Bank	36.32%	2.54%	-52.25%	-19.72%	-48.35%	18.26%	498.88%	3.85%
Jammu & Kashmir Bank	109.80%	25.05%	-47.50%	-41.15%	-50.32%	10.28%	465.04%	-0.27%
Karnataka Bank	46.62%	35.10%	-44.94%	-29.51%	-42.39%	14.44%	496.01%	-1.02%
Karur Vysya Bank	57.48%	15.53%	-49.57%	-35.20%	-46.27%	13.61%	534.00%	3.84%
Kotak Mahindra Bank	0.79%	-9.02%	-50.34%	-5.48%	-47.25%	60.75%	535.04%	-6.64%
Lakshmi Vilas Bank	73.39%	-1.79%	-54.51%	-38.09%	-49.94%	12.04%	506.15%	9.42%
Ratnakar Bank	302.44%	66.97%	-35.66%	-42.48%	-49.88%	5.80%	448.34%	-36.23%
South Indian Bank	72.07%	23.37%	-47.63%	-39.43%	-48.05%	11.42%	485.86%	6.08%
Tamilnad Mercantile Bank	63.51%	20.07%	-48.11%	-36.61%	-44.94%	17.90%	519.07%	0.15%
Yes Bank	34.62%	-2.23%	-52.08%	-18.12%	-53.02%	30.46%	525.33%	3.47%

It was found that all the sample private sector banks had excess liquidity in the 1–14 days time bucket, and that none of the sample private sector banks had liquidity deficiency in excess of 20% of total outflows in the 15–28 days time bucket. However, it was found that all of the sample private sector banks had liquidity deficiency in excess of 20% of total outflows in the 1–3 months time bucket.

The Table 5 shows the cumulative maturity gap position of the sample public sector banks in the different time buckets.

Table 5

(Rs. In crores)

Cummualtive Maturity Gap of Public Banks								
Bank	**1 - 14 days**	**15 - 28 days**	**29 days to 3 months**	**3 - 6 months**	**6 - 12 months**	**1 - 2 years**	**2 - 5 years**	**Over 5 years**
Allahabad Bank	9,985.83	10,332.14	10,424.58	6,800.91	-2,202.97	-17,057.25	-12,878.45	0.00
Andhra Bank	3,783.96	2,720.10	2,321.78	-4,250.37	-13,388.08	-17,094.71	-10,646.93	0.00
Bank of Baroda	8,818.69	6,021.18	5,578.72	-3,494.09	-26,327.97	-16,981.43	337.30	0.00
Bank of India	14,895.95	9,041.81	14,277.94	-796.15	-13,814.37	-11,213.50	-4,909.68	0.00
Bank of Maharashtra	6,331.62	6,206.75	2,429.30	-742.86	-7,263.48	-14,038.76	-8,925.98	0.00
Canara Bank	11,434.45	11,996.14	19,747.30	8,905.36	-9,465.04	1,015.73	-11,168.90	0.00
Central Bank of India	14,969.79	13,045.27	9,552.86	14,657.55	-478.88	-16,122.36	-13,316.42	0.00
Corporation Bank	9,416.78	9,803.62	15,165.41	11,779.62	6,509.34	13,846.76	8,309.24	0.00
Dena Bank	4,101.11	4,387.31	2,533.73	1,413.32	-1,712.26	-13,294.15	-9,040.54	0.00
Indian Overseas Bank	8,068.14	5,298.71	3,817.38	-3,567.01	-10,814.31	-25,386.38	-15,074.86	0.00
IDBI Bank Ltd.	5,195.85	-212.58	-13,771.99	-24,611.03	-62,931.20	-54,006.66	-38,953.66	0.00
Indian Bank	5,345.26	5,862.63	6,925.59	2,904.28	-3,637.55	-3,997.78	3,361.91	0.00
Oriental Bank of Commerce	12,393.18	12,749.54	10,787.45	-1,550.76	-26,387.24	-25,432.97	-14,365.08	0.00
Punjab and Sind Bank	187.85	-153.92	-618.31	-701.64	-6,768.43	-5,883.25	-3,384.12	0.00
Punjab National Bank	16,928.84	17,303.00	14,278.83	4,952.38	-1,684.21	-14,228.44	15,066.35	0.00
State Bank of Travancore	2,141.48	3,999.13	2,548.09	-598.66	-1,927.32	-6,562.45	-3,122.16	0.00
State Bank of Bikaner and Jaipur	2,760.64	2,636.22	-467.73	-1,512.60	-6,448.88	-573.96	-730.90	0.00
State Bank of Hyderabad	12,431.56	11,150.87	9,512.86	6,702.55	1,161.37	4,384.09	12,595.01	0.00
State Bank of India	85,876.77	72,725.31	62,860.29	43,372.61	-38,191.73	58,480.00	70,487.00	0.00
State Bank of Indore	2,143.08	1,602.96	804.93	-1,280.74	-3,422.47	-754.63	2,775.26	0.00
State Bank of Mysore	1,665.72	1,236.10	-386.75	-1,216.79	-2,826.13	2,090.65	1,187.24	0.00
State Bank of Patiala	5,728.63	4,829.29	3,320.14	-3,634.48	-8,410.76	-17,466.20	9,500.26	0.00
Syndicate Bank	10,683.31	11,123.15	5,391.52	-3,502.81	-21,878.39	-23,028.56	-12,982.77	0.00
UCO Bank	7,426.45	5,886.24	4,182.41	-409.46	-17,801.21	-16,880.69	-5,930.73	0.00
Union Bank of India	10,616.70	12,215.93	9,625.62	8,989.65	-2,692.08	9,772.70	17,794.45	0.00
Vijaya Bank	4,808.05	4,140.25	1,006.11	-5,318.25	-19,231.62	-16,553.34	-10,902.36	0.00

It was found that only two of the sample public sector banks, namely IDBI Bank and Punjab and Sind Bank, had severe liquidity deficiency starting from the 15–28 days time bucket. It was also found that two other sample public sector banks, namely State Bank of Bikaner and Jaipur and State Bank of Mysore, had liquidity deficiency starting from the 1–3 months time bucket. Further, it was found that ten of the sample public sector banks had excess liquidity until the 3–6 months time bucket, and that two of the sample public sector banks, namely Corporation Bank and State Bank of Hyderabad, had excess liquidity in all the time buckets.

The Table 6 shows the cumulative maturity gap position of the sample private sector banks in the different time buckets.

Table 6

(Rs. In crores)

Cummualtive Maturity Gap of Private Banks								
Bank	1 - 14 days	15 - 28 days	29 days to 3 months	3 - 6 months	6 -12 months	1 - 2 years	2 - 5 years	Over 5 years
Axis Bank	7,578.02	8,308.39	-1,650.57	-8,003.17	-20,761.12	-16,639.93	-2,129.32	0.00
Bank of Rajasthan	1,190.27	1,504.33	500.97	-334.38	-1,527.07	-1,437.95	33.18	0.00
Catholic Syrian Bank	585.54	671.38	223.81	-158.36	-694.44	-653.54	-10.69	0.00
City Union Bank	497.56	536.55	-90.14	-544.16	-1,219.18	-1,067.73	-103.97	0.00
Development Credit Bank	351.68	380.23	-8.26	-226.69	-707.13	-582.14	31.13	0.00
Dhanalakshmi Bank	415.91	457.63	89.05	-196.40	-609.81	-527.88	22.41	0.00
Federal Bank	1,969.67	2,347.18	60.04	-1,600.83	-4,138.76	-3,051.26	800.38	0.00
HDFC Bank	9,300.85	9,940.04	-2,641.15	-9,262.61	-22,257.74	-16,604.22	1,843.46	0.00
ICICI Bank	11,065.40	8,788.50	-18,231.91	-22,263.01	-51,962.14	-32,707.40	11,222.70	0.00
Indusind Bank	725.06	747.52	-1,258.11	-2,251.57	-4,437.56	-3,819.40	-839.86	0.00
ING Vysya Bank	938.60	976.76	-1,371.48	-2,211.42	-4,644.48	-3,877.06	-348.99	0.00
Jammu & Kashmir Bank	3,168.16	3,548.12	1,166.28	-955.88	-3,956.26	-3,404.65	29.57	0.00
Karnataka Bank	795.23	1,115.22	-252.41	-1,181.41	-2,668.00	-2,191.02	69.27	0.00
Karur Vysya Bank	723.51	826.75	-281.37	-1,100.16	-2,304.91	-1,972.06	-199.64	0.00
Kotak Mahindra Bank	19.39	-114.35	-2,079.82	-2,258.59	-4,429.06	-2,701.74	633.52	0.00
Lakshmi Vilas Bank	463.92	457.75	-159.04	-598.98	-1,240.69	-1,095.93	-226.20	0.00
Ratnakar Bank	331.02	370.12	300.51	214.65	102.27	114.59	245.43	0.00
South Indian Bank	1,123.58	1,314.75	18.68	-1,090.02	-2,641.02	-2,305.69	-358.86	0.00
Tamilnad Mercantile Bank	507.40	591.92	-89.49	-628.98	-1,372.22	-1,094.81	-5.08	0.00
Yes Bank	691.71	666.67	-1,005.75	-1,537.88	-3,621.17	-2,777.92	-223.73	0.00

It was found that only one of the sample private sector banks, namely Kotak Mahindra Bank, had severe liquidity deficiency starting from the 15–28 days time bucket. Apart from this bank, all other sample private sector banks had excess liquidity in the 1–28 days period wherein they are supposed to maintain a solid liquidity position as per the RBI guidelines. It was also found that eleven other sample private sector banks had liquidity deficiency starting from the 1–3 months time bucket. ICICI bank and HDFC bank, the major players in the private sector have liquidity deficiency starting from the 1–3 months time bucket till the 1–2 years time bucket. Further, it was found that one of the sample private sector banks, namely Ratnakar Bank, had excess liquidity in all the time buckets.

DISCUSSION

Asset-Liability Management has evolved as a vital activity of all financial institutions and to some extent other industries too. It has become the prime focus in the banking industry, with every bank trying to maximize yield and reduce their risk exposure. The Reserve Bank of India has issued guidelines to banks operating in the Indian environment to regulate their asset-liability positions in order to maintain stability of the financial system.

Maturity-gap analysis has a wide range of focus, not only as a situation analysis tool, but also as a planning tool. Banks need to maintain the maturity gap as low as possible in order to avoid any liquidity exposure. This would necessarily mean that the outflows in different maturity buckets need to be funded from the inflows in the same bucket. As per the RBI's guidelines, banks have to maintain a stable liquidity position in the short term duration, including both 1–14 days and 15–28 days time buckets, to ensure the stability and credibility of the banking system of the country.

The results of the study suggest that, overall, public sector banks had a better short-term liquidity position than the private sector banks and foreign banks.

Overall, the public sector banks were very conservative in their liquidity risk management. With the opening of banking domain to global players in Indian environment and increasing penetration of private sector banks, such a high short-term liquidity would be adverse for the public sector banks in terms of profitability, since the yield in this maturity bucket is lower than the yield in higher period maturity buckets, while the cost of the funds invested in the shorter period maturity buckets are higher, as they are sourced from higher period maturity buckets. There is great scope for the public sector banks to improve their profitability by reducing their short-term liquidity. Dash and Pathak (2011) have shown this scope using a linear programming model for asset-liability management.

Overall, the private sector banks also had a comfortable short-term liquidity position. They have managed their short-term liquidity better than the public sector banks. This could be a major factor contributing to the higher overall profitability of the private sector banks. Dash and Pathak's (2011) model can also be applied to further improve the profitability and liquidity of the private sector banks.

There are some limitations inherent in the present study. The actual maturity profiles of some of the balance sheet items were not available from the secondary sources. These balance sheet items were distributed in a pre-determined proportion for all the banks, based on overall demand patterns, as expressed by RBI. Also, the sample size was relatively small.

REFERENCES

Basel Committee on Banking Supervision (2001). *Principles for the Management and Supervision of Interest Rate Risk,* Bank for International Settlements.

Basel II (2004). *International Convergence of Capital Measurement and Capital Standards: a Revised Framework,* Bank for International Settlements.

Black, R. and Brown, K. (2002). *Asset And Liability Management: What Does The Future Have In Store?* Balance Sheet, Boston.

Dash, M. and Pathak, R. (2011). "A Linear Programming Model for Assessing Asset-Liability Management in Banks," *ICFAI Journal of Financial Risk Management,* 8(1), pp. 50–67.

Gardner, M.J. and Mills, D.L. (1991). *Managing Financial Institutions: An Asset/Liability Approach,* 2nd Ed., The Dryden Press, Chicago.

Giokas, D. and Vassiloglou, M. (1991). "A Goal Programming Model for Bank Assets and Liabilities," *European Journal of Operations Research,* 50, 48–60.

Gup, B.E. and Brooks, R. (1993). *Interest Rate Risk Management,* Irwin Professional Publishing, Burr Ridge.

Haslem, J.A., Scheraga, C.A. and Bedingfield, J.P. (1999). "DEA efficiency profiles of U.S. banks operating internationally," *International Review of Economics and Finance* 8(2).

Ranjan, R. and Nallari, R. (2004). "Study of Asset Liability Management in Indian Banks Canonical Correlation Analysis," *Spandan.*

Rao, A.V. (2005). "ALM systems in Banks," *Treasury Management.*

Ravikumar, T. (2002). *Asset Liability Management,* ICFAI Press.

Vaidyanathan, R. (1999). "Asset-Liability Management: Issues and Trends in the Indian Context," *ASCI Journal of Management,* 29(1).

Vaidyanathan, R. (1995). "Debt Market in India: Constraints and Prospects," Bangalore: Centre for Capital Markets Education and Research, IIM Bangalore.

Vaidya, P. and Shahi, A. (2001). "Asset Liability Management in Indian Banks," *Spandan.*

Foreign Banks in India: Need to Keep Banking Street Dull

K.V. Bhanu Murthy and Ashis Taru Deb[1]

Department of Commerce, Delhi School of Economics, Delhi

[1]Department of Economics, College of Vocational Studies University of Delhi, Delhi

ABSTRACT: *In recent years preceding the global financial crisis there has been a shift in the nature of the banking model. The aftermath of this shift has been the crisis itself, which was largely fueled by the kind of banking model that emerged insidiously. The consequence of such a shift had led to the new banking model wherein there was 'short-circuiting' of the loans from risk.*

With the help of extensive empirical exercises this paper clearly establishes that foreign banks in India follow a distinct business model which consists of a high exposure in off-balance sheet activities, a tendency to be footloose and fair-weather friends, practice exclusive banking, have great amount of internal rivalry precipitated by new banks. They reap high profits and use of ATM banking and contribute to the digital divide.

INTRODUCTION

There has been a recent interest shown in the nature and role of banking. Amongst others, the Governor, Reserve Bank of India has taken a view:

> *"Post-crisis, there is a deluge of ideas and suggestions on reforming banks, banking and bankers. Analysts with a historical perspective believe that the seeds of the 2008 crisis were sown when the separation of banking from securities dealing was undone." Subbarao (2011).*

BANKERS AND ECONOMISTS SPEAK

Schumpeter (1911) argued that financial services are paramount in promoting economic growth. He added that the services provided by financial intermediaries-mobilizing savings, evaluating projects, managing risk, monitoring managers, and facilitating transactions are essential for technological innovation and economic development. An integral part of the Schumpeterian story is that financial intermediaries make possible technological innovation and economic development. "The banker . . . authorizes people, in the name of society as it were, to... [innovate]" [Schumpeter, 1911, p. 741].

Keynes (1930), in his A Treatise on Money, also argued for the importance of the banking sector in economic growth. He suggested that bank credit "is the pavement along which production travels, and the bankers if they knew their duty, would provide the transport facilities to just the extent that is required in order that the productive powers of the community can be employed at their full capacity" (II, p. 220). In the same spirit Robinson (1952) argued that financial development follows growth, and articulated this causality argument by suggesting that "where enterprise leads finance follows" (p. 86).

Taking a long term historical view, Paul Krugman[1] argues that there is a negative correlation between the business model of banking and economic stability". Whenever banking got exciting and interesting, paid well and attracted intellectual talent, it got way out of hand and jeopardized the stability of the real sector. Conversely, periods when banking was dull and boring were also periods of economic progress.

Mervyn King, Governor of the Bank of England addressed the moral hazard issue: why were banks willing to take risks that proved so damaging to themselves and the rest of the economy? The problem, according to Governor King, was that financial institutions became too important to be allowed to fail. His solution: restrict banking to its traditional "utility" function—performing basic retail financial intermediation of deposit taking and lending, and providing payment and settlement services; and hive off the riskier financial services such as proprietary trading into a separate entity. In what has come quickly to be known as the 'utility and casino' model, the 'utility' will be heavily regulated and will enjoy implicit government guarantee while the 'casino' will be left to the discipline of market forces.

NEW BANKING MODEL

In recent years preceeding the global financial crisis there has been a shift in the nature of the banking model. The aftermath of this shift has been the crisis itself, which was largely fueled by the kind of banking model that emerged insidiously.

Existence of Banks

The global financial crisis has triggered a debate about the relevance of the traditional banking model, with the new banking model receiving some support but ultimately leading to a crisis.

[1]Subbarao (2011).

Post-crisis there has been a revival of the interest in the traditional banking model that arises out of the basic functions of banking, namely, receiving deposits and making loans and advances. The Arrow-Debrew (1954) framework argues that in a complete contingent market, banks would not exist. In contrast, Diamond (1984) rationalized the existence banks through the assertion that markets are neither complete nor contingent. Thus, banks would exist due to their special features like superior information (asymmetric information), potential for monitoring loans and risk bearing capacity. It is important to add a rider to the basic principle of the existence of banks. On the basis of their special features banks exist when they are able to make reasonable profit equal to opportunity cost. But, it is important to understand that such a justification for their existence has an inherent ethical dimension. In as much as banks exist because they facilitate individual borrowers and depositors under such circumstances they are entitled to reasonable profits. Instead if banks influence the banking markets so as to make them more risky or if they are opaque in their practices and transactions so as to create asymmetric information, the abnormal profits that they would reap by such behavior is ethically unjustified.

Crisis and the Banking Model

During the formation of the global financial crisis, there was an emergence of a new banking model. This was based on the shift in the paradigm of banking which could be spelt out as 'originate and sell' as opposed to the traditional principle of banking, namely 'originate and hold'. The consequence of such a shift had led to the new banking model wherein there was 'short-circuiting' of the loans from risk. It is ironic that while the existence of bank was attributed to their risk bearing capacity, the new banking model seeks to separate risk from loan. While banking markets are risky and banking business is about undertaking risk, banks operate on the basis of the prudence arising out of banking practices and principles that appropriately balance the bank's capacity to lend with its risk assessment and risk bearing capacity, both of which crucially depend upon the information content of the debt. The new banking model by separating the information from the loan was apparently aimed at the bank's capacity to lend, so that leads to a spread of banking, by weaning away the risk that the bank. In addition the implication is that if the risk is taken off the balance sheet of banks, the capital that is held as provision can be released for further loans. This lead to the securitization of risk. Unlike the traditional banking model where each loan was linked to the underlying information that was tagged to the loan in the new banking model the process of 'slicing and dicing' of such instruments lead to a 'massive loss of information'. An unanticipated impact of such a shift of the banking model was that the new structured products (credit debt swaps and hedge funds) lead to a situation that could best be described as 'unknown-unkown'. This made the banking markets extremely opaque. Neither did the seller (owner or creator) nor did the buyer of such instruments know about the information content of the new structured products.

A by product of such a phenomenon has been the explosion of a wide range of instruments which were meant to reduce the risk of the banking system but in fact infused risk into the banking system at a much a larger scale and led to systemic risk. Banks that pushed out the risk from the front door allowed a much greater risk to enter from the backdoor. The above analysis of the state of the banking system and the consequences for the banking model make it clear that either bank managers were blissfully ignorant of fundamental principles of banking or there was a deliberate attempt to gain supernormal profits while creating a moral hazard by shifting the risk to the shareholders, depositors and borrowers leaving the regulator in the lurch.

Democratization of Risk

The idea behind separating the risk from bank loans was that it would lead to the growth of banking market through the wider spread of loans. Certain structured products were created to facilitate this process. Such structured instruments like credit debt swaps were eulogized as a 'democratization' of risk. This meant that those who could should undertake risk according to their choice and in the process rid the banking system of the shackles of such risk. The new instruments were opaque and were not used in isolation but were highly leveraged. This led to deadly cocktail of a potentially explosive situation and insidious infiltration of toxic instruments into the banking system. The banking system was getting addicted to abnormal risk, abnormal profits and astronomical CEO salaries. The attempt to rid individual banks of their risk led to the potential to induce systemic risk. The induction of systemic risk, at once, converts democratization' of risk into 'universalization of risk.' Universalization implies that since the whole banking system is steeped in risky instruments whose information content is unknown; all participants in the banking system would be subjected to risk whether or not they choose to undertake such risk.

The New Banking Model

Theory of banking had evolved at a time when a lot of banking activity was restricted. The spread of banking, an imperative of modern day banking has lead to three implications-one, the spread of traditional banking activity; two, the spread of risk–taking of banks; and three, of the ambit and distribution of the gains of banking. In interpreting the spread of risk-taking function of baking the new banking model has erred in separating risk from the asset generating capacity of banks. This has been taken to be the basis of 'democratization' or 'inclusiveness' of banking. The origins of financial crisis owe themselves to the policy of giving loans to sub prime borrowers which was an attempt at 'inclusive banking'. In this banking model 'universalization' of banking cannot happen without 'universalization of risk'.

Thus, the features of the new banking model are:

1. Separation of risk from loan;
2. Securitization of risk;
3. Loss of information;
4. Off-balance-sheet exposure;
5. Aiming a high return at the risk of instability;
6. Generation of high returns with a narrower base of banking;
7. Use of e-banking.

The last two feature of the new banking model lead to the operation of banks on the basis of financial exclusion.

New Model and Foreign Banks

How new banking model spread? The foreign banks that adopted this model had a presence all over the world. In addition, in India there was new found emphasis on competition and profitability. Thus, other banking segments emulated foreign banks.

1. Through the spread for toxic assets—globally;
2. Through demonstration effect by imitating foreign banks;
3. Through spread of off-balance sheet activities;
4. Through aspiring for quick profits.

Foreign banks tend to cut down upon staff and hence have a very low branch network. To compensate they substitute branches with ATMs. The foreign banks show long-term conduct in terms of following a highly risky, and profit oriented banking. They indulge in financial exclusion. They have an urban bias. Most of all they are contributing to the digital divide.

Foreign banks, it is pointed out, are fair-weather friends at best and a potential source of instability at worst. Three other prominent effects of the new banking model adopted by foreign banks are:

1. Volatility in terms of terms of rivalry;
2. One branch banking; and
3. Footloose existence.

RISKY BANKING

The most distinctive characteristic of foreign banks has been captured in the trends relating to off balance sheet activities. Table 1 clearly show the risky nature of their banking activity. The minimum level of off balance sheet activities is large and significant in case of foreign banks, while in the case of all other banking segments it is significantly lower even to begin with. On an average off-balance sheet activities are growing at the rate of 17% in case of foreign banks which represents a highly significant trend. While to the contrary, all other banking segments show a declining trend with some varying levels of significance. This clearly shows that foreign banks are distinctly involved in a high level of off balance sheet activities along with a growing trend, in contrast to other banking segments. This shows long-tern behavior because it has been pointed out even as early as 1993 that such tendencies existed.

Table 1: Regression Results Related to Off-balance Sheet Activities

Regression Statistics					
Multiple R	0.986				
R Square	0.972				
Adjusted R Square	0.969				
Standard Error	0.243				
Observations	60				
ANOVA					
	df.	*SS*	*MS*	*F*	*Significance F*
Regression	7	107.422	15.346	260.786	0
Residual	52	3.06	0.059		
Total	59	110.482			
	Coefficients	*Standard Error*	*t Stat*	*P-value*	
Intercept	5.264	0.132	39.936	0	
T	0.171	0.014	11.779	0	
OPVTB	–2.187	0.186	–11.73	0	
NPVTB	–1.203	0.186	–6.456	0	
PSB	–2.115	0.186	–11.347	0	
Oldt	–0.111	0.021	–5.408	0	
Newt	–0.073	0.021	–3.541	0.001	
Psbt	–0.118	0.021	–5.752	0	

FAIR WEATHER FRIENDS

During the bond market boom between 2001 and 2003 almost all foreign banks with a sizeable presence in India shore up their business of primary dealership (PD from henceforth)

in government securities[2]. At that point the idea to enter the PD business was to take advantage of falling rate of interest. Foreign banks running a PD are HSB, Deutsche Bank, ABN-Amro Bank, Bank of America, JP Morgan and Stanchart, etc. As per RBI rules, each PD needs to be capitalized at a minimum of ₹ 50 crores. PDs need to meet minimum bidding commitment at the government securities auctions every year. Thy also play a market making role in government bonds through secondary market trades.

Most PDs have incurred losses during 2004–05. Aid plummeting bond prices, several foreign banks approached RBI wishing to exit the primary dealership business. While a PD can exit business by simply surrendering its license to RBI, the central bank is concerned about the exit of foreign banks from the business because it may encourage other PDs also to shut shop. The exit of foreign PDs could put a strain on government borrowing programme as primary dealers in government securities serve as underwriters at primary auctions of government securities. A few foreign banks want to retain PD licenses, while discontinuing the PD business. The idea is that when the cycle in the bond market turns, they can activate the primary dealership again to make profits.

FOREIGN BANKS ARE FOOTLOOSE

In an attempt to analyze the issue of stability of foreign banks in the country, we categorize them in a four-way classification: stable incumbents, unstable incumbents, stable entrants and lastly unstable entrants. If the bank is present during the first year of the study, i.e. 1991–92, we call it an incumbent bank. If this continues to exist throughout period of the study, it is called stable incumbent bank. If this makes an exit during a year covered by the study, it is called an unstable incumbent bank. If a bank enters during the period of the study, it is called an entrant. If an entrant continues to operate throughout the period of the study, it is called a stable entrant. Otherwise, it is called an unstable entrant. Table 2 provides the number of incumbents and entrants further sub-divided into two categories: stable and unstable.

Table 2: Different Categories of Foreign Banks: 1992–2009

	Stable	*Unstable*	*Total*
Incumbents	16(66.66%)	8(33.33%)	24
Entrants	15 (51.72%)	14 (48.27%)	29
Total	31	22	53

[2] Primary dealers in government securities are allowed to carry out certain core and non-core activities like dealing and underwriting G-Secs, dealing in interest rate derivatives, investments in units of equity oriented mutual funds and underwriting public issues.

During 1991–92, twenty four foreign banks were operating in the country out of which eight banks exited at different points of time. Twenty nine foreign banks entered during the period from 1992–2009, while as many as fourteen of them exited. Fifteen banks remained and the total count of foreign banks went upto thirty one from twenty four. Thus opening up of the economy raised the number of foreign banks by mere seven over a period of eighteen years from 1991–92 to 2008–09. Out of fifty three foreign banks which operated in the country over different stretch of time covered by during 1992–2009, only sixteen banks were present throughout the period of the study. To cap it all, twenty nine banks entered while twenty two banks exited, taking the total tally of foreign banks from twenty four to thirty one. The figures in brackets show the percentages. It is apparent that a greater proportion of incumbents prove to be more stable than the entrants with regard their commitment towards Indian economy. While in the case of public sector banks, there was no exit. In the case of private sector banks, there hardly exists any instance of an outright exit. However, there are a number of instances relating to merger. On the other hand, slightly more than forty percent of foreign banks present in the country from 1992– 2009 turned out to be unstable. This phenomenon of footloose banking is not found in other banking segments. Excessive entry and exit would lead to constant flux in the banking market. This would have several implications. First, long term incentives would be affected both with depositors and borrowers. It is therefore undesirable for the investment climate. It would also lead to information asymmetry as the stock of knowledge gathered by the banks about their clients would be lost. This may result in a situation to be exploited by other foreign banks for earning higher profits. Thirdly, even borrowers and depositors would be adversely affected by such asymmetric information. They face the consequences of moral hazard because the bank knows while they do not.

EXCLUSIVE BANKING

Foreign Banks in various ways practice exclusive banking:

1. One branch banks
2. Metro branches
3. ATM banking.

One Branch Banks

Table 3 shows the ratio of foreign banks that have only one branch, as a proportion of the total number of foreign banks. It is a commonplace observation that none of the public or private sector banks carry on banking activities with a single branch. However, a substantial proportion of foreign banks in the country have been conducting their operations with a single branch, as indicated by the table. This observation put together with the earlier results which demonstrate significantly lower average number of branch of foreign banks point out that foreign banks do not practice financial inclusion. Even at its lowest the ratio is 24%. This means that one of every 4 foreign banks have only one branch. Some of them are dubious because they deal with sensitive issues. Like Antwerp bank operates with one branch in Surat.

Table 3: Percentage of One Branch Foreign Banks

Year	*RMBTB*
1992	54.17
1993	54.17
1994	39.13
1995	33.33
1996	38.71
1997	38.46
1998	39.02
1999	47.73
2000	33.33
2001	30.95
2002	40.00
2003	44.44
2004	39.39
2005	41.94
2006	31.03
2007	24.14

Metro Branches

In the following table we have measured the proportion of branches in metro cities. The table shows the ratio of such branches with foreign banks as the base. Even PSBs which are the largest segment have only 5% of the metro branches as the foreign banks!! Old private banks are in the range of 3–4% and new private banks have only 2% of the number of metro branches as foreign banks. This clearly shows that FBs are having an urban bias. Not just urban but clearly in favor of large metro cities.

In Table 5 we have measured the number of ATMs per branch. The table shows the ratio of this number with foreign banks as the base. Even PSBs which are the largest segment have only 5% of the ATMs per branch as compared to the foreign banks!! Old private banks have grown from 3–20% for foreign banks. The new private banks had the same ratio but over time they have come down to 66% as compared to foreign banks. This clearly shows that FBs are having a technology bias. In the light of this they not only have an urban bias but also may be the cause of a digital divide. Poorer sections, socially backward classes and rural-folk would not be having the same reach as their counter-parts in terms of computers, education, and techsavyness. They would never be able to keep pace. We can expect a widening digital divide if such conduct persists as in the case of foreign banks.

Table 4: Proportion of Metro Branches of Foreign Banks as Percentage of Other Banking Segments

	PSBFB	*OLDFB*	*NEWFB*
2002	5.40	5.11	2.05
2003	5.30	4.84	2.12
2004	5.17	4.56	2.11
2005	5.26	4.38	2.22
2006	5.17	4.11	1.94
2007	4.28	4.04	2.10
2008	4.14	4.15	2.24
2009	4.01	3.98	2.26
2010	3.85	3.70	2.25
2011	3.85	3.79	2.35

ATM Banking

Table 5: ATMs per Branches in each Banking Segment

Year	*ATMs Per Branch: w.r.t. Foreign Banks (%)*		
	PSB	*Old*	*New*
2005	6.4159	8.3533	101.1288
2006	5.5606	9.9718	92.2499
2007	9.3572	9.9261	93.3163
2008	10.9168	12.5066	74.1653
2009	13.6781	15.9021	83.6252
2010	20.9000	20.6886	89.6104
2011	18.4369	19.8748	66.7440

RIVALRY

We compute Bodenhorn's measure of rivalry in the foreign banking industry to indicate level of competition in the industry. The measure is based on differences in rank of top banks between two adjacent years. To begin with foreign banks are ranked in terms of their profitability. In the present case, we consider the top five banks as the leading banks. In a particular year, the ranks of these banks are considered, their ranks in the preceding year are subtracted from them, their absolutes values are taken and added to construct the measure. In the second leg, we sought to quantify the contribution of new banks to rivalry created in foreign banking industry. With this end, we first identify new banks among the top five entities and repeat the procedure only for them to arrive at the relevant figure. This is divided by what we got in the first leg to identify the contribution of new foreign banks in generating rivalry in the foreign banking industry. Excepting just one aberration, contribution of new banks to competition in the industry has never gone below twenty five percent. In many as three instances they account for the entire rivalry generated. The implications of this phenomenon are clear. First, new banks enter the banking market with a view to earn quick profit and therefore they are able to create a churning in the ranks. Second, banking markets should not be fragmented. Therefore, such a churning does not augur well for the stability of the banking market. This clearly points towards a conflict between the two objectives of banks, profits versus stability. It must be understood that there are some limits to competition in banking unlike other industries. The Efficient Structure Hypothesis states that the structure of market depends upon the efficiency of firms. But in such a case, efficiency refers to productive efficiency. In case of banking, productive efficiency implies larger market share (deposits plus advances), not necessarily higher profits. In case higher profits are achieved, despite smaller market share, it implies that such banks are achieving these profits at the cost of creating riskier banking markets. This also implies that such banks enter for short term profits and not for long term banking development. Finally, it clearly shows that the new banks entering with a new banking model. With their new banking model, they are able to out compete the incumbents.

Table 6: Contribution of New Foreign Banks to Rivalry in the Industry

Year	*Measure of Rivalry*	*Contribution of New Banks to Rivalry*
1996	51	45.09
1997	54	96.29
1998	53	100.00
1999	32	96.87
2000	66	25.75
2001	25	100.00
2002	30	100.00
2003	26	0.00
2004	30	10.00
2005	7	57.14
2006	54	38.88
2007	33	75.75
2008	28	10.71
2009	16	87.5

PROFIT

The final test lies in a comparative study of the profitability of the three other banking segments as compared to foreign banks. The profitability has been measured as Net Profit/Asset ratio. The main objective of quick profit is driving the new banking model. For making such comparisons Table 7 shows the ratio of Net Profit of foreign banks to other

Table 7: Net Profit Ratio: Foreign to other Banking Segments

Year	*fb/psb*	*fb/opvtb*	*fb/npvtb*
1995	6.64	1.43	2.59
1996	–22.57	1.49	0.85
1997	2.09	1.31	0.69
1998	1.25	1.19	0.62
1999	1.64	1.44	0.67
2000	2.05	1.39	1.21
2001	2.21	1.58	1.15
2002	1.83	1.22	3.00
2003	1.63	1.33	1.73
2004	1.47	1.38	1.99
2005	1.49	3.94	1.24
2006	1.83	2.59	1.55
2007	2.05	2.43	1.87
2008	2.00	1.80	1.80
2009	1.89	1.70	1.55
2010	1.23	1.27	0.89
2011	1.87	1.57	1.17

Table 8: Net Profit Ratio of Foreign Banks and Public Sector Banks: Result of t-Test

t-Test: Two-Sample Assuming Unequal Variances		
	FB	*PSB*
Mean	1.37411765	0.69235294
Variance	0.10562574	0.08915662
Observations	17	17
Hypothesized Mean Difference	0	
Df	32	
t-Stat	6.36918951	
P(T<=t) one-tail	1.8718E-07	
t-Critical one-tail	1.69388875	
P(T<=t) two-tail	3.7436E-07	
t-Critical two-tail	2.03693334	

segments, namely, Old Private, Public Sector and New Private. Except for 1996 in the case PSBs all other ratios are positive. In no case are the foreign banks inferior to any of the banking segments. Sometimes the ratio is even 6.64 times that of PSBs. On an average in comparison to PSBs the FBs have double the profits. Table 8 shows that the t-test is significant. In the case of OPVTB and NPVTB the ratio is less dramatic on an average, but Tables 9 and 10 show that all comparisons favor FBs.

Table 9: Net Profit Ratio of Foreign Banks and Old Public Sector Banks: Result of t-test

t-Test: Two-Sample Assuming Unequal Variances		
	FB	*OPVT*
Mean	1.37411765	0.86823529
Variance	0.10562574	0.06596544
Observations	17	17
Hypothesized Mean Difference	0	
Df	30	
t Stat	5.0353135	
P(T<=t) one-tail	1.0543E-05	
t Critical one-tail	1.69726089	
P(T<=t) two-tail	2.1086E-05	
t Critical two-tail	2.04227246	

Table 10: Net Profit Ratio of Foreign Banks and New Public Sector Banks: Result of t-Test

t-Test: Two-Sample Assuming Unequal Variances		
	FB	*NPVT*
Mean	1.37411765	1.07882353
Variance	0.10562574	0.13486103
Observations	17	17
Hypothesized Mean Difference	0	
Df	32	
t Stat	2.48275386	
P(T<=t) one-tail	0.00923515	
t Critical one-tail	1.69388875	
P(T<=t) two-tail	0.01847031	
t Critical two-tail	2.03693334	

Another feature of the new banking model is not just quick profit but high profit. Banking as such has very low profit margins. If the ratio is as high as 2 to 6 times, this defies the basic intention of a bank. In addition, all other features discussed above make it clear that these high profits have been gained at the cost of instability, risk, rivalry and exclusive banking. Such high profits are not arising out of a wide banking base, development of banking market and steady growth lending stability to the banking system (Deb and Murthy, 2011).

Even though NPVT behave close to FBs there is a 30% difference in the margin. One argument might be that FBs are earning more profit because they are more efficient. First, our measure takes account of the asset base. Therefore, it implies that allocative efficiency cannot be vastly different. Managerial efficiency or technical efficiency can at the best account for 3–5% of the difference, not 3–5 times. It is therefore, obvious that such high profits are only due to off-balance sheet activities. Most of such activities are already discredited as an aftermath of the crisis.

In Figure 1, the thickset line represents FBs. Clearly it lies well above other banking segments, except from 1996 to 1999, where new banks are above. In spite of the volatility in graph it is clear that FBs are much better off. With the exception of 2010, where new private banks overtake briefly, from 2001 onwards all other segments show a declining trend, while FBS continue to gain.

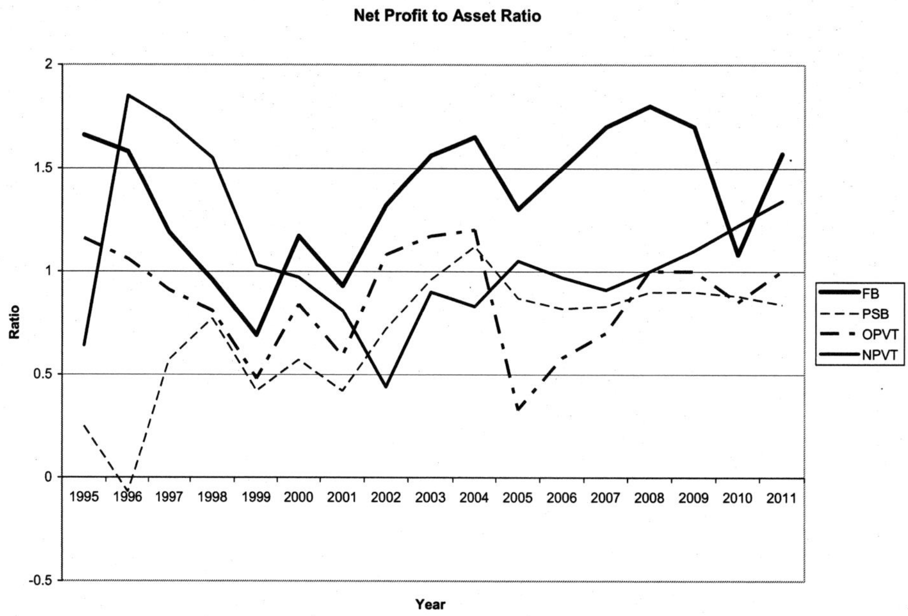

Fig. 1: Net Profit to Asset Ratio of Different Banking Segments: 1994–95 to 2010–2011

CONCLUSION

There has been a recent interest shown in the nature and role of banking. In recent years preceding the global financial crisis there has been a shift in the nature of the banking model. The aftermath of this shift has been the crisis itself, which was largely fueled by the kind of banking model that emerged insidiously. The consequence of such a shift had led to the new banking model wherein there was 'short-circuiting' of the loans from risk.

Thus, the features of the new banking model are: Separation of risk from loan; Securitization of risk; Loss of information; Off-balance-sheet exposure; Aiming a high return at the risk of instability; Generation of high returns with a narrower base of banking; and Use of e-banking.

With the help of extensive empirical exercises this paper clearly establishes that foreign banks follow a distinct business model which consists of a high exposure in off-balance sheet activities, a tendency to be footloose and fair-weather friends, practice exclusive banking, have great amount of internal rivalry precipitated by new banks. They reap high profits and use of ATM banking and contribute to the digital divide.

BIBLIOGRAPHY

Arrow, K.J. and Debrew, G. (1954). Existence of equilibrium for a competitive economy. Econometrica, 22, pp. 265–90.

Bhanu Murthy, K.V. and Ashis Taru Deb (2009). Sub Prime Crisis in US: Emergence, Impact and Lessons, SSRN Working Paper No http://ssrn.com/abstract=1303417

Bodenhorn, H. (1990). Entry, Rivalry and Free Banking, Review of Economics and Statistics, 724), pp. 682–686.

Charvaka (1993). Foreign Banks in India: The Drain, Economic *and Political Weekly*, January 30, pp. 155–57.

Deb, Ashis Taru and Bhanu Murthy, K.V. (2011) Corporate Governance in Foreign Banks in India in Corporate Governance in Banks, edited by Mridula Sahay, S. Sreenivasa Murthy and R.K. Mishra, Macmillan Publishers India Ltd, Macmillan Advanced Research Series, New Delhi.

Diamond, D.W. (1984). Financial Intermediation and Delegated Monitoring, *Review of Economic Studies, 51*(3), pp. 393–414.

Economic Times, *Fair-weather friends: Foreign banks seek to exit PD business*, 13th April, 2005, p. 1.

Keynes, John Maynard (1930). *A Treatise on Money*, London: Macmillan.

Reserve Bank of India, *Report and Trends of Banking in India*, various issues, Bombay.

Reserve Bank of India, *Statistical Tables relating to banks*, various issues, Bombay.

Robinson, J. (1952). *The Generalization of the General Theory in her the Rate of Interest and other Essays*, London: Macmillan.

Schumpeter, Joseph (1911). *The Theory of Economic Development: An inquiry into profits, capital, credit, interest and the business cycle.* London. Transaction Publishers.

Subbarao, Duvvuri (2011). "Financial Regulation for Growth, Equity and Stability in the Post-Crisis World", Governor, Reserve Bank of India at the First CAFRAL-BIS *International Conference on 'Financial Sector Regulation for Growth, Equity and Stability in the Post Crisis World'*, Mumbai, November 15.

Subbarao, Duvvuri (2011). "Should Banking Be Made Boring?—An Indian Perspective". *RBI Speeches*. http://rbidocs.rbi.org.in/rdocs/Speeches/PDFs/IMCS251109.pdf

Verma, Sunny (2011). RBI terns on off-balance sheet exposures of foreign banks, *Economic Times*, September 1, p. 2.

Vishwanathan, Aparna (1993). Foreign Banks: Need for Control, *Economic and Political Weekly*, March 22–27, pp. 503–04.

Indian Banking System and the Challenges Way Ahead

Manisha Raj

Amity University, Noida

ABSTRACT: *Indian financial setup began under the parental care of the government rules and regulations and privatization got a humungous fillip only after the liberalization era. But liberalization has its own responsibilities and challenges. This paper will basically explore the strengths and weaknesses of Indian banking system expanding its market on international arena and the vitality of Basel norms in Indian Perspective. The basic objectives of this paper are:*

1. *Banking system and the Indian economy in the pre-liberalized era.*
2. *Pros and cons of bank expansion in the current uncertain world economy.*
3. *Analyzing the extent of credit availability and its impact on Indian financial market.*
4. *Assessing the impact of Basel (III) norms on Indian banking system and its future.*

With the upcoming of Narasimham committee reports (i) and (ii) in 1992 and 1998 respectively, the Indian banking sector has become more resilient. But with time changes in its functional pattern is required to make the banking system more strong and capable to sustain itself in the changing world scenario. Therefore the role of bank expansion and proper regulation to maintain the diversity in its structure is need of the hour. Further a strong banking setup is a must for an emerging economy like India. Appropriate policies will not only make the financial market more strong but will also assist in financial inclusion so that the gross domestic product of the country can be enhanced.

Keywords: Basel Norms, Branch Expansion, Credit, Financial Markets, Growth, Monetary Policy, Regional Rural Banks.

BANKING SYSTEM AND THE INDIAN ECONOMY IN THE PRE-LIBERALIZED ERA

"A belief that the welfare costs of exclusion from the banking sector, especially for the rural poor, are high has led to widespread government intervention in the banking sector of low income countries "(Besley, 1995). India stands as a testimonial to this statement as

India took up financial inclusion as a matter of pride and development way back in 1969. The issue became pertinent due to the interest rate ceilings in the informal money market and weak financial condition of the rural poor. With further nationalization the public sector banking arms spread in 1980. The nationalization process no doubt synchronized the banking sector for the rural as well as urban people and assisted in the development of the country. The number of bank branches rapidly increased from 8,262 in 1969 to 13,622 in 1972, which subsequently increased to 45,332 by 1984.[1] During the pre-liberalization era, government rules and regulations were framed in such a way that banking habits could be developed among the rural poor. The unbanked areas were taken into notice and branches were expanded in such a way that all rural areas are also covered. Another important step of Indian banking system was directing bank lending towards the priority sectors (small scale industries, agriculture, exports and many more) so that weaker section of the society is empowered and in turn this will lead to economic growth of the nation.

A new banking era started with the post liberalization phase of the country. The opening up of the economy increased the already existent financial pressure on the economy. An expansion plan had to be taken up so that the public sector banks are assisted with the private sector and foreign banks to share the immense financial responsibility of the country. For eg: licenses were given to some private banks like Global trust bank, Axis bank. This helped in diversifying the banking structure of the country which in turn will meet the growing finance scarcity in the economy. Also India was least affected by the Asian crisis of 1997 as our banking system was much condensed at that time and capital account convertibility was rigorously being analyzed. The liberalization process had brought a new growth momentum in the economy and the private sector was very buoyant. The level of money supply managed by RBI through the policy mix of CRR and SLR was regulated in such a way that credit crunch is reduced and the private sectors also grow.

PROS AND CONS OF BANK EXPANSION IN THE CURRENT UNCERTAIN WORLD ECONOMY

Globalization has very much affected the structure of Indian banking system to that it adopts to the international exposure. The big question in front of RBI is that should Indian banks be allowed to expand its activities in the international market, especially when the western countries economic growth and financial viability is in doldrums. "Globalization is a double edged sword—it offers immense opportunities but also poses ruthless challenges.[i] Nothing illustrates this better than the global financial crisis of 2008/09.

Recall that in the years before the crisis—during the period of the 'Great Moderation'—we had Steady growth in advanced economies and accelerating growth in emerging and developing Economies, and low and stable inflation all around. This was a consequence of globalization—in Particular, of the tremendous boost to world production and productivity as a result of India and China joining the world labor markets. If the Great Moderation was the positive side of Globalization, the financial crisis of 2008/09 and the Great Recession that followed were its negative side. That a bubble in a quintessentially non-tradable sector like housing snowballed into a global financial crisis, taking a devastating toll on global growth and welfare, is a demonstration of the ferociousness of the forces of globalization." So globalization is a double edged sword which is hampering many emerging economies through detoriation of the key macro-economics variables. If we look into the major banking instruments then we see that there has been a declining trend in call money rate, deposit rates, interest rates etc. All these changes were mainly brought about after the recommendations made by the Narasimham committee on banking reforms which was set up with the aim to bring financial efficiency in the economy . The major finding of the committee set up in 1991 was as follows:

- In the pre-liberalization era banks had to maintain huge cash reserves in the form of statutory liquidity ratio of around 38.5%, and cash reserve ratio of around 15%. So a lump sum amount was locked within the banking sector which also dented on the profitability of banks.
- The directed lending schemes where in the banks lend loans to the agricultural sector and the small scale industries at concessional rates have affected the banking system in a bad manner. These sectors are maturing now and financial concessions should not be further provided.
- The committee also opined that there is no need of government intervention in the determination of interest rates. The deregulation of interest rate is the need of the hour.
- The committee focused on rationalization of Indian banking sector by reducing the number of banks functioning in the economy. It wanted four to five big banks along with SBI to be operational. This would lead to structural reorganization among banks and there should be a universal banking system with no more nationalization in future. In order to imbibe competition in the financial arena, private banks and foreign banks should also be promoted.
- There should be dual control mechanism by the reserve bank of India and the Banking division of ministry of finance.
- For upgrading banking technology and work culture banks should be given due autonomy so that they can respond to the changing market situations.
- The government did not accept the recommendation as a whole later on in 1998 second Narasimham committee was set up it was set up to review the progress and design of banks in India. The major recommendations were as such:
- The committee wanted to strengthen the banking system so that they are capable of handling problems regarding domestic liquidity and exchange rate management in the light of current account convertibility.

Capital adequacy should be improved so that the internal capacity of banks increases.

Non-Performing assets was a big problem for banks. Narrow Banking Concept should be undertaken where weak banks will be allowed to place their funds only in short term and risk free assets.

Bank autonomy should be enhanced through the adoption of professional corporate strategies.

The recommendations of *the Narasimham committee* have broadened the vision of banking and have rightly made an effort to incorporate it with the changing global situation. Another important feature that affects Indian financial scene is the rate of inflation. Inflation rate was brewing in the first quarter of 2010 and there after a moderating trend has been noticed. Inflation is a major issue for any emerging economy because it directly affects the demand of the economy which in turn has affect on the investment and saving rate of the economy. If the value of money is reduces due to high inflation then the exports and imports also undergo change as the terms of trade of the country detoriates. The Table 1 clearly shows that inflation is not an area of concern right now. But predictions are such that by the end of 2012, Indian economy will face the brewing inflation once again.

Table 1: Recent Inflation Record

Time Period	*Inflation Rate*
April 2010	14.86
June 2010	13.72
Aug 2010	9.88
Oct 2010	9.7
Dec 2010	9.47
Feb 2011	8.82
April 2011	8.76
April 2012	7.23

Source: http://indusfinance.com/2012/05

The above trend line basically shows that inflation is a major issue for an emerging economy like India. Its impact is felt on the value of money as well as the demand and supply of commodities in the market. The banking sector has to act judiciously to manage the credit availability and price stability in the economy. Even if we talk of GDP of India then it is noticeable that there is fluctuation in the growth rate according to the domestic performance of the country and the ongoing international trend. The western financial crisis of 2008 clearly dented on the growth rate of India as the GDP wrangled from around 10% in 2007 to 6.18% in 2008. But due to the controlled measures of Indian banking system and the fiscal management at the governmental end, the international upheaval did not affect the domestic scene for a long time as we saw a recovery in the growth rate to 10% by 2010 itself. In the quarter that lasted from July to September in 2011, Indian economy has seen a growth rate of 6.9 percent, which is the slowest in the past couple of years. The economic growth has been impeded by factors like the Euro zone crisis that is assuming threatening proportions by the day, and the high costs of borrowing in India itself. In the quarter encompassing January, February, and March in 2011, the national economy had grown by 7.8 percent. "We expect growth to fall below 7 per cent in 2011–12 from 8.5 per cent in 2010–11 due to the impact of an uncertain global funding environment, high domestic interest rates and the apparent lack of policy initiatives that can revive business confidence," Moody's said in a report. Also for the running year 2012 many economic and government organizations have come up with surprising and extremely disproportionate figures. The Table 2 shows that the growth rate in the first quarter of 2012 is very disappointing and a herculean task is ahead for the government to tackle this growth problem.

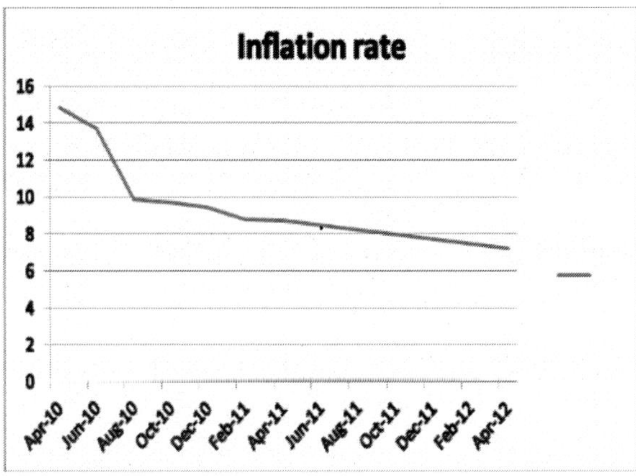

Fig. 1: Showing the Trend of Inflation in the Recent Times

Table 2: Showing GDP Growth of India in Recent Years

Year	*GDP Growth Figure*
2005	9.03%
2006	9.53%
2007	9.99%
2008	6.18%
2009	6.77%
2010	10.09%
2011	7.4%
2012	*5.3%

* The Gross Domestic Product (GDP) in India expanded 5.3 percent in the first quarter of 2012 over the same quarter of the previous year.

Source: http://business.com/india-gdp/growth-rate.html

Under such downtrend of economic growth, the role of financial system and per se the banking system becomes more important and the flow of money in the economy through measures like interest rate,inflation level,etc has to be managed in such a way that it keeps the tempo of investment at the required level for the economy.

Especially since 1980s the role of monetary policy has gained momentum and in the globalized ere every emerging economy will agree to the fact that stability in GDP and development can go simultaneously only when the monetary policy and fiscal policy are in tandem with each other. Earlier when we were kind of a closed economy then the role of fiscal policy was much emphasized and monetary mechanism of the nation was totally within the control of the government but now the economic scene has changed for the better where we have to give equal importance to the monetary policy. The banking system has been revamped to a great extent through the liberalization policy and Narasimham committee. Certain banking measures like Current account convertibility has made the banking system more streamlined but in order to process with the capital account convertibility, government has to move ahead very consciously because of the fragile financial markets in International market.

The Table 3 shows few banks who have set up their operations in foreign countries and are in an expanding mode but we will further see that within the domestic territory of India there is lot to be done. Indian banks have to achieve financial inclusion target for the urban as well as rural societies within the economy and then the banks should be allowed to cover the international markets. According to the RBI report based on 2001 population census India is still facing the problem of unbanked areas. The next table talks about it .Out of around 650 districts in India almost more than half of the districts are still unbanked. The nationalized banks should cover each and every district of the country and then only they should expand beyond the domestic territory. The private banks should be given the liberty to act on their moral and social responsibility to develop within or outside the economy. India being a welfare state has rightly come up with Regional Rural Banks that are meant to function in the rural areas so that the majority of population is out of the exploitation of the moneylenders.

Table 3: Showing the Share of Different Banks in the Country

Bank Names	*Share of Banks*
co-operative banks	29.74%
regional rural banks	35.34%
nationalized banks	8.62%
private banks	9.48%
sbi and its associates	3.02%
foreign banks	13.79%

Source: file:///H:/banks/India's%20Top%20Banks%202010%20%20Indian%20Banking%20Sector.htm

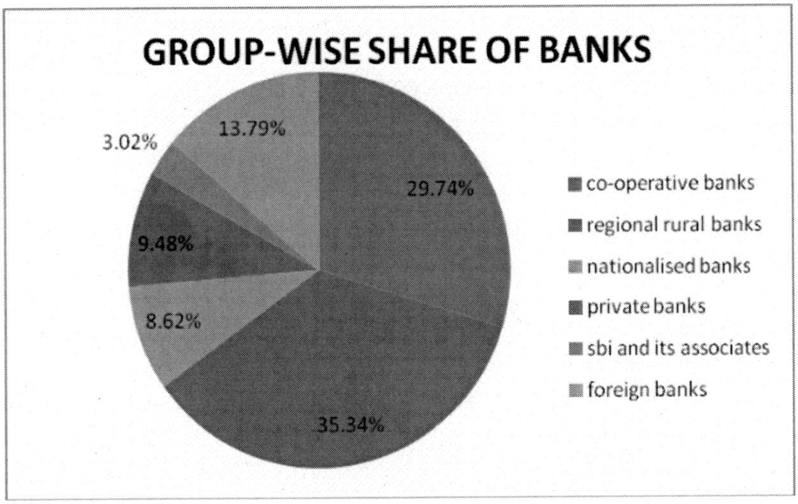

Fig. 2: Showing the Group-Wise Share of Banks

Many Indian origin banks have expanded their services in foreign countries and tried to gain international recognition and profit in the society. The numbers of foreign banks operating in India stood at 32 with 310 branches. Total business of foreign banks stood at ₹ 4,011.1 bn in FY10. The number of Indian banks operating outside India stood at 15 with 147 overseas branches and the overseas business of the Indian banks stood at ₹ 4,045.3 bn. (according to RBI and D&B Research). The Table 4 shows few major banks operating in the international markets.

Table 4: Showing Indian Banks Opreting in International Markets

Name of the Bank	*Operating Country*
Allahabad Bank	Hongkong
Axis Bankltd	Hongkong and Singapore
SBI (China) Ltd.	Sanghai
Bank of Baroda (Uganda) Ltd.	Uganda
Canara Bank	Hongkongand United Kingdom
Bank of Baroda	Muscat and Oman
Syndicate Bank	United Kingdom

ANALYZING THE EXTENT OF CREDIT AVAILABILITY AND ITS IMPACT ON INDIAN FINANCIAL MARKET

The Reserve Bank of India (RBI) issued an advisory note to Pubic Sector Banks (PSBs) for maintaining a Credit to Deposit Ratio (CDR) of 60% in rural and semi urban branches continuously to reduce inter-regional imbalances in credit delivery. The note is a critique of CDR as a yardstick of measuring bank's social responsibility like serving the poor, instead it suggests to develop an alternative measure that calculates credit as per utilization, which gives a far better picture of credit usage. It also proposes to build enabling environment for utilizing the vast banking network in India, which provide unique opportunity to achieve the MDGs and bring financial inclusion in the society because finance is the strongest link to achieve prosperity. Table 5 basically shows different banks operating in India and their credit-deposit ratio over five years.SBI and its Associates has the strongest credit-deposit ratio and foreign banks stand at the last, strong credit deposit ratio of at least above 60% indicates the soundness of the financial system and all the banks operating on Indian soil meet this criterion. The global meltdown and weak finance system in western countries should be a lesson for India to maintain balance in the functioning of the banking sector because it affects the overall growth of the economy.

Table 5: Credit-Deposit Ratio

Year	*State Bank of India and its Associates*	*Nationalized Banks*	*Other Scheduled Commercial Banks*	*Foreign Banks*	*All Scheduled Commercial Banks*
2006	68.52	68.01	73.04	85.77	70.07
2007	76.16	70.38	75.14	83.78	73.46
2008	76.72	71.66	76.80	84.29	74.61
2009	73.43	72.17	78.13	77.25	73.83
2010	77.45	71.34	76.87	68.64	73.58

Source: Trend and Progress of Banking in India 2000–2010.

The central bank of a country records and publishes the money supply data and in the mid of 2011 money supply (comprises currency in public circulation bank deposits and money invested in other saving plans) grew 16.4%.In case of high unemployment and excess capacity, though money supply acts as a demand stimulant, it does not affect the price level to a great extent. But if the economy is having full employment situation then impact of money supply is felt on prices. So the central banks has to consciously manage the liquidity level in the economy so that stability is not at stake.

ASSESSING THE IMPACT OF BASEL (III) NORMS ON INDIAN BANKING SYSTEM AND ITS FUTURE

The globalization process brought the necessity of synchronizing the financial mechanism of all the countries in such a way that proper regulation and functional viability is maintained throughout. For this purpose deliberations by central bankers from around the world, and in 1988, the Basel Committee (BCBS) in Basel, Switzerland, published a set of minimum capital requirements for banks and it came to be known as Basel Accord I. Further came Basel II in 2004. Its aim was to maintain sufficient consistency of regulations so that this does not become a source of competitive inequality amongst internationally active banks. It also set up the risk and capital management requirements so that adequate capital is maintained with the bank which leads to solvency and economic stability in the country. The proposed Basel III guidelines seek to improve the ability of banks to withstand periods of economic and financial stress by prescribing more stringent capital and liquidity requirements for them. ICRA views the suggested capital requirement as a positive for banks as it raises the minimum core capital stipulation, introduces counter-cyclical measures, and enhances banks" ability to conserve core capital in the event of stress through a conservation capital buffer. The prescribed liquidity requirements, on the other hand, are aimed at bringing in uniformity inthe liquidity standards followed by banks globally.

The key elements of the proposed Basel III guidelines include the following[ii]:

1. Definition of capital made more stringent, capital buffers introduced and Loss absorptive capacity of Tier 1 and Tier 2 Capital instrument of Internationally active banks proposed to be enhanced.
2. Forward looking provisioning prescribed.
3. Modifications made in counterparty credit risk weights.
4. New parameter of leverage ratio introduced.
5. Global liquidity standard prescribed.

The Basel Committee on Banking Supervision (BCBS) has issued comprehensive reform packages entitled "Basel III: A global regulatory framework for more resilient banks and banking systems" and "Basel III: International framework for liquidity risk measurement, standard and monitoring" in December 2010, with the objective of improving banking sector resilience by strengthening global capital and liquidity regulations, respectively.[iii] The reform package addresses the lessons of the financial crisis and aims at enhancing banking sector's ability to absorb shocks arising from financial and economic stress. Further, the BCBS, through the reform package also aims to improve risk management and governance as well as strengthen banks' transparency and disclosure standards relating to regulatory capital. The reforms also have a macro prudential focus, addressing system-wide risks which can build up across the banking sector as well as the procyclical amplification of these risks over time.

The financial turmoil since 2008 has raised the question over the liquidity prevailing in the markets and maintaining balance between credit and capital availability in the economy is a must. There is a wide body of evidence that the most severe economic crises are associated with banking sector distress.[iv] While there is variation in findings across studies, the Basel Committee's long-term economic impact study found that the central estimate in the economics literature is that banking crises result in losses in economic output equal to about 60% of pre-crisis GDP. Therefore strengthening the banking norms is the need of the our. The western economy crises has made the emerging economies to be alert in framing its macro and monetary policies.

The agreement is based on two assumptions that are judged as flawed.[v] The first one states that the crisis is a liquidity crisis when in fact it is a solvency crisis. This point is raised by Blundell-Wignall and Atkinson (2010):

> *"The liquidity proposals have some puzzling features. If banks are solvent, and have adequate capital, then the management of their liquidity and funding should, in principle, be left up to them. Maturity transformation is a key function of the banking system, and notwithstanding the crisis, banks should not be treated as being naïve in running their own business. The cause of the crisis was a solvency problem, after which uncertainty arose as to banks' ability to pay which, in turn, led to a buyers strike affecting short-dated funding".*

REFERENCES

[i] The Challenge of Globalization Some Reflections from the Reserve Bank Perspective—Address by Dr. Duvvuri Subbarao, Governor, Reserve Bank of India at the 37th Annual Convocation of the Indian Institute of Management, Bangalore on March 30, 2012.

[ii] ICRA Comment, Proposed Basel III Guidelines: A Credit Positive for Indian, Banks.

[iii] www.Rbi.org.in RBI/2011-12/331.
DBOD.No.BP.BC. 71/21.06.201/2011-12 December 30, 2011.

[iv] Conference on Basel III, Financial Stability Institute.
Basel 6 April 2011 , Basel III: Stronger Banks and a More Resilient Financial System, Stefan Walter, Secretary General, Basel Committee on Banking Supervision.

[v] The Basel III Agreement: A Critical Survey, Matthieu Méaulle, Economic Advisor, FEPS, This work has been done as part of the FEPS-IPD collaboration framework.

BIBLIOGRAPHY

1. RBI, Trends and Progress of Banking in India, various issues.
2. RBI, Statistical Tables relating to banks in India, various issues.
3. Shirai, S. (2001). "Assessment of India's Banking Sector Reforms from the perspective of the governance of the banking sytem", ESCAP-ADB Joint Workshop on "Mobilizing Domestics Finance fr Development: Reassessment of Bank Finance and Debt Markets in Asia and the Pacific", pp. 99–122.
4. Reserve Bank of India, 2010, Financial Stability Report—Financial Institutions (Chapter Five), RBI March 2010.

5. Ataullah, Ali, Cockerill, T. and Le, H. (2004). "Financial Liberalization and Bank Efficiency: A Comparative Analysis of India and Pakistan" Applied Economics.
6. Ketkar, Kusum W., Agarwal, M.L., Singh, G.K. and Mitra, S. (2005). "Liberalization and Deregulation: Performance of Banks in India," Under revision Economic and Political Weekly.
7. Narasimham Committee (1992). Report of the Committee on the Financial System, Reserve Bank of India Bulletin, Vol. XLVI, No. 2, February, 369–80.
8. Reserve Bank of India, Report on Trend and Progress of banking in India, Various issues, Bombay, India.
9. The Basel III Agreement: A Critical Survey Matthieu Méaulle, Economic Advisor, FEPS. This work has been done as part of the FEPS-IPD collaboration framework, 11th May 2011.

Fee-based Income for Public Sector Banks: Challenges and Opportunities

Smita Roy Trivedi

Department of Finance, National Institute of Bank Management (NIBM), Pune

The banking industry in Indian today is facing unique opportunities and challenges. A crucial issue concerning banks since the deregulation of interest rates and consequent increase in competition is the pressure on net interest margin. Banks are therefore now looking for fee-based income to fill the gap in interest income. Recently the RBI Governor, D Subbarao has urged banks to cut operating costs, raise fee-based income to pay more on deposits and charge less from lenders to help foster inclusive and higher economic growth.[1]

The importance of non-interest income for the banks cannot be overemphasized. In this context, this paper studies the growth in fee-based income as a proportion of total income for public sector banks in the last fifteen years. It provides a comparative analysis of fee-based income growth for public sector vis-à-vis old and new private sector banks. It is found that while both public sector and private sector banks have raised their fee-based income, the private sector banks have been more successful in increasing the income from fee-based activities.

Globally banks have been thought of as firms which take deposits and make loans, with profit difference between the costs of deposits and the earnings from lending. While banks performed other functions their main task was held to be intermediation, i.e. the conversion of short-term liabilities, such as deposits, into longer term assets, especially loans. However, in the last two decades the environment facing banks have been different, as Dammann (2008) points out. Thus, while traditionally most of bank's revenue has come from interest income, fee-based income now has an important position on the bank's income statement. As finance has become more globalised there has been an increasing shift from banking to securities markets, known as disintermediation. This

[1] Business Standard. "Subbarao asks banks to reduce margins". December 4, 2010. Retrieved from www.business-standard.com, accessed 7.12.2012.

has further increased competition among banks to find newer sources of fee-based income.[2]

Fund based income refers to income earned by the bank from use of its own funds, while fee-based income refers to income earned form services for which a fee is charged by the bank. Smith *et al.* (2003) examine the variability of interest and non-interest income and their correlation for banking systems of EU countries for the period 1994 to 1998. It is found that increased importance of non-interest income did for most bank categories stabilize profits in the European banking system in those years. However, the paper did not find that non-interest income is invariably more stable than interest income.[3] Uppal (2010) shows in the Indian context that interest income is continuously declining due to deregulation in interest rates and non-interest income is rising. Among the non-interest income components, commodity exchange and brokerage witnessed a large share while exchange transaction witnessed a meager part.[4]

This paper further identifies the top banks in each group who have successfully increased their income generated form fee-based activities. It must be underlined that while banks in India have recognized the importance of raising income from fee-based income activities and thereby reducing the dependence on fund-based income, there are many challenges in the way of moving to more fee-based activities and sustaining them, especially for public sector banks. This suggests that in future a framework must be developed to identify the opportunities for increasing fee-based activities and devising ways and means to successfully increase the income generated from such activities. We further briefly point out the challenges and opportunities present for public sector banks to raise fee-based income. In this context, we specifically highlight the possibility of financial planning services offering a viable source of revenue.

OBJECTIVES

Given the importance of fee-based income for banks in India today, and efforts by leading banks to raise income from fee-based services, this paper makes a comparative analysis of the proportion of income coming from fee-based and fund-based sources for public sector and private sector banks in India over the period 1998–2012. The post liberalization period is chosen here to understand the impact of reforms on income form fee-based activities. The paper further underlines the top banks in each group in terms of greater

---

[2] Dammann, N. (2008). The bidder competition for ABN AMRO: A strategic analysis and implications for the banking sector. Bachelor Thesis, ISBN 978-3-638-04944-3, pp. 3–4.

[3] Smith, R.; Staikouras, C. and Wood, G. (2003). Non-interest income and total income stability. Working Paper No. 198. Bank of England.

[4] Uppal, R.K. (2010). Stability in Bank Income through Fee-based Activities. *Information Management and Business Review,* Vol. 1, No. 1, pp. 40–47.

proportion of income coming from fee-based services. We further discuss the challenges faced by banks in the way of increasing fee-based income and the opportunities that can be tapped by these banks to raise such income, especially highlighting the move to financial planning and wealth management divisions as a viable source of fee-based income.

DATA AND METHODOLOGY

The paper compares the proportion of income coming from fee-based services for public sector and private sector (old and new) over a period 1998–2012. The list of banks in each group is given in Appendix A. For private sector banks the criterion fir classification into old and new has been the year of incorporation, with banks incorporated after 1980 taken as new private sector bank. Data on income earned by individual banks and its various components, as obtained from the CMIE Prowess database has been the secondary data source for the research.

FINDINGS OF THE STUDY

The finding of the study on the various aspects are discussed below:

Share of Income Coming from Fee-Based Services

Comparing public sector, private (old) and Private (new) sector banks. We find that the new private sector banks have the greatest proportion of income coming form fee-based income, with an average of 10.52% of total income coming from fee-based services over the period 1998–2012, while for public sector banks in India it is 6.11%. Table 1 shows

Table 1

Year	*1998*	*1999*	*2000*	*2001*	*2002*	*2003*	*2004*	*2005*
Percent of fee-based income in total income	6.78	8.42	6.42	7.26	8.14	6.69	7.61	8.94
Percent of fund-based income in total income	92.60	90.93	90.52	90.21	89.88	92.72	91.52	89.97
Year	*2006*	*2007*	*2008*	*2009*	*2010*	*2011*	*2012*	*Average*
Percent of fee-based income in total income	13.93	14.87	13.58	13.00	12.64	14.67	14.78	10.52
Percent of fund-based income in total income	84.92	83.74	84.79	85.78	86.05	83.75	84.06	88.10

for new private sector banks in Indian the proportion of income coming form fee-based sources have increased substantially, from 6.78% in 1998 to 14.78% in 2012. However, for the public sector banks, fee-based income has remained more of less constant at around 6%. Percentage of fee-based income in total income has decreased for public sector banks from 6.94% in 1998 to 5.47% in 2005 and then increased to a high of 6.31% in 2008 before falling again to 5.85% in 2002 and thereby marginally increasing to 6.22% in 2011 and 6.03 % in 2012. It can be seen from Table 3, that for old private sector banks

Table 2: Fee-based and Fund Based Income as Percentage of Total Income: Public Sector Banks

Year	*1998*	*1999*	*2000*	*2001*	*2002*	*2003*	*2004*	*2005*
Percent of fee-based income in total income	6.94	6.63	6.65	6.46	5.98	5.53	5.45	5.47
Percent of fund-based income in total income	91.11	89.43	91.49	91.90	92.36	92.82	92.02	91.60
Year	*2006*	*2007*	*2008*	*2009*	*2010*	*2011*	*2012*	*Average*
Percent of fee-based income in total income	6.07	6.17	6.31	5.87	5.85	6.22	6.03	6.11
Percent of fund-based income in total income	89.90	88.19	89.95	90.78	91.27	91.10	91.12	91.00

Table 3: Fee-based and Fund Based Income as Percentage of Total Income: Old Private Sector Banks

Year	*1998*	*1999*	*2000*	*2001*	*2002*	*2003*	*2004*	*2005*
Percent of fee-based income in total income	5.71	5.40	5.56	5.89	5.82	5.02	4.68	4.58
Percent of fund-based income in total income	91.27	92.61	92.51	92.11	92.14	92.94	93.33	93.19
Year	*2006*	*2007*	*2008*	*2009*	*2010*	*2011*	*2012*	*Average*
Percent of fee-based income in total income	5.15	5.27	5.39	4.81	4.33	4.06	4.15	5.06
Percent of fund-based income in total income	91.74	90.37	90.33	90.94	91.56	92.10	91.47	91.91

too, the percentage of income coming from fee-based services has hovered at around 5.06%. It fell from 5.71% in 1998 to 4.58% in 2005, and then increased to 5.39% to 2008, before falling to 4.06% before increasing marginally to 4.15%.

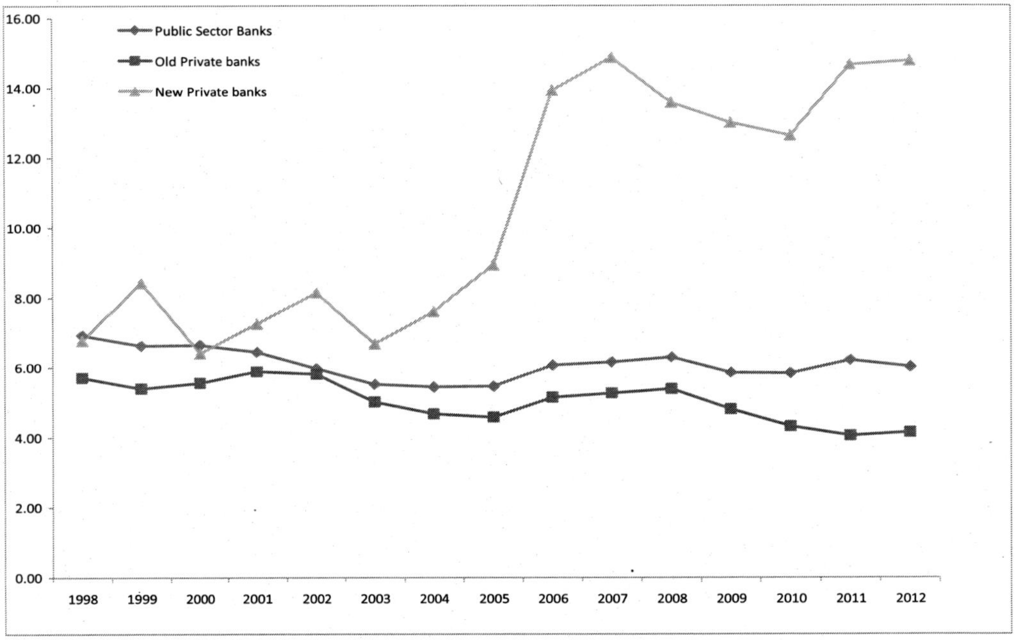

Chart 1: Fee-based as Percentage of Total Income: Public Sector and Private (old and new) Sector Banks

Top Performers for Public Sector Banks and New Private Banks

In this section we identify the top performers in each group who have a greater proportion of income coming from fee-based services. As seen in Table 4A, among public sector banks the State Bank group is the best performer, and State bank of India scores a high position with 9.73% of income generated from fee-based services. Table 4B gives the individual State percentages for top banks in the State Bank Group. The other banks following the State bank Group is given, with the average percentage of income coming from fee-based services over this period. This is also shown in Chart 2. We similarly find out for private banks the top performers in the group. We find that Yes bank since its inception has been successful in generating income from fee-based activities, with 13.06% of the income coming from fee-based services. It is followed closely by HDFC Bank and Axis bank, both with more than 10% income coming from fee-based services.

Table 4A: Public Sector Banks: Percentage of Income Coming from Fee-Based Services from 1998–2012

State Bank of India	9.73
State Bank Group	8.96
Punjab National Bank	6.28
Allahabad Bank	5.74
Corporation Bank	5.42
Indian Overseas Bank	5.40

Table 4B: State Bank Group: Percentage of Income Coming from Fee-Based Services from 1998–2012

State Bank of Bikaner and Jaipur	10.84
State Bank of India	9.73
State Bank of Mysore	9.49
State Bank of Indore	8.94
State Bank of Saurashtra [Merged]	8.86
State Bank of Hyderabad	8.28
State Bank of Patiala	7.92
State Bank of Travancore	7.59

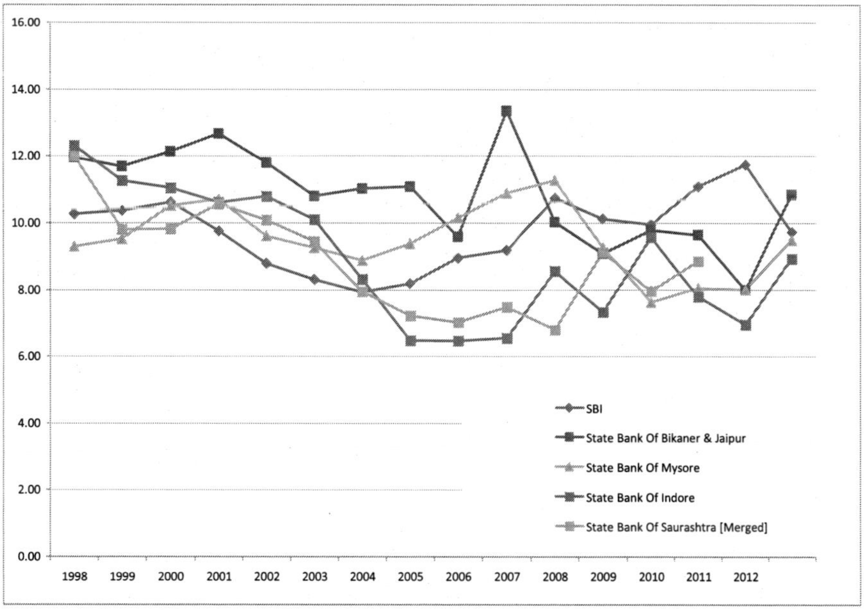

Chart 2: Fee-based Income in Public Sector Banks: A Comparison

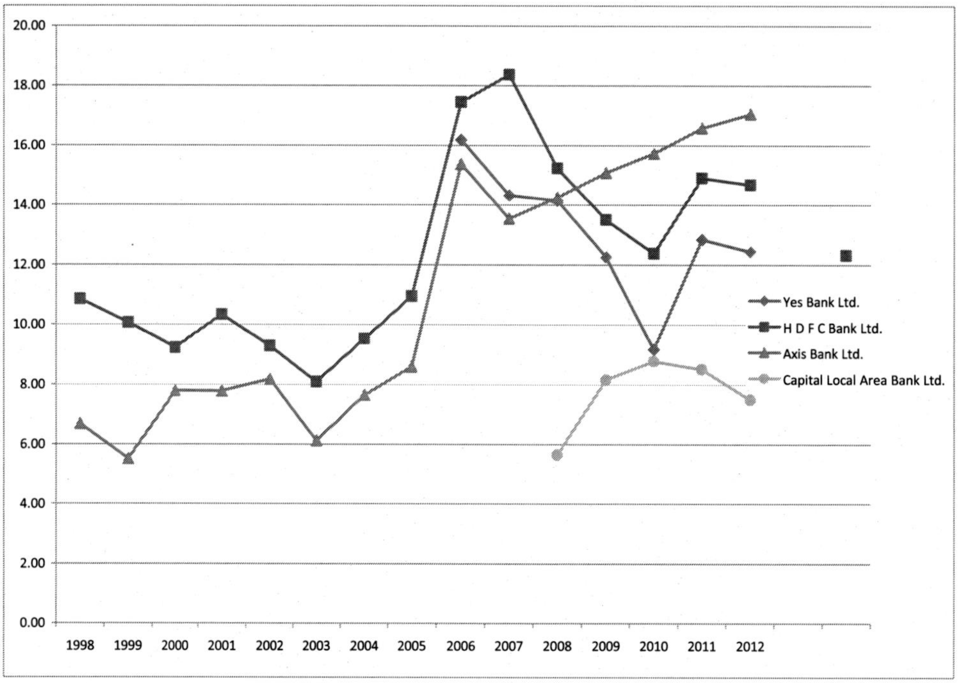

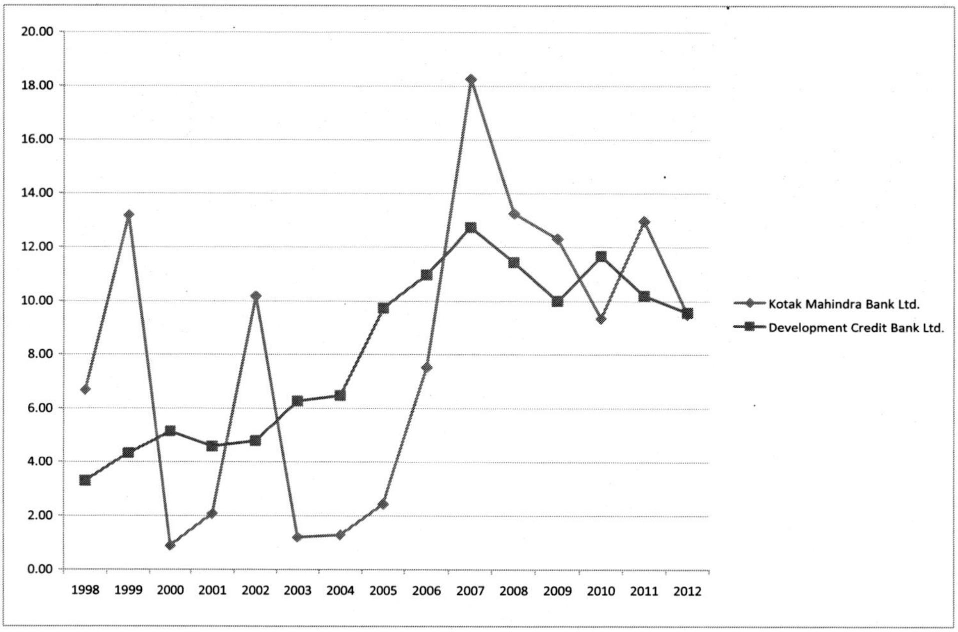

Chart 3: Fee-based Income in New Private Sector Banks: A Comparison

Table 5: Private Banks (New): Percentage of Income Coming from Fee-Based Services from 1998–2012

Yes Bank Ltd.	13.06
HDFC Bank Ltd.	12.32
Axis Bank Ltd.	11.06
Development Credit Bank Ltd.	8.07
Kotak Mahindra Bank Ltd.	8.06
Capital Local Area Bank Ltd.	7.71
Global Trust Bank Ltd. [Merged]	7.24
Centurion Bank of Punjab Ltd. [Merged]	7.00
Times Bank Ltd. [Merged]	6.84
IDBI Bank Ltd. [Merged]	6.81

CHALLENGES AND OPPORTUNITIES

It is seen that while new private sector banks have been very successful in increasing the income from fee-based activities the same cannot be dais about the public sector banks. We discuss the challenges and opportunities facing the public sector banks in this regard. One of the areas where banks can venture to raise the income from fee-based services is *financial planning and wealth management services.* The provision of wealth management services for the growing HNW and upwardly mobile Indian population affords an impressive opportunity for the public sector banks to increase their fee-based income and thereby enhance their competitiveness in the Indian financial market.

Globally and in India, there has been a huge growth in the assets of High Net Worth Individuals (HNWI) and Mid Net Worth population, as evidenced by several reports. The HNWI population is growing by leaps and bounds and India's population of HNWI has become one of the largest in the world. India's HNI population grew at 20.8 per cent in 2010 to 1,53,000 compared with 1,26,700 in 2009.[5] India mid net worth population is also on the rise turning the Indian market into one of the most lucrative markets for consumer goods. A new study by the McKinsey Global Institute (MGI) suggests that, if India continues its recent growth, average household income will triple over the next two decades and it will become the world's fifth largest consumer economy by 2025, up from 12th in 2007. Again, on account of changing demographics and increased access to higher education there are a larger proportion of young people in India earning considerably high incomes which could be channelized by banks into savings and investments through financial planning and wealth management services.

[5]Merrill Lynch - Capgemini Asia-Pacific Wealth Report (2011). Retrieved form www.ml.com/media/114333.pdf, accessed 23.2.2012.

The market for financial advisory services in India is waiting to be tapped. A plethora of financial products has flooded the Indian markets with varying risks and returns making the right choice of investment very difficult. This has led to a huge rise in the demand for financial advisory services. In India private banks including HDFC, Axis, ICICI and Kotak Mahindra have all been active in the provision of financial advisory services to individuals and corporates. Public sector banks have been late entrants in this area and only recently we have seen public sector banks venturing into full-fledged Financial Planning and Advisory Services divisions. The divisions aim at helping clients with professional advice to create, build and protect their wealth and minimize tax liability in a wealth preservation plan which they develop and monitor over a long-term, on-going relationship. Banks in India, in fact can explore quite a few organizational structures to tap this growing demand for financial advisory services.

State Bank of India has launched the Financial Planning and Advisory Services (FPAS) divisions in select cities across the country. Public sector banks like Bank of Baroda, Indian Bank, Punjab National bank, City Union Bank Ltd, The Development Credit Bank Ltd., The Federal Bank Ltd., ING Vysya Bank Ltd., The Lakshmi Vilas Bank Ltd. and Yes bank have now separate wealth management divisons which stress on designing specific financial plans keeping in mind the client risk profile, client financial goals and expected income streams.

However, without regulation coming out clearly regarding financial planning and wealth management division, public sector banks are finding it difficult to chart out a road map for provision of these services. With the Citi-bank fraud case of 2010 and reports of fraudulent practices followed in financial planning divisions, the Reserve Bank of India (RBI) and Securities and Exchange Board of India (SEBI) are coming out with a new and stricter set of rules for the wealth management industry as discussed in the Sub-Committee of Financial Stability and Development Council (FSDC) in August, 2011.[6] The anticipation of a newer set of guidelines has made the public sector banks who were in the plans of expanding into this sector somewhat wary of the new developments. It must be stressed here that not only do the public sector banks have a distinctive advantage in moving into this segment given their large customer base and branch network, they also have an advantage with respect to regulatory compliance with the already strict internal checks and balances in place at these banks.

SEBI Annual Report 2011 also made important changes to the mandated certification needed for executives in wealth management division. Earlier, agents/distributors of mutual fund units were required to obtain certification from Association of Mutual Funds in India (AMFI). From June 01, 2010, the certification examination for distributors, agents

[6] Post-scams, RBI plans wealth mgmt rules. The Financial Express, Aug 24, 2011. Retrieved www.financialexpress.com/news/postscams-rbi-plans-wealth, accessed 31.5.2012.

or other persons employed or engaged or to be employed or engaged in the sale and/or distribution of mutual fund products is to be conducted by the National Institute of Securities Markets (NISM). With the mandated certification being offered by NISM, the financial planning departments of banks will have train manpower for operation of the departments.[7]

Again, while many public sector banks do not have a functional wealth management or financial planning division though they are cross selling both insurance and mutual fund products through their retail division. The *cross-selling of mututal fund and insurance products* through retail division is another avenue through which fee-based income can increase. This also requires tarining of manpower but to an extent lesser than that required for financial planning divisions. *Corporate fee-based services offered by banks include treasury products; cash management services; letter of credit and bank guarantee; bill discounting; factoring and forfeiting services; foreign exchange services; merchant banking; leasing; credit rating; underwriting and custodial services.*[8] Most public sector banks in India are quite active in most of these services.

CONCLUSION

The paper shows that while new private banks have been successful in increasing income from fee-based services in India, the public sector banks have not been very sussessful in this regard. The percentage of income coming form fee-based services has remained more or less constant for both public sector banks and old private sector banks. In this regard regard, some banks like the State bank of India,and State Bank Group has been more sucessful than other public sector banks in raising revenue from fee-based services. Public sector banks must raise their fee-based income, some avenue of which has been discussed in this paper. This includes corporate fee-based services offered by banks include treasury products; cash management services; letter of credit and bank guarantee; bill discounting; factoring and forfeiting services; foreign exchange services; merchant banking; leasing; credit rating; underwriting and custodial services ansd reatil fee- based services like cross-selling of mututal fund and insurance products and the move to financial planning and wealth management services.

---

[7] Securities and Exchange Board of India (SEBI) (2011). Annual Report. Downloaded from http://www.sebi.gov.in › News/Publications › Annual Reports, accessed 28/11/2011.

[8] Structure of the Indian banking Industry. BFSI Sector in India. Retrieved from www.dnb.co.in/bfsisectorinindia/ BankC2.aspCached, accessed 31/5/2012.

APPENDIX–A: List of Public Sector Banks in India (Prowess Data)

Allahabad Bank
Andhra Bank
Bank of Baroda
Bank of India
Bank of Maharashtra
Bareilly Corporation Bank Ltd.
Bharat Overseas Bank Ltd. [Merged]
Canara Bank
Central Bank of India
Corporation Bank
Dena Bank
IDBI Bank Ltd.
Indian Bank
Indian Overseas Bank
Jammu and Kashmir Bank Ltd.
Nainital Bank Ltd.
Oriental Bank of Commerce
Punjab and Sind Bank
Punjab National Bank
SBI Commercial and International Bank Ltd.
State Bank of Bikaner and Jaipur
State Bank of Hyderabad
State Bank of India
State Bank of Indore
State Bank of Mysore
State Bank of Patiala
State Bank of Saurashtra [Merged]
State Bank of Travancore
Syndicate Bank
Uco Bank
Union Bank of India
United Bank of India
Vijaya Bank

APPENDIX–B: List of Private Sector Banks (New)

Axis Bank Ltd.
Bank of Punjab Ltd. [Merged]
Brink'S Arya India Pvt. Ltd.
Capital Local Area Bank Ltd.
Centurion Bank of Punjab Ltd. [Merged]
Development Credit Bank Ltd.
Ganesh Bank of Kurundwad Ltd. [Merged]
Global Trust Bank Ltd. [Merged]
HDFC Bank Ltd.
IDBI Bank Ltd. [Merged]
Kotak Mahindra Bank Ltd.
Krishna Bhima Samruddhi Local Area Bank Ltd.
South Gujarat Local Area Bank Ltd. [Merged]
Times Bank Ltd. [Merged]
Vinayak Local Area Bank Ltd.
Yes Bank Ltd.

APPENDIX–C: List of Private Sector Banks (New)

Bank of Rajasthan Ltd. [Merged]
Benares State Bank Ltd. [Merged]
Catholic Syrian Bank Ltd.
City Union Bank Ltd.
Dhanlaxmi Bank Ltd.
Federal Bank Ltd.
Karnataka Bank Ltd.
Karur Vysya Bank Ltd.
Lakshmi Vilas Bank Ltd.
Lord Krishna Bank Ltd. [Merged]
Nedungadi Bank Ltd. [Merged]
Ratnakar Bank Ltd.
Sangli Bank Ltd. [Merged]
South Indian Bank Ltd.
Tamilnad Mercantile Bank Ltd.
United Western Bank Ltd. [Merged]

Corporate Governance Reforms in Public Sector Banks in India

R.K. Mishra, S. Sreenivasa Murthy, J. Kiranmai and Md Azharuddin[1]

Institute of Public Enterprise, Hyderabad

[1]University of Hyderabad, Hyderabad

E-mail: rkmishra@ipeindia.org; ssmurthy@ipeindia.org; kiranmai@ipeindia.org

ABSTRACT: *The role of banks is integral to the growth of any Economy. They provide finance to commercial enterprises, access to payment systems, and a variety of retail financial services for the economy at large. Some banks have a broader impact on the macro sector of the economy, facilitating the transmission of monetary policy by making credit and liquidity available in difficult market conditions. The integral role that banks play in the national economy is demonstrated by the universal practice of states in regulating the banking industry and providing, in many cases, a government safety net to compensate depositors when banks fail. Financial regulation is necessary because of the multiplier effect that banking activities have on the rest of the economy. The large number of stakeholders (such as employees, customers, suppliers etc), whose economic well-being depends on the health of the banking industry, depend on appropriate regulatory practices and supervision. Indeed, in a healthy banking system, the supervisors and regulators themselves are stakeholders acting on behalf of society at large. Their primary function is to develop substantive standards and other risk management procedures for financial institutions in which regulatory risk measures correspond to the overall economic and operational risk faced by a bank. The paper tries to evaluate the Corporate Governance (CG) practices of five public sector banks in terms of strategic objective, roles and responsibilities, accountability, transparency, eligibility of board members, internal audit mechanisms, compensation policies, etc.*

INTRODUCTION

With the development of world economy, market structure has become much more complex and cohesive. In the present circumstances it is not easy to monitor the dynamics that come into play between the different agents. There always seems implicit form of tussle between the self-interest groups and the system, which is not productive in nature and may sometime come out to be perilous. The conventional idea of rational self-interest for the economic efficiency no longer rules until there is coordination on the part of the agents and principals. I think because of non-uniformity of interests between the groups in an organization the need for corporate governance arises. The concept of corporate governance catches the eyes of the public in more forceful form after the huge scandals and fraudulent in big capitalist industrial countries as well as developing countries. It is the system in which the interest of whole stakeholder is balanced. It not only brings the efficiency in the business but also one of the factors of high growth in an economy.

In this globalised world corporate need to access global pool of capital as well as best human capital to compete in cut-throat competitive world stage. Under such scenario the divergence of interest between managements and suppliers of capital bound to erupt. Through mutual understanding and fair distribution of share the divergence between the agents and principals can be neutralize. This could only be possible when there is effective corporate governance. The size of the corporate sector and their economic activities are huge and still growing, so the underlying mechanism and policy challenges faced by both regulators and policy makers are quite incomprehensible.

The term governance derives from the Latin word "gubernare", which means "to steer". So, the joint usage of the word corporate governance means to give direction to economic activities which should enhance the efficiency of the organization. Jerry McGuire's phrase "shows me the money!" remind us everything boiled down to numbers. Economic matters can be quantified and measured but corporate governance metrics are more elusive matter. Corporate governance guidelines are a mechanism that a firm can enact which should reduce agency costs and better align the interest of boards and suppliers of capital, fundamentally deals with agency problems caused by the separation of ownership from management. From financial perspective corporate governance is the construction of rules, practices and incentives to effectively align the interests of the agents with those of the principals. Corporate governance is beyond the realm of physical law, since it stems from the culture, ethic and mindset of management and cannot be regulated by legislation alone; it is about openness, integrity and accountability. Corporate governance is the list of practices indicating how the boards of director will attempt to oversee the management of the firm and carry out the responsibilities to the firm's suppliers of capital. Corporate governance cannot be separated from political structure of the country since it evolves from that generic framework.

CORPORATE GOVERNANCE IN BANKS

The role of banks is integral to any economy. They provide finance to commercial enterprises, access to payment systems, and a variety of retail financial services for the economy at large. Some banks have a broader impact on the macro sector of the economy, facilitating the transmission of monetary policy by making credit and liquidity available in difficult market conditions. The integral role that banks play in the national economy is demonstrated by the almost universal practice of states in regulating the banking industry and providing, in many cases, a government safety net to compensate depositors when banks fail. Financial regulation is necessary because of the multiplier effect that banking activities have on the rest of the economy. The large number of stakeholders (such as employees, customers, suppliers etc), whose economic well-being depends on the health of the banking industry, depend on appropriate regulatory practices and supervision. Indeed, in a healthy banking system, the supervisors and regulators themselves are stakeholders acting on behalf of society at large. Their primary function is to develop substantive standards and other risk management procedures for financial institutions in which regulatory risk measures correspond to the overall economic and operational risk faced by a bank. Accordingly, it is imperative that financial regulators ensure that banking and other financial institutions have strong governance structures, especially in light of the pervasive changes in the nature and structure of both the banking industry and the regulation which governs its activities. The World Bank report emphasis that the corporate governance initiatives win most supports when driven from the bottom up rather from the top down.

The globalization of banking markets has raised important issues regarding corporate governance regulation for banking institutions. There has been evaluation and re-evaluation of the norms of corporate governance in banks and other financial sectors in order to bring efficiency and transparency in its conduct. Banks are nerve center of whole economy, so they need special attention and monitoring. The traditional approach of corporate governance in the financial sector often involved the regulator or bank supervisor relying on statutory authority to devise governance standards promoting the interests of shareholders, depositors and other stakeholders. This is justified by the history of crises in the capitalist economy, we can conclude how banks are miserably failed in their operation. The great depression of 1929 was an example of series of banks failure, greed and misconduct on the part of agents. There has been a great deal of attention given recently to the issue of corporate governance in various national and international. In particular, the OECD has issued a set of corporate governance standards and guidelines to help governments "in their efforts to evaluate and improve the legal, institutional and regulatory framework for corporate governance in their countries, and to provide guidance and suggestions for stock exchanges, investors, corporations, and other parties that have a role in the process of developing good corporate governance". For example In US, corporate governance for banking institutions is regulated by federal and state statute and regulation. Federal regulation provides a prescriptive framework for directors and senior management in exercising their management responsibilities. US banking regulation also address governance problems in bank and financial holding companies.

The national banking law and regulation should permit the bank regulator to play the primary role in establishing governance standards for banks, financial institutions and bank/financial holding companies. The regulator is best positioned to represent and to balance the various stakeholder interests. They should be given some magnitude of power to draw their own mechanism of regulation which should be consistent with the regulatory board, keeping in mind the interest and the welfare of the society. The efficient banking regulation requires regulators to be entrusted with discretion to represent broader stakeholder interests in order to ensure that banks operate under good governance standards. Many countries traditionally adapted the principal-agent model to analysis the relationship between shareholders, directors and managers, and given the platform for broader investigation in policy framework to maintain financial stability and ensure that banks are operated in a way that promotes economic growth as well as enhance shareholder value. Corporate governance in the banking and financial sector differs from that in the non-financial sectors because of the broader risk that banks and financial firms pose to the economy. They finance much of their resource on the expectation that it will yield return on certain future date. This 'expectation' is venerable to future outcome and the mode of the markets. The asymmetric information in agency conflicts arises from the inability to write complete contracts. As a result regulators play more active roles in establishing standards and rules to make management practices in banks more accountable and efficient. But simultaneously the presence of regulators introduces a third party into the problem of asymmetric information between:

1. depositors, banks and regulators
2. owner, managers and regulators
3. borrowers, managers and regulators.

Corporate governance mechanism such as monitoring by equity holders and debt holders are hindered owing to lack of transparency and lack of market values for loans, thereby creating a more complex asymmetric information structure between insiders and outsiders in the banking sector. As insider ownership increases manger's interest become more aligned with the outside shareholders. Thus inside ownership is expected to have a positive effect on bank valuation. In regard to the bank risk, empirical investigation by Saunders *et al.* (1990), Knopf and Teall (1996) and Andreson and Fraser (2000) suggest a positive association between bank risk taking behavior and insider ownership, indicating that banks with high level of insider ownership are likely to be more risky.

If a bank is mismanaged and account manipulate then its consequences would be quite pervasive. Bank have contractual obligation to its customers and other member banks, if it fails to honors its obligation on time then the market could face serious liquidity crunch. Consequently, bank regulators place additional responsibilities on bank boards that often result in detailed regulations regarding their decision-making practices and strategic aims. These additional regulatory responsibilities for management have led some experts to observe that banking regulation is a substitute for corporate governance. Many propose improving banks' accountability and efficiency of operations by increasing the legal duties that bank directors and senior management owe to depositors and other creditors. This would involve expanding the scope of fiduciary duties beyond shareholders to include depositors and creditors. Under this approach, depositors and other creditors could sue the board of directors for breach of fiduciary duties and the standard of care, in addition to whatever contractual claims they may have. This would increase banks managers' and directors' incentive of bank managers and directors to pay more regard to solvency risk and would thereby protect the broader economy from excessive risk-taking. In this way agents, principal and other stakeholder will keep an eye on the organization. In some of the western countries like US and UK the major objectives of bank regulation involve, *inter alia,* capital requirements, authorization restrictions, ownership limitations, and restrictions on connected lending. These regulatory standards and rules compose the core elements of corporate governance for banking and credit institutions. As deregulation and liberalization has led to the emergence of global financial markets, banks expanded their international operations and moved into multiple lines of financial business. They developed complex risk management strategies that have allowed them to price financial products and hedge their risk exposures in a manner that improves expected profits, but which may generate more risk and increase liquidity problems in certain circumstances. The limited liability structure of most banks and financial firms, combined with the premium placed on shareholder profits, provides incentives for bank officers to undertake increasingly risky behavior to achieve higher profits without a corresponding concern for the downside losses of risk. Regulators and supervisors find it increasingly difficult to monitor the complicated internal operating systems of banks and financial firms. This has made the external model of regulation less effective as a supervisory technique in addressing the increasing problems that the excessive risk-taking of financial firms poses to the broader economy. This approach of making wealth was quite fascinating in the capitalist countries before the crisis of 2008. They developed financial instruments to attract investors from all over the world. When crisis hits it created havoc all over the world even the least exposed economy faced the consequences in large magnitude inform of unemployment and reduced GDP.

Bank exist because they are ready to take up the risk and challenges in financing. Beside with the rapid pace of financial innovation and globalization the structure of banking and other financial intermediaries is undergoing a sea-change. The regulation of banking firms should be taken in such a way that it does not hurt the interest of the managers, shareholders and stakeholder in one hand and economic activities in other. In India prior to 1991 big banks in public and private sectors incurred a substantial loss. This along with the massive failure of non-banking financial companies (NBFC) had adversely eroded the confidence of investors. The regulators the world over have recognized the variability of depositors to the whim of the managerial misadventure in banks and therefore have been regulated banks tightly than other corporation. Sound corporate governance can contribute to a collaborative working relationship between bank management and bank supervision and also reduced down the risk of principal-agent conflict.

BASEL 1

In its most recent corporate governance report, the OECD emphasized the important role that banking and financial supervision plays in developing corporate-governance standards for financial institutions. Consequently, banking supervisors have a strong interest in ensuring effective corporate governance at every banking organization. Supervisory experience underscores the necessity of having appropriate levels of accountability and managerial competence within each bank. Essentially, the effective supervision of the international banking system requires sound governance structures within each bank, especially with respect to multi-functional banks that operate on a transnational basis. A sound governance system can contribute to a collaborative working relationship between bank supervisors and bank management.

The Basel Committee on Banking Supervision (Basel Committee) has also addressed the issue of corporate governance of banks and multinational financial conglomerates, and has issued several reports addressing specific topics on corporate governance and banking activities. These reports set forth the essential strategies and techniques for the sound corporate governance of financial institutions, which can be summarized as follows:

(a) "Establishing strategic objectives and a set of corporate values that are communicated throughout the banking organization;"
(b) "Setting and enforcing clear lines of responsibility and accountability throughout the organization;"
(c) "Ensuring that board members are qualified for their positions, have a clear understanding of their role in corporate governance and are not subject to undue influence from management or outside concerns;"
(d) "Ensuring that there is appropriate oversight by senior management;"
(e) "Effectively utilizing the work conducted by internal and external auditors, in recognition of the important control function they provide;"
(f) "Ensuring that compensation approaches are consistent with the bank's ethical values, objectives, strategy and control environment;" and
(g) "Conducting corporate governance in a transparent manner."

These standards recognize that senior management is an integral component of the corporate-governance process, while the board of directors provides checks and balances to senior managers, and that senior managers should assume the oversight role with respect to line managers in specific business areas and activities. The effectiveness of the audit process can be enhanced by recognizing the importance and independence of the auditors and requiring management's timely correction of problems identified by auditors. The organizational structure of the board and management should be transparent, with clearly identifiable lines of communication and responsibility for decision-making and business areas. Moreover, there should be itemization of the nature and the extent of transactions with affiliates and related parties.

BASEL 2

The Basel Committee adopted the Capital Accord in 1988 as a legally non-binding international agreement among the world's leading central banks and bank regulators to uphold minimum levels of capital adequacy for internationally-active banks. The New Basel Capital Accord (Basel II) contains the first detailed framework of rules and standards that supervisors can apply to the practices of senior management and the board for banking groups. Bank supervisors will now have the discretion to approve a variety of corporate-governance and risk-management activities for internal processes and decision-making, as well as substantive requirements for estimating capital adequacy and a disclosure framework for investors.

Pillar One has been criticized as allowing large, sophisticated banks to use their own internal ratings methodologies for assessing credit and market risk to calculate their capital requirements. This approach relies primarily on historical data that may be subject to sophisticated applications that might not accurately reflect the bank's true risk exposure, and it may also fail to take account of events that could not be foreseen by past data

Pillar Two seeks to address this problem by providing for both internal and external monitoring of the bank's corporate governance and risk-management practices. Banks are required to monitor their assessments of financial risks and to apply capital charges in a way that most closely approximates the bank's business-risk exposure. Significantly, the supervisor is now expected to play a proactive role in this process by reviewing and assessing the bank's ability to monitor and comply with regulatory capital requirements

Pillar Three also addresses corporate governance concerns by focusing on transparency and market-discipline mechanisms to improve the flow of information between bank management and investors. The goal is to align regulatory objectives with the bank's incentives to make profits for its shareholders. Pillar Three seeks to do this by improving reporting requirements for bank capital adequacy. This covers both quantitative and qualitative disclosure requirements for both overall capital adequacy and capital allocation based on credit risk, market risk, operational risk, and interest rate risks. Pillar

Three sets forth important proposals to improve transparency by linking regulatory capital levels with the quality of disclosure. This means that banks will have incentives to improve their internal controls, systems operations, and overall risk-management practices if they improve the quality of the information regarding the bank's risk exposure and management practices. Under this approach, shareholders would possess more and better information with which to make decisions about well-managed and poorly-managed banks. The downside of this approach is that, in countries with undeveloped accounting and corporate-governance frameworks, the disclosure of such information might lead to volatilities that might undermine financial stability by causing a bank run or failure that might not have otherwise occurred had the information been disclosed in a more sensitive manner. Pillar Three has not yet provided a useful framework for regulators and bank management to coordinate their efforts in the release of information that might create a volatile response in the market.

RBI GUIDELINE AND ANNUAL REPORT

Government, usually, provide necessary framework and environment for its operation. Its value can be, further increased by using the developments of technological innovation, enhancement of productivity and optimality and optimal use of available resources by the corporate sectors.

The corporate governance of banks in developing economies is important for several reasons:

1. Banks have overwhelmingly dominant position in developing economy.
2. As financial markets are usually underdeveloped, banks in developing economy are typically the most important source of finance for the majority of firms.
3. Providing a general accepted means of payment, banks in developing countries are usually the main depositors for the economy's saving.
4. Many developing economies have recently liberalized their banking systems through privatization disinvestment and reducing the role of economic regulation.

The liberalization, privatization, and globalization and information technology are currently changing the Indian banking radically. Through a gradual, calibrated process, changes have been brought into the sector to make it more sound, competitive and vibrant, in line with international practices in terms of application of prudential standards. In this context governance in banks and financial institution has been attracting special attention in India. There are main two reasons:

Liberalization and globalization, the Indian economy while on the one hand is getting more and more integrated with the global markets on the other hand the development outside the country are also affecting are also effecting the domestic market. So the vulnerable, unstable and opaque banking and financial system can severally disrupt macro economics performance of the country. With increasing deregulation there is need for more self regulation, inspite of the fact that the banking and financial all over the globe including India are required to meet certain international bench marks or standards as per regulation, particularly in the areas of supervision, accountability and disclosures.

QUALITY AND CONCENTRATION OF OWNERSHIP

In the context of bank in India, certain dualities also need to be accommodated within the overall framework, particularly:

1. Majority government versus non-government ownership
2. Domestic versus foreign ownership.

The current legal framework with respect to voting rights restriction as per banking laws entails in public bank:

1. Nationalized Banks—No shareholder, other than the central government, shall be entitled to exercise voting right in respect of any shares held by him excess of 1 percent of the total voting rights of all the shareholders of the nationalized bank.
2. SBI—No shareholder, other than the central government shall be entitled to exercise voting rights in excess of 10 percent of the issued capital (government, in consolation with RBI, can raise the above voting right to more than 10 percent).
3. SBI Associates—No shareholder, other than SBI, shall be entitled to exercise voting rights in excess of 10 percent of the issued capital of the subsidiary bank concerned.

COMPARATIVE ANALYSIS OF PUBLIC SECTOR BANKS IN INDIA

Public sector banks (PBS), being the foundation of Indian banking system accounting for more than 78 percent of the total banking industries assets, have been selected where the five leading banks State Bank of India, Punjab National Bank, Bank of Baroda, Bank of India and Canara bank represent the industry. All these five banks are listed on the Mumbai/National Stoke Exchange. The study is based on the information extracted from the annual reports (2010–11) of the banks selected for analysis. The review on the composition and performance represent overall activities of banks during financial year. The financial performance of the five selected banks is discussed in Table 1.

Return on Assets

Return on assets measure how profitable a firm is relative to its total assets. In other word ROA indicates how efficient a management is at using its assets to generate wealth. Mathematically, ROA is the ratio of net income to the total assets. It is one of the best instruments for analyzing comparative performance of firms. Canara bank has the highest

ROA then followed by PNB and BOB. Being a market leader in banking sector SBI fails to reach like that of Canara Bank and other banks. The degree of non-performing assets also effects return, which is evident here.

Table 1: Financial Performance

Indicators	*SBI*	*PNB*	*BOI*	*BOB*	*Canara bank*
Return on Assets (%)	.71	1.32	.82	1.18	1.42
Profit per Employee (₹ in lkhs)	3.846	8.35	6.20	10.59	9.76
Earnings per Share (₹)	130.16	140.60	48.37	116.37	73.69
Net NPA as a percentage	1.63	.85	.91	.35	1.06
Net profit (cr)	8264.52	4433	2489	4241.68	4025.89
Dividend per share (₹)	30	22	7	16.50	11

Profit Per Employee

Net profit per employee or revenue per employee is a firm's net income divided by the total number of employees. In general, higher the numerical value, the more efficient the company uses its employee. It is also used for comparing firm's performance in the same industrial sector. All of the selected banks had scored well under this parameter but still they vary greatly. Bank of Baroda and Canara Bank have done for efficiently than other three banks. The lowest profit per employee is with SBI.

Earnings Per Share

Earnings per share are generally considered to be the single most important variable in determining a share price. It is also a major component used to calculate the price-to-earning valuation ratio. SBI and PNB were able to play well in stoke market as their Earnings Per Share (EPS) are considerably higher than the other banks. The BOI is not far away from these to banks but still behind it.

Net Non-Performing Assets

An asset, including a leased asset, becomes non-performing when it ceases to generate income for the bank. Non Performing Asset means an asset or account of borrower, which has been classified by a bank or financial institution as sub-standard, doubtful or loss asset, in accordance with the directions or guidelines relating to asset classification issued by RBI. Higher NPA is bad for banks because it reduce down the capacity of credit creation, thus effecting returns on assets. SBI, BOI and Canara Bank come in the same bracket as these banks have almost high net NPA. We can see the effect of NPA on the return of the banks, higher the NPA followed by lower return on assets or vice-versa.

Net Profit

Net profit is a measure of the profitability of a venture after accounting for all costs. In accounting net profit is the gross profit minus overheads minus interest payable for given period of time. SBI outpaced all other banks almost by half net profit. PNB, BOB and Canara Bank all come in the same platform. From this indicator we can at least say that SBI performing much better than all the other selected banks.

Dividend Per Share

Dividend Per Share (DPS) is the total dividends paid out over an entire year (including interim dividends but not including special dividends) divided by the number of outstanding ordinary shares issued. Dividends are a form of profit distribution to the shareholder. Having a growing dividend per share can be a sign that the company's management believes that the growth can be sustained. SBI has the highest dividend per share and still growing, and then followed by PNB and BOB. The other two banks are left behind in this parameter.

These statements include mandatory, non-mandatory as well as voluntary actions. The following are the seven parameters of governance:

1. Strategic objective.
2. Responsibility and Accountability.
3. Necessary Eligibility of Board Members.
4. Provisioning supervisioning of senior management.
5. Ensuring effective utilization of internal and external audit's work.
6. Establishing consistency in compensation policy with the bank's ethical values.
7. Ensuring transparency in operation.

To maintain sound corporate governance the introduction of disclosure requirement is necessary. So every national bank has to declare its performance and new policy framework under the rules of RBI every financial year. It is very difficult to quantify the theoretical abstract of corporate governance, but it is possible to study qualitatively because the standard corporate governance demands an ethical foundation which varies bank to bank. Under all these headings we find that almost all banks following mandatory guidelines of RBI. Some even adopted voluntary guidelines and strictly adhere to it. After the debacles of series banks failure in Western countries in 2008, banks in India puts more emphasis on audit committee and transparent accountancy because there was large scale of fraudulent with investors' money.

The studies of corporate governance of the selected banks are divided into seven broad categories highlighted in Basel 2 norms. This is also supported by pillar 3 disclosure requirements which allow participant to assess information necessary to them. Basel 2 also paid concern on the compatibility of norms with regulatory framework of the country. Some of the bank also adopted voluntary item in their policy for sound and efficient corporate governance. The following table notifies the compliance of variable among the selected sample. YES indicate compliance and NO indicates non-compliance.

Strategic Objective

Corporate governance is complex issue dealing with cultural, political, technological, and market valuation, cannot find strong footing unless the banks set a sound strategic objective in value and ethics. All these five banks specifically detailed about their philosophical view of corporate governance in their annual report. The philosophical clarity generates a sense of securities on the part of its customers. This is important base of corporate governance. In case of ethics, except two banks B.O.I. and Canara bank all the other three defined their code of ethics in their annual report as well as on their websites. Since these two banks are not following they failed to compliance with the codes of conduct. The policy of Human Resource development is a voluntary item under the strategic objective, is only adopted by P.N.B. and Canara Bank. It also reflects the sense of responsibility and development of qualitative workers in these two banks. The corporate social responsibility is in-built self regulating mechanism whereby day to day activities are monitored and ensure its active compliance with the spirit of law, ethical standard and international norms. Banks are contributing in the social development by introducing institutes in rural area and provide basic amenities; encouraging in setting up of rural clinics, drinking water facilities and engaging rural volunteers for betterment of communities. The CSR are being followed by all these five banks as mentioned in their annual report. If we analyze strategic objective in aggregate we would find that P.N.B., S.B.I. and B.O.B adopted it successfully and other two (B.O.I. and Canara Bank) fails to adhere even mandatory items.

Strategic Objective	*S.B.I.*	*P.N.B*	*B.O.I*	*B.O.B*	*Canara Bank*
Company's philosophy of corporate governance highlighted.	Yes	Yes	Yes	Yes	Yes
Code of ethics	Yes	Yes	No	Yes	No
Code of conduct reveled on its website	Yes	Yes	No	Yes	No
Affirmation of compliance of code of conduct	Yes	Yes	No	Yes	No
Policy on Human Resource Development (voluntary)	No	Yes	No	No	Yes
Policy on corporate social responsibility	Yes	Yes	Yes	Yes	Yes

Source: Compiled from Annual Reports.

RESPONSIBILITY AND ACCOUNTABILITY

The information about the composition of shareholders'/investors' grievance committee is disclosed by all the five banks but their composition of executive and non-executive directors varies. They are as follows:

Bank	*Executive-Directors*	*Non-Executive Directors*
SBI	3	2
PNB	2	1
BOI	1 and (2 independent)	0
BOB	1	4
Canara Bank	1	3

Source: Compiled from Annual Reports.

With regard to information about the meetings conducted in shareholders'/investors' grievance committee are also disclosed in an annual report of the banks. SBI conducted four meetings, PNB with six meetings, BOI with four meetings, BOB with four meetings and Canara Bank with four meetings.

All of the above five banks disclose the composition of Board of Directors and the number of meetings conducted during a financial year. In SBI central board of directors consist of five members of which one is chairman and other four are managing directors. The total number of meeting took place was ten. In PNB, Board consists of eleven members in 2010–11 and there were ten meetings held. In case of BOB there are twelve total numbers of directors and maximum of nineteen meetings were held. In Canara bank there are twelve members in Board and fourteen meetings had been conducted. The Bank of India has fifteen members in its Board and fourteen meetings were presided. No post Board meeting and annual meeting of non-executives and independent directors were held either of the above mentioned banks in 2010–11.

Only SBI, PNB and BOB comply with the minimum number of independent directors in Remuneration/Compensation Committee as curved out in RBI guidelines. All banks under the study except BOI don't have Independent directors as chairman of the Remuneration/Compensation committee. Since BOI don't have independent directors in this committee so the disclosure of number of meeting held by the Remuneration/ compensation committee were only reported by other four banks namely SBI, PNB, BOB, Canara bank. Last two items under the head of responsibility and accountability are voluntary in nature but is being followed strictly by all banks except BOB.

Responsibility and Accountability

Information about composition of Shareholders/Investors grievance committee.	Yes	Yes	Yes	Yes	Yes
Disclosure of composition of board	Yes	Yes	Yes	Yes	Yes
Disclosure of number of meetings held and attendance thereof	Yes	Yes	Yes	Yes	Yes
Post Board meetings	No	No	No	No	No
Information regarding number of meetings of shareholders/investors grievance committee and attendance thereof	Yes	Yes	Yes	Yes	Yes
Annual meetings of non-executives or independent directors	No	No	No	No	No
Compliance of minimum number of independent directors in Remuneration/Compensation committee	Yes	Yes	No	Yes	No
Independent directors as chairman of the Remuneration/Compensation committee	Yes	Yes	No	Yes	Yes
Disclosure of number of meeting held by the Remuneration/compensation committee	Yes	Yes	No	Yes	Yes
Compensation/remuneration committee comprising of at least three non-executive directors (voluntary)	Yes	Yes	Yes	No	Yes
An independent directors acting as chairman of the compensation/remuneration committee (voluntary)	Yes	Yes	Yes	No	Yes

Source: Compiled from Annual Reports.

NECESSARY ELIGIBILITY OF BOARD MEMBERS

All the five banks disclose selection procedure for Board members and the criteria on which they select required candidates. Board members are highly qualified people who have experience in financial market for a quit long time. Member includes researcher, financial advisers and even government nominated IAS officers. The training of Board members is voluntary item under this heading; we find that except SBI and PNB all other three banks BOB, BOI and Canara Bank undertook such training for its member. The evaluation of performance of non-executive or independent directors is voluntary item. Only two banks, BOI and Canara Bank evaluate such performance and report in their annual data but other three major banks SBI, PNB and BOB fails in this regard. The age limit imposed on its member is not disclosed by either of the banks. In PNB, BOI and BOB nomination committee consist of only non-executive directors or independent directors but in SBI and Canara Bank we find the presence of both executive as well as non-executives.

Necessary Eligibility of Board Members

Disclosure of membership criteria	Yes	Yes	Yes	Yes	Yes
Disclosure of selection procedure	Yes	Yes	Yes	Yes	Yes
Tenure of independent directors not exceeding, in aggregate, a period of nine years (voluntary)	No	No	Yes	No	No
A provision of training to board members (voluntary)	No	No	Yes	Yes	Yes
The board evaluates performance of non-executive directors or independent directors (voluntary)	No	No	Yes	No	Yes
Age limits of directors	No	No	No	No	No
Nomination committee consisting only of non-executive directors or independent directors (voluntary)	No	Yes	Yes	Yes	No

Source: Compiled from Annual Reports.

PROVISIONING SUPERVISIONING OF SENIOR MANAGEMENT

All banks had faced some penalties for not complying with certain guidelines imposed by RBI. They have mentioned in their annual report. There is no such succession planning in either bank as it isn't in their annual report. The certification of CEO/CFO is being followed by all banks except BOB. The whistle blower policy is voluntary and recently incorporated in corporate governance framework. Three banks SBI, BOI and Canara bank have their policy in their report but PNB and BOI does not have any framework on whistle blower policy.

Provisioning Supervisioning of Senior Management

Non compliance or penalties imposed on/and strictures passed during the last three financial years	Yes	Yes	Yes	Yes	Yes
The company has a succession planning	No	No	No	No	No
CEO/CFO certification	Yes	Yes	Yes	No	Yes
The company established a whistle blower policy (voluntary)	Yes	No	No	Yes	Yes

Source: Compiled from Annual Reports.

ENSURING EFFECTIVE UTILIZATION OF INTERNAL AND EXTERNAL AUDIT'S WORK

Internal audit as well as external audit must review the bank's operational and adherence to all applicable minimum requirements. Pillar 3 disclosure framework regarding bank's capital adequacy and the location of all related information about the accounting disclosure require a validation by the audit work. In conformity with the Revised Clause 49 of listing agreements and the directives of Reserve Bank of India should constitute an audit committee to monitor and provide effective supervision of the management's financial reporting process with a view to ensure accurate, timely and proper disclosures, and transparency, integrity and quality of financial reporting. The role of sound accounting and adequate disclosure in the creation of useful information for markets and investors is obvious. Sound auditing standards applied properly by auditors who also maintain high standards of professional conduct also contribute to market and investor confidence. In turn, these disciplines are also responsive to the changing needs of market, investors and other external stakeholders. Compliance with accounting standards also contributes to transparency with regard to certain aspects which are relevant to corporate governance.All of the above five banks have independent directors in audit committee as required by RBI. In the investigating period (2010–11) chairman of audit committee is an independent director in all these banks and there exist at least one financial expert in the committee. There is no information regarding the participation of head of financial, chief internal auditor and independent auditor in the meeting. These banks are following the minimum number of meeting audit committee should conduct as prescribed by RBI. SBI conducted eleven meetings, PNB conducted ten meetings, BOI conducted eleven meetings, BOB eleven meetings and Canara Bank also conducted eleven meetings during the financial year 2010–11. In the matter of securities these banks are safe yet they haven't reached the regime of unqualified financial statement.

Ensuring Effective Utilization of Internal and External Audit's Work

Compliance of minimum number of independent director in audit committee	Yes	Yes	Yes	Yes	Yes
Chairman of audit committee is an independent director	Yes	Yes	Yes	Yes	Yes
Existence of at least one financial expert in the audit committee	Yes	Yes	Yes	Yes	Yes
Adoption of audit committee charter	Yes	No	No	No	No
Information relating to participation of head of finance, chief internal auditor and independent auditor in the meeting	No	No	No	No	No
Compliance of minimum number of meetings held by audit committee	Yes	Yes	Yes	Yes	Yes
Company reached at the regime of unqualified financial statement	No	No	No	No	No

Source: Compiled from Annual Reports.

ESTABLISHING CONSISTENCY IN COMPENSATION POLICY WITH THE BANK'S ETHICAL VALUES

Since these banks are public sectors banks so the remuneration of whole time Directors is paid in accordance to the Notification No. F No. 20/1/20015- BO.I dated 9th March 2007 and non-executives are paid in accordance to the section 17 of the Nationalized Banks (Management and miscellaneous Provisions) Scheme, 1970. All selected banks pay specific sitting fees to non-executive directors as commanded by Central government in consultation with RBI. There is no disclosure of remuneration policy that determines the incentives given to whole time Directors based on Performance Evaluation Matrix. While all banks provide details of remuneration paid to directors in their annual report except PNB.

Establishing Consistency in Compensation Policy with the Bank's Ethical Values

Specific criteria for directors' remuneration	Yes	Yes	Yes	Yes	Yes
Disclosure of remuneration policy	No	No	No	No	No
Detail of remuneration to all directors as per format in the main report	Yes	No	Yes	Yes	Yes

Source: Compiled from Annual Reports.

ENSURING TRANSPARENCY IN OPERATION

Shareholders and other stakeholders are highly depended on managers and the board of directors for their management of capital investment. Transparency in day to day activities and financial accountings of banks will keep moral trust high among the participants. So smooth working of banks is only possible if fairness and corporation exist on both sides. Information will become cheap consequently reducing down the cost of principal-agent conflicts. All the banks comply with the requirement of independent directors in board as put forth by RBI guidelines. There is no such disclosure of appointment of lead independent directors or non-executive independent directors as chairman in either bank. SBI, BOI and BOB provide details about the other companies where its directors also held position. The other two banks PNB and Canara Banks do not show such information in their annual report. The information related to party transaction is only disclosed by SBI, BOI and BOB. In case of resolving complaints these selected banks did not disclosed the 'nature' of complaints received but rather they just indicated the number of complaint received and the proportioned solved. All banks specifically disclose the location and time of general meetings held in last three years. Only three banks PNB, BOI and Canara Bank provide details about the special resolution passed in their last three AGMs/EGMs in their current report (2010–11). Only SBI and PNB showed their zeal in disclosing the list of top ten shareholders.

Ensuring Transparency in Operation

Compliance of number of independent directors in board	Yes	Yes	Yes	Yes	Yes
Appointment of Lead Independent Director or Non-executive Independent directors as chairman	No	No	No	No	No
List of companies where the directors also hold position	Yes	No	Yes	Yes	No
Disclosure of related party transactions	Yes	No	Yes	Yes	No
Disclosure of nature of complaints and queries by share holders received and disposed-item wise	No	No	No	No	No
Proportion of such complaint resolved (if more than 50 percent)	Yes	Yes	Yes	Yes	Yes
Location and time of general meetings held in last three years	Yes	Yes	Yes	Yes	Yes
Details of special Resolution passed in the last three AGMs/EGMs.	No	Yes	Yes	No	Yes
Details of resolution passed last year through postal ballot	No	Yes	No	No	Yes
Listing on stoke exchanges with stoke code	Yes	Yes	Yes	Yes	Yes
Top 10 shareholders	Yes	Yes	No	No	No
Registrar and transfer agent- address, phone, fax, email.	Yes	Yes	Yes	Yes	Yes
Maintenance of non-executive chairman's office	No	No	No	No	No
Half yearly report on financial performance sent to each household of shareholders.	No	No	No	No	No

Source: Compiled from Annual Reports.

CONCLUSION

In the years to come, the Indian financial system will grow not only in size but also in complexity as the forces of competition gain further momentum and financial markets acquire greater depth. In this circumstances role of corporate governance become much more crucial than the previous generation. The corporate governance standard should be improved to encourage banks in creating value through entrepreneurism, innovation, development, and exploration and provide accountability and control system commensurate with the transparency involved. The bank may find the cost of increasing disclosure could be quite high but the cost is nothing compared to the inefficiency suffered by the banks to damage the confidence of the shareholders and other stakeholder. Corporate governance is not merely fulfilling certain norms stipulated by the regulatory authorities rather it is complex and dynamic issue involving cultural, political, technological, and market variations whose strong existence represents a safety value to minimally control fraud and mismanagement to gain confidence of investors and other claimants. Corporate governance practice of the banks become apparent only, that reveals even in complying mandatory requirement the banks find inconvenience banishing the relevance of non-mandatory and voluntary requirements. There is an increasing trend of fraud committed in the banks internally. Sometime the cost of these frauds gradually developed into corers of rupees even the central author keeps mum sometime fearing that its public would erode the confidence. With the technological development we find opposite result, instead of reduction of such occurrence we indeed facing surmountable challenges of manipulation and maneuvering for personal gains. The mechanism that can tackle information asymmetry is the need of the time.

Foreign Direct Investment in Banking and Finance Sector

Kahkashan Tabassum and A. Damodaram[1]

Department of CS and IT, Maulana Azad National University, Hyderabad

[1]Department of CSE, Director SCDE, JNTUH, Kukatpally

ABSTRACT: *Foreign Direct Investment in banking and finance sector now-a-days is an important source for creating and increasing the global interconnectivity and is a way of attaining competitive efficiency. Foreign Direct Investment (FDI) plays a vivacious role in the economy since it not only facilitates the host countries to enhance their economic growth but also creates new openings to the local/home countries to optimize their income envelope by utilizing their superlative resources. Allowing the foreign involvement in the banking sector is anticipated to increase real output, irrespective of the imperfect competitive nature of the current industrial trends.*

Thus Foreign Direct Investment is a contributing factor to the enormous popularity and favorably apparent foreign competition in the banking and financial sectors and is also responsible for the increase and the overall efficiency of the inherent local or domestic financial institutions (DFIs). The strong competition faced by domestic companies with foreign banks leaves them with no choice except to improve their services along with matching the cost efficiency with respect to the foreign competitors so that they can have long–term establishment in the services sector. This new competition corresponds to the successful expansion of the wide range of financial products and services in the domestic firms.

This paper mainly:

1. *Provides an overview of the various trends in Foreign Direct Investments in banking and financial sectors in developing economically underdeveloped countries.*
2. *Their impacts and importance within the service sector*
3. *It explains the role of technology in FDI and how its international growth (whether B2B, B2C or C2B) can raise infrastructure gap within a service sector and how the countries that are economically backward can make a successful future with the use of technology (e-commerce) by participation. The type as well as the volume of the FDI which is directly proportional to the development attracted in the particular service sector.*

4. *The technical or socio-economic problems that FDI faces and the diminishing growth of e-commerce in under-developed countries are also classified.*
5. *The aspects that identify the macro constraints for a particular economy that curb FDI in e-commerce are also highlighted.*

INTRODUCTION

Foreign Direct Investment in banking and finance sector now-a-days is an important source for creating and increasing the global interconnectivity and is a way of attaining competitive efficiency. Foreign Direct Investment (FDI) plays a key role in the economy since it not only facilitates the host countries to enhance their economic growth but also creates new openings to the local/home countries to optimize their income envelope by utilizing their superlative resources. Allowing the foreign involvement in the banking sector is anticipated to increase real output, irrespective of the imperfect competitive nature of the current industrial trends.

Foreign Direct Investments in the Banking and Finance Industry in our country is based on the overriding appropriate policies for recovery and for future sustainable development, which includes the treatment of foreign investors. This paper briefly discusses the benefits and risks (or costs) linked with foreign direct investments in the banking and financial services sector. Based on the profit side, the financial services face the entry of foreign competition through FDIs, thus the overall efficiency corresponding to existing domestic/local financial institutions (DFIs) is increased. The sturdy competition from immense foreign banks or insurance companies, local/domestic financial corporations motivates them to enhance their services and strive to match the cost effectiveness of overseas challengers for their long-lasting endurance. This advent of innovative competition provides the growth of the variety of financial products and services available to local or domestic companies and customers. To enhance foreign technology-domestic access, collaboration can be done with the foreign financial service providers foreign trade financing, risk management and different types of managerial expertise. Domestic consolidation in the financial sector is the result of the foreign competition and it allows for financial regulation and supervision.

The management and increased risks are a source for liberalization. The regulatory standards are to be fixed so as to manage risks. Some foreign service providers can precisely take advantage of weaker or lenient regulatory instructions in developing countries not complying with the strict regulatory system standards within their in-house markets, therefore, financial regulation becomes poor that can reduce attraction of foreign investments. If the domestic or local financial industry is insufficiently prepared for the attack of foreign competition in the market then there is a net loss to FDI. As a result there is foreign displacement of DFIs. This can also have unfavorable impact on banking and financial flows. The issue to derive maximum profits ate the costs of minimized risks from liberalizing Foreign Direct Investment in the financial services sector remains.

The paper is organized as follows: Section 2 gives an overview of trends in FDI in section 3, the FDI restrictions and banking scenario are highlighted. Section 4 specifies the role of FDI in development of a country, advantages of FDI in banking and finance sector. Section 5 provides the guidelines and section 6 concludes the paper.

RECENT TRENDS IN FDI IN FINANCIAL SERVICES IN THE ASEAN

In terms of foreign direct investments (FDI), the statistics at a regional level shows trends in the sectoral breakdown of FDI are scanty and to understand it each country has to be individually examined. For instance, FDI stocks in Asia over the 1990s away from primary and secondary sectors towards the tertiary sectors reflects increasing investment liberalization and opening up of sectors such as financial services that were typically restricted. In fact, an increasing amount of FDI has been going into the finance sector in Asia. The increased activities of foreign banks in emerging markets can be measured either in terms of foreign bank participation in domestic banking markets or in terms of how effectively foreign banks control banking activities. The foreign banks might participate in a number of joint ventures as minority shareholders, the overall operations of the banks might be controlled by the local majority shareholders. It is also clear that the level of assets under the control of foreign bank subsidiaries and branches in the foreign participation is highest in Malaysia and fairly low in the other regions. The less of foreign participation is due to restrictive regulations on foreign bank entry. The restrictions on foreign bank entry have typically involved limitations on both the number of foreign banks that could enter the market and the number of branches they could establish within the market.

FDI RESTRICTIONS AND BANKING SCENARIO

Private sector banks limit in FDI is relaxed to 74 per cent including investment by foreign investment in India and the cumulative foreign asset in a private bank from all sources is also allowed at 74 per cent of remunerated capital of the bank. In nationalized banks DI and Portfolio investment are restricted to 20 per cent. In modern times, the multi-national banks economy is increasing in the banking and insurance sector.

But the involvement of foreign investors is a threat that may cause the insurers loose their business. Likewise it is also cause the workers to loose their job. Thus it cannot be encouraged to have greater rights of these in private banks whish results in less privatization. If the foreign or domestic investors obtain a large share in any bank and work out proportionate rights, it creates potential problems in the banking sector and can also render the economy to more serious financial crisis. FDI in banking sector can solve various problems of the overall banking sector as follows:

1. Pioneering Financial Products
2. Technological, Scientific and Systematic Developments in Foreign Marketplace
3. Problem of Incompetent and Ineffective Management
4. Non-executing, non-yielding and non-performing Assets
5. Financial Insecurity, Unsteadiness and Instability
6. Deprived and Poor Capitalization
7. Varying Financial Market Circumstances.

These problems specified owe to low-capital support but FDI on the other hand is a non-debt inflow that solves the problem of capital support along with entailing profit. Due to the globalization, the domestic banks are contending in the worldwide market. Whereas, the development of a domestic bank has the key limiting factor that can be characterized by innovative financial yield of multinational banks, they are trying to keep tempo with the technological development ahead. In the present days banks are prominent and cautious in the fast expansion of consumer providing support both in domestic as well as in foreign markets. Authorities in-charge of financial stability of the banks and credit management are assessed by appropriately with the help of tools. Some extra information and techniques may also be required to monitor other pecuniary and financial vulnerabilities. The FDI technically facilitates the monetary transfers, training programs, data sharing and various forms of technical support.

Risk Management, Financial Stability and Better Capitalization

Banks are escalating their vicinity of operation, this necessitates a transformation of their approaches to apply spirited stress and expression effect on domestic or local organizations, by re-assessing business practices. Thus the banking sector entirely is striving for a strategic policy for RM. With the assistance of FDI, the host countries will be acquainted with the proficient management technique. The improvement of RM can make most of the financial banking system more secure.

Host countries may benefit immediately. From foreign entry, if the foreign bank re-capitalize a struggling local institution. In the process also provides needed balance of payment finance. In general; more efficient allocation of credit in the financial sector, better capitalization and wider diversification of foreign banks along with the access of local operations to parent funding, may reduce the sensitivity of the host country banking system and lead towards financial stability.

THE ROLE OF FOREIGN DIRECT INVESTMENT IN DEVELOPMENT

There are four perspectives that play vital role to support the development in FDI. They are given below:

1. Relationship between FDI and Development:
   (a) The reigning orthodoxy in neo-liberal economics
   (b) FDI is neither good nor bad; it all depends on how you deal with it
   (c) Aid Created Debt Crisis; FDI Will Create an Even Greater Crisis of Development
   (d) FDI is Not a Development Tool at all; it is a Response to Systemic Crisis of the Developed Countries.
2. Does FDI Bring Development? The Experience of Mexico, East Asia and Argentina.
3. The Truth about FDI in Africa.
4. FDI is an Answer to West's Profitability Crisis, Not an Answer to Development Countries' Development Crisis.

Advantages of FDI

Assimilation with the Global Economy

FDI provides access to an extensive global access to financial growth and improved platform in the world economy to the developing countries. These major sectors can be massively promoted with the help of foreign direct investment. A remarkable inflow of FDI in various financial and banking sectors in India has enhanced the economic life of not only our country but also other countries around the world.

Expansion of Trading

Foreign Direct Investments have opened a broad variety of opportunities in the banking and financial sectors. Services of superior quality are planned and offered by various domestic as well as foreign industries in India due to greater amount of FDI inflows in the country. The same scenario exists for other countries of the world.

Knowledge Transmission and Technology Dissemination

FDI in fact helps in the outsourcing of knowledge from India mainly in the Information Technology Segment. World class technology and technical expertise are the outcome of most of the developing countries that has invited FDI to their on hand working practice. Foreign expertise in banking and finance can be an important factor in raising the existing technical processes.

Increased Competition

FDI enhances the intensity of struggle in the country. As discussed in section 1 other companies or banking and financial sectors will have to progress with respect to their processes and services in order to continue in the market. The results are very obvious that because of FDI quality of financial services are enhanced within a particular sector. Linkages and spillover to domestic firms- Various foreign firms are now occupying a position in the Indian market through Joint Ventures and collaboration concerns. The maximum amount of the profits gained by the foreign firms through these joint ventures is spent on the Indian market.

Human Resources Development and Employment

Employees of the country which is open to FDI get acquaint with globally valued skills. FDI has also ensured a number of employment opportunities by aiding the setting up of industrial units in various corners of India.

GUIDELINES FOR FDI IN BANKING

In the private banking sector of India, FDI is allowed up to a maximum limit of 74% of the paid-up capital of the bank. On the other hand, Foreign Direct Investment and Portfolio investment in the public or nationalized banks in India are subjected to a limit of 20% in totality. This ceiling is also applicable to the investments in the State Bank of India and its associate banks. FDI limits in the banking sector of India were increased with the aim to bring in more FDI inflows in the country along with the incorporation of advanced technology and management practices. The objective was to make the Indian banking sector more competitive. The Reserve Bank of India governs the investment matters in the banking sector. Three channels execute Indian operations by foreign banks:

- Branches in India
- Wholly owned subsidiaries
- Other subsidiaries.

In case of wholly owned subsidiaries (WOS), the guidelines for FDI in the banking sector specified that the WOS must involve a capital of minimum ₹ 300 crores and should ensure proper corporate governance.

Problems Faced by Indian Banking Sector

FDI in Indian banking sector resolves the following problems often faced by various banks in the country:

- Inefficiency in management
- Instability in financial matters
- Innovativeness in financial products or schemes

- Technical developments happening across various foreign markets
- Non-performing areas or properties
- Poor marketing strategies
- Changing financial market conditions.

Benefits of FDI in Banking Sector in India

- Transfer of technology from overseas countries to the domestic market
- Ensure better and improved risk management in the banking sector
- Assures better capitalization
- Offers financial stability in the banking sector in India.

CONCLUSION

FDI seems to be "solution" to the underdevelopment with respect to developing countries. But actually the development is a multifaceted process. One cannot single out FDI as the primary means to development. There is in fact no evidence that FDI brings development. There is also no evidence that FDI transfers technology. All that happens is a pseudo-transfer of technology. But still many governments seek for FDI because of the influence of International Financial Institutions (IFI). Also may be because of the bureaucrats are educated in innovative economics. FDI should be used intelligently by the companies throughout the world so that it brings development and benefits.

REFERENCES

"Economic Review" Foreign Invest flows to India, RBI Annual report 2005–06 (September).

Foreign Direct Invert in the Financial Sector of emerging market economics "CGFS publication No. 22".

FDI in Financial Sector, CGFS publication No. 25.

IMF's study on India, Business Line.

Insurance FDI: Left to oppose like, Business Line

RBI guidelines for FDI in Banking Sector, Dr. P.K. Shrivastava

Oxfam Briefing paper No. 46, April 2003.

The Economist, February 24, 2001—Special Survey of South Africa.

The Economist, February 8, 2003.

David Woodward, Financial Effects of Foreign Direct Investment in the Context of a Possible WTO Agreement on Investment, Third World Network, 2003.

Martin Khor, "Monterrey Spirit in Search of a Body to Avoid Being a Ghost", New York, 31 October 2003 (A report on the Monterrey Conference on Finance for Development).

Yash Tandon, Fallacies about the Theory of FDI: Its Ideological And Methodological Pitfalls, SEATINI publication, 2002.

Examining Regulatory Compliance in Indian Banking: Some Issues in the Context of Anti-Money Laundering Regulation

G. Sreekumar and L. Prakash Sai[*]

Department of Management Studies, Indian Institute of Technology, Madras Adyar, Chennai

E-mail: gsreekumar@rbi.org.in

ABSTRACT: *Regulation would be effective only when it is complied with by the regulatee institutions in both letter and spirit. There could be various impediments to voluntary compliance by banks, as well as the effectiveness of enforcement strategies, resulting in varying degrees of compliance. There are different strands of literature explaining compliance in various industries from different perspectives. Literature on compliance management in the context of banking is limited. This paper explores the factors influencing compliance in Indian banking. Given the differences with regard to size, ownership and operational complexity, among other things, Indian banking offers a rich context against which the mechanics of compliance and the effectiveness of the compliance function in banks could be studied from a banker's perspective. The research focus has been confined to 'Anti-Money Laundering' regulation, which serves both social objectives as well as internal objectives of preventing fraud, money laundering and related operational risks. Select senior bankers were interviewed to identify, modify and validate the variables influencing compliance in banks by studying and contrasting the same with the extant research literature. The paper presents the insights and the important determinants of compliance emerging from the interviews. On the strength of these insights, directions for further research are identified along with a discussion on the theoretical, methodological and policy contributions that could be made.*

Keywords: Regulation, Compliance, Regulatory Compliance, Money Laundering, Anti-Money Laundering, Know Your Customer.

---

[*] The authors are, respectively, General Manager, Reserve Bank of India, on sabbatical at the Indian Institute of Technology Madras, and Professor, Department of Management Studies, Indian Institute of Technology Madras. Views are personal and do not represent those of the institutions they are working for.

"20 per cent of the regulated population will automatically comply with any regulation, 5 per cent will attempt to evade it, and the remaining 75 per cent will comply as long as they think that the 5 per cent will be caught and punished"—Chester Bowles (1971)
"I don't know what the government is coming to. Instead of protecting businessmen, it pokes its nose into business! Why, they're even talking now about having bank examiners. As if we bankers don't know how to run our own banks!"

—**Gatewood**, the banker in John Ford's
"Stagecoach" (1939) (quoted in Krugman, 2012b)

INTRODUCTION

The global financial crisis of 2007–09 is widely accepted as to be the most severe since the Great Depression of 1929–33, calling for government and central bank intervention on an unprecedented scale. As was noted in one of the books on the crisis (Johnson and Kwak, 2010):

> *"Although the financial crisis was similar to earlier meltdowns, especially in emerging markets, it was unique in its complexity and scale... Given the panic that seized financial markets, it was possible that a sudden evaporation of credit, coupled with rapid de-leveraging by financial institutions and corporations everywhere, could have led to a second Great Depression."*

The major policy initiatives arising out of the crisis include an increased focus on financial stability. As an expert committee set up by the United Nations observed:

> *"The crisis has exposed fundamental problems, not only in national regulatory systems affecting finance, competition, and corporate governance, but also in the international institutions and arrangements created to ensure financial and economic stability. These institutions have proven unable to prevent the crisis and have been slow to design and implement adequate responses. Indeed, some policies recommended by these institutions have facilitated the spread of the crisis around the world."*
>
> ***—United Nations, 2009***

As recommended in various reports (Financial Services Authority, 2009, and Larosière, 2009) and implemented through legislation in some countries (for instance, the "Dodd-Frank Wall Street Reform and Consumer Protection Act" of the United States, commonly referred to as the Dodd-Frank Act), there will be greater control over banking activities in general through stronger regulation and closer monitoring and supervision of their functioning. There would also be more specific focus on the activities of systemically important financial institutions which are "too big to fail" in view of the impact that the risks posed by these institutions have on the rest of the financial sector and the real economy. As stated by Paul Krugman in a recent column, "...we need a return to much stronger financial regulation, stronger even than the Dodd-Frank regulations passed back in 2010" (Krugman, 2012a).

As financial stability concerns are intertwined with overall macro-prudential considerations and micro-prudential stability of individual institutions, it would be incumbent on banking regulators worldwide to closely monitor their health (Borio, 2003, and Bank for International Settlements, 2001). Regulation would be effective only as far as they are complied with by the regulatee institutions in a very substantive sense.

LITERATURE

There could be various impediments to voluntary compliance by banks, as well as the effectiveness of enforcement strategies, resulting in varying degrees and extent of compliance. The importance of eliciting adequate levels of compliance is highlighted in the following quote (United Nations, 2009):

> *"The underlying challenge to effective global economic governance originates from the absence, in a world of sovereign states, of an adequate body or bodies as a locus of coordination and accountability and no way to enforce transparency and elicit compliance" (Emphasis added).*

There are different strands of literature explaining compliance in various industries from different perspectives which straddle economic, sociological, political, psychological, organizational, institutional, criminological and management theories. From an economic expected utility perspective, following Becker (1968) and Stigler (1970), it has been postulated that the decision to comply would be the outcome of comparing the benefits of non-compliance with the probability of non-compliance being detected and punished, and the severity of such punishments. An effective enforcement would, therefore, have to make the punishment severe enough to make compliance attractive to these "amoral calculators" (Kagan and Scholz, 1984). "Bounded rationality" and behavioural organization theory postulated that there are limits to the ability of organizations to process information (March and Simon, 1958) which meant that big operational risk events may have to occur before organizations sit up and take notice of the need to be compliant. The deterrence approach has also been criticised based on empirical studies that have proved that the underlying assumptions do not hold good in practice, giving way to a search for other factors that determine compliance. These alternative explanations include social norms (Coffee, 2001), negative effect of formal sanctions, deterrent impact of informal sanctions, legitimacy and trust (Tyler, 2001; Scholz and Lubell, 1998), moral obligations and social influence (Sutinen and Kuperan, 1999; Kuperan and Sutinen, 1998; Ayres and Braithwaite, 1992). The three motivations for compliance have been labelled by Winter and May (2001) as "calculated", "normative", and "social". In keeping with the changing views on what drives compliance, the policy prescriptions for enhancing compliance has also moved from a pure "command and control" approach to one favouring a mix of enforcement strategies described in the literature as "regulatory pyramid" and "responsive regulation" (Ayres and Braithwaite, 1992). These and various other theories have been tested empirically across different industries and in different contexts. While these have been largely in the areas of environment regulation, tax compliance, and health and safety, empirical studies in the area of compliance by financial institutions with regulations have been very limited.

PRESENT STUDY

The present study is a preliminary step towards a more detailed understanding of the mechanics of regulatory compliance by banks in India. Indian commercial banks, with its unique mix of size, ownership and complexity, among other factors, offers an interesting policy perspective against which compliance behaviour could be studied. The size varies from very small banks to a very large one whose total assets constitute around 17% of the Indian Gross Domestic Product. In terms of ownership, there are Indian, private and foreign banks, with the newer private banks being in stark contrast to the older ones, and the foreign banks themselves being a mix of the large and the small. There are those which undertake traditional commercial banking and those which are more complex in terms of the type of activities that they undertake and the network of subsidiaries that they have. The literature suggests that some of these factors could have an impact on compliance. For instance, in keeping with the consistent finding in empirical research that larger firms are more likely to have compliance systems in place and be more compliant (Ashby and Diacon, 1996) and that they are more mindful of their image (Genn, 1993)' one could expect larger banks to be more compliant with regulation.

Banks in India are governed by regulations of various types, from entry to exit, that affect activities ranging from traditional banking to complex financial products and risk management. These regulations serve various objectives, social, economic and political. Of these, regulations relating to Know Your Customer (KYC) procedures serve very important internal and external objectives. A customer enters into a long term relationship with a bank at the point of entry, or customer acquisition, which is when detailed KYC procedures, by whatever name called, were traditionally carried out in banks. Compliance with these requirements serve as important controls in preventing money laundering, frauds and other operational risk events. In a training session on frauds, addressed by the first author, a group of 20 experienced bankers were asked as to what were the factors that resulted in fraud and the group was more or less unanimous in its view that non-compliance with KYC requirements was the single most important contributor to fraud.

The fact that 93% of the respondents in a survey indicated that fraud has been on the rise in the last one year underlines the importance of the issue (Deloitte, 2012). Yet another report found that "increasingly, the financial services industry is looking at anti money laundering compliance as a key concern area, with it figuring as an important point of discussion for board of directors and senior management on a frequent basis. Organizations are using AML compliance as a parameter to measure senior management performance, which in turn is ensuring accountability across organizational processes and products. Increasing internal focus by the organizations on AML coupled with the external factors such as high profile corruption cases, terrorism, heavy fines paid by global financial institutions and FATF membership is gradually leading to tighter AML compliance." (KPMG, 2012). Thus, increasing compliance with AML regulation will continue to be high on the agenda of bank management for some more time to come.

Risks resulting from KYC non-compliance may be borne not just by the bank, but also by the entire system, both within the country and across jurisdictions. Poorly implemented KYC norms could result in frauds involving other banks and even other segments of the financial system. Such non-compliance could also result in money laundering which could have deleterious effects on both the society and the economy (Unger, 2007). Even though it is highly unlikely that anti-money laundering (AML) policies and strategies would result in reducing crime, as newer methods of money laundering are emerging (Unger and Hertog, 2012), AML would remain one of the important elements in fighting crime. With the increased focus on AML policies and compliance in the last one decade, the KYC procedures followed by banks over the years have got subsumed under the overarching strategy towards tackling money laundering. India was following the global trend in this regard (Levi, 1991) when passing a legislation on money laundering in the year 2002 (Government of India, 2002). Given the cross-border diseconomies associated with crime and money laundering, the implementation of such AML legislation and the effectiveness of the overall AML regime in different countries are being monitored by the Financial Action Task Force (FATF) and various other multilateral agencies.

The three main stages in money laundering are termed in the literature as placement, layering and integration (Levi and Reuter, 2006). Banks play an important role, often unwittingly, in all stages of laundering in different types of money laundering as pointed out in various reports brought out by the Financial Action Task Force (www.fatf-gafi.org). It is keeping this in view that one of the first internationally coordinated efforts in countering money laundering through banks was made by the Basel Committee on Banking Supervision (BCBS, 1988), a work which has been carried forward both by the BCBS (2001, 2003) itself and by other agencies. Regulations are in place in India also in terms of which responsibility is cast on banks to comply with the AML regulations.

Notwithstanding the importance of AML regulation, compliance with the same by banks in India has not been of the desired level as may be seen from the following observation made by Governor, Reserve Bank of India, while making the annual monetary policy statement in April 2012 (Reserve Bank of India, 2012):

> *"Risk categorisation of customers as also compilation, periodic updation of customer profiles and monitoring and closure of alerts in accounts by banks are very important for effective implementation of KYC, anti-money laundering (AML) and combating of financing of terrorism (CFT) measures apart from helping their business development. It is, however, observed that there are laxities in effective implementation of the Reserve Bank's guidelines on KYC/AML measures. Any weakness in the KYC/AML process would leave banks vulnerable to operational risk. Banks should, therefore, ensure compliance with the regulatory guidelines on KYC/AML in both letter and spirit."*

The above statement shows the concern of the Reserve Bank of India as regards the effective implementation of AML/KYC guidelines. Thus, having established that regulatory compliance in banks, especially in the context of AML, is an ideal area to study how banks in India respond to regulation, it was decided to collect grounded information from experienced bankers as to different aspects of regulatory compliance in this area. Assessing compliance related information based on a survey/interview of the target population, including employees of regulated firms, is an accepted method which has been used widely in the compliance literature (Parker and Nielsen, 2009; May, 2005). This has been reckoned to be even superior to that of data collected by the regulators which tend to be non-representative for various reasons.

RESULTS OF INTERVIEWS

Interviews were done with senior bankers covering different sizes of banks and also public sector, old private sector, new private sector and foreign banks. The bankers were those who were having direct hands on experience in the matter of compliance with the AML regulations and/or related compliance function. The objective of the interviews has been to validate, modify and identify the variables influencing compliance management in banks by studying and contrasting the same with the extant research literature. The interviews were semi-structured with check list and open ended questions, which revolved around causes of operational risk events, factors leading to poor AML compliance, role of management, organization and compliance function, ingredients of a good compliance culture, role of regulators and regulation, processes and controls, costs and benefits of compliance/non-compliance, role of audit, third parties, technology and HR policies, and indicators of non-compliance.

One of the senior bankers interviewed stated that the "Main challenge over next five years would be compliance. Overcoming this is key to profitability and efficiency." This highlighted the importance of compliance to the overall functioning of banks. The interviews also confirmed that non-compliance with KYC norms was one of the major reasons for frauds, complaints and other operational risk events in banks.

The most important determinants of compliance, as brought out by the responses from the bankers, have been grouped and classified under 12 categories as given in Figure 1. These are generally along the lines as anticipated in theory, but the precise strengths of the relationships could vary due to various factors, such as age, size, complexity and ownership of banks. For instance, if one looks at the disaggregated data, the issues of "legacy" and "volume of transactions" were brought out by large public sector banks and not by either foreign banks or private sector banks which are relatively newer and thus have less of a legacy challenge, and also higher levels of technology induction, indicating better ability to deal with a higher volume of transactions.

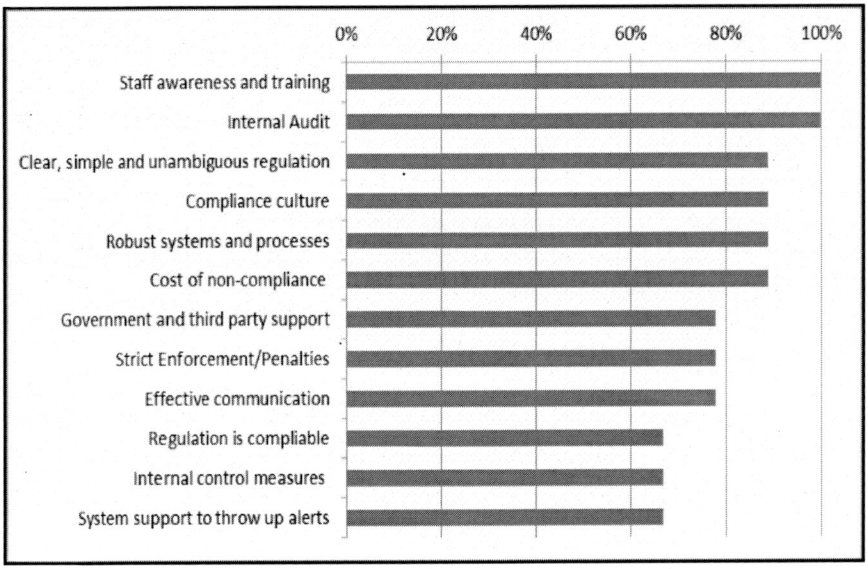

Fig. 1: Top 12 Determinants of Compliance

The following also turned up as important determinants of compliance though ranking below the above set of factors:

1. Different levels of approval for new products, processes, systems
2. Trust/confidence in regulator
3. Regulation flexible to specific requirements
4. HR Policies

5. Effective monitoring
6. Management commitment
7. Proactive in training
8. Adequate skilled, experienced and committed staff
9. System support to processes
10. Effect of compliance in controlling frauds and unethical practices.

In a more detailed survey of bankers, some of the above factors, along with a few others, are likely to become more important as, intuitively, these are important factors in ensuring higher levels of compliance.

Among the other major highlights of the interviews, a significant one was a comment that banks did not seem to look into the costs and benefits of implementing AML regulation before deciding on compliance. It was generally seen as something to be complied with and as part of the "cost of doing business". This view ruled out the relevance of the expected utility theory in explaining compliance in banking, at least in the context of AML regulation, even though costs of non-compliance was identified as an important determinant. However, certain other important determinants which have a basis in theory, such as trust/confidence in the regulator and that of the regulator in the regulatee, social norms, legitimacy and deterrence, have not been brought out in the above exercise. This calls for a more detailed exercise to capture the perceptions of bankers.

The interviews had included questions on the impact of non-compliance with AML regulation. Based on the responses, the major effects were as depicted in the graph below:

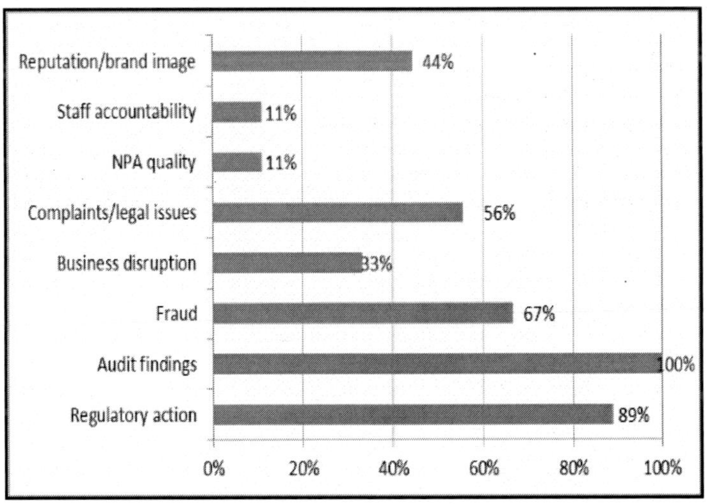

Fig. 2: Effects of Non-compliance

Thus, while all respondents felt that non-compliance would result in audit findings, 89%, 67% and 56% of the respondents felt that non-compliance would result in regulatory action in one form or the other, frauds and complaints/legal issues respectively. However, only 11% felt that it would result in staff accountability. One of the issues here is whether the low level of staff accountability is by itself also a determinant of non-compliant behaviour in banks.

The following were some of the other insights that were gained from the interviews:

1. Compliance with AML regulations is also linked to issues in compliance with related legislation such as the Foreign Contributions Regulation Act, 2010.
2. Though the levels of compliance with AML regulation was low in the initial years after introduction of the Prevention of Money Laundering Act 2002, quality of compliance has been increasing over time.
3. There seems to be a trade-off between ensuring AML compliance and increased business.
4. Ensuring AML compliance for smaller customers is fraught with different challenges and may call for different remedies.
5. The type of branch could have an impact on its level of compliance and the related risks.
6. Over reliance on technology could be counterproductive as it could delay identification of patterns in banking transactions and overshadow the role of judgement, which is also important.
7. Similarly, an over reliance on third parties to aid AML compliance could also be counterproductive unless it is supplemented by ability to independently verify documents produced before banks.

Based on the above preliminary assessment, it was concluded that the following areas need to be explored further in order to obtain a better understanding of the dynamics of compliance by banks in India in the context of AML regulation:

1. Assessment of the nature and extent/level of compliance with AML regulation
2. Response of the target population to AML/KYC regulation
3. Short term and long term effects of non-compliance
4. Effectiveness of self-regulation by banks
5. Performance of attributes affecting regulatory compliance.
6. Differences in compliance across different bank types.

CONCLUSIONS

AML regulation serves important socio-economic objectives and also helps prevent frauds, money laundering and other operational risks in banks. However, compliance with the regulation is not to the desired extent. The paper has identified, based on interviews with senior bankers, various determinants that determine levels of compliance. Further investigations exploring the above need to be done to draw more conclusive evidence. Such an exercise could have theoretical, methodological and practical implications. The theoretical novelty would lie in applying new institutional, behavioural and sociological perspectives in the context of compliance with AML regulation. While such analyses have been made in the context of other industries, it would be interesting to study and analyse the results based on data from the banking system.

From a methodological perspective, the assessment of regulatory compliance and its effects could be studied using interviews, surveys and experiments. Multivariate analytical tools could also be used. The surveys could be done relying in perceptions of bankers, as has been done in the extant literature on regulatory compliance. Such an exercise would provide unique insights into the effectiveness of different styles of regulation.

The study could also have practical policy implications for both the regulator and the regulated banks. From a regulatory perspective, it is hoped that conclusions could be drawn on the regulatory and enforcement strategies that would be more effective. From a compliance management perspective for banks, insights could be drawn on what compliance strategies would be optimal for increasing levels of compliance to meet regulatory expectations as there apparently exists a trade-off between business growth and levels of AML compliance.

As discussed above, there is increased interest in the area of regulatory compliance in banking, especially in the wake of the financial crisis of 2007–09. Further study into the subject in the context of AML regulation would, among other things, provide insights into improving compliance with the regulation apart from strengthening the effectiveness of the compliance function in banks and their overall compliance risk management.

REFERENCES

Ashby, S.G. and Diacon, S.R. (1996). "Motives for Occupational Risk Management in Large UK Companies", *Safety Science*, 22(1–3): 229–243.

Ayres, I. and Braithwaite, J. (1992). *Responsive Regulation: Transcending the Deregulation Debate,* Oxford University Press, New York.

Bank for International Settlements (2001). Marrying the macro- and microprudential dimensions of financial stability, BIS Papers No. 1, Monetary and Economic Department, Basel.

Basel Committee on Banking Supervision. *Compliance and the Compliance Function in Banks.* Bank for International Settlements, Basel, 2005.

Basel Committee on Banking Supervision. *Customer Due Diligence for Banks.* Bank for International Settlements, Basel, 2001.

Basel Committee on Banking Supervision. *General Guide to Account Opening and Customer Identification.* Bank for International Settlements, Basel, 2003.

Basel Committee on Banking Supervision. *Prevention of criminal use of the banking system for the purpose of money-laundering*, Bank for International Settlements, Basel, 1988.

Basel Committee on Banking Supervision. *Sound Practices for the Management and Supervision of Operational Risk.* Bank for International Settlements, Basel, 2011.

Becker, Gary S. (1968). "Crime and punishment: An economic approach", Journal of Political Economy, 76(2): 169–217.

Borio, Claudio (2003). Towards a macroprudential framework for financial supervision and regulation? Working Paper No. 128, Bank for International Settlements, Basel.

Bowles, C. (1971). *Promises to Keep – My Years in Public Life, 1941–1969.* Harper Collins, New York.

Coffee Jr., John C. (2001). "Do Norms Matter?: A Cross-Country Examination of the Private Benefits of Control", Columbia Law School Working Paper Series.

Deloitte (2012). India banking fraud survey – 2012: Navigating the challenging environment, February.

Financial Services Authority (2009). "The Turner Review: A Regulatory Response to the Global Banking Crisis", London.

Genn, H. (1993). "Business responses to the regulation of health and safety in England" *Law and Policy,* 15: 219–233.

Government of India (2002). Prevention of Money Laundering Act, New Delhi.

Johnson, Simon and James Kwak (2010). "13 Bankers: The Wall Street Takeover and the Next Financial Meltdown", Pantheon Books, New York.

Kagan, R. and Scholz, J. (1984). "The 'criminology of the corporation' and regulatory enforcement strategies" in Hawkins, K. and Thomas, J. (ed.) Enforcing Regulation, Kluwer Nijhoff Publishing, Boston, pp. 67–95.

KPMG (2012). India Anti-Money Laundering Survey 2012.

Krugman, Paul (2012a). "Dimon's Déjà-Vu Debacle", New York Times, May 20, http://www.nytimes.com/2012/05/21/opinion/dimons-deja-vu-debacle.html. Accessed May 21, 2012.

Krugman, Paul (2012b). "End this Depression Now", W.W. Norton and Co., New York.

Kuperan, K. and Jon G. Sutinen (1998). Blue Water Crime: Deterrence, Legitimacy, and Compliance in Fisheries. *Law and Society Review,* 32(2): 309–338.

Larosière, Jacques de (2009). "Report of the High-Level Group on Financial Supervision in the EU", European Union, Brussels.

Levi, Michael (1991) *Pecunia non olet*: Cleansing the money-launderers from the Temple. *Crime, Law and Social Change,* 16: 217–302.

Levi, M. and Reuter, P. (2006). Money laundering, *Crime and Justice*, 34: 289–376.

March, J. and Simon, H. (1958). *Organizations*, Wiley, New York.

May, Peter J. (1995). Compliance Motivations: Perspectives of Farmers, Homebuilders, and Marine Facilities. *Law and Policy.* 27(2): 317–347.

Parker, Christine and Nielsen, V.L. (2009). Corporate Compliance Systems: Could They Make Any Difference. *Administration and Society,* 41(1): 3–37.

Scholz, John T. and Mark Lubell (1998). Trust and Taxpaying: Testing the Heuristic Approach to Collective Action, *American Journal of Political Science,* 42(2): 398–417.

Stigler, G. (1970). "The optimum enforcement of laws", Journal of Political Economy, 78(3): 526–536.

Sutinen, J.G. and Kuperan, K. (1999). A Socio-economic Theory of Regulatory Compliance. *International Journal of Social Economics*, 26 (1/2/3), 174–193.

Tyler, Tom R. (2001). *Trust and Law-Abidingness: A Proactive Model of Social Regulation.* Australian National University and Australian Taxation Office, Centre for Tax System Integrity, Working Paper No. 16, August.

Unger, Brigitte and Johan den Hertog (2012). *Water always finds its way: Identifying new forms of money laundering*, Crime, Law and Social Change, open access at springerlink.com. http://www2.econ.uu.nl/users/unger/publications/Water_always_finds_its_way_Identifying_....pdf

Unger, Brigitte (2007). *The Scale and Impacts of Money Laundering*, Edward Elgar, London.

United Nations (2009). "Report of the Commission of Experts of the President of the United Nations General Assembly on Reforms of the International Monetary and Financial System (Chairman: Joseph Stiglitz), New York.

Winter, Soren C. and Peter J. May (2001). "Motivation for Compliance with Environment Regulations", *Journal of Policy Analysis and Management* 20(4): 675–698.

Performance Analysis of Commercial Banks in India: A Study of State Bank of India and Andhra Bank

G.V. Bhavani Prasad and D. Veena

Department of Commerce and Business Management,
Kakatiya University, Warangal
E-mail: bhavaniprasadgv@gmail.com; sunil_veena10@yahoo.co.in

ABSTRACT: *Indian Banking sector has been witnessing a sea change in the operating environment due to the changes in the economic environment in general and the environment for Banking and Financial Services. There is the impact of the globalization on the performance of the Banks. This compels all the banks to be competitive by adhering to the norms of financial performance as prescribed the Reserve Bank of India and International agencies. This paper is on the comparative analysis of State Bank of India (the first Public Sector Bank in India) and Andhra Bank (which was nationalized in 1969). All the key financial ratios are analyzed to arrive at the relative efficiency of these two banks. A cross analysis with the RBI norms is attempted to understand whether these banks perform in accordance with the prescribed norms. The Key ratios such as Investment Valuation Ratios, Profitability Ratios, and Management Efficiency Ratios for the years 2007–2011 are analyzed to give an insight into the Performance efficiency of the select banks.*

INDIAN BANKING INDUSTRY OVERVIEW

The Indian banking sector has emerged as one of the strongest drivers of India's economic growth. The banking system of India should not only be hassle free but it should be able to meet new challenges posed by the technology and any other external and internal factors. Post-Independence era, India's banking system has several outstanding achievements to its credit. The most striking is its extensive reaches not only metropolitans or cosmopolitans but even to the remote corners of the country. This is one of the main reasons of India's growth process.

The history of Indian Banking System can be segregated into three distinct phases. They are as mentioned below:

- *Phase I Pre-Nationalization Era:* Early phase from 1786 to 1969 of Indian Banks
- *Phase II Nationalization Stage:* Nationalization of Indian Banks and up to 1991 prior to Indian banking sector Reforms.
- *Phase III Post Liberalization Era:* New phase of Indian Banking System with the advent of Indian Financial and Banking Sector Reforms after 1991 and Liberalization.

Phase I

The General Bank of India was set up in the year 1786. The East India Company established Bank of Bengal (1809), Bank of Bombay (1840) and Bank of Madras (1843) as independent units and called it Presidency Banks. These three banks were amalgamated in 1920 and Imperial Bank of India was established which started as private shareholders banks, mostly Europeans shareholders.

In 1865 Allahabad Bank was established and first time exclusively by Indians, Punjab National Bank Ltd. was set up in 1894 with headquarters at Lahore. Between 1906 and 1913, Bank of India, Central Bank of India, Bank of Baroda, Canara Bank, Indian Bank, and Bank of Mysore were set up. Reserve Bank of India came in 1935. During the first phase the growth was very slow and banks also experienced periodic failures between 1913 and 1948. There were approximately 1100 banks, mostly small. To streamline the functioning and activities of commercial banks, the Government of India came up with The Banking Companies Act, 1949 which was later changed to Banking Regulation Act 1949 as per amending Act of 1965 (Act No. 23 of 1965). Reserve Bank of India was vested with extensive powers for the supervision of banking in India as the Central Banking Authority. During those day's public has lesser confidence in the banks. As an aftermath deposit mobilization was slow. Not only that. The banks were selective in inviting the customers for transacting with the banks. Only those wealthy and strong financial backgrounds were invited to be part of the clientele for the banks. Abreast of it the savings bank facility provided by the Postal department was comparatively safer. Moreover, funds were largely given to traders.

Phase II

Government took major steps in this Indian Banking Sector Reform after independence. In 1955, it nationalized Imperial Bank of India with extensive banking facilities on a large scale especially in rural and semi-urban areas. It formed State Bank of India to act as the principal agent of RBI and to handle banking transactions of the Union and State Governments Seven banks forming subsidiary of State Bank of India was nationalized in

1960 on 19th July, 1969, major process of nationalization was carried out. It was the effort of the then Prime Minister of India, Mrs. Indira Gandhi. 14 major commercial banks in the country were nationalized.

Second phase of nationalization Indian Banking Sector Reform was carried out in 1980 with seven more banks. This step brought 80% of the banking segment in India under Government ownership.

The following are the steps taken by the Government of India to Regulate Banking Institutions in the country:

- 1949: Enactment of Banking Regulation Act.
- 1955: Nationalization of State Bank of India.
- 1959: Nationalization of SBI subsidiaries.
- 1961: Insurance cover extended to deposits.
- 1969: Nationalization of 14 major banks.
- 1971: Creation of credit guarantee corporation.
- 1975: Creation of regional rural banks.
- 1980: Nationalization of seven banks with deposits over 200 crores.

After the nationalization of banks, the branches of the public sector bank India raised to approximately 800% in deposits and advances took a huge jump by 11,000%. Banking in the sunshine of Government ownership gave the public implicit faith and immense confidence about the sustainability of these institutions.

Phase III

This phase has introduced many more products and facilities in the banking sector in its reforms measure. In 1991, under the chairmanship of M Narasimham, a committee was set up by his name which worked for the liberalization of banking practices. The country is witnessed with the advent of foreign banks and their ATM stations. Banks started putting efforts to give a satisfactory service to customers. Phone banking and net banking was introduced. The entire system became more convenient and swift. Time is given more importance than money and the customer service has become the focal point of all banking operations. The financial system of India has shown a great deal of resilience due to strong monetary policies and banking innovations. The public policy related to the economy as well as financial sector also added to the changing phase of banking system. It is sheltered from any crisis triggered by any external macroeconomics shock as other East Asian Countries suffered. This indicated the strength of the Indian Financial System of which Banking system is also a part. Innovative financial management of Banks, Value added services offered by the banks and focus on market orientation have all added to the need for efficient management of banks to be competitive and to survive in the intense and dynamic financial system.

TRENDS IN INTERNATIONAL ENVIRONMENT FOR BANKING SECTOR

The strategic nature of banking sector necessitated the development of International norms in order to ensure the effective functioning of Commercial Banks. This led to evolution of Basel I, II and III.

Basel I Norms

The history of the Basel Accord started by the end of 1974 with Basel Committee on Banking Supervision (BCBS) under the auspices of the Bank for International Settlements (BIS), comprising of Central Bank Governors from the participating countries.

BCBS has been instrumental in standardizing bank regulations across jurisdictions with special emphasis on defining the roles of regulators in cross-jurisdictional situations. The committee meets four times a year. It has around 30 technical working groups and task forces that meet regularly.

Basel I norms, were set out in 1988 and accepted over the years by around 100 Central Banks across the globe under what came to be known as the Basel Accord. The original accord, now known as Basel-I, was quite simple and adopted a straight-forward `one size fits all approach' that does not distinguish between the differing risk profiles and risk management standards across banks. The Indian monetary authorities implemented the Basel II by 1999.

The banks were to assess their assets and off-balance-sheet risks taken and incorporate them on their balance-sheet. Basel I norms prescribed a minimum capital adequacy ratio (CRAR)

[1] Of 8% for Banks which were signatories to the Basel Accord.

Basel I framework was confined to the prescription of only minimum capital requirements for banks, the Basel II framework expands this approach not only to capture certain additional risks in the minimum capital ratio but also includes two additional areas, Supervisory Review Process and Market Discipline through increased disclosure. Thus emerged RBI guidelines on investments and operations risk, paving the way for adoption of what have come to be known as Basel II norms.

Basel II Norms

According to the 1996 amendments to the Basel I accord, in June 1999 BCBS issued a proposal for a New Capital Adequacy Framework to replace the 1988 Accord. The proposed capital framework consists of three pillars:

- *Pillar 1:* ***Minimum capital needed and its requirements,*** which seek to refine the standardized rules, set forth in the 1988 Accord.

- *Pillar 2:* ***Supervisory review process*** of an institution's internal assessment process and capital adequacy.
- *Pillar 3:* Market Discipline.

The accord has been finalized in June 2004. For banks adopting advanced approaches for measuring credit and operational risk the deadline has been shifted to 2008.

The role of Basel II, both before and after the global financial crisis, has been discussed widely. While some argue that the crisis demonstrated weaknesses in the framework, others have criticized it for actually increasing the effect of the crisis http://en.wikipedia.org/wiki/Basel_II -cite_note-14. In response to the financial crisis, the BCBS published revised global standards, popularly known as Basel III http://en.wikipedia.org/wiki/Basel_II -cite_note-15. The Committee claimed that the new standards would lead to a better quality of capital, increased coverage of risk for capital market activities and better liquidity standards among other benefits.

Basel III Norms

Basel III released in December, 2010 is the third in the series of Basel Accords. According to Basel Committee on Banking Supervision "Basel III is a comprehensive set of reform measures, developed by the Basel Committee on Banking Supervision, to strengthen the regulation, supervision and risk management of the banking sector". Thus, we can say that Basel III is only a continuation of effort initiated by the BCBS to enhance the banking regulatory framework under Basel I and Basel II. This latest Accord seeks to improve the ability OF banking sector's to deal with financial and economic stress, improve risk management and strengthen the banks' transparency.

Three Pillars of Basel Still Stand under Basel III: Basel III has essentially been designed to address the weaknesses that become too obvious during the 2008 financial crisis world faced. The intent of the Basel Committee seems to prepare the banking industry for any future economic downturns. The framework enhances bank-specific measures and includes macro-prudential regulations to help create a more stable banking sector.

The basic structure of Basel III remains unchanged with three mutually reinforcing pillars.

- *Pillar 1:* ***Minimum Regulatory Capital Requirements based on Risk Weighted Assets (RWAs):*** Maintaining capital calculated through credit, market and operational risk areas.
- *Pillar 2:* ***Supervisory Review Process:*** Regulating tools and frameworks for dealing with peripheral risks that banks face.
- *Pillar 3:* ***Market Discipline:*** Increasing the disclosures that banks must provide to increase the transparency of banks.

Comparison of Capital Requirements under Basel II and Basel III

Requirements	*Basel II (in Percentages)*	*Basel III (in Percentages)*
Minimum Ratio of Total Capital To RWAs	8	10.5
Minimum Ratio of Common Equity to RWAs	2	4.5 to 7
Tier I capital to RWAs	4	6
Core Tier I capital to RWAs	2	5
Capital Conservation Buffers to RWAs	None	2.5
Leverage Ratio	None	3
Countercyclical Buffer	None	0 to 2.5
Minimum Liquidity Coverage Ratio	None	TBD (2015)
Minimum Net Stable Funding Ratio	None	TBD(2013)
Systemically important Financial Institutions Charge	None	TBD (2011)

CHANGING ENVIRONMENT FOR INDIAN BANKING SECTOR

Current and emerging economic environment offers a number of opportunities and challenges for the Indian banking sector. Factors like expected positive economic performance, strong savings growth spurred by the favorable demographic dividend, emphasis on expansion of physical Infrastructure and the extent of financial exclusion to be bridged will ensure growth of the banking sector in medium term. To exploit emerging opportunities and to benefit from their Strengths, Indian banks need to be globally competitive. From a strategic perspective,

Competitiveness can be achieved by balancing factors such as scale, scope, prudence and knowledge and by successful adoption of Basel III norms with higher and better quality capital; an internationally harmonized leverage ratio to constrain excessive risk taking; capital buffers which would be built up in good times so that they can be drawn down in times of stress; minimum global liquidity standards; and stronger standards for supervision, public disclosure and risk management. Quick assessments show that at the aggregate level Indian banks will not have any problem in adjusting to the new capital rules both in terms of quantum and quality but few individual banks may fall short of the Basel III norms. Migration to Basel III requires a high level of liquidity to be maintained through a pool of liquid assets. Converging to International Financial Reporting Standards (IFRS) global accounting standards facilitates comparability between enterprises operating in different jurisdictions. Convergence would help to reduce both the cost of capital and cost of compliance for industry. Training, education and skill development are cornerstones of a successful implementation of IFRS. To face the challenges and complexities of IFRS banks has to upgrade their infrastructure, IT and human resources.

RBI POLICY

Various developmental and regulatory policy measures announced by the Reserve Bank in the policy statements from time to time sets out new measures of improving the operational efficiency of Banking Sector in India. Reforms in Monetary Policy have been continued with a view to building a robust and resilient financial system. More stringent capital and liquidity measures for commercial banks have been implemented and steps have been taken to build provision buffers. Basel III capital and liquidity standards for banks are in the process of being prescribed. New prudential compensation practices have been adopted. Various institutional mechanisms and tools for monitoring systemic risks have been put in place. Efforts are being made to develop effective macro prudential supervision.

The Reserve Bank instituted a systemic risk survey (SRS) to supplement its assessment of systemic risks through wider consultation. The findings of the SRS also reaffirmed the stability of the system. Over half the respondents were 'confident' or 'very confident' about the stability of the Indian financial system. However, according to the survey, deterioration in asset quality was identified as one of the major risks faced by banks.

PERFORMANCE ANALYSIS OF SBI AND AB

The changing economic scenario coupled with liberal competitive structure has compelled the banks to become more prudent in the management of assets and liabilities. The banks are mandated to think in terms of leveraging the cost structure in favor of increasing operating profit. This has become all the more important in the light of reduced interest spread and intense competition to capture the available customer base. In the following sections the performance of commercial banks, especially the public sector banks, is analyzed to understand the relative performance of these banks in the changing global environment. For the purpose, State bank of India and Andhra Bank are taken as the case examples. The performance of these banks is analyzed for the period 2007–11.

The performance is evaluated in terms of Management Efficiency Ratios, Profitability Ratios, and Investment Valuation Ratios. The mean difference test is conducted in order to find out whether there is any significant difference in the performance of both the banks, though both of them work under the same environment.

Table 1: Management Efficiency Ratios

		2007	*2008*	*2009*	*2010*	*2011*	*mean*	*S.D*	*T-test*
Interest income/Total fund	SBI	8.27	8.82	8.88	8.52	8.39	8.58	0.25	0.33
	AB	7.83	8.77	9.06	8.85	8.8	8.66	0.43	
NIM = NII/Total Fund(TF)	SBI	3.85	3.87	3.79	3.82	4.1	3.89	0.18	3.28
	AB	3.53	3.26	3.07	3.58	3.71	3.43	0.23	

		2007	*2008*	*2009*	*2010*	*2011*	*mean*	*S.D*	*T-test*
Non-interest income/TF	SBI	0.19	0.14	0.11	0.1	0.09	0.13	0.18	2
	AB	0.56	0.56	0.47	0.45	0.02	0.41	0.22	
Interest expended/TF	SBI	4.42	4.96	5.09	4.69	4.29	4.69	0.3	1.68
	AB	4.3	5.51	5.99	5.26	5.09	5.23	0.57	
Operating expenses/TF	SBI	2.39	2.16	2.06	2.38	2.67	2.33	0.24	2.28
	AB	2.2	1.89	1.91	1.96	2.07	2.01	0.14	
Profit before provisions/TF	SBI	1.54	1.74	1.75	1.46	1.43	1.58	0.14	0.97
	AB	1.76	1.82	1.5	1.95	1.95	1.8	0.44	
Net Profit/TF	SBI	0.86	1.04	1.08	0.91	0.65	0.91	0.14	0.604
	AB	1.22	1.11	1.04	1.32	1.27	1.19	0.22	
Loans Turnover	SBI	0.15	0.15	0.16	0.15	0.14	0.15	0.15	0.1
	AB	0.14	0.15	0.14	0.14	0.14	0.14	0.14	
Total income/ Capital Employed (CE)	SBI	8.46	8.96	8.99	8.62	8.48	8.7	0.42	1.42
	AB	8.39	9.33	9.35	9.29	9.22	9.25	0.47	
Interest expended/CE	SBI	4.42	4.96	5.09	4.69	4.29	4.69	0.3	1.68
	AB	4.3	5.51	5.99	5.26	5.09	5.23	0.57	
Total assets turnover Ratio	SBI	0.08	0.09	0.09	0.09	0.08	0.09	0.06	0
	AB	0.08	0.09	0.09	0.09	0.09	0.09	0.05	
Assets turnover Ratio	SBI	5.44	6.32	7.2	7.26	7.24	6.69	0.71	1.56
	AB	6.23	7.6	8.01	20.08	10.58	10.52	4.98	

Interest Income/Total Fund

This ratio is very useful to know the percentage of interest income over total funds. The higher the ratio the more will be the ability of the bank in generating the more interest income from total funds. During the years 2007–11 the ratio showed a growth rate of 1.01 percentage with mean 8.58 and Standard Deviation (SD) 0.25 percentages for SBI and 1.11 percentage with a mean 8.66 and SD 0.43 percentages for AB. It indicates there are insignificant differences in the performance of both the banks' Interest income/total funds ratio. This is supported by the t-test conducted. The calculated t-value is 0.33 which is less than the table value 2.1315 (at 5% significance level).

Net Interest Margin (NIM)

For banks, interest expenses are their main costs and interest income is their main revenue source. The difference between interest income and expense is known as net interest income earned by the bank on its Funds. This ratio indicates as to how effectively the banks deploy all their funds to generate income from credit and investment operations. Higher the ratio, the more efficient is the bank. During the years 2007–11 the ratio showed a growth rate of 1.01 percentage with mean 3.89 and SD 0.18 percentages for SBI and 1.05 percentage with a mean 3.43 and SD 0.23 percentages for AB. It indicates there are *significant* differences in the performance of both the banks' NIM. This is supported by the t-test conducted. The calculated t-value is 3.28 which is greater than the table value 2.1315 (at 5% significance level).

Non-interest Income/Total Funds

This ratio is used to indicate the growing importance of other sources of income such as off-balance sheet exposures and non-traditional sources of income such as fees and commission. Thus, in a way the ratio is an indicator of diversification of operations of banks. Fee based income account for a major portion of the banks other income. The bank generates higher fee income through innovative products and adapting the technology for sustained service levels. This stream of revenues is not depended on the banks capital adequacy and consequently, potential to generate the income is immense. The higher ratio indicates increasing proportion of fee-based income.

During the years 2007–11 the ratio showed a declining rate of 0.48 percentage with mean 0.13 and SD 0.18 percentages for SBI and 0.73 percentage with a mean 0.41 and SD 0.22 percentages for AB. It indicates there are *insignificant* differences in the performance of both the banks' Non-interest income/Total funds ratio. This is supported by the t-test conducted. The calculated t-value is 2 which is less than the table value 2.1315 (at 5% significance level).

Interest Expended/Total Fund

This ratio is to know the interest expenses on total funds, the lower the ratio the higher will be the income. During the years 2007–11 the ratio showed a declining rate of 0.97 percentage with mean 4.69 and SD 0.3 percentages for SBI and increasing trend 1.18 percentage with a mean 5.23 and SD 0.57 percentages for AB. It indicates there are *insignificant* differences in the performance of both the banks' ratio. This is supported by the t-test conducted. The calculated t-value is 1.68 which is less than the table value 2.1315 (at 5% significance level).

Operating Expenses/Total Fund

Operating expenses vary widely with the type of funds. The largest component of operating expenses is the fee paid to a fund's investment manager/advisor. Other costs include recordkeeping, custodial services, taxes, legal expenses, and accounting and auditing fees. Some funds have a marketing cost referred to as a 12b-1 fee, which would also be included in operating expenses. A fund's trading activity, the buying and selling of portfolio securities, is not included in the calculation of the expense ratio. The lower the ratio better will be the income.

During the years 2007–11 the ratio showed an increasing rate of 1.12 percentage with mean 2.33 and SD 0.24 percentages for SBI and decreasing trend 0.94 percentage with a mean 2.01 and SD 0.14 percentages for AB. It indicates there are *significant* differences in the performance of both the banks' ratio. This is supported by the t-test conducted. The calculated t-value is 2.28 which is greater than the table value 2.1315 (at 5% significance level).

Profit before Provisions/Total Funds

This ratio helps the banks to know the movement in profit mainly reflects an increase in the value of the Bank's share investments holdings and lower loan loss provisions. During the years 2007–11 the ratio showed a declining rate of 0.93 percentage with mean 1.58 and SD 0.14 percentages for SBI and 1.11 percentage with a mean 1.8 and SD 0.44 percentages for AB. It indicates there are *insignificant* differences in the performance of both the banks' ratio. This is supported by the t-test conducted. The calculated t-value is 0.97 which is less than the table value 2.1315 (at 5% significance level).

Net Profit/Total Fund

Net profits are the profits net of provisions, amortization and taxes. So this ratio shows the banks pure profits on total funds. Higher the ratio reflects the ability of the bank to generate more income from funds. During the years 2007–11 the ratio showed a declining rate of 0.75 percentage with mean 0.91 and SD 0.14 percentages for SBI and increasing trend 1.04 percentage with a mean 1.19 and SD 0.22 percentages for AB. It indicates there are *insignificant* differences in the performance of both the banks ratio. This is supported by the t-test conducted. The calculated t-value is 0.604 which is less than the table value 2.1315 (at 5% significance level).

Loans Turnover Ratio

This ratio estimates how quickly the banks can convert the loan portfolio to cash. The lower the result the faster the loan portfolio matures. During the years 2007–11 the ratio showed a declining rate of 0.93 percentage with mean 0.91 and SD 0.14 percentages for SBI and stable with a mean 0.15 and SD 0.15 percentages for AB. It indicates there are *insignificant* differences in the performance of both the banks' ratio. This is supported by the t-test conducted. The calculated t-value is 0.1 which is less than the table value 2.1315 (at 5% significance level).

Return on Capital Employed (ROCE)

ROCE compares earnings with capital invested in the company or banks. It is similar to Return on Assets (ROA), but takes into account sources of financing.

ROCE = Total income/Capital employed

During the years 2007–11 the ratio showed a growth rate of 1.00 percentage with mean 8.7 and SD 0.42 percentages for SBI and 1.09 with a mean 9.25 and SD 0.47 percentages for AB. It indicates there are *insignificant* differences in the performance of both the banks' ratio. This is supported by the t-test conducted. The calculated t-value is 1.42 which is less than the table value 2.1315 (at 5% significance level).

Interest Expended/Capital Employed

This ratio is useful to know the operating expenses percentage on capital employed. Increase in the ratio decreases the income of the banks. . During the years 2007–11 the ratio showed a declining rate of 0.97 percentage with mean 4.69 and SD 0.3 percentages for SBI and increased rate1.18 percentage with a mean 5.23 and SD 0.57 percentages for AB. It indicates there are *insignificant* differences in the performance of both the banks' ratio. This is supported by the t-test conducted. The calculated t-value is 1.68 which is less than the table value 2.1315 (at 5% significance level).

Total Assets Turnover Ratio

This ratio is a measure of how efficiently a bank can generate income from total assets.

Total Assets turnover ratio = revenue/average total assets

During the years 2007–11 the ratio showed a growth rate of 1.33 percentage with mean 6.69 and SD 0.71 percentages for SBI and 1.7 percentage with a mean 10.52 and SD 4.98 percentages for AB. It indicates there are *insignificant* differences in the performance of both the banks' ratio. This is supported by the t-test conducted. The calculated t-value is 1.56 which is less than the table value 2.1315 (at 5% significance level).

Table 2: Profitability Ratios

		2007	*2008*	*2009*	*2010*	*2011*	*Mean*	*S.D*	*T-test*
Interest spread	SBI	4.2	4.32	4.32	3.82	4.12	4.16	0.31	0.67
	AB	4.72	4.04	3.78	4.48	4.59	4.32	0.36	
Adjusted cash margin (%)	SBI	11.43	12.81	13.04	11.62	9.6	11.7	1.23	2.86
	AB	16.03	13.1	12.32	15.54	14.95	14.39	1.43	
NPM	SBI	10.12	11.65	12.03	10.54	8.55	10.58	1.23	2.62
	AB	14.53	11.84	10.96	14.7	13.79	13.06	1.44	

		2007	*2008*	*2009*	*2010*	*2011*	*Mean*	*S.D*	*T-test*
Return on long-term fund (%)	SBI	99.2	86.83	100.35	95.02	96.72	95.62	4.7	1.97
	AB	84.98	116.48	126.87	127.15	102.46	111.59	16.07	
Return on net worth	SBI	14.5	13.72	15.74	13.89	12.71	14.11	0.99	4.49
	AB	17.78	17.71	17.9	23.71	19.51	19.32	2.29	
Adjusted return on net worth	SBI	14.47	13.7	15.74	13.91	12.74	14.11	0.99	3.91
	AB	17.03	17.7	17.89	23.7	19.5	19.16	2.4	
ROA	SBI	594.69	776.48	912.73	1038.75	1023.4	869.21	166.36	2.81
	AB	65.08	67.5	75.2	90.93	116.02	82.85	109.53	

Interest Spread

This ratio is the difference between the average lending rate and the average borrowing rate for a bank or other financial institution. This is the excess of total interest earned over total interest expended. This ratio shows the efficiency of bank in managing and matching interest expenditure and interest income effectively. Interest spread is critical to a bank's success as it exerts a strong influence on its bottom line.

Interest Spread = (Interest income/interest earning assets) – (interest expenses/ interest bearing liabilities)

During the years 2007–11 the ratio showed a declining rate of 0.98 percentage with mean 4.16 and SD 0.31 percentages for SBI and 0.97 percentage with a mean 4.32 and SD 0.36 percentages for AB. It indicates there are *significant* differences in the performance of both the banks' interest Spread. This is supported by the t-test conducted. The calculated t-value is 0.67 which is greater than the table value 2.1315 (at 5% significance level).

Adjusted Cash Margin

The Adjusted Cash Flow Margin ratio is an important ratio as it expresses the relationship between cash generated from its operations. The company or bank needs cash to pay dividends, suppliers, service debt, and invest in new capital assets. During the years 2007–11 the ratio showed a declining rate of 0.84 percentage with mean 11.7 and SD 1.23 percentages for SBI and 0.93 percentage with a mean 14.39 and SD 1.43 percentages for AB. There are *significant* differences in the performance of both the banks' Adjusted Cash Margin ratio. This is supported by the t-test conducted. The calculated t-value is 2.86 which is greater than the table value 2.1315 (at 5% significance level).

Net Profit Margin (NPM)

A ratio of profitability calculated as net income divided by revenues. Profit margin is very useful when comparing companies in similar industries. A higher profit margin indicates a more profitable company or bank that has better control over its costs compared to its competitors. During the years 2007–11 the ratio showed a declining rate of 0.84 percentage with mean 10.58 and SD 1.23 percentages for SBI and 0.95 percentage with a mean 13.06 and SD 1.44 percentages for AB. It indicates there are *significant* differences in the performance of both the banks NPM ratio. This is supported by the t-test conducted. The calculated t-value is 2.62 which is greater than the table value 2.1315 (at 5% significance level).

Return on Net Worth (RON)

Return on Net worth reveals how much profit a company or bank earned in comparison to the total amount of shareholder equity found on the balance sheet A b has a high return on equity is more likely to be one that is capable of generating cash internally. During the years 2007–11 the ratio showed a declining rate of 0.88 percentage with mean 14.11 and SD 0.98 percentages for SBI and 1.14 percentage with a mean 19.16 and SD 2.4 percentages for AB. It indicates there are *significant* differences in the performance of both the banks RON. This is supported by the t-test conducted. The calculated t-value is 4.49 which is greater than the table value 2.1315 (at 5% significance level).

Return on Assets (ROA)

The Return on Assets ratio is an important profitability ratio because it measures the efficiency with which the company is managing its investment in assets and using them to generate profit. It measures the amount of profit earned relative to the firm's level of investment in total assets. As per the Base II norms it should be more than 1 percentage. Both the banks are satisfying these norms.

ROA = Net income/total assets

Table 3: Investment Valuation Ratios

		2007	*2008*	*2009*	*2010*	*2011*	*mean*	*S.D*	*T-test*
Dividend per share	SBI	14	21.5	29	30	30	24.9	6.31	6.63
	AB	3.8	2	4.5	5	3.5	3.76	1.04	
Operating profits PS per share	SBI	147.72	173.61	230.04	229.63	255.39	207.28	40.03	9.27
	AB	12.08	14.76	14.93	26.67	29.12	19.51	6.97	
Net Operating profit PS	SBI	833.38	899.83	1179.45	1353.15	1504.34	1154.03	257.08	8.04
	AB	71.21	94.18	116.79	144.83	156.65	116.73	31.51	
Free reserves PS	SBI	184.43	356.61	373.99	412.36	468.29	359.14	93.39	6.64
	AB	34.66	32.68	34.25	41.42	64.32	41.47	11.82	

During the years 2007–11 the ratio showed a declining rate of 1.72 percentage with mean 869.21 and SD 166.36 percentages for SBI and 1.78 percentage with a mean 82.85 and SD 109.53 percentages for AB. It indicates there are *significant* differences in the performance of both the banks' ROA. This is supported by the t-test conducted. The calculated t-value is 2.81 which is greater than the table value 2.1315 (at 5% significance level).

Dividend Per Share

During the year dividend per share shown a growth rate of 2.14 with mean 24.9 SD 6.31 for SBI and decreasing rate of 0.92 with mean 3.76 and 1.04 for AB. It indicates there are *significant* differences in the performance of both the banks' ROA. This is supported by the t-test conducted. The calculated t-value is 6.63 which is greater than the table value 2.1315 (at 5% significance level).

Operating Profit Per Share

During the year operating profit per share shown a growth rate of 1.73 with mean 207.28 SD 40.03 for SBI and 2.41 with mean 19.51 and SD 6.97 for AB. It indicates there are *significant* differences in the performance of both the banks' Operating profit per share. This is supported by the t-test conducted. The calculated t-value is 9.27 which is greater than the table value 2.1315 (at 5% significance level).

Free Reserves Per Share

During the year free reserves per share shown a growth rate of 2.54 with mean 359.14 SD 93.39 for SBI and 1.86 with mean 41.47 and SD 11.82 for AB. It indicates there are *significant* differences in the performance of both the banks' Free reserves per share. This is supported by the t-test conducted. The calculated t-value is 9.27 which is greater than the table value 2.1315 (at 5% significance level).

CONCLUSION

The preceding analysis shows that the select banks have shown significant differences in their performance with reference to NIM, Operating Expenses, Adjusted Cash Margin, NPM, RON, ROA, Operating Profit per Share and Net Operating Profit per Share, Free Reserves per Share. The Profitability, Investment Valuation Ratios and Management Efficiency Ratios indicate that both the banks perform differently inspite of the similar business environment in which they are operating. SBI seems to have better edge over Andhra Bank. The insistence on the implementation on BASEL I, II and III seem to have had better effect on the performance of the banks. They are compelled to be more competitive, efficient and lean in order to improve their operating profits and compete with global organizations. A further analysis of the Asset and Liability Management and Risk Management is needed to have a deeper understanding of the impact of global standards on the Banking Sector in general and the select banks in particular.

REFERENCES

[1] Jayaditya Sharma, K. (Feb. 06, 2012). "Basel 2: Challenges for The Indian Banking Industry", Published on Coolavenues.com.

[2] Vibha Batra, Karthik, Puneet Maheshwari, "Indian Banking Sector: Challenges unlikely to derail the progress made", ICRA, June, 2011.

[3] "Evolution of Indian Banking Industry", Available at; www.southasiananalysis.org/%5cpapers.

[4] Narendra Jadhav, "Emerging Issues in Banking and Financial Sector in India", DBOD. No. BP. 256/21.04.098/2007–08, September 5, 2007.

[5] Kamath, Kohli; Shenoy, Ranjana and Nayak, Kuppuswamy (2003). "Indian Banking Sector: Challenges and Opportunities", VIKALPA, Vol. 28, No. 3, July 2003.

[6] Rajesh, Goyal, "Basel III Accord—Basel 3 Norms", Available at: www.allbankingsolution.com.

[7] Subba Rao, Governor, "RBI Monetary Policy Statement 2012–13".

[8] Report on Trend and Progress of Banking in India 2010–2011.

[9] Highlights of RBI nonetary policy, Available at: www.fingyan.com/repo-and-reverse-repo-rates-in-monetary-policy-2012-13.

[10] Key Financial Ratios of SBI, Available at: www.moneycontrol.com>banks-publicsectorbanks-sbi.

[11] Key Financial Ratios of Andhra Bank, Available at: www.moneycontrol.com>banks-publicsectorbanks-andhrabank.

[12] Fridson, Martin and Fernando Alvarez. Financial Statement Analysis: A Practitioner's Guide. New York: John Wiley, 2002.

[13] Mohanty, R.K., Ratio Analysis, Available at: www.iibf.orf.in/documents/caiib_fm_modc.ppt.

[14] "Financial Ratios", Available at: www.netmba.com/finance/financial/ratios.

[15] "SBI scales up core banking linkage for Basel II", Available at: www.business-standard.com/india/news/sbi-scalescore-banking-linkage-for-basel-ii.

PART–II

Challenges Relating to Competition, Technology and CRM

Indian Public Sector Banks in the Post-Reforms Period: An Analytical Study Using S-C-P Approach

Ashis Taru Deb and Sonia Koushik[1]

College of Vocational Studies, University of Delhi
[1]Bharti Mahila College, University of Delhi

ABSTRACT: *The study adapts S-C-P paradigm to analyse the emergence and evolution of competition in public sector banking industry in India. It argues that developments in the industry followed expectation of the policy makers the paper demonstrated change in all the four aspects of the market in which PSBs have been operating: basic conditions, market structure, conduct and performance. It explains how a pseudo competitive market in the pre-reforms period got replaced by an oligopoly in the post reforms period.*

Keywords: Banking, S-C-P Paradigm.

INTRODUCTION

Financial sector reforms are regarded as basic policy reform in any developing countries like India. Efficiency in the mobilisation and allocation of resources by the financial sector influence the performance of the real sector of the economy. A prerequisite for capital account convertibility is a sound financial sector (Ahluwalia, 1999; Sarkar, 1999). The earlier Latin American debt crisis and the East Asian crisis a few years ago reminded the policy makers of the need for strengthening the financial system. There are two kinds of financial system: bank-based and market-based. In a bank based financial system, banks mobilise savings, provide risk management vehicles and allocate capital. As opposed to it, in a market-based financial systems, securities market are active as banks in allocating society's savings to firms and helping management of risk. In India, like many developing countries, we have a bank-based financial system. The commercial banking sector has been the most dominant component of the country's organized financial system, which has accounted for the bulk of financial intermediation process. Naturally, a major component of financial sector reforms consists of banking reforms. Public Sector Banks (PSBs) have been the most dominant component of our bank-based financial system and deserve a substantial research interest in any meaningful analysis of the financial system.

The paper is divided into a number of sections. Next section develops the rationale of the study after an analysis of policy framework confronting PSBs and the theoretical foundation underlying it. The section after that traces the evolution of PSBS in India up to the deregulated era. This section also reviews the extant literature relating PSBs in the post reforms era from a critical perspective. Next section seeks to develop a suitable theoretical framework necessary to analyse the research issue in hand. The next section spells out the detailed objectives of the study in the context of the theoretical framework developed in the earlier section. The section after develops the hypotheses to be tested in the study. Data and methodology to be used are discussed in the next section. Results are contained in next section. Summary and conclusions of the study are contained in last section.

EVOLUTION OF PSBS IN INDIA

India had a fairly well developed commercial banking system in existence at the time of independence in 1947. The Reserve Bank of India (RBI) was established in 1935. While the Reserve Bank became a state owned institution from January 1, 1949, the Banking Regulation Act was enacted in 1949 providing a framework for regulation and supervision of commercial banking activity. The first step towards the nationalization of commercial banks was the result of a report (under the aegis of RBI) by the Committee of Direction of All India Rural Credit Survey (1951) which till today is the locus classics on the subject. The Committee recommended one strong integrated state partnered commercial banking institution to stimulate banking development in general and rural credit in particular. Thus, the Imperial Bank of India was taken over by the Government and renamed as the State Bank of India (SBI) on July 1, 1955 with the Reserve Bank acquiring overriding substantial holding of shares. A number of erstwhile banks owned by princely states were made subsidiaries of SBI in 1959. Thus, the beginning of the Plan era also saw the emergence of public ownership of one of the most prominent of the commercial banks. There was a feeling that though the Indian banking system had made considerable progress in the '50s and '60s, it established close links between commercial and industry houses, resulting in cornering of bank credit by these segments to the exclusion of agriculture and small industries.

To meet these concerns, in 1967, the Government introduced the concept of social control in the banking industry. The scheme of social control was aimed at bringing some changes in the management and distribution of credit by the commercial banks. The close link between big business houses and big banks was intended to be snapped or at least made ineffective by the reconstitution of the Board of Directors to the effect that 51 per cent of the directors were to have special knowledge or practical experience. Appointment of whole-time Chairman with special knowledge and practical experience of working of commercial banks or financial or economic or business administration was intended to professionalize the top management. Imposition of restrictions on loans to be granted to the directors' concerns was another step towards avoiding undesirable flow of credit to the units in which the directors were interested. The scheme also provided for the take-over of banks under certain circumstances.

Political compulsion then partially attributed to inadequacies of the social control, led to the Government of India nationalizing, in 1969, 14 major scheduled commercial banks which had deposits above a cut-off size. The objective was to serve better the needs of development of the economy in conformity with national priorities and objectives. In a somewhat repeat of the same experience, eleven years after nationalization, the Government announced the nationalization of six more scheduled commercial banks above the cut-off size. The second round of nationalization gave an impression that if a private sector bank grew to the cut-off size it would be under the threat of nationalization.

Profitability of public sector enterprises during the heydays of nationalization was the not the concern of the policy makers. PSBs in India were no exception. Large private sector banks were nationalized in 1969 and again in 1980 to achieve social objectives. As result, banks were concerned about achievement of some targets related to social banking and the quality of their loan portfolio declined. Absence of any income recognition and asset classification norms helped the PSBs to conceal their real status from the rest of the world. However, during thirty years succeeding the first bout of nationalization, many of the PSBs ate up their net worth. Mindless pursuit of social banking by PSBs took its toll. Since the beginning of banking reforms in the early eighties, the government has contributed ₹ 20,046 crores towards re-capitalization and allowed banks to write off ₹ 3,978 crores. Clearly, in the pre-reform era, when provisioning was not done, the profits of PSBs were overstated in their accounts. However, it is interesting to note that re-capitalization started as early as 1985–86, as noted by Mathur (2002). This is indicative of the malfunctioning of the banks that started much before Narasimham Committee and continued throughout the nineties.[1]

RATIONALE OF THE STUDY

An indispensable parameter of any analysis of PSBs in the post reforms era is a reference to Narasimham Committee (1991). After years of unprofitable operations which ate up their

[1]Biswas and Deb (2004).

net worth in a controlled regime which was far from being competitive, there emerged an overwhelming emphasis on the performance of PSBs in terms of their profitability. Narasimham committee (1991) wanted the new private sector banks to create a cold shower effect on public sector banks by way of subjecting them to competitive forces, which was absent so far in the banking industry. The policy makers expected the new banks to conduct their operations differently, compared to public sector. It was expected that new banks would work on the basis of leaner structures with lower operating costs to total asset, and outperform the public sector banks in terms of numerous parameters including funds management, service and introduction of new technology. They would start with a clean slate and would be devoid of any of the weaknesses of the existing ones. It was expected that possible that public sector would curve out a profitable niche for them in the industry and, when faced with competitive forces unleashed by the new private sector banks.

Clearly, Narasimham Committee (1991) visualized new private banks to be the agents of transformation for PSBs. This is in line with classic economic writing by Alfred Marshall which suggest that older firms are prone to inertia that go along with age and thus are unlikely to flexible enough to make rapid changes in the contemporary environment. There exists two strands in literature, which attribute innovation with new firms. Schumpeter in his two books "The Theory of Economic Development" (1934) and "Capitalism, Socialism and Democracy" (1942) had expressed two different views about innovation. In the first work, Schumpeter points out that innovation is not associated with an established firm but is typically created by a newcomer. As opposed to this, the other view suggests that innovation is the product of efforts of existing large or monopolistic enterprises. These two views of Schumpeterian innovation may be linked to two modes of development of an industry. The first one is an "entrepreneurial mode of development of an industry" in which innovation is associated with the entry of new firms while the other is "routinised mode of development" in which innovations typically come from established large firms. The distinction between the two Schumpetarian regimes involves a reversal of relative roles of innovation by entrants and established firms. The entrepreneurial regime is one that is favourable to innovative entry and unfavourable to innovation by established firms while a routinised regime is one in which the conditions are other way around. Clearly in a situation where PSBs were stuck in a non-innovative set up in a a regulated regime, Narasimham Committee (1991) was in favour of "entrepreneurial mode of development of an industry" in the form of entry of new private banks.

Hawtrey (1943) argued that the potential competition of newcomers is the primary competitive factor in the determination of profit. He went on to add that competition from inside is important when firms in an industry are struggling to maximize their share in a shrinking business. But, in the case of a growing industry[2], demand is found to be

[2]This implies existing firms are enjoying external economies. We shall pursue this argument later.

outstripping capacity, and the immediate result is to enable all the producers to secure high prices and augmented profit margins. If all the established producers prefer to hold back, perhaps from a tacit understanding that no one of them should endanger the excess profits enjoyed by them, the initiative is likely to come from outside, and newcomers would enter the industry with innovation. Gerosky (1989) also argues that entry and innovation are undoubtedly intertwined in the case of new firms.

Along with entry of new private banks, Narsimham Committee (1991) introduced new norms of conduct relating to capital adequacy, asset classification and income recognition norms. More changes were brought in over a period of time. They began with deregulation in interest rates on deposit followed by advances and freeing of service charges. Deregulation in lending rates, has been followed by lifting of different quantitative restrictions on credit allocation. Such a step has led to more autonomy on the part of the banks, in formulating their own method of assessing working capital needs of borrowers, within the prudential guidelines and exposure norms prescribed by RBI. All instructions relating to Maximum permissible bank finance and Credit Monitoring Arrangement schemes have been withdrawn since April 1997. Similar deregulations have also been made with respect to term finance, by virtue of which RBI has withdrawn its stipulation both on time and quantum of loans, that can be granted by banks either individually or in consortia, for a single project. By September 1999, service charges charged by the banks from their customers were freed.

The above changes were introduced with a view to provide them with the needed flexibility in their operations in their attempt to cope up with new competitive impulses generated by entry of new private banks. Entry of new private banks, it may be argued, may be also expected to create a rivalry amongst PSBs in a new situation when they all are threatened by competition emanating from entry. Each one of them of them will need to work out their new status in the new scenario, which may lead to change in their position relative to their competitors in the industry. There is likely to be adjustment among PSBs in favor of those PSBs which adapts itself faster in the new situation. This may lead one expect change in the market structure of public sector.

The forgoing analysis throws up the research question to be pursued in our study in the following form: Whether the expectation of the policy makers have been realized? Could new private banks act as agents of change for PSBs through exposing them to competition? An anslysis of such an expectation of the policy makers may be decomposed at three related levels. For an easy comprehension:

- First, entry of new private banks will squeeze market share of PSBs.
- Secondly, reduction of market share of PSBs will force them to reorient their conduct.
- Thirdly, such a change in conduct will lead to improved profitability.

SURVEY OF LITERATURE

The literature on post reforms phase of public sector banks is quite vast and varied in nature. A number of issues relating to banking have engaged the attention of the researchers. They include Non-performing Assets, risk and productivity change, net interest margin, asset liability management, stability of interest and non interest income, implication of Basel accord, corporate Governance, Off-balance sheet activities, and last but no the least the issues related to performance. The later issues span through total factor productivity, technical and allocative efficiency, total revenue efficiency, profit efficiency, cost efficiency and profitability. However, the studies of interest to our research question relate to those which attempted an analysis of public sector banks in a comparative perspective.

Koeva (2003) examined a variety of financial indicators of banks and concluded that ownership has a significant effect on some of the performance indicators and reforms have led to lower intermediation costs and profitability. Bhowmik and Dimova (2004) analyzed performance in terms of return on assets of all banks and concluded that by 2000, competition helped PSBs to reduce the gap in performance that existed between them and private banks. Rammohan and Ray (2004) compared revenue maximizing efficiency of three groups of banks: public, Indian private and foreign banks during 1992–2000. They found that PSBs were significantly better than private sector banks on revenue maximization efficiency, but between PSBs and foreign banks, the differences in efficiency was not significant. A study by Sensharma (2005) used the method of stochastic frontier analysis to estimate cost and profit efficiencies in Indian banking over a long period of time extending up to eighteen years. The results may be summarized as follows. PSBs have shown higher cost efficiency than private banks, whereas it has been the other way round in the case of profit efficiency. New private and foreign banks show the least efficiency in terms of both measures. Cost efficiency improved during the sample period while profit efficiency underwent a decline. The authors attributed this result to deregulation of the economy. In terms of bank groups, domestic banks appear to be more efficient than foreign banks.

The initial attempt to analyze efficiency in banking industry was made by Keshari and Paul (1994) to examine whether foreign banks on an average operate with greater efficiency. The authors took the sum total of the amount of the total deposits and advances of a bank as output measure and labour, capital and materials as inputs. The results show that the foreign banks as a group was one percent less efficient than domestic banks while the standard deviation of technical efficiency was a little higher than that of domestic banks. Though the authors used econometric frontier approach, their study took only a single cross section data and did not make any attempt to link performance of the banking industry through liberalization.

Noulas and Ketkar (1996) examined technical and scale efficiency of Indian PSBs for the year 1993 using a non-parametric production function approach. They followed intermediation method of measuring output and took labour, capital and funds as inputs of production. Overall technical inefficiency was approximately 3.75 percent of which only 1.5 Percent was on account of pure technical inefficiency and 2.25 percent inefficiency was due to scale inefficiencies. The majority of banks were found to be opera rating under increasing returns to scale. They concluded that increasing the scale of operations could further enhance efficiency of Indian PSBs.

Das (1997) examined the efficiency of the PSBs in India since nationalization using longitudinal data and compared the efficiency of banks prior to deregulation with the efficiency after regulation. A non-parametric programming approach was used to calculate various types if efficiency. The inputs included in calculation of various efficiency measures were labor and loan-able funds-deposits and borrowing. Te author used margin and commission, exchange, brokerage etc as output measure. The results indicate that State Bank group was more efficient than the nationalized banks. The mean technical efficiency of the sample of banks for the period 1984, 1990 and 1996 were .85, .89 and .77 respectively. Most of the PSBs improved their allocative efficiency significantly in the deregulation period. Finally inefficiency that existed in these banks was merely the results of technical rather allocative efficiency. They analyzed overall technical efficiency-technical, allocative and scale of Indian PSBs and found a decline in overall efficiency.

Bhattacharya *et al.* (1997) used DEA methodology to examine the productive efficiency of seventy commercial banks over a period of six years from 1984 to 1991. The authors used a stochastic frontier approach to attribute variation in calculated efficiencies to a set of temporal ownership and government regulatory policy variables. They used advances, deposit and investment as output measure and interest expenses and operating expenses as resources. They found publicly owned to be the most efficient and privately owned banks the least efficient, in utilizing the resources at their disposal to deliver services. The average efficiencies over the period were 80.35, 87.40, 75.88 and 75.37 for the banking industry, publicly owned, privately owned and foreign-owned banks respectively. They also found a temporal improvement in the performance of foreign banks, virtually no trend in the performance of privately owned and a temporal decline in the performance of publicly—owned banks.

Another Study was conducted by T.T. Ram Mohan (2002), to study the impact of deregulation on the performance of the PSBs. He has evaluated the performance of PSBs both in absolute and in relative terms. The period of his study is 1991–92 to 1999–2000. the variables used by him are: interest spread, intermediation cost, NPA, provisions and contingencies, net profit. For the evaluation of performance in absolute terms, he has compared the last year of his study with 1991–92 as well as 1992–93 and for evaluation in relative terms, he has used the data from 1994–95 to 1999–2000. It is interesting to note that, he has left the first two years of deregulation for the relative evaluation to make the data comparable as the profitability of the PSBs was severely impacted by the new accounting and prudential norms and the consequent cleaning up of the balance sheets, while the private and foreign banks did not carry the same kind of baggage from the past. For comparative evaluation, he has used the Wilcoxon Rank Sum Test, which is a non-parametric test and works with medians rather than means. In his study he has concluded that: the efficiency of the banking system as a whole, measured by declining spreads, has improved and that PSBs have improved their performance both in absolute as well as in relative terms. He also claims that though there has not been a clear trend towards improved efficiency over the decade of the 1990s, there is a clear trend in the recent period from 1996–97 to 1999–2000, when the interest spread has declined. Second, a decrease in provisions (due to the cleaning up of bank balance sheets) improved profitability of the public sector banks. Finally, for the latter half of the decade the public sector banks have done better than private sector banks in terms of the spread or the net interest income. This is true, he claims, no matter what combination of public sector banks and private banks we take public sector banks minus three weak banks with old private sector banks, public sector banks with old private sector banks, or public sector banks with all private sector banks.

However, Errol D'souza (2002) has also attempted an analysis on the on the performance of the PSBs and he counters the work of T.T. Ram Mohan by arguing that the efficiency of the banking sector has not improved as measured by interest spreads which have been rising and not declining (he has used spread to working funds ratio as against the spread to asset ratio). He further argues that PSBs have been behind this declining efficiency as their spreads have risen at a faster rate than the decline in the spreads of the private and foreign banks. Though the turnover/employee ratio has risen in the public sector banks, the turnover per employee in the private and foreign banks doubled relative to the ratio for the public sector banks during this decade. Also, this is not due to the presence of a large rural and semi-urban concentration of bank branches amongst public sector banks but rather due to technological up-gradation in the private and foreign banks and their resorting to changing the structure of their employment towards a higher skilled workforce by increasing the recruitment of officers and reducing their clerical and subordinate staff—the combination of higher technology and higher skills have posted a higher turnover for these banks as they have been able to provide better customer support and manage assets better. The profitability of the public sector banks improved relative to that of the private and foreign banks but this has been partly because of their declining asset base as they are losing ground in their ability to attract deposits at favorable net interest rates. Also, private and foreign banks have been more prudent in their expenditures on provisioning and their operating expenses have risen in the latter half of the decade as they have made large investments in technological up-gradation—a pointer to them sacrificing current returns for greater long-term returns. The improved relative profitability of public sector banks is better read in this light

A study by De (2004) attempted to empirically investigate the ownership-liberalization—efficiency issue of the Indian banking Industry using a panel data set for the years 1985 to 1995–96. Das, Nag and Ray (2005) empirically estimated and analyzed various efficiency scores of Indian banks during 1997–2003 using DEA, In spite of gradual liberalization aimed at strengthening the operational efficiency of the financial system in the 1990s, it is observed that Indian banks are still not differentiated in terms of input or output oriented technical efficiency and cost efficiency. Nevertheless, they differ sharply in respect their revenue and profit efficiencies. Bank size, ownership and listing on the stock exchange are some of the factors which have been found to exert a positive impact on average profit efficiency and to some extent revenue efficiency scores. Finally, the median efficiency scores of Indian banks, in general, and of bigger banks, in particular, have improved during the post reform period.

An important empirical studies regarding performance of banks is Sarkar *et al.* (1998). It used a number of financial variables to compare performance of various categories of banks: PSBs, private and foreign banks. The variables used to measure performance are as follows:

- Net profit as a ratio of assets
- Operating profit as a ratio of assets
- Operating profit as a ratio of staff expense
- Net-interest margin deflated by assets.
- Operating cost/assets
- Staff expenses as a ratio of assets.

After controlling for effects of a number of concomitant variables, they conducted regression analysis to find the effect of ownership type on different measures of performance. It suggests a weak ownership effect of private banks over PSBs. The study confirmed the expectation of the authors that in absence of well functioning capital markets, there may not be significant differences between performance of PSBs and private banks. However, the study does not include new private banks since data was available only till 1994–95. Hence it is perhaps a little premature to judge the relative performance of different kinds of banks on the basis of this study.

A critical analysis of the literature on PSBs reveals the following points:

- First, it is heavily biased towards performance of PSBs in a comparative perspective. it is almost entirely concerned with impact on ownership on performance This is attributed to the fact that very charged debate is going in the country whether PSBs should be privatized or not. Performance of PSBs is a very important component of the debate relating to privatization of banks. It is argued that PSBs should be privatized if they continue make losses or perform worse than private sector banks[3] and that if social banking is the reason behind poor performance of PSBs, such activity should not be thrust upon PSBs and government should use its fiscal instruments to achieve a better distribution of income. The administrative machinery needs to be revamped in order to collect more direct tax so that its proceeds can be used meet social objectives. Clearly the performance of PSBs has attracted most research attention as it is at the center of the debate related to privatization of PSBs.

- Secondly, concentration of attention solely on the impact of ownership takes away the whole perspective on competition, which needs to be a critical focus in any post reforms study of public sector banks.
- Thirdly, a serious lacuna in the literature is absence of a well laid out theoretical framework within which the research question needs to be posed. For example, differential performance of two different groups of banks needs to use an underlying theory of strategic groups, where differential conduct between two groups lead to differential performance.
- Finally, a glaring gap in the literature is absence of relates to a detailed analysis of various aspects of functioning of PSBs in the post reforms era. Such a detailed and focused study should proceed any analysis of PSBs in a comparative perspective, on which much research effort has been devoted. The initial requirement for such an analysis is development of a suitable theoretical framework to which we will turn in the next section.

THEORETICAL FRAMEWORK

Pure theory of fractional reserve banking treats banks as mere passive entities leading to a mechanical modeling of their responses. Banks are assumed to acquiesce in supplying whatever quantity of demand deposits is dictated by public's desire for demand deposits on the one hand and the monetary authority's reserve requirements on the other. Clearly, the micro foundations of banking theory were weak. Even the H theory of money supply, which apparently attributes an active role to commercial banks in the endogenous determination of money supply, does not present an explicit model of the banking firm. Gurley and Shaw (1960) and Tobin (1963) observed that the theory of money creation neglected the role of banks as firms.[4] However, early analysis of banks treated it as a

[3]This is a component of a liberal line of thinking which argues that even the lender of last resort function should be dispensed with (Gongopadhaya and Singh, 2000).

[4]Identification of banks as firms provides a natural rationale behind application of industrial organisation framework to banking.

mere rational investor operating in an environment characterized by risk or uncertainty and not primarily as a firm. Conceptual difficulties in drawing analogy between a bank and the typical firm in neoclassical analysis led researchers to concentrate on only one specific problem of a bank: allocation of bank's funds among competing stocks of assets This approach is grossly inadequate as it completely neglects the production and cost constraints under which banks operate and the role they play in determining the equilibrium output mix and scale size of a bank.

Instead of simply considering the banking sector as a passive aggregate, as in the standard approach to monetary policy often found in macro textbooks, commercial banks need to be modeled as independent entities that optimally react to their environment. In Industrial economics, a bank, like a firm, is conceptualized as operating under a certain kind of market structure providing a service to its customers and in the process incurs costs in order to produce this service. In the process, it has to compete with other banks in the industry, using price and non-price instruments and earn a return enough to justify its existence in the industry. Industrial organization framework is a general expression of relationship between the attributes, which seem to characterize an industry. The unit of analysis is market or industry on the one hand or the firm on the other. The framework uses a technique of analysis called partial equilibrium, which is introduced by Marshall. The S-C-P paradigm assumes that certain attributes, designated as basic conditions, are given and a chain of causation logically determines all the other attributes as follows.

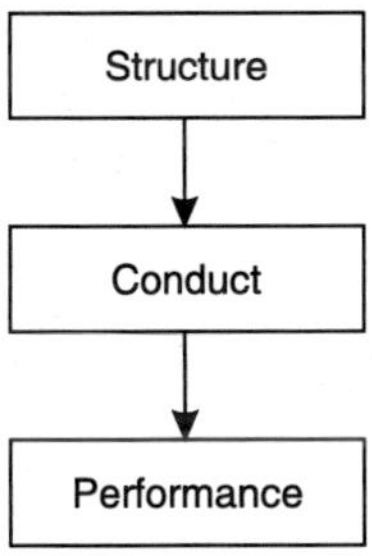

Fig. 1: Schema of Traditional S-C-P Paradigm

The basic content of the paradigm is captured by the following few lines. The basic conditions are the primary determinants of the market or industry structure. In the next step, the structure of the industry influences the conduct by participants in the industry. Conduct, in turn influences performance.

Basic Conditions

In a discussion of S-C-P paradigm, the phenomenon of basic conditions does not ordinarily receive much attention (Hay and Morris, 1979; Ferguson and Ferguson, 1994).

Basic conditions shape market irrespective of market forms. It is determined by the basic conditions of demand and supply. Demand side conditions include: direct and cross-elasticities of demand; market growth in its trend, cyclical and seasonal aspects; taste, requirement and purchasing habit of customers. Supply side conditions include: location and ownership of raw materials; technology; unionization; product durability; industry history; availability of substitutes and the legal, ethical and political framework within which business activity takes place. The usual attitude is to regard basic conditions consisting of taste, technology and institutions as given and concentrate structure, conduct and performance.

In terms of the view of industrial organization contained in the figure above, basic conditions are shown to influence structure alone as opposed to conduct or performance. Clearly change in technology; a component of the basic condition has an impact on the conduct of firms. Again, change in taste of consumer will force the firms to change in behavior of the firm. Once more, with introduction of new substitutes, conduct of firms in the industry would change. In all such cases, conduct of firms would change directly as a result of change in basic conditions. Such a change could not be discussed in the traditional framework of S-C-P as it treats basic conditions as given. The traditional paradigm needs to be adapted to render it suitable for analyzing an industry where basic conditions have undergone a change. It will be argued below that public sector banking industry is one such industry.

An examination of emergence of competitive forces as a result of reforms in public sector banking must start from an analysis of basic conditions in the said industry. Analysis of basic demand and supply conditions will provide interesting insights into the phenomenon of entry of new private banks. In absence of such a study, it appears that entry mechanically follows amendment of Banking Regulation Act in 1993. However, in reality, thing are complex and while a legal enactment is necessary for initiation of a new economic activity, it is by no means a sufficient condition.

In order to understand the dynamics of basic conditions confronting PSBs, In order to understand the supply side factors related to entry, a quick look at the relevant feature of the situation relating to PSBs during the period succeeding nationalization is necessary. Till the initiation of reforms in 1992, Indian PSBs had been operating as if they were subsidiaries of the government, whose objective was to meet the financial requirements of the state. They operated under the strict guidelines of the RBI, which were all encompassing. Although most of their deposit came from the private sector, i.e., households, a major part of their lending was confined to the government, and they also made substantial investment in government bills/securities. RBI acted as the mediator between the state and PSBs more or less determining the amount/share of the deposit to be allocated to the state and the private sectors. For the private sector lending it fixed ceiling and floor rates of interest depending on the type of loan, size of loan, type of borrower, nature of collateral, etc.[5] The interest rates often did not reflect the risks of lending. RBI also fixed interest rates on deposits. The bank had little room for making independent decisions in adjusting interest rates with the risks of lending, especially to the private borrowers. Under this system, there was very limited scope for making profitable innovations in terms of both organizational changes and seeking new sources of fund and new avenues of investments/lending[6]. For a long period, real interest rates were negative for many of these loans; obviously, vested interest, political and local intervention would creep in, in order to extract surplus in the system (i.e., difference between the opportunity costs and actual cost of borrowing). Since it was not mandatory on the part of the banks to declare NPA or recover loans, and since, RBI was happy so long as the banks were able to finance state expenditure, a laxity crept into the banking sector. This happened particularly for the kind of private sector lending mentioned above and, in general, profit earning/meeting the interests of the depositors became the secondary objective of the banks. Often the non-intended borrowers received the loans, and even for the case of some target borrowers, the influential brokers who arranged the loans would take away a sizeable amount of the loan disbursed. The borrowers would not be able to repay the loans; even if they could, they would not be interested in doing so. The broker had to manipulate the system in such a way that the bank could not penalize the borrowers. On the contrary, the bank granted fresh loans to the defaulters so that the debt would roll on (known as ever greening of accounts). Under these circumstances, it was quite obvious that some personnel of the bank would also try to extract some surplus.

Thus a new institution evolved. The institution involved a nexus of some personnel of banks, brokers, and borrowers that would siphon off public money through manipulating banking machinery, state machinery, mobilizing political and local forces. The banks on the other hand showed this lost money, or the rolling loans, as normal assets. The banking institution and their institutional environment that evolved over the decades were therefore not supportive of healthy and innovative ways of making progress by the banks. This being the status of existing PSBS, the policy favour was not in favour creating new PSBs through nationalization and relied on "entrepreneurial mode of development of an industry" in the form of entry of new private banks to rejuvenate PSBs.

[5]For instance minimum of the key lending rates was 13.50 percent in 1980, which increased to 16 percent in 1989 and then to 19 percent in 1991–92. Thereafter it declined slowly. Similarly, the ceiling rate was 19.50 percent in 1980–81, which declined to 16.50 percent in 1987-88. The minimum rate for selective credit control also varied over the years, which was freed in 1994–95 (Hand Book of Statistics on the Indian Economy, 2003).

[6]Chakravarty committee (1985) mentions three essential characteristics of a sound financial system. They include high levels of allocation and operational efficiency, stability and innovations in instruments and financial techniques to meet the ever-changing preferences of the community of savers and investors.

The shortcomings of the public sector banking system, as discussed by the Narasimham Committee (1991), provide the rationale for financial sector reforms. Despite impressive quantitative achievements in resource mobilization and in extending the credit reach, several distortions have crept in, especially in the financial system. Productivity and efficiency has been eroded and its portfolio quality has deteriorated. Customer service has been poor, work technology remains out-dated and transactions cost high. In the process, several banks have become weak financially and unable to meet the challenges of a competitive system. Among other things, it was argued in the Narasimham committee (1991), the objective of the financial sector should be competitive efficiency and accordingly it was suggested that entry into the financial system should be liberalized. This led to amendment of Banking Regulation Act in 1993 and the legal barrier to entry into the private banking industry was removed. It represented a supply side factor, which by itself was not enough to lead to entry. There had to be some demand side factors, which would lead to entry, when supply bottlenecks were removed.

The indifferent quality of service provided by the public sector banks and the supply of such services by foreign banks at high prices created a high level of dissatisfaction among the upper middle class segment in the metros. This section had a high opportunity cost of visiting a branch and was ready to pay a higher price for better service instead of an indifferent quality of service at a low price. At the same time, they could not shift to foreign banks, the primary reason being the insistence on a large sum as the account opening and lock-in requirement. It was a situation comparable to landing between the devil and the deep blue sea. There existed a demand for better quality of standard services of a bank, new services and even of new modes of providing the old services, which could only be accomplished through vigorous use of information technology. New entrants entered with new products and services based on information technology because they believed there would be a market for their new output and expected that economic benefit, net of the incurred cost.

To sum up, it may be said that in response to a change in basic conditions of demand in favor of more user friendly banking service, basic conditions of supply changed in the form of emergence of substitutes of public sector banks in the form of new private banks when entry was deregulated through a new legislation and supported by easy availability of new information technology. The traditional S-C-P paradigm with unchanged basic conditions can not analyze the impact of entry of new private banks on public sector banks till basic condition itself is treated as a variable through changing taste, regulation and technology which led to a situation where a change in demand was met by means of expansion of substitutes for services produced by public sector banks. Treating basic conditions as a variable rather than a parameter is the first significant change incorporated in the traditional S-C-P paradigm.

Structure

The structure of an industry or market is by far the most important, though not sole determinant of business conduct. Therefore an economic analyst cannot adequately describe or fully understand the conduct of a business firm without putting it into the context of the industry's structure. It is important to point out that perfectly contestable markets may also be used as a benchmark for analysis of industry structure. Such markets are open to entry by entrepreneurs who face no disadvantages vis-à-vis incumbent firms and who can exit without loss of any costs that entry requires to be sunk. There are no legal restrictions on market entry and exit and there are no special costs that must be borne by an entrant that do not fall on the incumbent firm as well. In such markets, competitive pressures from potential entrants exercise strong constraints on the conduct of incumbent firms. Hence in a perfectly contestable market, absence of features like sunk costs and entry barriers, structure of an industry is rendered inconsequential for the conduct and performance of the firms operating in that industry. It may be pointed out; contestable markets do not serve as a useful reference point for analysis of banking industry, which is apparently characterized by sunk cost and entry barriers.

Conduct

Conduct is the term used in reference to the behavior of firms in the market. It refers to how firms react to the conditions imposed by market structure and interacts with rivals. In course of interaction with competitors, the firm has to take into account the dependence of other firm's actions on its behavior. Conduct includes a strategic move, which is one that influences the other person's choice, in a manner available to one's self, by affecting other person's expectations on how one's self will behave. In principle, many types of conduct may be distinguished, some of which may be extended beyond the strictly economic. Under conduct, one conventionally looks at: how price is set; the way in which the volume, quality and range of products are determined; advertising and marketing strategy; research and development planning and implementation; and legal tactics.

Performance

Performance is a judgment about the results of market behavior (Burgess, 1988). The dimensions of market performance about which industrial organization is concerned include efficiency, fairness and progress. Efficiency involves how well a market makes use of available resources. Fairness involves how equitably market distributes benefits of economic activity to the participants. Progress concerns how effectively the market nurtures and yields better products and production techniques.

OBJECTIVES OF THE STUDY

The objective of this thesis is to conduct a comprehensive study of the public sector banking industry in the post-reforms phase through an analysis of changes in basic conditions, market structure, conduct and performance in public sector banks.

In sum, the objectives of the study are as follows:

- To classify different reform measures depending on whether they impact basic conditions, market structure and conduct.
- Impact on basic conditions.
- Impact of market structure.
- Impact on conduct.
- Impact on performance.

HYPOTHESES

Primary Hypotheses

- Competition in banking industry can be understood in terms of S-C-P.
- Entry of new private banks will lead to rivalry between them and PSBs leading to decline in market Share of PSBs.
- PSBs will improve their profitability.

Selected Secondary Hypotheses

- Pattern of market dominance will change.
- PSBs will reorient their conduct in direction of improved profitability.

DATA SOURCES AND METHODOLOGY

The study relates to the period from 1992 to 2011 for which data is provided by two sources, first the RBI and second, the Indian Banking Association. The data for the study is collected from two data sources published by RBI, including Statistical Tables for banks and Trend and second, Progress of Banking in India. The data for these two sources is available on the RBI website from 1998 onwards.

The precise elements in the methodology of the study are mentioned as under.

- Identification of variables related to basic conditions, structure, conduct and performance categories.
- Calculation of share of public and private sector banks in the market as well as their incremental market share over time.
- Calculation of market share of leading banks.

- Use of paired t-test to test for existence of significant difference between mean values of relevant conduct and performance variables over time.

RESULTS OF THE STUDY

Here we will report the results of a number of exercises conducted to test the hypotheses developed in an earlier section.

Basic Conditions

We begin with calculation of two sets of ratios: the share of public and private sector banks in the total banking market and in the expanded market. Movement of shares of a banking segment in the aggregate market depends on its share in the expanded market. Introduction of new private banks in the banking market by itself need not depress the market share of PSBs. New banks have have either cut into the existing market served by PSBs or grown by creating new markets. In either case, it was imperative for PSBs to react to new private sector banks and expand their market share. In fact, if PSBs can maintain their market share achieved in the preceding year in the expanded market in the current year as well, its market share will remain unaffected. A falling market share in the expanded market will pull down the market share in the aggregate market. The relevant ratios are provided in Table 1 in the appendix, which clearly points out to existence of

Table 1: Share pf Public Sector and Pubic Sector Banks in Aggregate as well Expanded Market: 1993–94 to 2003–05

	Share in Agrregate PSB	*Share in Market Pvt. Banks*	*Share in Expanded PSB*	*Share in Market Pvt. Banks*
1994	0.937700259	0.062299741	0.818856089	0.181143911
1995	0.921331794	0.078668206	0.83550531	0.16449469
1996	0.910857024	0.089142976	0.840608497	0.159391503
1997	0.893666524	0.106333476	0.771359794	0.228640206
1998	0.882954152	0.117045848	0.82846089	0.17153911
1999	0.878488066	0.121511934	0.854496132	0.145503868
2000	0.865421628	0.134578372	0.794311447	0.205688553
2001	0.861553349	0.138446651	0.839408619	0.160591381
2002	0.835262055	0.164737945	0.683733439	0.316266561
2003	0.82536125	0.17463875	0.753194791	0.246805209
2004	0.809035604	0.190964396	0.709949997	0.290050003

rivalry in the banking market to capture a larger market share. New private sector banks entered in 1995 and the year 1994 was used in the table as a benchmark. It may be seen that private sector banks has been consistently raising their share in the expanded over the period from 1993–94 to 2003–04. Clearly pressure exerted by private sector banks in the form of trebling their share have led to lowering of share of PSBs from 93% to 80%.

Market Structure

In the second leg of this section, we calculate share of the leading PSB in respect of total assets, business and branches of public sector banking industry.

It needs to be clarified that application of S-C-P paradigm to banking industry has to recognize the difference between an ordinary firm and a bank. While asset may be an appropriate indicator of market size for a firm, the same need not be true for a bank. A bank is a financial intermediary, which accepts deposit and provides advances. It operates simultaneously in the market for acceptance of deposit and provision of advances and competes with other banks in the process. It appears that sum of deposit and advances are likely to an appropriate indicator of size of bank.

Secondly, there is an impression that PSBs operate on the basis of branches and it is more dependent on manpower, unlike new private banks or foreign banks. It seems to be an interesting idea to explore these aspects as well by means of an analysis of changes in concentration ratio in terms of employment as well as branches. The changes in concentration ratio in public sector banking industry in terms of employment and assets need not mirror changes in concentration ratio based on asset, deposit and advances. The implementation of voluntary retirement scheme in PSBs may impact each PSB differently and changes in concentration ratio in terms of employment may be different compared to other concentration ratio. A similar impact may be expected for concentration ratio in terms of branches, in view of branch rationalization adopted by PSBs. Organizational restructuring including branch rationalization as well as manpower rationalization was undertaken in PSBs to make banking services product and customer friendly.

The regulated phase of development of public sector banking in India was characterized by administered interest rate and service charges as well as tight credit allocation mechanism coupled with restricted entry into domestic private banking sector. The domestic private banks were operating on the basis of a large number of branches and uniform products. While entry of new banks was restricted by government policy, the private banks competed with one another solely on the basis of efficiency. Clearly, exit was the only option of unprofitable branches. For them, entry was restricted but exit was allowed. The situation of a public sector bank during this period appears to be akin to an atomistic producer whose status is that of a price taker. The interest rate on liabilities and assets were not fixed by profit motive, but by RBI regulation through the system of administration spreads. An "uniform price" was artificially prevalent during the regime. It may be appropriate to call the then market structure of the domestic private banking industry "pseudo competitive" in which the profits enjoyed by the banks due to existence of administered spreads which could not be competed away by new entrants. Apart from regulation of interest rate, RBI also regulated the credit allocation by banks through different mechanisms. Presence of interest controls as well as rigorous credit allocation mechanisms, eliminated price competition. Credit allocation mechanisms included capital authorization scheme, credit-monitoring arrangement, consortium financing and lead bank system.

The "pseudo competitive" market structure, which prevailed during the regulated period is not conventional text book market structure. Let us make an attempt to analyze market structure of PSBs during the post reforms period with references to three standard elements: nature of the product, number of firms and conditions of entry and exit. The deregulated regime allowed PSBs to move away to differentiated products from uniform products thrust upon them by the regulated regime. Narasimham Committee (1991) ruled out nationalization leading to entry blockade and exit of PSBS, as the in the earlier phase was not allowed. This led to an unchanged number of PSBs in the industry. The implication of number of banks of market structure is as follows. If a market is divided among large number of firms, one expects them to have smaller market share and not heavy enough to influence the market through their conduct. However, in a situation where a few firms exist in the market, then few top markets may dominate the market through their conduct. These big firms will influence each other by virtue of their large size and will conduct themselves in anticipation of how their rivals will retaliate to what do they do. They may compete or collude depending upon what appears to be them optimal for attaining their objectives. They may compete in fast growing markets, while collude in slowing growing or stagnant markets. It is here concentration ratio appears to be useful to comment on market structure. If it is high, it indicates few firms dominate the market. The literature uses concentration ratio to distinguish between a tight as loose oligopoly. A four-firm ratio above 60% and below 40% have been identified with tight and loose oligopoly respectively (Shepherd, 1987). A threshold value of four-firm concentration ratio percent range should present a clear divide between effective competition seen in loose oligopoly and high market power that tight oligopoly may create. In tight oligopoly, collusion is likely to crystallize effectively into strong cooperation, as the oligopolist's common interest overwhelm the rewards from cheating. Loose oligopoly, on the other hand, is seen a setting for disintregation, where many oligopolists are unable to jointly unable to avert price cutting.

It may be mentioned that dominance in the industry by a few leading banks is quite common. Banking is dominated by ANZ, Westpac, NAB, and Commonwealth Bank in Australia.

Six companies including Royal Bank of Canada, Toronto Dominion Bank, Bank of Nova Scotia, Bank of Montreal, Canadian Imperial Bank of Commerce and National Bank of Canada control the banking industry in Canada. Five banks dominate the UK banking sector, they were accused of being an oligopoly by the relative newcomer Virgin bank.

Usually, four or five firm concentration ratios are used. It is popular because it is easy to understand and has limited data requirements. However, there are a few problems with this measure. First, traditional concentration ratio is not inspired theoretically. Secondly, it ignores identity of firms. This may lead to problems. For example, an unchanged four firm concentration ratio may be taken to mean that there is no change in concentration even when four different firms may replace the four largest firms. Thirdly, the choice of particular value of k is arbitrarily and has little direct economic significance. It reports only one point on the cumulative concentration curve. Comparison of concentration in an industry at two points of time depends on the arbitrarily chosen value of k.

Concentration is usually second in importance to individual markets, as an element of market structure. For example, a firm A may have a 50% while it along with other three firms B, C and D have a combined concentration ratio of 90%. A's price-profit, innovation and other results are likely to be influenced more closely by its own 50% share-giving it a dominant-firm than by the fact that it is in a market with high concentration in four firms. It is clear that it is not meaningful to calculate a concentration ratio with an arbitrary number of leading firms without examining the importance of the leading firm absolutely and relatively. In case the leading firm is overwhelmingly important, it does not need to collude with other leading firms, since it may call the shots on its own.

In the empirical component of the attempt to identify the market structure of PSBs, let us begin by looking at the market share of the leading PSB and changes therein over a period of time. Let us look at Table 2 which provides the share of SBI, the leading PSB in the total assets, business, branch network and employment of all PSBs. It may be observed that the share of SBI has gone up in two cases, while it has gone down in the other two. It is important to test whether such changes in case of leading PSB is statistically significant. Results of the regression exercises are provided in Tables 3–5. While the share of SBI in total assets and business have falling significantly, its share in total branches have remained flat over the period 1991–2 to 2010–11. This is the absolute picture relating to SBI which provides a declining status for the leading bank.

Table 2: Share of SBI in Total Assets, Business and Branch of Public Sector Banks

	State Bank of India's Share in		
	Assets	*Branches*	*Dep+Adv*
1992	0.317373767	0.20646659	0.275158099
1993	0.301400397	0.20651994	0.271085529
1994	0.294467431	0.203660904	0.261893069
1995	0.277984267	0.202011199	0.253752035
1996	0.285601035	0.20050097	0.261082412
1997	0.281294617	0.198574588	0.258272837
1998	0.276765922	0.197054667	0.25938329
1999	0.288852377	0.195856956	0.269106162
2000	0.293511928	0.195376472	0.270715075
2001	0.306519257	0.195971763	0.279762515
2002	0.30130413	0.195864953	0.270014176
2003	0.292457249	0.194654034	0.266390226
2004	0.277156185	0.188777414	0.25626911
2005	0.271698641	0.18767157	0.248573908
2006	0.256463968	0.189146725	0.235214856
2007	0.242521274	0.187772326	0.225039316
2008	0.249529862	0.195235738	0.224438456
2009	0.268321598	0.20856716	0.24909013
2010	0.250380332	0.213586093	0.235911034
2011	0.242783583	0.216334175	0.230301694

Table 3: Fitting a Linear Trend to Share of SBI in Total Assets of all PSBs

Regression Statistics	
Multiple R	0.7852
R Square	0.6166
Adjusted R Square	0.5953
Standard Error	0.0139
Observations	20.0000

ANOVA					
	df	*SS*	*MS*	*F*	*Significance F*
Regression	1.0000	0.0056	0.0056	28.9501	0.0000
Residual	18.0000	0.0035	0.0002		
Total	19.0000	0.0090			

	Coefficients	*Standard Error*	*t-Stat*	*P-value*	*Lower 95%*	*Upper 95%*
Intercept	0.3092	0.0064	48.0201	0.0000	0.2957	0.3227
Time	–0.0029	0.0005	–5.3805	0.0000	–0.0040	–0.0018

Table 4: Fitting a Linear Trend to Share of SBI in Total Business of all PSBs

Regression Statistics	
Multiple R	0.7314
R Square	0.5349
Adjusted R Square	0.5091
Standard Error	0.0119
Observations	20.0000

ANOVA					
	df	*SS*	*MS*	*F*	*Significance F*
Regression	1.0000	0.0029	0.0029	20.7010	0.0002
Residual	18.0000	0.0025	0.0001		
Total	19.0000	0.0055			

	Coefficients	*Standard Error*	*t-Stat*	*P-value*	*Lower 95%*	*Upper 95%*
Intercept	0.2771	0.0055	50.1721	0.0000	0.2655	0.2887
time	–0.0021	0.0005	–4.5498	0.0002	–0.0031	–0.0011

Table 5: Fitting a Linear Trend to Share of SBI in Total Branches of all PSBs

Regression Statistics	
Multiple R	0.0190
R Square	0.0004
Adjusted R Square	–0.0552
Standard Error	0.0084
Observations	20.0000

ANOVA					
	df	*SS*	*MS*	*F*	*Significance F*
Regression	1.0000	0.0000	0.0000	0.0065	0.9367
Residual	18.0000	0.0013	0.0001		
Total	19.0000	0.0013			

	Coefficients	*Standard Error*	*t-Stat*	*P-value*	*Lower 95%*	*Upper 95%*
Intercept	0.1993	0.0039	50.7743	0.0000	0.1910	0.2075
Time	0.0000	0.0003	–0.0806	0.9367	–0.0007	0.0007

The above absolute picture needs to be supplemented by an attempt where we will examine the importance of SBI with regard to other banks down the line. A few simple calculations are made for this purpose. During the first year of the study, assets owned by SBI were more than the total assets owned by five banks succeeding SBI. The relative importance of the bank over the period of the study has declined as it is found that the bank has more assets compared to three following banks put together in the terminal year of the study. So far the share of SBI in total business is concerned, it continues to more assets owned the three banks taken together in both initial and terminal years of the study. Same is picture with regard to share of SBI in total number of branches. Clearly, creation of new substitutes in the form of entry of new private banks failed to adversely impact the share of leading bank across the board. Entry of new banks took place in 1994–95 and even seventeen years after entry, SBI, the leading bank remains more important than three banks in respect of assets, business and branch network. Thus SBI remains the leader as before even in the new scenario. This needs to be contrasted against the private banking industry, where entry of new banks have re-written the rules of the game through change in the leadership in the form of emergence of ICICI bank. The pattern of dominance in the industry remains same and hence the change in the industry can not be attributed to change in leadership but to competitive impulses generated by new private banks affecting all leading PSBs across the board. SBI remains the market leader and market structure evolves into an oligopolistic structure in the liberalized banking regime which evolved after 1993 since the implementation of Narasimham Committee (1991) reforms.

Conduct of PSBs

The next of exercises relate to conduct. A number of thirteen conduct variables were selected. They are stated in the next Table 6. A paired t test is selected as a methodology to test whether change in the variables occurring over the period of the study is statistically significant. Results of the statistical exercises relating to conduct are reported in Tables 7(a)–(m).

The objective to banking sector was to revitalize the banking so that they conduct their operations along efficient lines. It is observed that the banks have become leaner, as reflected in reduction in three variables which include of staff to branch ratio, wages and salaries as a proportion to operating expenditure and the ratio of operational expenditure to total expenditure. Overstaffing was recognized as one of important ills of PSBs by Narasimham Committee (1991). Voluntary Retirement Scheme was launched by the government to right-size the overstaffed banks. The reduction in staff to branch ratio demonstrates the impact of such an effort. However, significant reduction in staff to branch ratio was not accompanied by a reduction in wages to branch ratio. On the other hand, there occurred a significant rise in the ratio. It may be noted that there is nothing wrong in such a rise if it contributes to higher productivity of branches.

Table 6: Definition of Conduct Variables Used in the Study

BRNCH	No. of branches
NPA	Ratio of net NPA to net advances
WAGEOP	Ratio of wages and salaries to operational Expenditure
ADV	Ratio of advertising expenditure to operational Expenditure
SIZE	Sum of advances and deposits
MB	Ratio of number of branches in metro to total no. of branches
OPEX	Ratio of operational expenditure to total Expenditure
OFABR	Ratio of other fixed asset to no of branches
WAGEBR	Ratio of wages and salaries to no of branches
ADVBR	ratio of advertising expenditure to total income
DIV	Ratio of non-interest income to total income
SPRD	Ratio of difference between interest earned and Interest expended to assets
STAFFBR	Ratio of no of staff to no of branches
G-SECINV	Ratio of investment in g-sec in India to total investment
TLNADV	Ratio of term loan to total advances

Table 7(a): Branches

t-Test: Paired Two Sample for Means

	br92	*br2011*
Mean	1644.84	2456.2
Variance	2699922	6233143
Observations	25	25
Pearson Correlation	0.989681	
Hypothesized Mean Difference	0	
Df	24	
t-Stat	–4.49897	
P(T<=t) one-tail	7.42E-05	
t-Critical one-tail	1.710882	
P(T<=t) two-tail	0.000148	
t-Critical two-tail	2.063899	

Table 7(b): Metro Branches to Total Branches

t-Test: Paired Two Sample for Means

	mb92	*MB*
Mean	0.13532	0.209615
Variance	0.001185	0.001995
Observations	25	25
Pearson Correlation	0.859136	
Hypothesized Mean Difference	0	
Df	24	
t-Stat	–16.0123	
P(T<=t) one-tail	1.3E-14	
t-Critical one-tail	1.710882	
P(T<=t) two-tail	2.6E-14	
t-Critical two-tail	2.063899	

Table 7(c): *Wages* to Branches

t-Test: Paired Two Sample for Means

	wagebr92	*wagebr2011*
Mean	11.608	79.68118
Variance	5.576258	180.6654
Observations	25	25
Pearson Correlation	0.568775	
Hypothesized Mean Difference	0	
Df	24	
t-Stat	–27.7782	
P(T<=t) one-tail	4.64E-20	
t-Critical one-tail	1.710882	
P(T<=t) two-tail	9.28E-20	
t-Critical two-tail	2.063899	

Table 7(d): Staff to Branches

t-Test: Paired Two Sample for Means

	staffbr92	*staffbr2011*
Mean	19.4392	11.10568
Variance	9.929033	4.53056
Observations	25	25
Pearson Correlation	0.749285	
Hypothesized Mean Difference	0	
Df	24	
t-Stat	19.84474	
P(T<=t) one-tail	1.07E-16	
t-Critical one-tail	1.710882	
P(T<=t) two-tail	2.14E-16	
t-Critical two-tail	2.063899	

Table 7(e): Other Fixed Assets to Branches

t-Test: Paired Two Sample for Means

	ofabr92	*ofabr2011*
Mean	1.8528	13.79049
Variance	0.339721	23.98499
Observations	25	25
Pearson Correlation	0.096993	
Hypothesized Mean Difference	0	
Df	24	
t-Stat	–12.2424	
P(T<=t) one-tail	4.13E-12	
t-Critical one-tail	1.710882	
P(T<=t) two-tail	8.25E-12	
t-Critical two-tail	2.063899	

Table 7(f): Advertising to Branches

t-Test: Paired Two Sample for Means

	advbr92	*advbr2011*
Mean	0.0368	0.010046
Variance	0.000393	2.94E-05
Observations	25	25
Pearson Correlation	0.048927	
Hypothesized Mean Difference	0	
Df	24	
t-Stat	6.592269	
P(T<=t) one-tail	4.05E-07	
t-Critical one-tail	1.710882	
P(T<=t) two-tail	8.09E-07	
t-Critical two-tail	2.063899	

Table 7(g): Wages to Operating Expenses

t-Test: Paired Two Sample for Means

	wageop92	*wageop2011*
Mean	0.69584	0.663354
Variance	0.001701	0.002624
Observations	25	25
Pearson Correlation	0.335842	
Hypothesized Mean Difference	0	
Df	24	
t-Stat	3.013237	
P(T<=t) one-tail	0.003007	
t-Critical one-tail	1.710882	
P(T<=t) two-tail	0.006013	
t-Critical two-tail	2.063899	

Table 7(h): Advertising to Operating Expenses

t-Test: Paired Two Sample for Means

	adv92	*adv2011*
Mean	0.002359	0.010046
Variance	1E-06	2.94E-05
Observations	25	25
Pearson Correlation	0.24396	
Hypothesized Mean Difference	0	
Df	24	
t-Stat	–7.30142	
P(T<=t) one-tail	7.65E-08	
t-Critical one-tail	1.710882	
P(T<=t) two-tail	1.53E-07	
t-Critical two-tail	2.063899	

Table 7(i): Operating Expenses to Total Expenses

t-Test: Paired Two Sample for Means

	opex92	*opex2011*
Mean	0.28984	0.256256
Variance	0.001716	0.001004
Observations	25	25
Pearson Correlation	0.028179	
Hypothesized Mean Difference	0	
Df	24	
t-Stat	3.264415	
P(T<=t) one-tail	0.001642	
t-Critical one-tail	1.710882	
P(T<=t) two-tail	0.003285	
t-Critical two-tail	2.063899	

Table 7(j): Size = Dep + Adv

t-Test: Paired Two Sample for Means

	size92	*size2011*
Mean	1489482	29364131
Variance	4.21E+12	1.07E+15
Observations	25	25
Pearson Correlation	0.983449	
Hypothesized Mean Difference	0	
Df	24	
t-Stat	–4.55024	
P(T<=t) one-tail	6.52E-05	
t-Critical one-tail	1.710882	
P(T<=t) two-tail	0.00013	
t-Critical two-tail	2.063899	

Table 7(k): Diversification

t-Test: Paired Two Sample for Means

	DIV	*DIV*
Mean	0.097684	0.101189
Variance	0.00051	0.000397
Observations	25	25
Pearson Correlation	0.431466	
Hypothesized Mean Difference	0	
Df	24	
t-Stat	–0.76987	
P(T<=t) one-tail	0.224445	
t-Critical one-tail	1.710882	
P(T<=t) two-tail	0.44889	
t-Critical two-tail	2.063899	

Table 7(l): Spread to Total Assets

t-Test: Paired Two Sample for Means

	SPRD	*SPRD*
Mean	0.00032	0.026022
Variance	1.12E-08	9.54E-06
Observations	25	25
Pearson Correlation	0.157125	
Hypothesized Mean Difference	0	
Df	24	
t-Stat	–41.8076	
P(T<=t) one-tail	3.09E-24	
t-Critical one-tail	1.710882	
P(T<=t) two-tail	6.19E-24	
t-Critical two-tail	2.063899	

Table 7(m): Net NPA/NET Advances

t-Test: Paired Two Sample for Means

	NPA1996	*NPA2011*
Mean	9.604	1.0056
Variance	27.62788333	0.155409
Observations	25	25
Pearson Correlation	0.068071659	
Hypothesized Mean Difference	0	
df	24	
t-Stat	8.198075502	
P(T<=t) one-tail	1.02074E-08	
t-Critical one-tail	1.710882067	

An attempt towards branch rationalisation was made during reforms. While it had taken the form of closing of unprofitable branches or swapping of branches, one need not to expect the branch network to diminish as an impact of reforms. ATMs and other modern methods of delivery of banking service were intended to supplement branch network of PSBs and not substitute it. With rise in population, income and spread of banking habit, PSBs needed to expand their branch network as a part of their commitment to the general public. However, they are not expected to expand their branch network as was done in the post nationalisation phase, remaining completely oblivious of the profitability consideration. Branch expansion is expected to reoriented to pursue the objective of profitability. A significant rise is branch network as well as proportion of metro branches to total branches is observed. A rise in the ratio of number of branches in metro to total no. of branches reflects that profitability is an important concern of PSBs, as metros provide opportunities for profits. Clearly branch expansion of PSBs has proceeded along with a rise with the ratio of metro branches to total branches in the new regime.

It is observed that the new private sector banks introduced new ways of banking based on information and communication technology. To stay afloat in such a situation, it was imperative for PSBs to go for adoption of new technology on a war footing. A significant rise in the ratio of other fixed asset to branches is a reflection of attempts by PSBs to go for new technology, spurred by competitive rivalry.

In September 1999, the RBI removed service charges paid by banks. During 2000, the new private banks started promoting their different brands of high tech banking. Not to be left far behind, PSBs, which were selling uniform products during the regulated era began attempts towards product differentiation in form of advertising to stay in the competition. Two ratios relating to advertising were constructed. The rise in the ratio for PSBs over time turned out to be statistically significant.

Branches operated by public sector banks have increased significantly over the period of the study. Consequently a rise in business conducted by PSBs is expected. Table 7(j) of the appendix shows that the business of PSBs have significantly increased over the time period covered. With the rise in population, income, spread of banking habit and commitment to inclusive banking, business conducted by public sector banking industry is growing as they collecting more deposits and advances. However, while PSBs are increasing their core business of collecting deposits and provision of advances, they have to contend with rising rivalry from both within and outside the industry. Such rivalry has forced them to diversify into non-funded business generating fee income to shore up their bottomline. Accordingly one expects the ratio of non-interest income to total income for PSBs to rise significantly over the period covered by the study.

The non-performing assets are expected to fall as a result of better tackling of issues relating to information asymmetry like adverse selection and moral hazard in the post-reforms regime. Putting a check on growth of NPA is a situation, where PSBs have to compete with their private counterparts both for deposits as well as for equity capital has made them demonstrate spectacular improvement on NPA front. A significant fall in NPA of PSBs has been observed over the period of the study.

Performance of PSBs

Now we will analyse the profitability aspect of PSBs operating in the country. Two measures of profitability are used: Operating profit as a ratio of asset and return on capital. There exists s debate in the literature about selection of initial years for comparing profitability of PSBs over a period of time and for comparing profitability of PSBs with other banking groups. The recommendations of Narasimham Committee (1991) were implemented in 1992–93. This rules out 1991–92 as the initial year of comparison. Since the year 1992–93 saw imposition of new norms of prudential conduct, it is perhaps makes sense to provide PSBs a breathing space before comparison of profits is made. Positive profits in 1991–92 in absence of prudential norms and negative profits in 1992–93 as well as 1993–94 supports our contention. This led us to use three years as initial years and compare profitability accordingly. The results are reported in Tables 8(a)–(b). The null hypotheses of equality of profitability is rejected by one tailed t test irrespective of measure of profit used the process of reforms has led to a positive impact on the profitability of PSBs. Thus one may argue that broadly speaking, the objective of reforms has been achieved.

Table 8(a): Comparing Operating Profit to Asset of PSBs: Results of t-Test

	1992	*1993*	*1994*	*1995*	*2011*
Mean	0.002757401	–0.016031298	–0.01635541	0.000935828	0.018378983
Variance	6.39801E-06	0.000536811	0.000552871	5.04959E-05	1.37912E-05
Observations	25	25	25	25	25
Pearson Correlation	0.434902278	0.53695397	0.389941035	0.226869788	
Hypothesized Mean Difference	0	0	0	0	
df	24	24	24	24	
t-Stat	–22.53015997	–8.037675183	–7.77803396	–12.05838555	
P(T<=t) one-tail	5.9015E-18	1.45193E-08	2.58711E-08	5.65155E-12	
t-Critical one-tail	1.710882067	1.710882067	1.710882067	1.710882067	

Table 8(b): Comparing Return over Equity of PSBs: Results of t-Test.

	1992	*1993*	*1994*	*1995*	*2011*
Mean	0.346723435	–0.454059621	–0.144860397	0.359903531	14.77196762
Variance	0.156555274	1.340042791	0.495775993	0.401963244	517.329699
Observations	25	25	25	25	25
Pearson Correlation	0.422142741	0.492033241	0.650064132	0.84269415	
Hypothesized Mean Difference	0	0	0	0	
df	24	24	24	24	
t-Stat	–3.194153113	–3.429564688	–3.345542637	–3.244026701	
P(T<=t) one-tail	0.001947712	0.001096096	0.001347289	0.001725858	
t-Critical one-tail	1.710882067	1.710882067	1.710882067	1.710882067	
P(T<=t) two-tail	0.003895423	0.002192192	0.002694579	0.003451716	
t-Critical two-tail	2.063898547	2.063898547	2.063898547	2.063898547	

CONCLUSION

Narasimham committee report (1991) was implemented with the objective of revitalization of PSBs. The revitalisation programme consisted of improvement of profitability of PSBS through exposing them to competition unleashed by entry of new private banks in he arena. With a view to analyse whether the scenario in public sector banking industry has changed in accordance with the expectations of the policy makers, a modified Structure-Conduct-Performance was chosen as the theoretical framework. It treated the underlying basic conditions as a variable, unlike the traditional framework treated it unchanged. The study identifies change in basic conditions, conduct and most importantly performance of the industry. No fundamental change was observed in market structure of public sector banking industry because SBI remains the leader as before even in the new scenario. This needs to be contrasted against the private banking industry, where entry of new banks have re-written the rules of the game through change in the leadership in the form of emergence of ICICI bank. The pattern of dominance in the industry remains same and hence the change in the industry can not be attributed to change in leadership but to competitive impulses generated by new private banks, affecting all leading PSBs across the board. However, market structure of public sector banks evolved from pseudo-competitive market structure during the pre-reform period into an oligopolistic structure in the post reform period.

REFERENCES

Ahluwalia, M.S. (1999). Reforming India's Financial Sector: An Overview, in J. Hansen and S. Kathuria, ed. *India: A financial sector for the twenty-first century.* New Delhi: Oxford University Press, pp. 29–54.

Biswas, P.K. and Deb, A.T. (2004). Determinants of NPAs in the Indian Public Sector Banks, *The ICFAI Journal of Bank Management*, 3(3), pp. 15–45.

Deb, A.T. (2004). *Market Structure and Entry: A Study of the Determinants of Market Concentration in Private Domestic Banking Industry in India,* Paper presented in 6th annual conference on money and finance, Indira Gandhi Institute for Development Research, Mumbai.

Hawtrey, R.G. (1943). Competition from Newcomers, *Economica*, 10(new series: 37–40), pp. 219–222.

Marshall, Alfred (1920). Principles of Economics, 8th edition, Macmilan, London.

Narasimham, M. (1991). *Report on the Financial System,* government of India.

Sarkar, J. (1999). India's banking sector: Current Status, Emerging challenges, and policy imperatives in globalized environment, in J. Hansen and S. Kathuria, eds. *India: A financial sector for the twenty-first century.* New Delhi: Oxford University Press, pp. 71–131.

Schumpeter, J. (1934). *The Theory of Economic Development*, Cambridge, Mass: Harvard University Press.

Schumpeter, J. (1942). Capitalism, Socialism and Democracy. New York: Harper and Row.

An Evaluation of Quality of Service of Indian Banks from Consumers Perspective and Consumer Satisfaction

Sri Ram Khanna[1] and Paramjit Singh

Department of Commerce, Delhi School of Economics, University of Delhi

[1]Jago Grahak Jago PI, National Consumer Helpline Managing Editor, Consumer Voice

INTRODUCTION AND BACKGROUND OF THE STUDY

In the year 2005, Voice Society (VS) initiated assessing the quality of service studies under sponsorship from Consumer Welfare Found (CWF), Ministry of Consumer Affairs and Public Distribution (MOCA&PD), Govt. of India. The first study which was initiated was on Quality of Banking Sector in India in the year 2006, in which altogether 3100 banking consumers having deposit accounts in various public, private and foreign banks were interviewed. Before conducting the survey, a stakeholders' conference was organised to seek suggestions and comments from Indian banks on the methodology adopted. The methodology adopted for assessing the quality of banking service was also sent to the banks and other stakeholders to seek their comments. Finally, with the active involvement of Reserve Bank of India (RBI) a workshop was organised in Delhi, where officials of the banks presented their perception on the results of the study as well as their efforts to enhance the quality of their banking services. During the workshop, it was felt that VS should periodically conduct these studies on consumer perception. Therefore it was decided to select banking as one of the sector which requires periodic assessment.

The current study is based on the identical methodology to that in VOICE 2006 study. However, in the 2012 study on which this paper is based more thrust has been given on the online banking, phone banking and credit card operation.

Since 2006 the growth in Indian banking industry has been more of qualitative than quantitative. As per the RBI statistics released on 20 August 2010, number of commercial banks in India has come down from 222 in March 2006 to 170 in March 2009. The banking industry in India has experienced consolidation as a result of various mergers and acquisition in the recent years. The aggregate deposits of the schedule commercial banks during the same period has increased from Rs. 21,09,049 crores to 33,34,110 crores, a growth of 81.8%. The nationalised banks have a major share in aggregate bank deposits, at 49.4% in 2009. The number of deposit accounts, as per RBI, is estimated to be over 66 crores in 2009.

The recent development in the information technology sector have led to major changes in the way the services are delivered to the customers. Although there is no authentic data on number and nature of internet banking users in India, RBI estimates that share of electronic payment is about 35% of the total number of transactions (Banknet). The bankers are now offering innovative and attractive technology-based services and products such as 'Anywhere Anytime Banking', 'Tele-Banking', 'Internet Banking', 'Web Banking', etc. to cope up with the competition (Khan, Mohapatra and Serrkimar, 2009). Online Banking Service (OBS) is increasingly becoming popular as compared to visiting bank branches. Some of the reasons for customers to prefer online services (as online banking services) are: convenience, feeling more in control of the service process and saving time. Due to the growing competition in the market, Banking operations have seen fundamental changes and the credit goes to the advent of high speed internet service and growing internet competition. Taking into consideration the huge investments, that the banks make in Internet infrastructure, customer satisfaction and retention are turning into the crucial factors for success in online banking meaning that the generation of positive customer value on the Internet requires the establishment of long-term customer relationships (Bauer, Hammerschmidt and Falk, 2005). Therefore an effective internet banking service (e-services) requires not only acquiring new customers but also retaining the existing ones. Secondly, with the introduction of internet banking services, the consumer expectation from banks as well as perception of their services are also changing. Therefore e-service quality provided by the banks has become increasingly important. The current study, therefore, gives more thrust on the internet banking, mobile banking and credit card operation.

LITERATURE REVIEW

Research has shown that improvement in efficiency of bank branches is obtained through potential improvement in service quality *(Athanossopoulous, University of Cyprus),* BAI, USA established linkages between marketing, operations, organizational structure and Human Resource Management. Wharton School, USA found plausible links in service-profit chains.

Parasuraman, Zeithaml and Berry, 1985 attempted to present a model of service quality. The paper acknowledged that the consumers have more difficulty on evaluating service quality as compared to product quality and that service quality perceptions resulted from comparison of their expectations with service performance. The empirical data in this paper was from in-depth interviews with executives and consumers related to four firms. These were retail banks, credit card, securities brokerage and product repair and maintenance. This was accompanied by 12 focus group of consumers where service quality experiences were discussed. The authors postulated a general model of service quality based on commonalities among service perceptions while ignoring perceptions that were specific to the industries. They identified four specific impacts of expectation-management perception gaps. They postulated that service quality perception depended on size and direction of these gaps aggregated. They proposed that regardless of service, consumers used basically similar criteria in evaluating service quality which they divided into 10 categories which they labeled as "service quality determinants" namely, Reliability, responsiveness, competence, access, courtesy, communication, credibility, security, understanding and tangibles. In a later paper *(Parasuraman, Zeithaml and Berry, 1988)* they felt that because service quality was being measured by whims of researchers and measures used were not meaningfully related to "an explicit concept statement of the phenomena or variable in question", they needed "to be preceeded by and rooted in a sound conceptual specification of the construct being scaled". They proceeded to propose Servqual as a multiple item scale composed of five dimensions namely, Tangibles, Reliability, Responsiveness, Assurance and empathy. These five were assumed to capture all 10 originally conceptualized dimensions from their 1985 paper. On the basis of their data from five service categories they claimed scale reliability based on factor analysis which was based on items that were common and relevant to the different services included in the sample. Certain "good" items, which were not common to all firms were deleted in the process. They developed a SERVQUAL scale consisting of 22 items and it was proposed that the scale also had content validity. In a later paper *(Parasuraman, Zeithaml and Berry, 1991)* they used data from five firms (one telephone Co., two Insurance Companies and two Banks) drawn from a sample of 1936 customers. They postulated a modified servqual instrument consisting of 22 items in expectations and perceptions.

In *1992 Cronin and Taylor* in their paper in Journal of Marketing proposed an alternative SERVPERF scale based only on evaluation of services on service performance. This paper was criticized by *Parasuraman, Zeithaml and Berry in their 1994 paper* in Journal of Marketing. Cronin and Taylor in their 1994 paper SERVPERF Vs SERVQUAL in the same journal addressed the critique of Parasuraman *et al.* and went a long way in suggesting that future research could focus on measuring performance only perceptions of consumers as compared to perceptions minus expectations based SERVQUAL.

These models have been used by a number of academic researchers to empirically test their validity. However, the present study was carried out from the consumers angle with a view to compare their satisfaction levels with service quality across national brands. Its purpose was not to test the empirical validity of either of these models.

European Consumer Organisations have been conducting studies in quality of service from consumer perspective. Consumers association, UK carried out studies on quality of service of banks in UK and Euroconsumer, Belgium carried out large scale studies in five European Countries on Quality of Service in banking sector. Their focus was on identifying the differential consumer satisfaction levels with Quality of Service of Banks operating in their markets. Surprisingly, they did not adopt Servqual/Servperf models. Their approach focuses on Key Performance Indicators (KPIs), when the predecessor study on Quality of Service of banks in India was developed the authors contacted these two organizations in 2005. The methodology used by Consumer Association, UK was discussed with Terese Fritz, head of Finance and Banking sector who provided details of their recent study (June 2004) and informed that apart from publishing the results of the studies in their magazines, UK banks and consumers consider these results for their future planning. (WHICH: Current Accounts 2004 (21234) Final Market Research Report) prepared by Judy Aidam for Mathew brown). The highlight of this study was a focus on 10 KPIs shown in the figure below:

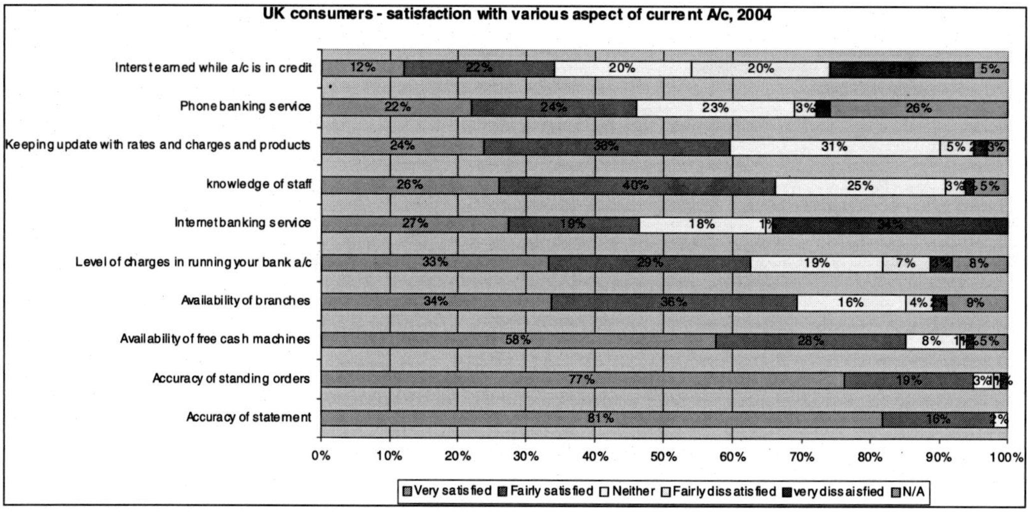

Fig. 1: A Snap Shot of QoS in UK

The Euroconsumers Study which inspired the Indian study was conducted in France, Portugal, Spain, Netherlands and Italy. A discussion with Sermeus. Guido was held in their office in Brussels during 2005 on the methodology used. This study also compared different banks on KPIs. The following figure shows the one KPI—Consumer Awareness on the fees of their Banks.

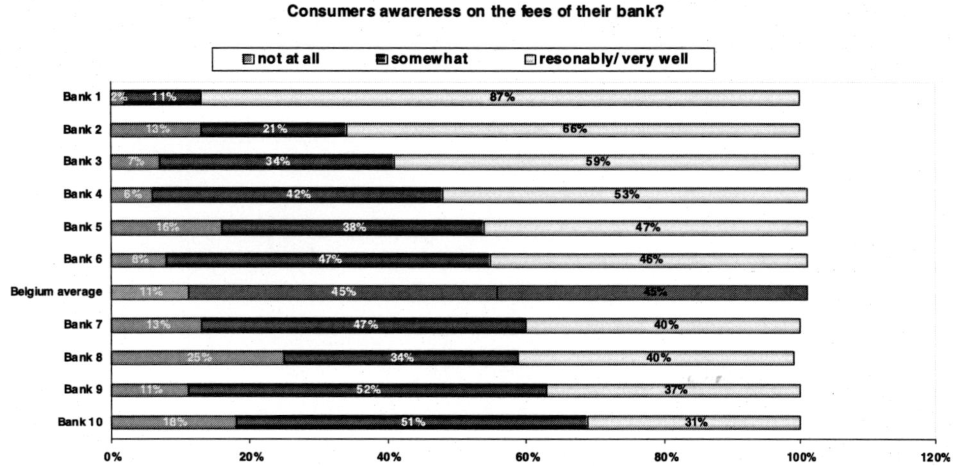

Fig. 2: A Snap Shot of Euroconsumer Survey: Belgium

The conclusions of this study were published in the Euroconsumer magazines published in these five countries. The detailed reports were widely circulated among European Banks who value them as an important consumer feedback and incorporate the findings in their future planning.

At that time there was no such study conducted in India. Few studies on Quality of Service in Banking were conducted as part of University research degrees and most of the studies focused on management and operational efficiency of banks designed to assist better management of banks. An inventory of common consumer complaints with a typical private sector Indian Bank branch in 2005 showed the following common consumer complaints with banks:

Table 1: In India Common Disputes Releate to

- **quarterly/ monthly statements of saving account**
- **ATM card/pin no./cheque book**
- **clearing cheque funds not credited/ timely credited**
- **TDS amount deducted**
- **deduction for various charges without the consent of clients**
- **account closure charges**
- **cash deposited at branch not credited in account**
- **standing instruction for recurring deposits not set**
- **fixed deposit not linked to account**
- **outstation cheque collection**
- **Issues related to transfer of account**
- **Issues related to address change**

Soruce: ICICI, a branch in Delhi in 2006.

The following list of frequently occurring problems of consumers with Indian banks was recorded at the National Consumer Helpline at the time.

Table 2: Frequently Occuring Problem (2006)

Debit Cards
▪ Unauthorised withdrawal listed in statement
▪ Stealing of PIN No. in transit (post)
▪ Hidden Charges
▪ Non-working of ATM machines
▪ Non-cooperation from bank staff/ delay in redressal
▪ Non-installation of cameras in ATMs

Sourece: National Consumer Helpline.

Table 3: Frequently Occuring Problem

Credit Cards
▪ Hidden Charges
▪ Terms/ condition of sanction never made available to card holder
▪ Problem with DSA's/ Recovery agent/ Call centre
▪ Unsolicited add-on cards issued and then charged for
▪ Cheque put in drop-box not cleared in time and interest applied for transit period of delayed clearance
▪ Non clarity in calculation of interest and rate of interest
▪ Redressal mechanism not in place/ publicised

Source: National Consumer Helpline.

The methodology to measure Quality of Service of Indian banks was developed keeping in view the experience of Indian Consumer with their banks. The type of Quality complaints that they had and the mechanism to deal with such complaints. The two main objectives of the study were:

1. Indian Consumer loyalty was direct result of customer satisfaction with quality of service of their banks.
2. Customer Satisfaction, on the other hand, was largely influenced by perception of value of service provided to customers by the bank concerned.

With these objectives the study focused on Quality of Service as perceived by consumers. In doing so it was decided to adopt the KPI model used by Euroconsumers and not the Servqual/Servperf models on the following grounds:

(a) The Servperf/Servqual model was pre occupied with the objective of enhancing goals of management as most studies using the model were aimed at assisting better management of the services and not in guiding consumers to identify service providers with excellent Quality of Service.

(b) The models provided an academic analysis to guide managements of service provider's rather then specific measurement of key performance indicators which could be easily identified and understood by key consumers of these services.

(c) The five perceived dimension of service quality in the servqual model, namely, Reliability, Responsiveness, Assurance, Tangibles and empathy were and remain meaningless to key consumers of these services. Most Indian consumers of bank services would not be able to understand these terms. However, they could easily understand key performance indicators based on their personal experience of their bank's service.

In view of the above it was decided to focus on perceived measures of Quality of Service as represented by KPI's: Key Performance Indicators. The methodology also focused on cross- firm comparison to measure the difference in consumer perception across firms on available Quality of Service delivered to the customer-respondents. The methodology used in Euro consumer studies were suitably adapted to the Indian banking market.

Therefore the Indian study of 2006 and its present successor study rely on key performance Indicators to measure Quality of Service of Indian Banks. The following two figures explain the relationship of the methodology adopted in the present study and the servqual/servperf models:

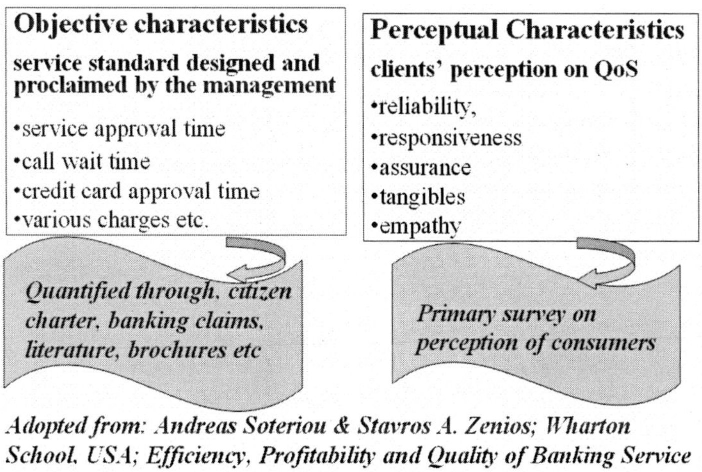

Fig. 3: Model for Assessing Quality of Service—Adopted form Servqual and Sevperf Model

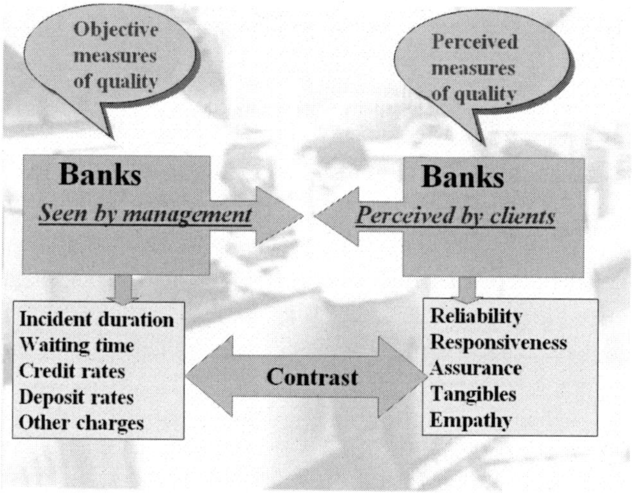

Fig. 4: Analysis and Benchmarks

The list of KPIs was developed by situation appraisal of Indian banking Quality of Service. This involved an in depth discussion with about 100 bank customers A pilot survey of consumers was also conducted to finalise the key performance indicators to be used in the study. The indicative list of KPIs in the pilot survey was based on the Consumer Association, UK and Euroconsumer studies in Europe and was adapted to the Indian market during situation appraisal and pilot survey. This list is shown in Table 4 below:

Table 4: Coverage of Study (Primary survey)

Satisfaction level to be measured on following parameters:

- *Accessibility to bank branches*
- *Public opening hours*
- *Investment advice given by bank staff*
- *perceived competence of staff*
- *client oriented attitude of staff*
- *correct follow up and correct execution of ordered transaction*
- *facility for correcting errors*
- *received information on bank products*
- *privacy inside the branches*
- *safety feeling inside the branches*
- *speed of service*
- *waiting time*
- *account opening charges*
- *Timely receipt of ATM/ debit card/pin no./chq book*
- *Receipt/ non-receipt quarterly/monthly statements*
- *accuracy/ clarity of statements,*
- *timely clearing of cheque funds and credited to a/c*
- *proper deduction of TDS amount*
- *knowledge/ dealing of staff, updating information on rates and charges,*
- *ATMs and branches,*
- *interest rates,*
- *home banking services*
- *ease of using ATM/ Debit card*
- *annual charges for ATM/ debit/ credit card*
- *updating charges for using ATM/ debit/ credit card*
- *security of using debit/ credit cards*
- *customer support related to debit/ credit cards*

Adapted from Which? UK, and Euroconsumer Model.

Sampling and Data Collection Procedure

Data for this "Banking Survey" has been collected by means of face to face interview using a questionnaire. The survey was conducted during 2nd half of 2011 in parallel in eight cities of India (Delhi, Pune, Mumbai, Kolkata, Ahmedabad, Bangalore, Hyderabad, Chennai). The criteria used in selecting a representative sample of 3773 banking consumers in the 8 cities is explained in Annexure **A** herewith. The actual sample exceeded the target sample of 3710.

SAMPLE CHARACTERISTICS

Gender Profile: Out of the total achieved sample of 3773 consumers covered in eight cities, 1140 (30.2%) were female as against 2633 (69.8%) male, showing a predominance of male customers among banks.

The highest proportions of women were found in Kolkata (42.4%), followed by Delhi (37.6%) and Chennai (31.9%).The lowest female ratio was found in Ahmedabad (20.0%) followed by Bangalore (21.9%), Hyderabad (22.8%), Pune (26.4%) and Mumbai (26.7%).

Age Profile: Majority of the target respondents (about 75%) were found to be youngsters (less than 35 years of age). Around one fifth (20.2%) of the respondents fell in the age group of 36 to 50 years. Whereas only 3.5% were over 50 years of age.In Delhi nearly half (48.8%) of the respondents were up to 25 years of age. This was followed by 28.1% in Bangalore, 23.7% in Mumbai, 23.4% in Hyderabad, 22.2% in Ahmedabad and 22% in Pune. In Pune over 70% of the respondents were in the age group of 25–35 years. Similarly majority of respondents in Chennai (65.1%) and Mumbai (51.8%) were found in the age group of 26–35 years. Highest proportion of the respondents over 50 years of age were found to be in Bangalore (13.2%), followed by Hyderabad (9.8%) and Kolkata (7.4%).

Financial Situation

Around 48% of the respondents revealed their financial status as 'comfortable', followed by 35.5% describing it to be 'very comfortable'. However, 12.7% also disclosed that they 'somehow make their two ends meet'. Remaining 4% quoted their financial status as 'difficult', 'very difficult' and 'problematic'.Respondents with 'problematic' financial situation were found only in Bangalore, Kolkata and Mumbai.

Respondents of Chennai were found to be financially sound as 97% of the surveyed respondents revealed their financial situation to be either 'very comfortable' or 'comfortable'. Likewise, respondents of Pune (96.7%), Delhi (91.8%), Hyderabad (88.6%) and Ahmedabad

(78.9%) were also found to be financially comfortable.In comparison to this, respondents of Kolkata were found to be financially weaker as only 58% revealed their financial status to be either 'very comfortable' or 'comfortable'.

Educational Profile

More than half (55.6%) of the respondents approached were found to be graduates followed by under graduates (28.6%). Around 11.4% of the respondents were post graduates and other 4.4% were professionally qualified such as IT professionals, engineers, management or medical professionals.The percentage of professionally qualified respondents were found to be highest in Hyderabad (15.2%), followed by Bangalore (13.8%).Highest percentage of undergraduates having a bank account were found in Bangalore (40.7%), followed by Ahmedabad (33.3%) and Mumbai (29.8%).

Professional Profile

Majority of the respondents covered in the sample were employed in private service (51.5%). The proportion of sample for Government and Public Service was 13.5%. Other 18.6% had their own business or self employed. Rest were housewives (7.4%), students (5%) and others (3.9%).

Bank Wise Profile

As explained in the methodology, majority consumers of the banks covered were with Nationalised Banks (49.1%), followed by Private Sector Banks (24.7%), SBI %& Associates (18.0%) and Foreign Banks (8.2%). The bankwise d etails are shown in the Table 5 below:

Table 5: Bank Wise Sample Distribution

Banks	*Count*	%
State Bank of India	516	76.1%
State Bank of Hyderabad	61	9.0%
State Bank of Mysore	55	8.1%
State Bank of Bikaner and Jaipur	46	6.8%
Total SBI and Associates	678	18.0%
Punjab National Bank	319	17.2%
Canara Bank	305	16.5%
Bank of Baroda	289	15.6%
Central Bank of India	247	13.3%

Banks	*Count*	*%*
Union Bank of India	246	13.3%
Bank of India	233	12.6%
Syndicate Bank	215	11.6%
Total Nationalised Banks	1854	49.1%
Indian Overseas Bank	192	20.6%
HDFC Bank	262	28.1%
ICICI Bank	218	23.4%
Axis Bank	123	13.2%
ING Vysya Bank	63	6.8%
Karnataka Bank	74	7.9%
Total Private Sector Banks	932	24.7%
Standard Chartered Bank	167	54.0%
HSBC	79	25.6%
Citibank	63	20.4%
Total Foreign Banks	309	8.2%
Total All Banks	3773	100.0%

Source: Question no. 1 of the questionnaire.

MAIN REASON TO CHOOSE THE BANK

Respondents were asked to indicate the reasons for choosing their main bank. Three different reasons were be indicated. Location of the branch, nearby home or work place, was cited as the most important main reason for choosing the bank. This was indicated by more than half of the respondents (55.6%). This reason was indicated by majority of respondents across all the cities.

The good reputation of the bank was found to be second most important main reason as this was indicated by 7.4% of the total respondents.There was some difference for the second most important main reason amongst few the cities. In Mumbai 6.5%, Hyderabad 15.2% and Chennai 11.1% of respondents indicated that they did not choose their bank but it was suggested or imposed by their company or employer. In Ahmedabad 10% and Pune 17.6% had indicated that they chose their main bank on advice given by their friends or relatives. In Delhi (8.3%), the operating hours of the branch was cited as the second most important main reason.

Bank wise analysis shows that the location of branch (near home and working place) was found be the most important reason for choosing main bank by the respondents of all the main banks.

The bank "was advised by a friend or relative" was indicated as the second most important reason for choosing a bank by the clients of nearly all the main banks except State Bank of India and Citibank. In the case of State Bank of India, good reputation of the bank, reported by 48% of its clients, was the second most important reason for choosing this bank. Whereas in the case of Citibank easy access to the bank such as car parking, layout etc. (39.7%) was found to be the second most important reason.

As far as the third most important reason to choose a bank is concerned, good reputation of the bank was indicated by clients of most of the bank except State Bank of India, State Bank of Hyderabad, State Bank of Bikaner and Jaipur, ING Vysya Bank, Karnataka Bank, Standard Chartered Bank and Citibank.

No of Years with Bank

More than 56% (2118) of respondents are clients of their main bank for than less 5 years. Nearly 35% are clients between 5–10 years. This was followed by 7.7% respondents who are clients between 11–20 years. Only 1.2% (46) respondents said they were with the banks for more than 20 years. The analysis shows that Bangalore topped the list as far as number of years is concerned. Around 7% of respondents were with the main banks for more than 20 years. This could also be because of highest number of aged respondents (over 50 years) were interviewed in Bangalore.

Respondents with highest average number of years were found in Karnataka Bank with 6.45 years. This was followed by Canara Bank (5.85 years) and Standard Chartered Bank (5.66 years) Average years were found to be lowest in State Bank of Bikaner and Jaipur (4.09 years) followed by ICICI Bank (4.18 years) and ING Vysya Bank (4.30 years).

CHANGING FOR ANOTHER MAIN BANK

Less than 3% respondents indicated that they had changed their main bank during the past 10 years. This suggests a high degree of bank loyalty of consumers. In Hyderabad over one out of ten (11.4%) respondents had changed their main bank in the last ten years, closely followed by Kolkata (8.9%). In Pune none of the respondents indicated change in their bank in the last ten years. Similarly very few in Delhi and Chennai indicated the same.

Out of 108 respondents who had changed their main bank during the past ten years, 87% had changed once. Therefore only 13% (14) reported that they had changed more than once. All respondents in Delhi, Hyderabad and Chennai, who had reported that they had changed their main bank in the last ten years, had done so only once.

Age wise analysis reveals that amongst the respondents in the age group of over 50 years (6.1%) and 36–50 years (5%) have changed their main banks. Changing the main bank was also found to be more popular among males (3.1%) as compared to female respondents (2.4%)

Changing main bank was found to be higher amongst the professionally qualified degree holders (7.2%). The trend of changing the main bank was highest among the respondents with average financial situation (4.2%), followed by those with difficult financial situation (3.8%). Around 3.1% of the respondents having comfortable financial also changed their main banks. The trend of changing more than once was found more among females (22.2%) as compared to males (9.9%).

Education wise analysis reveals that one fourth of respondents having professional qualification degree had changed their main bank more than once. Similarly, changing main bank more than once was also found higher among respondents having comfortable financial situation

The data collected reflects that clients from both public and private banks have shifted their main bank in the last 10 years. Therefore, it is clear that the change is for public as well as private sector banks. This should dispel an impression that quality of service of private banks was superior and that only public sector clients left for private sector banks.

WHERE DO NEW CLIENTS COME FROM?

Altogether 108 respondents had reported they had changed their bank in the last 10 year. The largest migration has taken from State Bank of India and ICICI Bank (13 each) followed by Canara Bank (12) and Bank of India (11). *However, the churning is not one way but two way process.* The data collected shows the State Bank of India and Canara Bank had also received highest number of clients (17 each), followed by Union Bank of India (11) and HDFC Bank (10). The clients of state Bank of India have gone to private, foreign as well as public sector banks. Such as ING Vysya, Standard Chartered Bank, Punjab National Bank, Canara Bank, Union Bank of India etc. In the case of ICICI Bank, 9 out its 13 clients migrated to public sector banks such as Canara Bank (3, 23.1%)), State Bank of India (2, 15.4%) and one each to State Bank of Mysore, Punjab National Bank, Bank of Baroda and Union Bank of India. Remaining 4 migrated to HDFC (3, 23.1%) and Karnataka Bank (1, 7.7%).

Why Change Bank?

Inconvenient location coupled with few numbers of branches, near home and working place, was found as the most important reason for changing the main bank – cited by 51% and 31.5% of respondents who had changed their main banks. This was found across most of the cities covered in survey. The dissatisfaction with the efficiency of staff and efficacy of the bank were the other two important reason indicated by nearly 30% of total respondents who changed their banks. These reasons were reported by respondents in almost all the cities covered under the survey.

PROBLEM, COMPLAINTS AND REDRESSAL BY BANKS

City Wise Problems

This analysis of data on problem–related experiences with the bank based on all aspects that were detailed in question 57 of the questionnaire (including problems with internet banking/phone banking/mobile banking/debit/credit cards).shows that one fourth of the total respondents interviewed reported to ever have experienced some problems with their banks. The highest percentage of problems were reported from Delhi (41.3%), followed by Pune (40.7%) and Ahmedabad (37.8%).

The data collected also shows the respondents who lodged complaints regarding their problem and response from the bank. All respondents in Ahmedabad, Pune and Chennai, who ever had a problem, lodged complaints. Where as in other cities most of the respondents (89.7%–98.7%) who experienced deficiency in the services had reported they had put their complaints. This shows almost every consumer who has a problem, complains to their respective banks.

As far as responses from banks are concerned, all complaints were responded to in Ahmedabad, Pune and Chennai followed by Delhi (98.7%), Mumbai (98.6%), Hyderabad (96.2%) and Kolkata (95.9%).

The data collected also shows the data related to problems which were completely solved, partly solved or not solved at all. Overall, 94.3% were completely solved, 4.9% partly solved and 0.8% not solved at all. City wise analysis shows all problems were completely solved was reported from Bangalore, Ahmedabad and Pune. In Delhi 4 (1%) and Chennai 1 (2%) and Mumbai 3 (0.9%) complainant reported that their problem was not solved at all.

Bank Wise Problems

Bank wise analysis shows that Citibank topped the list with 36.5% of respondents reported they had some problem with their main bank. This was followed by State Bank of Hyderabad (34.4%) and Syndicate Bank (33%).Nearly all respondents who had problem with their banks reported they had lodged their complaints. It was only in State Bank of Bikaner and Jaipur and where 25% did not put up complaints. As far as responses from banks are concerned, nearly all complaints were responded by the concerned banks.

As far as redressal is concerned, best record goes to State Bank of Bikaner and Jaipur, where all 9 clients who got response from the bank reported that their problem was completely solved. In the case of Karnataka bank this was reported by 77.3%. of respondents.

Frequent Occurring Problems

Most of nationalized bank respondents complained about delay in cheque credit. In the case of Syndicate Bank, this problem was reported by almost 10% of respondents followed by 8.7% from State Bank of Bikaner and Jaipur and 8.1% from Central Bank of India. This problem was also reported from private bank customers such as ING Vysya Bank (9.5%) and Citibank (7.9%)

Unauthorized transaction was reported by mostly reported by the customers of State Bank of Bikaner and Jaipur (8.7%), Central Bank of India (7.7%), State Bank of Mysore (7.3%), ING Vysya and Citibank (6.3% each) and Axis Bank (5.7%). Customers of Private Banks also reported problems related to cash withdrawal/deposit. In the case of ING Vysya this was reported by 16% of the customers, followed by Axis Bank (13%), HSBC (8.9%) and Karnataka Bank (8.1%).

Problems in Internet Banking

In the case of internet banking; non receipt of pin numbers, delayed transaction, non receipt of one time password (OTP) and unauthorized transactions were reported by respondents from almost all banks included in the study. HSBC (3.8%) tops the list in case of Non receipt of PIN numbers followed by Axis Bank (3.3%), ING Vysya Bank (3.2%) and Standard Chartered Bank (3%). In the case of non receipt of OTP, ING Vysya Bank (4.8%) topped the list followed by State Bank of Mysore (1.8%), ICICI Bank (1.4%) and Bank of India (1.3% each). Delayed transactions were reported highest in the case of Standard Chartered Bank (3.6%) followed by State Bank of Hyderabad, Union Bank of India, ING Vysya Bank and Citibank (1.6% each). Unauthorised transaction was reported highest in the case of HSBC Bank (3.8%) followed by ICICI Bank (1.8%) and Syndicate Bank (1.4%).

Telephone Banking Problems

In the case of telephone banking, respondents have reported problems mainly related to provision of incorrect information and also unauthorized transactions. Unauthorised transactions were reported mainly from the clients of Syndicate Bank (1.9%) followed by ING Vysya Bank and Citibank (1.6% each). Citibank Bank (3.2%) and Syndicate Bank (1.9%) also topped the list whose clients reported about incorrect information supplied.

Mobile Banking

In the case of mobile phone banking, respondents have reported problems mainly on non receipt of transaction passwords and failure to carryout instructions.

Problems with Debit Cards

In the case of debit card, non receipt of card was reported by respondents from all the Bank's clients—ING Vysya Bank (19%) topped the list followed by State Bank of Hyderabad (13.1%) and Axis Bank (13%). The problem of hidden charges related to using other banks' ATM was mostly reported by the clients of Syndicate Bank (5.6%), followed by Central Bank of India (5.3%), ING Vysya Bank and Citibank (4.8% each) and HDFC Bank (4.6% each).Unauthorized transaction was reported by 1.2% (46) of respondents. This was mainly from the clients of ING Vysya Bank (4.8%) and HSBC (3.8%) and Axis Bank (3.3%).

Problems with Credit Cards

In the case of credit cards, non receipt of pin number was the major problem reported. In the case of clients of ICICI Bank and Axis Bank, this was reported by over 4.8% of their customers. In the case of Citibank this was reported by 4.6%.

Delays in Cheque collection from drop box and then charging late fees and interest from the card holders was also found as one of the frequent occurring problem. This was mainly reported by the clients of HSBC (9.1%), ICICI Bank (4.8%), Standard Chartered Bank (2.6%), Citibank (2.3%) and HDFC Bank (2.1%).

PATTERN OF ONLINE BANKING AND SATISFACTION

Overall 83% respondents reported that their bank provides the facility of internet banking. Rest 17% were either unaware or reported that their bank does not provide such facility.Those who reported that their banks provide the internet banking service were asked on the frequency of use of Internet banking. one third (33.7%) were using Internet Banking with different frequency. There were 30 (1%) respondents who were using it daily. Most of the respondents were using it once a month (18%) followed by a couple of times a year (7.3%) and weekly (6.5%). This shows the growing adoption of internet banking in India.

Maximum users of internet banking were found in Ahmedabad (51%) followed by Hyderabad (42.4%) and Kolkata (40.3%).Daily users were also found more in Hyderabad (5.7%) followed by Bangalore (3.1%). No daily users were found in Ahmedabad, Pune and Chennai. majority of internet banking users were in the age group 26–35 years.

Majority of respondents who are using internet banking with lesser frequency such as a couple times a year are over 50 years. Respondents having their own business and also with private sector were found to be using internet banking. Education wise analysis reveals that internet baking is being used more by post graduates (38.1%) followed by graduates (34.3%). It is a more popular mode of transaction amongst respondents having very comfortable (38.8%) and comfortable (33.9%) financial situation. Bank wise analysis shows that over half of the HSBC (54.6%) and Karnataka Bank (50.1%) were using internet banking with different frequency. In the case of Standard Chartered Bank (46.6%), HDFC Bank (43.7%) and Citibank (42%) over 2 out of 5 were using internet banking. Majority of the respondents using internet banking, check their balance (69.8%), book their railway or air tickets (64%) and pay their bills (62.1%). This trend was found in all the cities covered. In Delhi, Mumbai, Kolkata and Chennai, people also seek information about products and services through net banking. Transfer fund between own accounts was found to highest in Delhi (53.9%), followed by Mumbai (43%), Chennai (36.4%) and Bangalore (35.5%). Whereas third party transfer was highest in the case of Chennai (43.2%) followed by Mumbai (37.1%).

Satisfaction with Internet Banking

The respondents were asked to score 1 to 10 on 9 aspects of banks' web site, listed in question no. 12 of questionnaire, where "1 stands for absolutely dissatisfied ... to ... 10 for absolutely satisfied." Post survey, the exploratory factor analysis (EFA) was applied in order to reduce variables (aspects) in to common factors. The total numbers of variables were then reduced from nine to six as three of the variables were merged in to one common factor.

All banks attained scores between 7–7.99 on overall satisfaction. Therefore the overall satisfaction levels with the web site of their main banks were found to be similar. This is because consumers do not find any significant difference on various aspects of the web site such as speed, design and information on the web site. It was only in the case of Bank of Baroda that the satisfaction with query resolution was found to bit low at 6–6.99. On all the other aspects the satisfaction level was reported at 7 – 7.99.

In the case of State Bank of Bikaner and Jaipur, satisfaction score on 'fast and quick website' were higher at 8–8.99. Similarly, State Bank of Hyderabad scored high (8–8.99) on 'Aesthetic design of website'.

The respondents were asked to score 1 to 10 on 6 aspects of internet banking operation, listed in question no. 16 of questionnaire, where "1 stands for absolutely dissatisfied ... to ... 10 for absolutely satisfied." Post survey, the exploratory factor analysis (EFA) was applied in order to reduce variables (aspects) in to common factors. The total numbers of variables were then reduced from six to five as two of the variables were merged in to one common factor.

Most of the banks attained scores between 7–7.99 on overall trust. There were four banks which attained low scores (6–6.99) on overall trust with their main banks on online banking services. These were—State Bank of Hyderabad, Central Bank of India, Union Bank of Indi and HSBC Bank.

State Bank of Hyderabad, Punjab national Bank, Central Bank of India, Union Bank of India and Standard Chartered Bank scored low (6–6.99) on the aspect of misuse of personal information. All other Banks scored 7–7.99.

On the accuracy of online transaction all except three banks score 7–7.99. The three banks which score low (6.–6.99) were ICICI Bank, Standard Chartered Bank and HSBC Bank.

On the speed of completion of ordered transaction, six banks attained low score (6–6.99) and rest of the 14 banks scored 7–7.99. All these 6 Banks were Public sector banks—State Bank of Hyderabad, State Bank of Mysore, State Bank of Bikaner and Jaipur, Punjab National Bank, Central Bank of India and Union Bank of India.

The following figure shows the over all trust on the bank with respect to online banking on as 10 point scale.

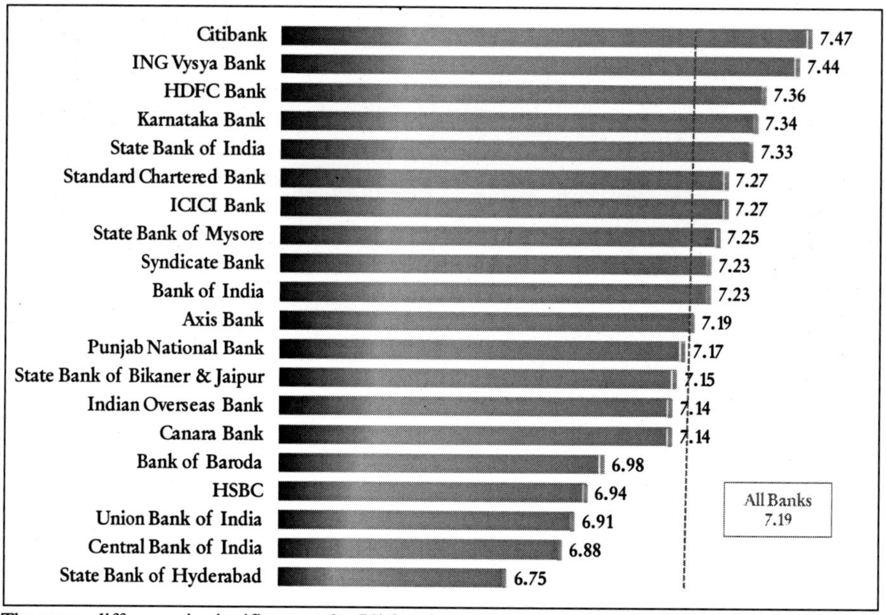

The mean difference is significant at the 5% level.

Fig. 5: Overall Trust on Online Banking Service of the Main Bank

All the main banks analyzed received score in the range of 6.75 to 7.47 on the overall trust on online banking service provided to their clients.Banks have been put under three different groups using Post Hoc (Duncan) homogenous subsets where one group was different from another at different significance level.

In the first group there were 17 banks and Citibank topped the list with the mean value of 7.47. Citibank was followed by ING Vysya Bank (7.44) and HDFC Bank (7.36)

In the second group there were two banks—Union Bank of India (6.91) and Central Bank of India (6.88).

In the lower segment group there was only State Bank of Hyderabad with the mean value of 6.75.

Table 2: Duncan New Multiple Range Tests Find Difference among Following Groups of Banks at Different Significance Level

Group I			*Group II*			*Group III*		
Bank	*N*	*Mean*	*Bank*	*N*	*Mean*	*Bank*	*N*	*Mean*
Citibank	24	7.47	Union Bank of India	42	6.91	State Bank of Hyderabad	19	6.75
ING Vysya Bank	13	7.44	Central Bank of India	58	6.88			
HDFC Bank	101	7.36						
Karnataka Bank	29	7.34						
State Bank of India	132	7.33						
ICICI Bank	68	7.27						
Standard Chartered Bank	68	7.27						
State Bank of Mysore	19	7.25						
Bank of India	51	7.23						
Syndicate Bank	57	7.23						
Axis Bank	27	7.19						
Punjab National Bank	74	7.17						
State Bank of Bikaner and Jaipur	12	7.15						
Indian Overseas Bank	62	7.14						
Canara Bank	98	7.14						
Bank of Baroda	66	6.98						
HSBC	35	6.94						
Significance level	*0.06*		*Significance level*	*0.065*		*Significance level*	*0.091*	

PATTERN OF TELEPHONE BANKING AND SATISFACTION

Overall 78.5% respondents were of the opinion that their bank provides the facility of Telephone banking. Rest 21.5% were either unaware or reported that their bank does not provide such facility. Overall only 4.6% of the total respondents were using telephone banking facility. Pune topped the list where 7.6% were using telephone banking, followed by Kolkata (6.7%) and Hyderabad (6.4%). The shown the telephone banking is yet to come of age.

Most of the phone banking users belonged to the age group of up to 26–35 years followed by 36–50 years. Respondents with professional qualification degree (8.6%) and post graduates (7.2%) were found to be using this facility more as compared to under graduates (1.6%) and graduates (4.9%). Telephone banking users were also found more amongst Business/self employed (5.4%) and respondents in private service (5.3%). Secondly clients having comfortable financial situation were found to be using it more as compared to those having average and problematic financial situation.

Bank wise analysis shows that Citibank has the highest Telephone banking users. Nearly one out of ten Citibank's clients (9.3%) were found to be using telephone banking facility. This is followed by the clients of State Bank of Mysore (6.4%), Bank of Baroda (6.1%) and Indian Overseas Bank (6%) who were using telephone banking. Majority of the respondents using telephone banking are using telephone banking to check their balance, request for cheque books and transfer funds between their own accounts. This trend was found in all the cities covered.In Delhi, Mumbai, Kolkata and Chennai, people also seek information about products and services through telephone banking.

Transfer fund between own accounts was found to be highest in Kolkata (86.7%) followed by Hyderabad (62.5%) and Delhi (60.5%). Third party transfer was also found highest in Kolkata (60%) followed by Hyderabad (37.5%).

Satisfaction with Phone Banking

All banks attained scores between 7–7.99 on overall satisfaction with the telephone banking service provided by their main bank. Four banks scored low (6–6.99) on accessibility of telephone banking service. They were -State Bank of India, Punjab National Bank ICICI and Citibank. Citibank also scored low on the aspect of availability of service for information and transaction purpose. Punjab National Bank and Central Bank of India also score low on this aspect.

State Bank of India along with Central Bank of India scored low (6–6.99) on effortless mechanism using telephone banking service. In other words their service is considered to have cumbersome process and consumers have to put some effort in for seeking information and making transaction. In the case of private sector banks, ICICI had also scored low.

The respondents were asked to score 1 to 10 on 6 aspects of telephone banking operation, listed in question no. 26 of questionnaire, where "1 stands for absolutely dissatisfied … to … 10 for absolutely satisfied.

Almost all banks, except Standard Chartered Bank, attained scores between 7–7.99 on overall trust with the telephone banking service provided by their main bank. Standard Chartered attained scored between 8–8.99. The major public sector bank—State Bank of India and Punjab National Bank—had attained low score (6–6.99) on four out of six aspect related to confidence with the telephone banking. Both the banks had low score on safety of the transaction, quickness in service, on delivery of services which are promised by banks. State Bank of India had also attained low on the trust on the misuse of clients' personal information. Punjab National Bank had attained low score on confidence on telephone banking service. Indian overseas Bank, another public sector Bank, had also attained low on four aspects—Confidence on service, trust on misuse of personal information; speed of service and on delivery of services which are promised by banks.

Citibank was the only private sector bank to attain low score (6–6.99) on few aspects such as confidence of service, safety of transaction and delivery of services promised by bank. HDFC has scored high (8–8.99) on trust that clients' personal information is not misused by bank.

PATTERN OF USAGE OF MOBILE PHONE BANKING AND SATISFACTION

Overall 81.2% were of the opinion that their bank provides the facility of Mobile phone banking. Rest 18.8% were either unaware or reported that their bank does not provide such facility. Overall only 11.5% of the total respondents were using mobile phone banking facility. Delhi topped the list where 14.8% were using mobile phone banking, followed by Mumbai (12.4%) and Hyderabad (10.3%). Most of the phone banking users belonged to the age group of up to 25 years followed by 26–35 years.

Gender wise analysis shows that percentages of male respondents (12.7%) were higher than the female respondents (8.6%) who were using mobile phone banking. Respondents with post graduate (16.2%) and professional qualification degree (14.9%) were found to be using this facility more as compared to under graduates (8.8%) and graduates (11.5%). Mobile banking users were also found more amongst Business/self employed (15.9%), students (11.9%) and respondents in private service (11%). Secondly clients having comfortable financial (13.2%) situation were found to be using it more as compared to those having average and problematic financial situation.

Bank wise analysis shows that Karnataka bank has the highest mobile banking users. More than one fourth of Karnataka Bank's clients (27.1%) were found to be using mobile phone banking facility. This is followed by the clients of ING Vysya Bank (23.4%), Axis Bank (17%) and HDFC Bank (16.4%) who were using mobile banking.

Majority of the respondents using mobile phone banking, check their balance and get transaction alert through SMS. 22–24% of the banks' customers pay their bills via mobile phone, book their rail and air tickets and transfer funds between their own bank accounts. Around 17–18% also use stop payment facilities and do online purchase. Other 13–14% use third party transfer, seek information about bank services and products.

Transaction alert through SMS was found to be used highest in Kolkata (94.7%) followed by Mumbai (85.9%) and Bangalore (82.6%). Checking account balance through mobile phone banking was found to be highest in Ahmedabad and Pune where all the three customers using mobile phone banking use this option. These customers were also using the option of bill payment and booking rail of airline tickets. In terms of number, bill payment was found highest in Delhi 33% and Mumbai 32%.

Third party transfer through mobile phone banking is considered the advanced usage of online banking transaction. Overall only 48 respondents had reported that they were using this facility. In terms of number, this was found to be highest in Mumbai (27) followed by Delhi (16).

The respondents were asked to score 1 to 10 on 4 aspects of mobile banking operation, listed in question no. 34 of questionnaire, where "1 stands for absolutely dissatisfied … to … 10 for absolutely satisfied.

All banks, except four, attained scores between 7–7.99 on overall satisfaction with the mobile phone banking service provided by their main bank. Four banks scored 6–6.99. They were Punjab National Bank, Canara Bank, Indian Overseas Bank and ING Vysya Bank. All these four banks had scored low (6–6.99) on accessibility of mobile phone banking service. Punjab National Bank and Canara Bank along with State Bank of Hyderabad also scored low (6–6.99) on effortless mechanism of using mobile phone banking service. In other words their service is considered to have cumbersome process and consumers have to put some effort in for seeking information and making transaction.

Five banks scored low (6–6.99) on the aspect of continuous availability for information and transaction purpose. These banks included –Punjab National Bank, Canara bank, Bank of India, ING Vysya and Standard Chartered Bank. Confirmation of transaction on Mobile phone through SMS is an important aspect in the Mobile Banking service. In fact RBI has made this facility as mandatory provision because this builds confidence among the online banking consumers. However, five banks had scored low (6–6.99) on this aspect. They are Punjab National Bank, Canara bank, Bank of Baroda, Central Bank of India and HSBC Bank.

The respondents were also asked to score 1 to 10 on 6 aspects of mobile banking operation, listed in question no. 36 of questionnaire, where "1 stands for absolutely dissatisfied … to … 10 for absolutely satisfied.

All banks, except five, attained scores between 7–7.99 on overall trust with the mobile phone banking service provided by their main bank. Five banks attained low score (6–6.99). They were—Punjab National bank, Canara Bank, Indian Overseas bank, ING Vysya Bank and Standard Chartered Bank. The major public sector bank –Punjab National Bank – had attained low score (6–6.99) on all 6 aspect related to confidence with the mobile phone banking. Similarly Indian Overseas Bank, another public sector Bank, scored low (6–6.99) on 5 of the 6 aspects.

Standard Chartered Bank scored low (6–6.99) on three aspects –accuracy in transaction, quickness in completion of service, delivery of whatever has been promised. Similarly ING Vysya Bank and ICICI Bank also scored low (6–6.99) on quickness in completion of service, delivery of whatever has been promised.

State Bank of Hyderabad attained high score (8–8.99) on confidence on service. Secondly, HSBC Bank also scored high (8–8.99) on safety of transaction.

PATTERN OF USAGE OF DEBIT CARDS AND SATISFACTION

Overall 48% of debit card holders were using it once a month. This was reported by over 70% in Pune. In Ahmedabad, Hyderabad, Chennai and Mumbai this was reported by half of the respondents covered. Whereas in Delhi and Bangalore 40–44% of respondents were using their debit card once a month. Over one fourth (25.3%) indicated that they use their debit card weekly. The trend was reported highest in Bangalore and Chennai (36.2% each) followed by Ahmedabad and Kolkata (around 30% in each city).23.5% had been using their debit card less frequently (less than monthly). This was found to be highest in Delhi (36%) followed by Kolkata (25.3%) and Mumbai (22.8%).

CONSUMER SATISFACTION ON WITH DEBIT CARDS

The respondents were asked to score 1 to 10 on 9 aspects of main bank's debit card, listed in question no. 51, where "1 stands for absolutely dissatisfied and … to.. 10 for absolutely satisfied. Two of the foreign banks (Standard Chartered Bank and HSBC Bank) and two public sector banks (State Bank of Bikaner and Jaipur and Central Bank of India) included in the study attained low score (6–6.99) on overall satisfaction as compared to the rest of the private and public banks, which attained 7–7.99.

State Bank of India and other three private banks—HDFC Bank, ICICI Bank and Axis Bank—attained high score (8–8.99) on the aspect of "number of ATMs in which one can withdraw money without paying any fee. The lowest score (3–3.99) on this aspect was attained by State Bank of Bikaner and Jaipur and Standard Chartered Bank. HSBC and Citibank also scored low (4–4.99), whereas State Bank of Hyderabad, Bank of Baroda, Central Bank of India, Indian Overseas Bank and Union Bank of India scored 5–5.99. Rest of the Banks attained 6–6.99 and 7–7.99.

On the remaining aspects, such as Fees to pay for withdrawing money from ATMs of other networks/banks, Number of places where one can pay with the card, Rewards/benefits that one gets when using the card, Yearly fee for having the card, Obtaining information regarding the use of the card (summary of charges), Customer service/assistance help line, Online (internet/telephone) services (e.g.: see balances, reviews past statements, etc) and Safety at the bank ATM's, most of the banks had attained score of 7–7.99. However, there were few banks which attained low score of 6–6.99.

The highest recommendation score (definitely or probably) was scored by HDFC Bank (86.6%) closely followed by State Bank of India (85.7%) and Axis Bank (85.3%). Around 18% of HDFC clients have strongly recommended the debit card of their bank. This was followed by 16.5% of State Bank of India's clients.

Overall 511 (13.5%) were not in favour of recommending (probably + definitely) debit card of their bank. Non recommendation was highest in the case of HSBC (26.6%) followed by Standard Chartered Bank (22.8%) and Citibank (22.2%). All these three are foreign banks and had very few ATMs.

Other 573 (15.2%) were not sure about recommending the debit card of their bank.

PATTERN OF USAGE OF CREDIT CARDS AND SATISFACTION

All together only 32% respondents were credit card holders. The highest percentage were found in Mumbai (39.8%) followed by Hyderabad (33.7%) and Ahmedabad (33.3%). Most of them were having one credit card (82%). In Bangalore over 1 out 10 (12.5%) card holders were having 3 or more credit cards.

Age wise analysis shows that percentage of respondents having credit card were found more in the age group of 26–50 years as this was reported by over one third (over 35%) as compared to 25–27% in the other group. More men (33.8%) were having credit cards as compared to female respondents (27.8%)

Over 4 out of 10 professionally qualified and post graduates were having credit card as against 33.8% of graduates and 22.3% of undergraduates.Nearly 4 out of 10 (36.8%) of respondents having very comfortable financial situation were credit card holders as against 30.2% having comfortable, 28.6% with average and 20.7% with problematic financial situation.

Most of the respondents were having only one credit card. Respondents having more than 3 credit cards were mainly men in the age group of 26–50 years, having their own business or employed in public as well as private service with average or comfortable financial situation. 9 out of 10 credit card holders were using only one credit card. 3 (4.2%) of the credit card users in Bangalore were found to be using 3 or more credit cards. In Bangalore 16.7% were using 2 credit cards In Delhi, Mumbai and Kolkata 1 out of 10 were using 2 credit cards.

Out of 317 female respondents, who were using credit cards, 291 (91.8%) were using only 1 credit card. None of them were found using 3 or more credit cards. 2 credit card users were found more among respondents with professional qualification degree (12.2%) but surprisingly having problematic financial situation (20.7%).

47.8% of credit card users were using their card once a month, followed by 36.8% who were using their card less than monthly. Only 14.5% were using their card on weekly basis. In Ahmedabad over 25% were using their credit cards weekly whereas in Mumbai and Hyderabad, 1 out of 5 respondents were found using their credit card on weekly basis. Nearly 45.0% of the Delhi card users followed by 40.0% of Hyderabad card users were using their card less frequently (less than monthly).

The analysis shows that majority of daily card users were above 50 years followed by the age group 26–35, post graduates and professional degree holders, students and business community with a comfortable financial situation. Users with problematic financial situation were mostly using their card with less frequency monthly (55.2%) or less than monthly (41.4%).

Brands of the credit cards used by respondents were led by Canara Bank (11.6%). This was followed by State Bank of India (8.8%) and Punjab National Bank (8.7%). Most of the credit cards used by respondent were found to be VISA (59%). 3 out of 10 respondents were having Master Card. Other 8.4% were using American Express Card. Only 10 (0.8%) were found with Diners Club and most of them were from Bangalore.

19.4% had chosen their card because it was offered them on free of charge. However, the most important reason was cited as their card offers a wide range of extra services/benefits (23.2%) followed by it has a 24-hours help line for cardholders (20.7%). The card is free of charge was reported more by youngsters (up to 25 years) and also aged (over 50 years), graduates and post graduates, students and others such as retired and with average and problematic financial situation. The card offers a wide range of services was mostly reported by youngsters (25.6%), under graduate (32.5%), housewives and others (over 30%) but having comfortable as well as problematic financial situation.

Highest level of satisfaction ranking was given on the aspect of yearly fee for having the card (7.82) followed safety at the bank ATMs (7.46). Lowest level of satisfaction ranking was given on aspect of Customer service/assistance help line (6.78) and on obtaining information regarding the use of the card (summary of charges) (7.10). On overall satisfaction level mean rank of 6.9 was given by the credit card users. Highest mean rank was given by Ahmedabad card users (8.23) followed by Chennai users (7.64), Bangalore (7.25) and Kolkata users (7.18).The lowest mean ranking was given by Delhi card users (6.8).

The respondents were asked to score 1 to 10 on 10 aspects of credit card, listed in question no. 51, where "1 stands for absolutely dissatisfied and ... to.. 10 for absolutely satisfied. The table also shows the overall satisfaction score (Question no. 52) received by the banks.

Five banks—two public sector and three private banks—attained score of 7–7.99 on overall satisfaction with the credit cards. They were State bank of India, Union Bank of India, HDFC Bank, ICICI Bank and Axis Bank. Rest eleven banks attained low score (6–6.99). State Bank of India and two private banks—HDFC Bank and ICICI Bank—attained high score (9–9.99) on the aspect of "number of ATMs in which one can withdraw money without paying any fee. Axis Bank also scored relatively high score (8–8.99) than the other banks.

State Bank of India also scored high (9–9.99) on Yearly fee for having the card. Three other banks—Punjab National Bank, HDFC Bank and ING Vysya—also scored relatively high (8–8.99) on this aspect. Three banks scored very high (9–9.99) on payment Flexibility. They were HDFC Bank, Axis Bank and Citibank.

State Bank of India, Punjab National Bank and HSBC Bank scored low (6–6.99) on the aspect of obtaining information regarding the use of the card such as summary of charges etc. Similarly, State Bank of India and Punjab National Bank also scored quite low (5–5.99) on customer services. Other to score relatively low (6–6.99) on customer services included Union Bank of India, Indian Overseas Bank, ICICI Bank and HSBC Bank. Nearly 80% of total credit card users indicated that they probably/definitely recommend their credit card to a friend or relative. Highest recommendation percentage was found in Pune where all the 28 credit card users indicated that they would probably/definitely recommend their card to a friend. This was followed by Ahmedabad users (90%) and Hyderabad users (85.5%). Highest recommendations (91.4%) were achieved by Central Bank of India. This was followed by State Bank of India (89.6%) and HDFC Bank (86.3%).

All the main banks analyzed received relatively high scores (8–8.44), except State Bank of Hyderabad. Banks have been put under three different groups using Post Hoc

(Duncan) homogenous subsets where one group was different from another at different significance level. In the first group, there was only one bank—Axis Bank, which scored the highest overall satisfaction level with the mean value of 8.44. In the second group there are ten banks the Bank of India scored the highest mean value of 8.39 followed by State Bank of India (8.37) and Union Bank of India (8.32)

The following figure shows the rank of the banks on a 10 point scale:

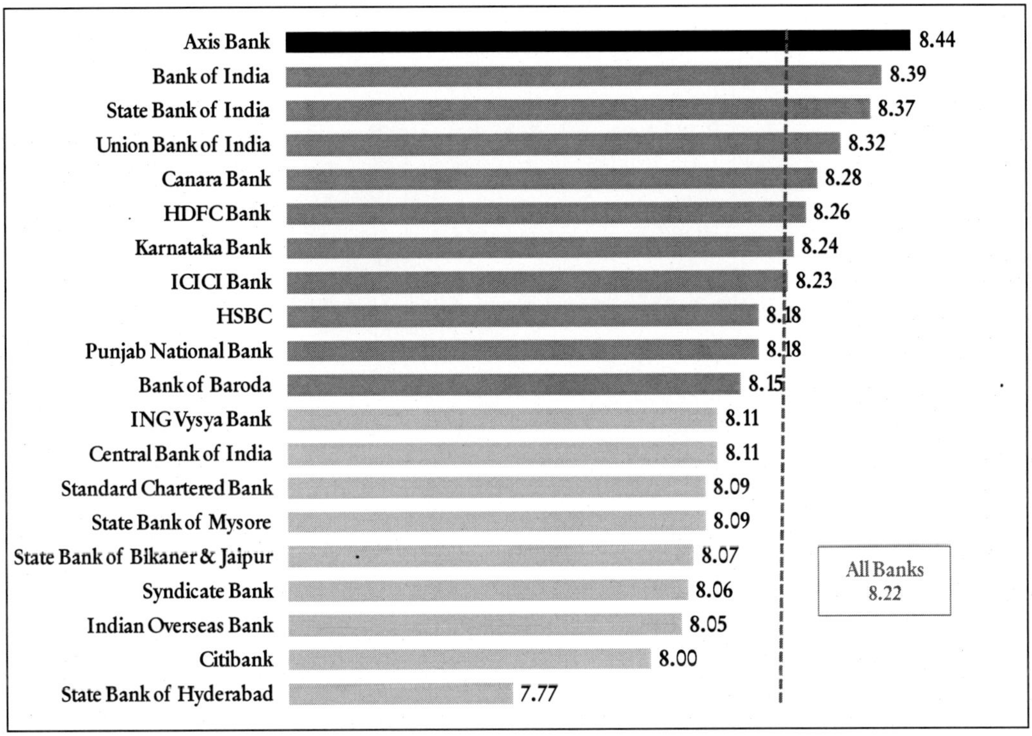

Fig. 6: Overall Satisfaction with Main Bank

The mean difference is significant at the 5% level.

Source: Question No.60 of Questionnaire.

In the lower segment group there were nine banks and highest score was attained by ING Vysya Bank and Central Bank of India with mean value of 8.11 each, followed by Standard Chartered Bank and State Bank of Mysore (8.09 each).

Table 3: Duncan's New Multiple Range Tests Finds Difference among Following Groups of Banks at Stated Significance Levels

Group I			*Group II*			*Group III*		
Bank	*N*	*Mean*	*Bank*	*N*	*Mean*	*Bank*	*N*	*Mean*
Axis Bank	123	8.44	Bank of Baroda	289	8.15	State Bank of Hyderabad	61	7.77
			HSBC	79	8.18	Citibank	63	8
			Punjab National Bank	319	8.18	Indian Overseas Bank	192	8.05
			ICICI Bank	218	8.23	Syndicate Bank	215	8.06
			Karnataka Bank	74	8.24	State Bank of Bikaner and Jaipur	46	8.07
			HDFC Bank	262	8.26	Standard Chartered Bank	167	8.09
			Canara Bank	305	8.28	State Bank of Mysore	55	8.09
			Union Bank of India	246	8.32	ING Vysya Bank	63	8.11
			State Bank of India	516	8.37	Central Bank of India	247	8.11
			Bank of India	233	8.39			
Significance level	*0.65*		*Significance level*	*0.62*		*Significance level*	*0.57*	

Respondents were asked to rate their overall satisfaction with their Bank on a ten point scale. The following figure shows the satisfaction cover for the respective banks (Figure 7).

A reliable satisfaction is the recommendation of the bank to a close friend or relative.

Canara Bank is the highly recommended bank amongst the 20 banks analysed. 91.2% of the clients recommended it. It may be pertinent to point out that although 24.3% consumers had said they would probably recommend this bank a much larger share of 66.9% had strongly recommended this bank.

Axis Bank takes second position with 91.1% of the customers recommending it.

Indian Overseas Bank is the most favored bank as 67.7% customers would definitely recommend it. Although the lowest score goes to State Bank of Mysore (81.8%), however, 63.6% of its clients would definitely recommend this bank which is higher than most of the other banks.

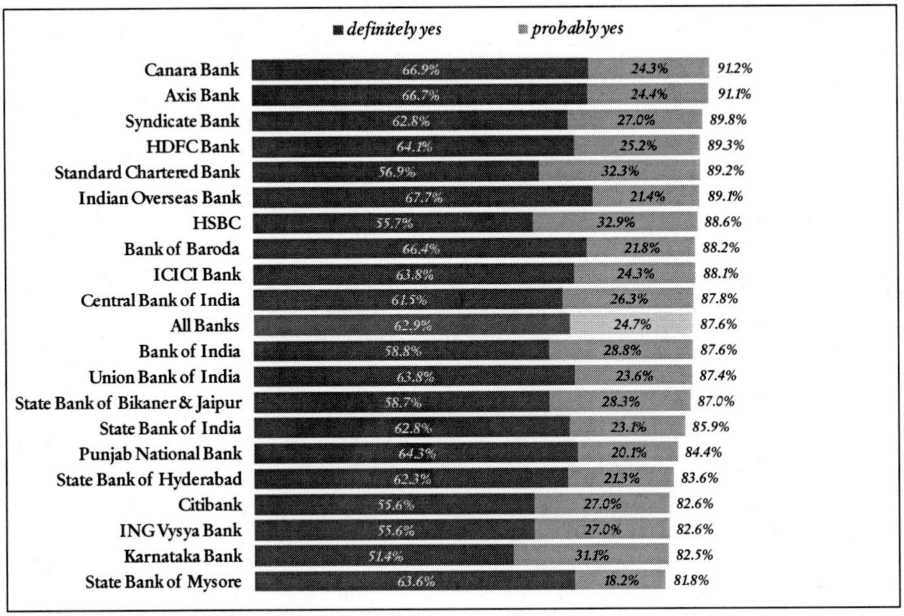

Fig. 7: Would You Recommend Your Main Bank to a Friend or Relative?

The mean difference is not significant at the 5% level.

87.6% would definitely/probably recommend their main bank to a relative or a friend. This was found to be highest in Pune where 97.8% of respondents recommend their main bank. This was followed by Chennai (95.3%) and Mumbai (91.6%). Overall 338 (9%) respondent indicated they would probably/definitely not recommend their main bank. In Hyderabad 15.2% would not recommend their main bank followed by 13.5% in Bangalore and 12.4% in Delhi.

During the interaction with banks after the completion and release of this study it was discovered that some private banks pay considerable emphasis on this aspect and describe this variable as "Net Promoter Score (NPS)". The Net Promoter Score is computed by some private banks by monitoring customer satisfaction rates of their customers.

CONCLUSION

The study has shown that banking service quality levels in the Indian Banking Market are high. The difference between high and low quality of service levels is small. There is hardly any significant difference between public, private and foreign banks quality of service levels. Consumer loyalty rates among banks are high and consumers seem to be getting a good quality of service from banks. The inter-bank comparison show marginal difference in quality of service levels and consumer satisfaction levels.

ANNEXURE

ANNEXURE–A

Sampling Procedures

Selection of Cities

As per the latest RBI statistics available, all India aggregate deposits of all the commercial banks in India stood at Rs. 45,40,130 crores in June 2010. Eight cities were selected whose share of the all India deposits stood at more than 1%. These cities were Greater Mumbai (20.4%), Delhi (12.3%), Bangalore (4.2%), Kolkata (3.2%), Chennai (2.9%), Hyderabad (2.2%), Ahmadabad (1.4%) and Pune (1.3%). *A sample of 3710 (considering the financial constraints) was divided among these 8 cities in the proportion.*

Sample Distribution among the Bank Group

City wise sample has been further distributed among the "Bank Groups" based on the RBI statistics on Bank-Group and Population Group-Wise Number of Branches of Scheduled Commercial Banks—March 2010, which were the latest available statistics at the time.

Selection of Banks

(a) *State Bank and Associates*

Only those banks among particular "State Bank Group" have been selected whose share of number of branches in that group is 7% and above at all India level. This is based on RBI statistics on Branches and ATMs of Scheduled Commercial Banks, as at the end-March 2010.

(b) *Other Nationalised Banks*

Only those banks among particular "Nationalised Bank Group" have been selected whose share of number of branches in that group is 5% and above at all India level. This is based on RBI statistics on Branches and ATMs of Scheduled Commercial Banks, as at the end-March 2010.

(c) *Private Sector Banks*

Only those banks among particular "Private Bank Group" have been selected whose share of number of branches in that group is 5% and above at all India level. This is based on RBI statistics on Branches and ATMs of Scheduled Commercial Banks, as at the end-March 2010.

(d) *Foreign Banks*

Only those banks among particular "Foreign Bank Group" have been selected whose share of number of branches in that group is 10% and above at all India level. This is based on RBI statistics on Branches and ATMs of Scheduled Commercial Banks, as at the end-March 2010.

The following table shows the target sample distribution that was created using the sampling criteria explained above:

Annexure Table 1: Target Sample: City Wise and Bank Wise Sample

Sl.No.		*Delhi*	*Pune*	*Mumbai*	*Kolkata*	*Ahmedabad*	*Bangalore*	*Hyderabad*	*Chennai*	*Total*
	SBI and Its Associates	170	15	290	50	15	60	30	45	675
1.	State Bank of India	130	15	220	35	15	45	25	30	515
2.	State Bank of Hyderabad	15		25	5		5	5	5	60
3.	State Bank of Mysore	15		25	5		5		5	55
4.	State Bank of Bikaner and Jaipur	10		20	5		5		5	45
	Nationalised Banks	535	55	845	135	55	175	95	125	2020
5.	Punjab National Bank	80	10	125	20	10	30	15	20	310
6.	Canara Bank	80	10	120	20	10	25	15	20	300
7.	Bank of Baroda	80	10	110	20	10	25	15	15	285
8.	Central Bank of India	65	5	110	15	5	20	10	15	245
9.	Union Bank of India	65	5	110	15	5	20	10	15	245
10.	Bank of India	60	5	100	15	5	20	10	15	230
11.	Syndicate Bank	55	5	90	15	5	20	10	15	215
12.	Indian Overseas Bank	50	5	80	15	5	15	10	10	190
	Other Scheduled Commercial Banks	185	15	300	55	15	65	35	45	715
13.	HDFC Bank Ltd.	70	5	110	20	5	25	10	15	260
14.	ICICI Bank Ltd.	55	5	90	15	5	20	10	15	215

Sl.No.		*Delhi*	*Pune*	*Mumbai*	*Kolkata*	*Ahmedabad*	*Bangalore*	*Hyderabad*	*Chennai*	*Total*
15.	Axis Bank Ltd.	30	5	50	10	5	10	5	5	120
16.	ING Vysya Bank	15	0	25	5	0	5	5	5	60
17.	Karnataka Bank Ltd.	15	0	25	5	0	5	5	5	60
	Foreign Banks	75	5	130	20	5	25	20	20	300
18.	Standard Chartered Bank	40	5	70	10	5	15	10	10	165
19.	HSBC Ltd.	20	0	35	5		5	5	5	75
20.	Citibank N.A.	15	0	25	5	0	5	5	5	60
	Total	965	90	1565	260	90	325	180	235	3710

(e) *Sample Distribution among the Selected Bank*

The sample has been distributed among the selected banks based on their proportion in the Group Wise selected banks.

(f) *Bank Sample Distribution in the Selected Cities*

Further the banks' sample has been distributed among the selected cities based on RBI statistics on top two hundred centres arranged according to size of aggregate deposits/gross bank credit, June 2010.

(g) *Bank Sample Distribution in the Selected Cities*

Further the banks' sample has been distributed among the selected cities based on RBI statistics on top two hundred centres arranged according to size of aggregate deposits/gross bank credit, June 2010.

For assessing the quality of *online banking service* it was decided to target at least 1000 respondents who are aware and using online banking services for at least 12 months, at the time of survey.

For assessing the quality of *credit card services* it was decided to target at least 1000 respondents who are using credit card services of any bank for at least 12 months, at the time of survey.

Since *telephone and mobile banking* is a very new phenomenon, therefore, quota for these respondents were not specified, however, it was decided to include variables and attributes on these services.

As all the banks included in the sample are issuing *debit cards* to their saving account holders, therefore, quota for the debit card holders was not fixed.

MODE OF INTERVIEW

It was decided to target 100% of the respondents using Face to Face technique. Respondents were selected based on well defined sample distribution method using PIN numbers of the cities. Most of the respondents were interviewed outside their bank branches, houses and offices in the selected PIN areas. The actual sample achieved in face to face interviews was 3773 as shown in Table.

1. Banknet India, a group promoted and managed by senior bankers is focused on disseminating banking and financial information through Online, Offline, Print and Mass Media. http://www.banknetindia.com/banking/101025.htm
2. Mohammed Sadique Khan, Siba Sankar Mahapatra and Sreekumar; Service quality evaluation in internet banking: an empirical study in India; Int. J. Indian Culture and Business Management, Vol. 2, No. 1, 2009.
3. Hans H. Bauer, Maik Hammerschmidt, Tomas Falk, (2005) "Measuring the quality of e-banking portals", International Journal of Bank Marketing, Vol. 23 Iss: 2, pp. 153–175.
4. Parasuraman, Zeithaml and Berry (1985), Journal of Marketing: A conceptual Model of Service Quality and Its Implications for Future Research.
5. Parasuraman, Zeithaml and Berry (1988), Journal of Retailing: SERVQUAL: a Multiple Item Scale for Measuring Consumer Perceptions of Service Quality.
6. Parasuraman, Zeithaml and Berry (1991), Journal of Retailing: Refinement and Reassessment of the SERVQUAL Scale.
7. Cronin and Taylor (1992), Journal of Marketing: Measuring service quality: A re-examination and extension.
8. Cronin, Joseph and Taylor (1994). Journal of Marketing: SERVPERF versus SERVQUAL: Reconciling performance-based and perceptions-minus-expectations...
9. Judy Aidam for Mathew Brown, WHICH: Current Accounts 2004 (21234) Final Market Research Report.
10. Euro Consumer Study.
11. CV Study 2006.
12. Andreas Soteriou and Stavros A. Zenios; Wharton School, USA; Efficiency, Profitability and Quality of Banking Service.

A Comparison of Relationship Marketing in Public and Private Sector Banks in India

Mihir Dash and Vineetha Rajshekhar[1]

Quantitative Techniques School of Business, Alliance University

[1]Banking and Finance School of Business, Alliance University

ABSTRACT: *Relationship Marketing is a new phenomenon in marketing. It is a multifunctional approach, describing marketing as "an integrative activity involving functions across the organization, with emphasis on facilitating, building and maintaining relationship over time." This trend has been catalyzed by the general shift to information highway, IT, database management, whereby marketers have leveraged this new technology to create closer ties with their customers. The overall objective of relationship marketing is to build and facilitate long-term/life-time customer relationships.*

The present study examines Relationship Marketing in the context of banking. The primary objective of the study is to analyze customer. perceptions of Relationship Marketing in public and private sector banks in India. It further discusses various barriers to the implementation of Relationship Marketing in Indian Banking Sector. The study is based on a survey of a random sample from the of customer databases of five public sector and five private sector banks. The data was collected using a structured questionnaire, pertaining to five dimensions of Relationship Marketing, viz. Trust, Bonding, Communication, Relationship Quality, and Conflict-handling, and the overall Customer Satisfaction with the service.

The findings of the study indicate that Relationship Marketing in both public sector and private sector banks has to go a long way to go to become effective. There was found to be a significant gap between expectations and perceptions in the Bonding, Communication, and Conflict-handling aspects of Relationship Marketing. Further, Communication and Conflict-handling aspects were found to be significant drivers of overall Customer Satisfaction.

Keywords: Relationship Marketing, Trust, Bonding, Communication, Relationship Quality, Conflict-Handling, Drivers of Customer Satisfaction.

INTRODUCTION

New age marketing is aimed at winning customer forever, when companies greet the customers, create the product to suit to their needs, and work hard to develop lifetime customers through the principle of "consumer delight." The success of any business depends solely on the quality of product and/or service and customer organization relationship. Instead of running after the customer, there is a need to run with the customer. Customer's active participation and attitude is also essential to project success as quality of service depends upon the customer's disclosure of his/her exact requirements, cooperation, prompt decisions and actions at every stage. While customer's attitude and perceptions have changed, many organizations are yet to respond to the change in the desired manner, though, they have recognized the need to be more relationship-oriented.

Even though marketing has always been based on relationships, Relationship Marketing is thought to be a new phenomenon in the province of Marketing. The advent of mass marketing and mass production obscured the idea of Relationship Marketing for quite a long time. However, with fierce competition, eroding brand loyalty, and heightened expectations of the customers, there has been a trend in favour of Relationship Marketing. Relationship Marketing is especially immensely used by B-to-B marketers. However, Relationship Marketing as a marketing approach is still ambiguous to many practitioners.

Berry and Parasuraman (1991) defined Relationship Marketing as a marketing approach that concerns attracting, developing, and retaining customer relationships. Coviello (1997) further elaborated Relationship Marketing to be a multifunctional and integrative approach, "an integrative activity involving functions across the organization, with emphasis on facilitating, building and maintaining relationship over time." The overall objective of relationship marketing is to facilitate and long term customer relationships, which leads to changed focal points and modifications of the marketing management process. The common superior objectives of all strategies are enduring unique relationships with customers, which cannot be imitated by competitors and therefore provide sustainable competitive advantages (Berry and Gresham, 1986).

Some of the tools used in Relationship Marketing include financial bonds, social bonds, promises, trusts, commitment, and structural bonds. Financial Bonds attempt to tie the customer primarily through financial incentives that may be in the form of lower prices for greater volumes purchases or lower prices for customers who have been with the firm for a long time. For example, in airline industry and related travel service industries like hotels and also in car rental companies, "Frequent Flier Programs" provide financial incentives and rewards for travelers who bring more of their business to a particular airline. Unfortunately, financial incentives do not generally provide long term advantages to the firm, especially if it is not combined with another relationship strategy, so they don't serve to differentiate the firm from its competitors in the long run. For instance, many travelers belong to several "Frequent Flier Program" and don't hesitate to trade-off among them and there has been considerable switching every month among the major telecommunication suppliers.

Social bonds are investments of time and energy that produce positive interpersonal relationships between partners, although this can be range from formal organizational contacts to informal, personal contacts. They are are more personal than organizational. Social exchange is viewed as a dynamic process and plays a central role in ongoing exchange episodes by fostering symbiotic adaptation. Such a bond can be strengthened through multilevel contacts between parties. The most important elements of social bonds are promise, trust and commitment.

An integral element of the relationship marketing approach is the promise concept. Grönroos (2009) argued that marketers should not only give promises and then persuade the customers for a certain desired outcome. Apart from making only promises they should attract new customers and initially build relationships. However, if promises are not kept, the evolving relationships cannot be maintained and enhanced. Fulfilling promises is equally important as means of achieving customer satisfaction, retention of customer base. And long term profitability.

Trust can be defined as "a willingness to rely on an exchange partner in whom one has confidence." Trust can lead to the commitment to a relationship that results from an exchange partner exerting all his/her efforts to preserve an important relationship. The resources of the seller—personnel, technology and systems—have to be used in such a manner that the customer's trust in the resources involved and, thus, in the firm itself is maintained and strengthened. This means that there has to be belief in the other partner's trustworthiness that results from the expertise and reliability of that partner. Maintaining and strengthening trust is essential to the long-term success of a relationship. Where trust is absent relationship will deteriorate.

Another key element of social bond is commitment. Both affective commitment (which is based on a sense of liking and emotional attachment to the relationship) and calculative commitment (which is based on cognitive evaluation of the worth of the relationship) are constructive for developing mutually beneficial relationships, with affective commitment being the more effective.

Structural bonds are developed when two organizations adapt to each other in some economic or technical way such as products or process adjustments. These bonds are forged when two parties adapt themselves to the other by making investments that are difficult to retrieve when the relationship breaks down, and are often strengthened through joint investment in products and process development.

Lindgreen (2001) provided a comprehensive framework of Relationship Marketing, where he identified objectives, defining constructs, and instruments as three major conceptual constructs of Relationship Marketing. This framework can be represented using a simple analytical model as shown in Figure 1 below.

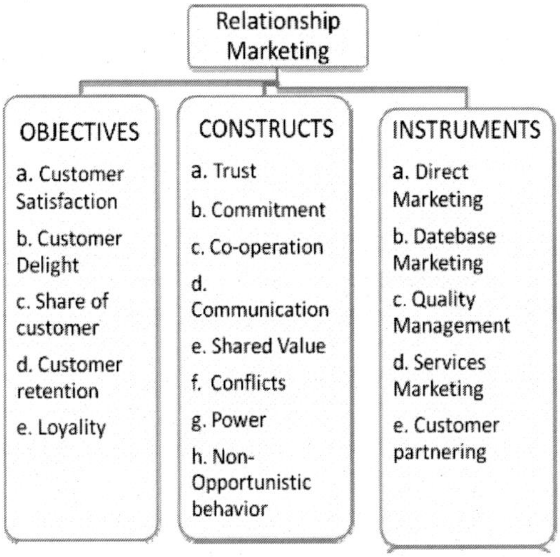

Fig. 1: Breakdown of Relationship Marketing into Objectives, Defining Constructs, and Instruments

LITERATURE REVIEW

There is a vast literature on Relationship Marketing, discussing the benefits of Relationship Marketing, the dimensions of Relationship Marketing, and strategies for implementation of Relationship Marketing.

Jain *et al.* (2002) argued that, though Customer Relationship Management (CRM) has emerged as a core business process for maintaining and enhancing competitive edge in modern business warfare, in spite of meticulous planning and implementation, a large number of CRM programs fail to accomplish their goals. They suggest that a deeper understanding of the behavioral dimensions of relationship marketing and careful evaluation can help organizations to make their relationship building efforts more effective. Service providers need to be customer-oriented and trained in displaying a genuine care and concern for customer welfare. A relationship based on mutual trust and faith lasts longer.

Mittal (2006) discussed the evolution of relationship marketing approach as a evolution of a revolution in the marketing. He suggests that marketing is no longer just about developing, selling and delivering products; it is increasingly concerned with customers. In fact, relationship marketing is based upon the premise that it makes economic sense to satisfy and retain customers as the strength and duration of relationship is directly proportional to the resultant profitability.

Shaineesh and Mohan (2001) addressed certain issues in Relationship Management such as quality and customer centric processes; employee empowerment; technology selection; customer knowledge strategies and individualization of market programs.

Rich (2000) highlighted that the evolution from transaction marketing to relationship marketing in recent years has resulted in the need for more rigorous databases and greater utilization of current computerized tracking systems, with long-term perspectives of the dyadic exchange process to enhance sales results. He suggested that the role of trust and culture in the Relationship Marketing process would require a deeper understanding of the customer; for example, seeking knowledge of a customer's personal feelings concerning their comfort level with various communication approaches could enhance the reception of messages crafted for them.

Sheedy (1997) proposed that Relationship Marketing emphasizes long-term relationships between providers and customers, rather than individual transactions. For example, commercial banks have pursued Relationship Banking programmes to target key corporate and institutional clients, and this has been extended to other customer groups including retail customers. Relationship Banking can be described as the antithesis of "transaction banking." The objective is to increase long-term profits by maintaining and enhancing client relationships.

Colgate and Alexander (1998) suggested that Relationship Marketing is becoming increasingly important within the banking industry. In particular, competition is driving banks to look at forms of defensive marketing rather than offensive marketing strategies. Maintaining and enhancing relationships with personal customers is one way banks have sought to use defensive marketing and increase customer retention. However, at the same time that banks are looking to create more effective and efficient relationships with their customers, competitors from outside the industry are seeking to establish their own financial service relationships with these customers. They argued that customers greatly value their relationships with their banks. They found that customers are increasingly concerned about having a high quality experience of banking. They expect atmosphere and entertainment and prefer banks with a personality rather than those perceived as offering a commodity. Quality of service is becoming an increasingly important differentiator between banks.

Though Relationship Marketing is a well-studied area, there is little literature on Relationship Marketing in India, and especially on Relationship Marketing in Indian banks. The present study addresses this gap.

METHODOLOGY

This study examines the linkage between Relationship Marketing and the customer satisfaction variables in the Indian banking sector (between public and private sector bank). In order to do so, a survey was conducted in Bangalore city to understand customer perceptions of Relationship Marketing dimensions and customer satisfaction in five Indian public sector banks and five private sector banks. The specific objectives of the study were to find out whether customers believe that their banks are relationship centric or not, to compare the Relationship Marketing orientation of public and private sector banks, and to study and compare the customer's satisfaction of public and private sector banks. The data collected through a structured questionnaire, comprising questions pertaining to the dimensions of Relationship Marketing, including Trust, Bonding, Communication, Relationship Quality, and Conflict-handling, and Customer Satisfaction. The data was collected from a sample of 40 customers of the five public sector banks and 40 customers of the five private sector banks under study.

FINDINGS

The descriptive statistics for the expectation and perception levels of the Relationship Marketing variables and the perception level of Overall Satisfaction are given in the Table 1.

Table 1

Dimension	*Expectation*		*Perception*			
	Mean	*Std. Dev.*	*Mean*	*Std. Dev.*	*t-stat*	*p-value*
Trust	3.68	1.053	3.54	0.751	1.021	0.1550
Bonding	3.75	1.037	3.30	0.824	3.459	0.0005
Communication	3.89	0.955	3.48	0.880	3.401	0.0005
Relationship Quality	3.91	0.957	3.78	0.951	0.337	0.3685
Conflict Handling	3.86	1.003	3.26	0.983	4.093	0.0000
Overall Satisfaction			3.36	0.836		

There were found to be above average levels of expectation and perception in all of the dimensions of the Relationship Marketing variables and in Overall Satisfaction. The dimension with highest expectation level was Relationship Quality, followed by Communication, Conflict-handling, Bonding, and Trust. On the other hand, the dimension with highest perception level was Relationship Quality, followed by Trust, Communication, Bonding, and Conflict-handling.

The paired-samples t-test was performed to compare the perception levels with the expectation levels (i.e. gap analysis). The results showed that there was a statistically significant gap between expectations and perceptions in Bonding, Communication, and Conflict-handling. The gap between expectations and perceptions of Trust and Relationship Quality were not statistically significant.

Multiple linear regression was performed to identify the impact of perceptions of the Relationship Marketing variables on Overall Satisfaction. The model was statistically significant, explaining 60.0% of the variation in Overall Satisfaction. The coefficient Table 2 is shown below.

Table 2

	Coefficient	*Beta*	*t-stat*	*p-value*
Trust	0.199	0.179	1.447	0.152
Bonding	0.101	0.099	0.702	0.485
Communication	0.366	0.385	2.965	0.004
Relationship Quality	–0.030	–0.122	–1.573	0.120
Conflict-handling	0.186	0.219	2.058	0.043
(Constant)	0.557		1.850	0.068

Dependent Variable: Overall Satisfaction.

The only significant Relationship Marketing variables having a statistically significant impact on Overall Satisfaction were Communication and Conflict-handling. The other variables did not have a statistically significant impact on Overall Satisfaction.

The descriptive statistics for the expectation and perception levels of the Relationship Marketing variables and the perception level of Overall Satisfaction in public and private sector banks are given in the Tables 3 & 4 below.

Table 3

(expectations)

	Public Sector		*Private Sector*			
Dimension	*Mean*	*Std. Dev.*	*Mean*	*Std. Dev.*	*t-stat*	*p-value*
Trust	3.68	0.797	3.68	1.269	0.000	0.5000
Bonding	3.55	1.154	3.95	0.876	–1.747	0.0475
Communication	3.83	1.010	3.95	0.904	–0.583	0.2805
Relationship Quality	3.98	0.891	3.85	1.027	0.582	0.2815
Conflict Handling	3.85	1.027	3.88	0.992	–0.111	0.4610

Table 4

(perceptions)

	Public Sector		*Private Sector*			
Dimension	*Mean*	*Std. Dev.*	*Mean*	*Std. Dev.*	*t-stat*	*p-value*
Trust	3.48	0.862	3.61	0.625	0.780	0.2190
Bonding	3.07	0.849	3.54	0.735	2.640	0.0050
Communication	3.25	0.890	3.72	0.813	2.480	0.0075
Relationship Quality	3.85	0.821	3.72	0.762	0.734	0.2337
Conflict Handling	3.06	1.069	3.46	0.856	1.846	0.0345
Overall Satisfaction	*3.01*	*0.818*	*3.71*	*0.704*	*4.102*	*0.0000*

The independent-samples t-test was performed to compare the perception levels and the expectation levels of public and private sector banks. The results showed that there was a statistically significant higher level of expectation of Bonding in private sector banks than in public sector banks. On the other hand, there was a statistically significant higher level of perception of Bonding, Communication, and Conflict-handling in private sector banks than in public sector banks. Interestingly, there was a higher level of perception of Relationship Quality in public sector banks than in private sector banks, but this was not statistically significant. Finally, there was a statistically significant higher level of Overall Satisfaction in private sector banks than in public sector banks.

The descriptive statistics for the expectation and perception levels of the Relationship Marketing variables and the perception level of Overall Satisfaction for private sector banks are given in the Table 5 below.

Table 5

Dimension	*Expectation*		*Perception*			
	Mean	*Std. Dev.*	*Mean*	*Std. Dev.*	*t-stat*	*p-value*
Trust	3.68	0.797	3.61	0.625	0.546	0.2940
Bonding	3.95	0.876	3.54	0.735	2.685	0.0055
Communication	3.95	0.904	3.72	0.813	1.717	0.0470
Relationship Quality	3.85	1.027	3.72	0.762	0.794	0.2160
Conflict Handling	3.88	0.992	3.46	0.856	2.386	0.0110

For private sector banks, the dimensions with highest expectation levels were Bonding and Communication, followed by Conflict-handling, Relationship Quality, and Trust. On the other hand, the dimensions with highest perception levels were Communication and

Relationship Quality, followed by Trust, Bonding, and Conflict-handling. The results of the paired-samples t-test showed that there was a statistically significant gap between expectations and perceptions in Bonding, Communication, and Conflict-handling in private sector banks. The gaps between expectations and perceptions of Trust and Relationship Quality in private sector banks were not statistically significant.

Multiple linear regression was performed to identify the impact of perceptions of the Relationship Marketing variables on Overall Satisfaction in private sector banks. The model was statistically significant, explaining 44.7% of the variation in Overall Satisfaction. The coefficient Table 6 is shown below.

Table 6

	Coefficient	*Beta*	*t-stat*	*p-value*
Trust	0.183	0.163	0.738	0.465
Bonding	–0.123	–0.128	–0.619	0.540
Communication	0.339	0.392	1.918	0.064
Relationship Quality	0.236	0.256	0.986	0.340
Conflict-handling	0.053	0.065	0.323	0.749
(Constant)	1.163		2.139	0.040

Dependent Variable: Overall Satisfaction.

The only significant Relationship Marketing variable having a statistically significant impact on Overall Satisfaction in private sector banks was Communication. The other variables did not have a statistically significant impact on Overall Satisfaction in private sector banks.

The descriptive statistics for the expectation and perception levels of the Relationship Marketing variables and the perception level of Overall Satisfaction for public sector banks are given in the Table 7 below.

Table 7

Dimension	*Expectation*		*Perception*		*t-stat*	*p-value*
	Mean	*Std. Dev.*	*Mean*	*Std. Dev.*		
Trust	3.68	1.269	3.48	0.862	0.860	0.1975
Bonding	3.55	1.154	3.07	0.849	2.296	0.0135
Communication	3.83	1.010	3.25	0.890	2.979	0.0025
Relationship Quality	3.98	0.891	3.85	0.843	0.670	0.2535
Conflict Handling	3.85	1.027	3.06	1.069	3.346	0.0010

For public sector banks, the dimensions with highest expectation levels were Relationship Quality, followed by Conflict-handling, Communication, Trust, and Bonding. On the other hand, the dimension with highest perception levels was Relationship Quality, followed by Trust, Communication, Bonding, and Conflict-handling. The results of the paired-samples t-test showed that there was a statistically significant gap between expectations and perceptions in Bonding, Communication, and Conflict-handling in public sector banks. The gaps between expectations and perceptions of Trust and Relationship Quality in private sector banks were not statistically significant.

Multiple linear regression was performed to identify the impact of perceptions of the Relationship Marketing variables on Overall Satisfaction in public sector banks. The model was statistically significant, explaining 71.1% of the variation in Overall Satisfaction. The coefficient Table 8 is shown below.

Table 8

	Coefficient	*Beta*	*t-stat*	*p-value*
Trust	0.279	0.294	1.479	0.148
Bonding	0.127	0.132	0.531	0.599
Communication	0.306	0.333	1.875	0.069
Relationship Quality	–0.030	–0.172	–1.637	0.111
Conflict-handling	0.129	0.168	0.927	0.361
(Constant)	0.383		1.195	0.240

Dependent Variable: Overall Satisfaction.

The only significant Relationship Marketing variable having a statistically significant impact on Overall Satisfaction in public sector banks was Communication. The other variables did not have a statistically significant impact on Overall Satisfaction in public sector banks.

DISCUSSION

The findings of the study show that overall the gap of perceptions among the customers of private and public sector banks is quite wide with respect to the Relationship Marketing implementation, especially in terms of Bonding, Communication, and Conflict-handling.

The findings clearly show that the Relationship Marketing approach is not effectively implemented in public sector banks. The poor implementation of Relationship Marketing approach in public sector banks is reflected in the poor perception of Conflict-handling, Bonding, and Communication dimensions, and has resulted in poor Customer Satisfaction.

Thus, the public sector banks must work hard to improve their Relationship Management systems, especially in these areas.

The private sector banks must also work to improve their Relationship Marketing systems. Though they have fared better than public sector banks in terms of the different dimensions of Relationship Management, they still have to improve their systems especially in terms of Relationship Quality.

Relationship Marketing requires a drastic change in organizations. Firms may have to move from processing customers in groups to serving individual needs. To do so, the organization must be redesigned and decentralized, giving line managers the chance to respond to customer issues. Other changes in policies and procedures to improve the way in which customer needs are addressed may also be needed. Human resource policies should focus on encouraging employees to build relationships. Employees should be encouraged to consider the long-term effects of how they treat customers, rather than viewing the customers as a one-time buyer. Salespeople, in particular, play a key role in developing customer service that leads to loyalty.

However, the biggest change that is required is that of top management. The greatest challenge for the top management is to install among its employees, a deep sense of commitment towards the customers. In order to foster a customer-centered organizational culture, top management must be customer-focused and convey that attitude to employees. Employees, in turn, must be trained in customer service. Firms can offer incentives to encourage good service, but they must also empower employees to address customer concerns this will not only help to improve customer service, but also make. employees more satisfied with their work.

Along with these changes, organizations need to establish an effective customer service system that not only responds to customer complaints, but also encourages customers to complain. Such a service quality information system enables managers to hear and understand customer complaints, track performance, reward good service and determine what is important to customers.

There are some limitations in the present study. The sample size of the study was relatively small, and the coverage of private and public sector banks was limited. There is great scope to extend the present study and consider individual banks. In particular, the banks themselves should regularly conduct customer satisfaction surveys. With better understanding of customers' perceptions, the banks can determine the actions required to meet the customers' needs. They can identify their own strengths and weaknesses, where they stand in comparison to their competitors, chart out path future progress and improvement.

REFERENCES

Berry, L.L. and Parasuraman, A. (1991). *Marketing Service—Competing through Quality*, The Free Press, New York, NY.

Berry, L.L. and Parasuraman, A. (1993). "Building a new academic field—the case of service marketing", *Journal of Retailing*, 69(1), 13–60.

Booms, B.H. and Bitner, M.J. (1981). "Marketing Strategies and Organisation Structure for Services Firms," in Donnelly J and George W.R. (eds), *Marketing of Services*, AMA.

Cowell, D. (1999). *The Marketing of Services,* Heinnemann, London

Grönroos, C. (2009). "Marketing as promise management: regaining customer management for marketing", *Journal of Business and Industrial Marketing*, 24(5/6), 351–359.

Jain, R., Jain, S. and Dhar, U. (2007). "CUREL: A scale for measuring customer relationship management effectiveness in service sector," *Journal of Services Research*, Vol. 7, No. 1, pp. 37–58.

Levitt, T. (1975). "Marketing myopia," *Harvard Business Review*, Sept–Oct., 26–38.

Lindgreen, A. (2001). "A framework for studying relationship marketing dyads," Qualitative Market Research: An International Journal, 4(2), 75–87.

Mittal A. (2006). "Relationship Marketing—Evolution of Revolution," *Synthesis*, 3(3), 63–70.

Peppers, D. and Rogers, M. (2000). "The direction of marketing relationships," *Journal of Business and Industrial Marketing*, 15(2/3), 170–191.

Schoell, K.F. and Ivy, J.T. (1981). *Marketing: Contemporary Concepts and Practices*, Allyn and Bacon; Boston.

Sheth, J.N. and Parvatiyar, A. (1995). "The evolution of relationship marketing", International Business Review, Vol. 4, No. 4, pp. 397–418.

CRM Index: An Effective Weapon for Indian Banks

Arun Kumar, Agariya and Deepali Singh

Atal Bihari Vajpayee-Indian Institute of Information Technology and Management, Gwalior

ABSTRACT: *The aim of this paper is to develop a reliable and valid CRM (Customer relationship management) index specifically catering to Indian banking sector. An exhaustive review of literature on CRM was followed by depth interview and questionnaire survey. Exploratory factor analysis was followed by confirmatory factor analysis which was presented in three forms; the single factor model, covariance model and the structural model. The covariance model shows CRM in Indian banking sector as a multidimensional construct comprising of factors namely organisational structure and customer support, service quality, trust, technology, personalisation and market orientation. The structural model validates the previously extracted factors along with their indicators. The validation of CRM scale is done through a case based method for development of CRM Index along with the customer and service provider weights with the help of questionnaire design and survey conducted. The findings of this study validate the long held belief that CRM is a multidimensional construct and serves as a critical success factor for business performance. Since this study was conducted in context of Indian banking sector, the generalizability of the CRM index has to be tested in other business segments at national level.*

Keywords: CRM Scale, CRM Index, Indian Banking Sector, Exploratory Factor Analysis, Confirmatory Factor Analysis, Structural Equation Modelling.

SUMMARY STATEMENT OF CONTRIBUTION

A fair amount of literature on Indian banking sector dealt with identifying factors explaining the constructs of quality, value or satisfaction. But there is paucity of research pertaining to industry specific CRM index development and validation. This study is an attempt to bridge this gap in the existing literature. It provides a conceptually validated CRM index specifically catering to Indian banking sector, which can help the managers in implementing the CRM in an effective manner and also can be used as a tool to identify the major areas requiring attention.

INTRODUCTION

Reforms initiated in 1991 have changed Indian economy significantly in a span of 20 years and is expected to reach top league in coming years, according to McKinsey research report, 2009. In most emerging economies the regulatory changes are structured to facilitate a threefold agenda which includes liberalization, privatization and globalization. The banking index has shown a highly impressive compounded annual growth rate of more than 51% since April, 2001. As on 31st March, 2010 there were 167 commercial banks operating in India out of which 163 are scheduled commercial banks and 4 were non-scheduled commercial banks. Out of 163 scheduled commercial banks 82 are regional rural banks (RBI Report, 2011). Apart from the public sector/nationalized banks there are private and foreign players which are contributing significantly to Indian banking sector. Foreign banks also grow faster at 30 per cent due to a relaxation in regulations. The contribution of banking sector in GDP increases to over 4.7 per cent. In the current Indian banking scenario of intense competition, deregulation and the availability of internet, the customers have a diversified array of banking and financial products and services to choose from. Indian rural banking sector contributes only 3 percent of the market of Indian banks (Kamath, 2007). Dynamic changes in the competition as well as customer expectations have resulted in a dramatic shift from one time transaction based approach to long term relationship orientated approach. Increasing demands of the customers as well as the intense competition in the marketplace forced banks to device their strategies accordingly to tap the growing market potential. One example of such strategy that has been adopted by banks in varying degrees is the implementation of a superior market

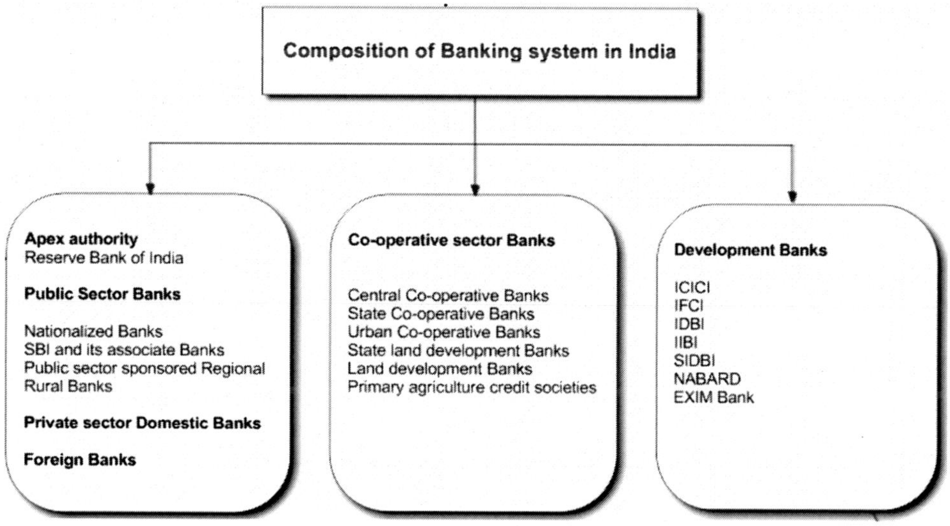

Fig. 1: Composition of Indian Banking System (Kamath, 2007)

orientation. Market orientation draws its relevance from marketing concept which clearly indicates that to maintain the consistency in the success; firms should do the need assessment of its customers and satisfy them more effectively than their competitors in the marketplace (Day, 2000). Initially the financial services industry believed less in the marketing philosophy (Howcraft and Durkin, 2003). The past decade has seen substantial and rapid changes in the way the customer relationship is dealt with in financial services (Berger, 2009). Indian banks are realising the importance of implementing customer relationship management (CRM) for acquiring and retaining their customers. This clearly indicates the need for identifying and addressing the major dimensions that plays a crucial role in the effective CRM implementation. This study has three fold objectives comprising of Identification of the current status, preparedness, implementation and other related issues of CRM through the survey of Indian banks; Development and empirical validation of CRM scale from customers point of view and Development of CRM index through a case based method.

LITERATURE REVIEW

The recent studies on Indian banking industry have concentrated only on the efficiency measurement of banks in terms of utilization of resources (i.e. operating efficiency), but the main aspects of effectiveness of banks in achieving their pre-determined policy objectives is completely ignored (Debnath and Shankar, 2008; Ram Mohan and Ray, 2004; Sanjeev, 2006; Sathye, 2003; Sensarma, 2006; Shanmugam and Das, 2004). As indicated from the work of prominent authors it can be safely concluded that the overall performance of the organization appraisal should take into consideration both the criteria i.e. resource utilization efficiency and effectiveness in achieving pre-decided goals (Asmild *et al.,* 2007; Mouzas, 2006). Many of the researchers have already validated the positive associations between performance outcomes and levels of market orientation (Jaworski and Kohli, 1993; Kumar *et al.,* 1998; Narver and Slater, 1990). However some of the researchers have found that performance is related to market orientation only under moderate environmental conditions (Harris, 2000). Customers do complain when they are not satisfied with the products or services of the organizations which clearly indicates the absolute number or percentage of the dissatisfied customers.

Like zero defects in manufacturing organisations, if the organisations succeed in reducing the customer complaints to zero, this itself will indicate that customer dissatisfaction is eliminated. However the organisations have to recognise that reduction in customer dissatisfaction not always be considered as same as achieving satisfaction (Brige, 2006). Rowley (2005) urges researchers to focus on managing the value offered to the customer. The institutional characteristics along with the behaviour of the managers are the major factors influencing customer satisfaction, service innovation, market orientation and outreach performance within regional rural banks (Megicks *et al.,* 2005). As validated by the previous researchers that the main pillar of organisational success is the market-led approach which has triggered the necessity for investing the nature of market orientation (Deshpande *et al.,* 1993; Siguaw and Diamantopoulos, 1995), the barriers and antecedents faced while implementation (Avlonitis and Gounaris, 1999; Harris, 2000; Slater and Narver, 1995), its key components (Kumar *et al.,* 1998) and the relationship of performance outcomes with it (Doyle and Wong, 1998; Harris, 2001; Pelham, 1999).

In the service firms the market orientation is now considered as a failure-prevention factor sometimes called as a hygiene factor (Barnabas and Mekoth, 2010). Similar to the concept of zero defects in the manufacturing industries, some of the researchers have suggested the concept of flawless performance during service encounters for service industries (Berry and Parasuraman, 1991). Some of the research findings from hospitality sector clearly indicate that disposition and behaviour of the service provider are crucial in the final determination of consumer's evaluation of the services delivered as well as the level of satisfaction and sometimes act as a part of the product experience itself (Collie and Sparks, 1999; Reisinger, 2000). For financial services sector especially the banks the above suggestion holds true (Sobti, 2003). As identified by previous researchers that the employees of the organisations i.e. internal customers have a crucial role in influencing the end customers perceptions i.e. external customers about the quality service (Berry *et al.,* 1983; Bitner *et al.,* 1990).

This is the main reason because of which the concept of market orientation is getting momentum (Jaworski and Kohli, 1993; Narver and Slater, 1990), as it deals with the implementation of the marketing concept through the generation, dissemination and responsiveness to market intelligence throughout the organization. Moreover, employees of an organization have the tendency to replicate the same behavior to the customers as they receive from the organization (Carter and Gray, 2007; Straughan and Cooper, 2002). The terms relationship marketing and customer relationship management are almost used interchangeably in many of the previous works of prominent authors. Still there exist differences between the concepts of relationship marketing and customer relationship management as highlighted by Sin *et al.,* 2005. Fournier *et al.,* 1998 have pointed out in his study that without a precise understanding of when and why consumers respond favorably and strongly to the relationship-building efforts of the business organizations, customer relationship management remains elusive. The study done by Kumar and Gulati, 2010 clearly indicates that high efficiency does not stand for high effectiveness in the Indian public sector banking industry. One of the research study on Indian banking shows that the private and foreign banks are performing relatively better in offering a diversified range of products and services including e-banking facilities as compared to public sector banks.

The experience, size, financing pattern and ownership of the bank were found out to be major factors influencing the extent of e-banking services for urban customers (Malhotra and Singh, 2010). Das *et al.,* 2009 has proposed a list of 29 CRM best practices, for helping the business organizations in achieving comprehensive CRM deployment. The findings also indicate that going for CRM deployment may not be a profitable strategy for Indian retail banks.

Although CRM has now become as a powerful concept to align the interests of a firm and its customers (Boulding *et al.,* 2005), its success depends upon the appropriateness of the firms CRM strategy as well as the effectiveness of CRM implementation. There is very little research which has been done on defining constructs of CRM and development of index specifically catering to Indian banking sector (Agariya and Singh, 2011a, 2011b).

CRM RESPONSIVENESS IN INDIAN BANKS (CUSTOMER PERSPECTIVE)

In the first model (Figure 2) CRM is represented as a uni-dimensional construct and all the extracted dimensions from the factor analysis are leading to CRM. This model is verified through confirmatory factor analysis by using the second half of the data (Sample size: 224). This model is discarded because of poor fit based on the calculated absolute measures, incremental fit measures and parsimonious fit measures. The calculated statistics of these measures is shown in Table 1. In the second model (Figure 3) CRM is represented as a multi-dimensional construct explained by the six factors extracted through exploratory factor analysis. This measurement model is verified through confirmatory factor analysis by using the second half of the data (Sample size: 224).

This model is accepted because of much improved level of fit as compared to model-1 based on the calculated absolute measures, incremental fit measures and parsimonious fit measures (Anderson and Gerbing, 1988). The comparative calculated statistics of these measures are shown in Table 1. In addition to this all the indicators loaded significantly on the corresponding latent constructs. The values of the fit indices indicate a reasonable fit of the measurement model with the sample data (Byrne, 2001).

Table 2 clearly indicates that the composite reliability of all the constructs is more than 0.6, which is quite acceptable (Carmines and Zeller, 1988). Construct validity is established in this study by establishing the content validity, convergent validity and discriminant validity. Content validity is verified through existing literature and expert's interaction in the area of CRM. Convergent validity is assessed by examining the average variance extracted and factor loadings (Fornell and Larcker, 1981). All the indicators have shown significant loadings onto their respective latent constructs with values varying in between 0.51 to 0.85. In addition, the average variance extracted (AVE) for each construct is greater than or equal to 0.50, which further supports the convergent validity of the constructs. As suggested by Fornell and Larcker (1981) the discriminant validity can be assessed by comparing the average variance extracted (AVE) with the corresponding inter-construct squared correlation estimates. AVE values for each latent construct were found more than the square of the inter-construct correlations. Thus, the measurement model reflects good construct validity and desirable psychometric properties (Ganguli and Roy, 2011). In the third model (Figure 4) the structural CRM model is validated by using structural equation modeling. In short, the structural model confirms the six-factor structure of Customer relationship management (Table 3).

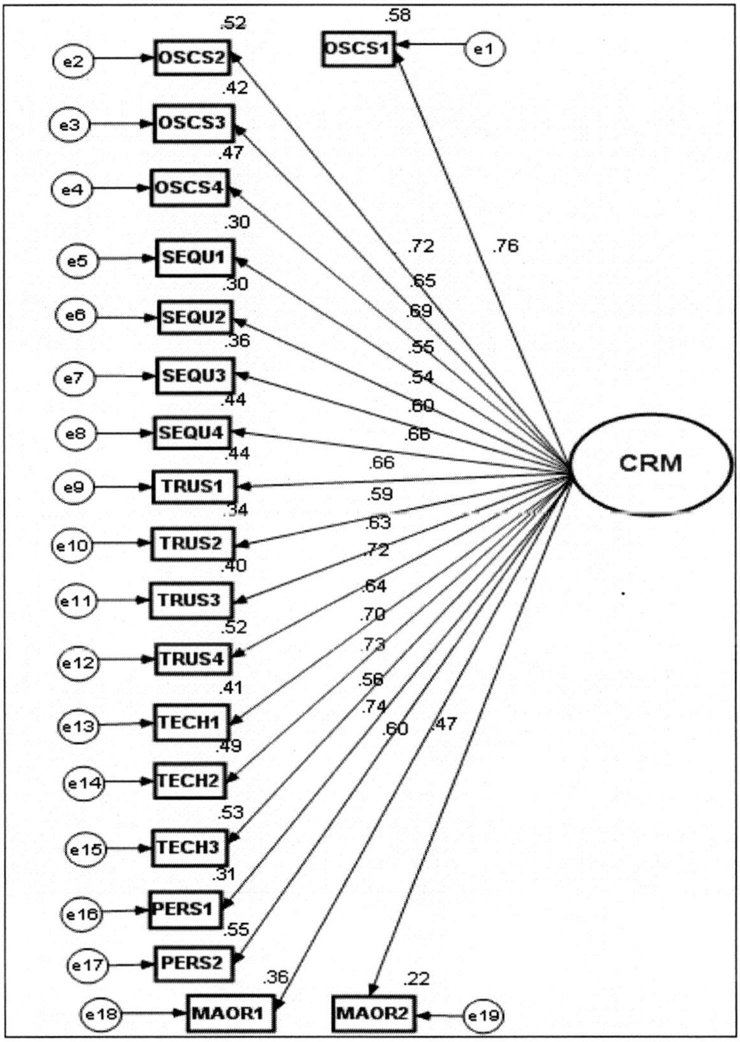

Fig. 2: Model 1-CRM as an Unidimensional Construct

OSCS: Organisational structure and customer support, SEQU: Service quality, TRUS: Trust, TECH: Technology, PERS: Personalisation, MAOR: Market orientation

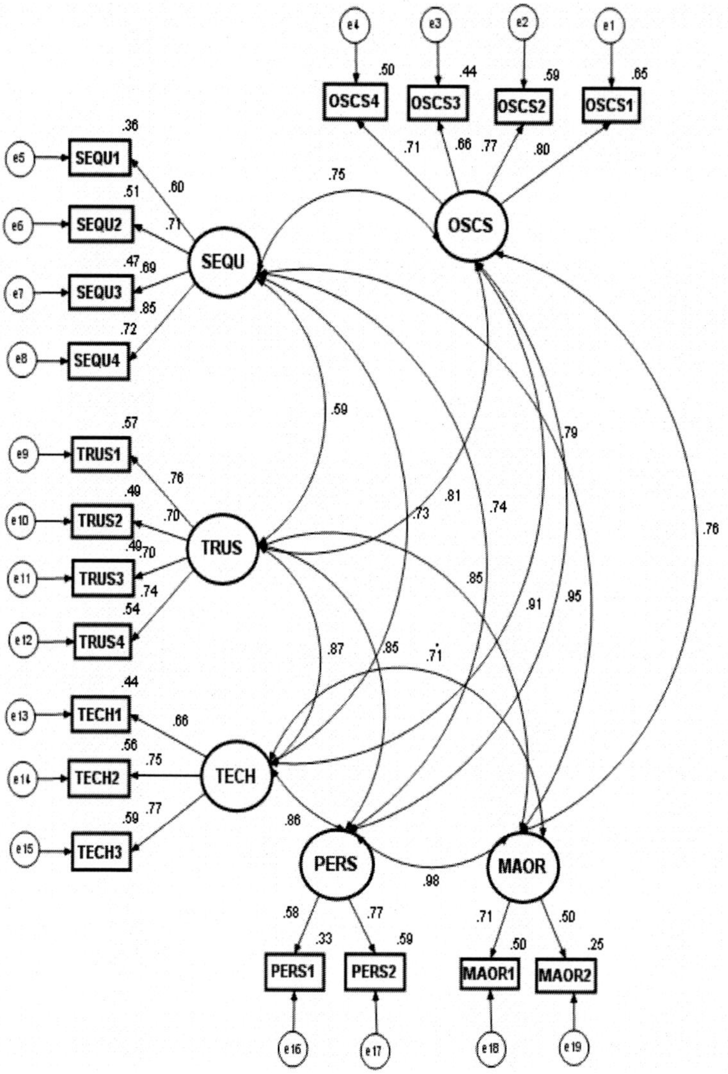

Fig. 3: Model 2-Six Factor Model (Measurement Model)

Table 1: Comparison of the Calculated Statistics of the Models

S. No.	*Model Fit*		*Absolute Measures*			*Incremental Fit Measures*		*Parsimonious Fit Measures*	*RMSEA*
	χ^2	χ^2/df	*RMR*	*GFI*	*AGFI*	*CFI*	*TLI*	*PCFI*	
Model 1	491.49	3.24	0.05	0.81	0.76	0.84	0.82	0.74	0.10
Model 2	305.18	2.23	0.04	0.88	0.84	0.92	0.90	0.74	0.07

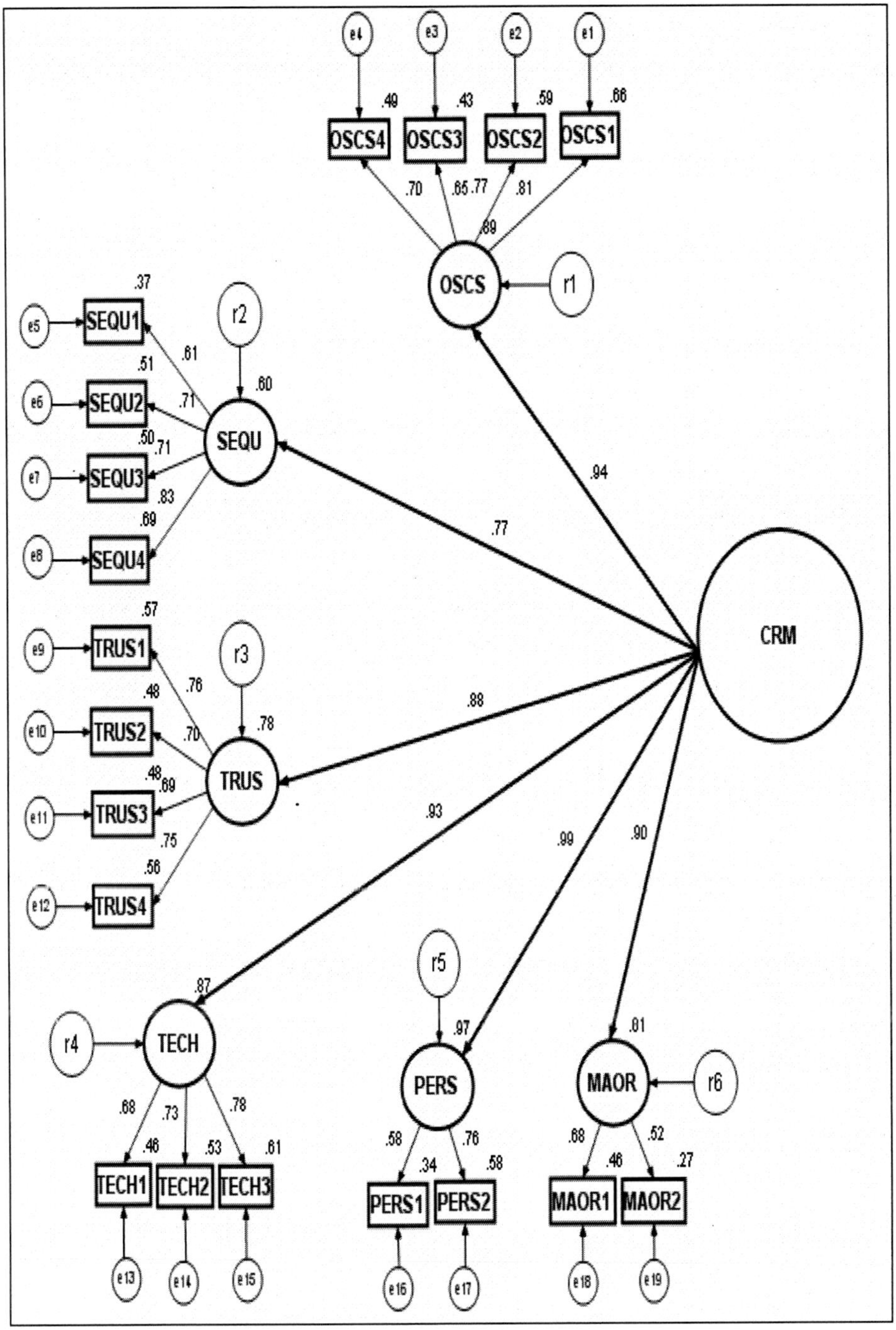

Fig. 4: Model 3-Six Factor Model (Structural Model)

Table 2: Composite Reliability of the Constructs

Construct	*Composite Reliability*
OSCS	0.79
SEQU	0.79
TRUS	0.80
TECH	0.75
PERS	0.67
MAOR	0.66

Table 3: Calculated Statistics of Model-3

S. No.	*Model Fit*		*Absolute Measures*			*Incremental Fit Measures*		*Parsimonious Fit Measures*	*RMSEA*
	$\square^2$	$\square^2/df$	*RMR*	*GFI*	*AGFI*	*CFI*	*TLI*	*PCFI*	
Model 3	348.13	2.38	0.04	0.87	0.83	0.91	0.88	0.77	0.07

CRM INDEX DEVELOPMENT USING THE CASE BASED METHOD IN THE PUBLIC AND PRIVATE SECTOR BANKS IN INDIA

The comparison matrix (Table 4) clearly indicates that there exist a gap between the importance given to the factors by customers and service providers. The weights given by the customers should be duly taken care of and the bank should work upon to minimize the gaps as indicated from the table by devising proper CRM strategies so as to get the

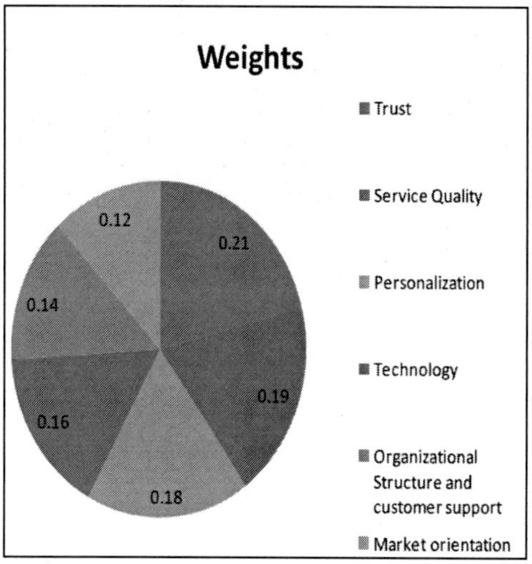

Fig. 5: Weightage given by Public Sector Bank (Customers perspective)

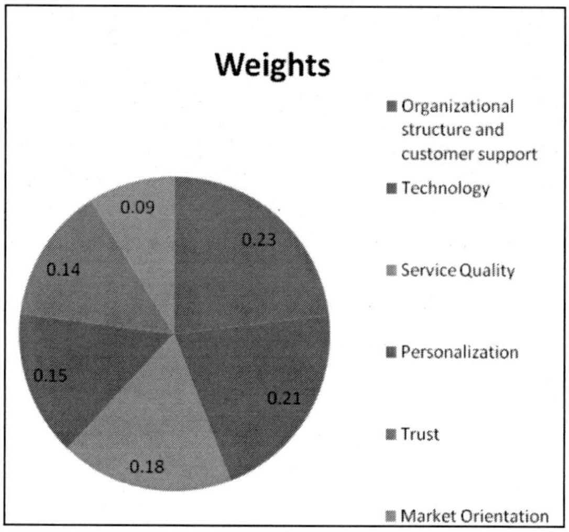

Fig. 6: Weightage Given by Public Sector Bank (Service providers perspective)

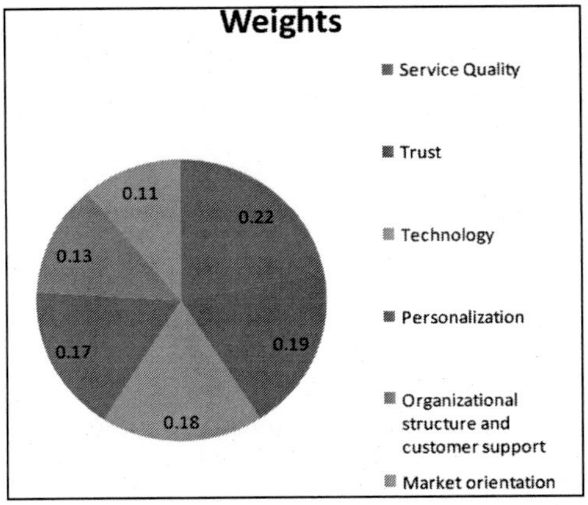

Fig. 7: Weightage given by Private Sector Bank (Customers perspective)

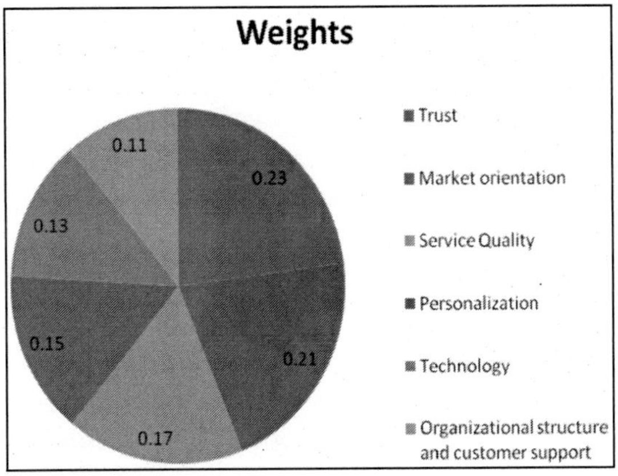

Fig. 8: Weightage given by Private Sector Bank (Service providers perspective)

Table 4: Comparison Matrix

S. No.	*Factors of CRM*	*Public Sector Bank*		*Private Sector Bank*	
		Customers Perspective	*Bank ·Perspective*	*Customers Perspective*	*Bank Perspective*
		Weights (W_{Ai})	*Weights* (W_{Ai})	*Weights* (W_{Ai})	*Weights* (W_{Ai})
1.	Trust	0.21	0.14	0.22	0.23
2.	Service Quality	0.19	0.18	0.19	0.21
3.	Personalization	0.18	0.15	0.18	0.17
4.	Technology	0.16	0.21	0.17	0.15
5.	Organizational structure and customer support	0.14	0.23	0.13	0.13
6.	Market orientation	0.12	0.09	0.11	0.11

maximum benefit of CRM implementation and side by side use this index from time to time to get the feedback of the customer to check the level of effectiveness of the devised and implemented CRM strategies.

INFERENCES AND STRATEGIC IMPLICATIONS

The study verified the long held belief that CRM is a multi dimensional construct. The critical factors that explain CRM in Indian banking sector have been identified as organizational structure and customer support, service quality, trust, technology, personalization and market orientation.

Organisational Structure and Customer Support

This factor includes dimensions such as *working conditions of staff* i.e. the workload and satisfaction level of the employees, so banks have to ensure that there is reasonable workload and proper incentives and career growth policy so as to increase the satisfaction level and foster the sense of belonging to the organization in the employees. R*esponsiveness* i.e. willingness of bank employees to help the customers and providing prompt service to them, *assurance i.e.* The competence and courtesy of employees and their ability to foster confidence and trust in the minds of the customers, *conflict handling i.e.* includes the top management ability to avoid conflicting situation by creating a favourable work culture and in case of any unavoidable conflict solve it before it create problems and the ability of discussing the same openly, practicing them in the organisation will attract large number of customers in future and propagate a positive word of mouth improving the goodwill of the company. This will also play a big role in retaining the customers of the companies.

Service Quality

This factor is of vital importance in the light of more enlightened and demanding customers than ever before who put lot of emphasis on getting a better quality of service which they avail from a particular bank. They in fact are even prepared to pay a premium for getting a better quality service from their bank but will not compromise on inferior or poor service quality. This factor includes dimensions such as *promise fulfilment i.e.* it is the experience of the customer with the bank that whatever has been promised earlier is always fulfilled, *empathy/market orientation i.e.* It is the individualised care and attention provided to the customers, *commitment i.e.* The extent to which a customer perceives the demand to maintain a relationship, *service recovery* i.e. Banking organisation response in case of service failure and all of them play a pivotal role in improving the service quality.

Trust

Customers now-a-days being more enlightened and assertive than ever before, expect consistency in the services which they receive from their bank. Additionally by embarking upon benchmarking and rendering the services which are compared with those of the best in class companies in the world, the banks can maintain its competitive posture and in turn improve its reputation in the eyes of its customers. The dimensions such as *reliability i.e.* It is the ability of the bank to perform the promised service dependably with accuracy, *privacy and security i.e.* privacy is the claim of customers to determine for themselves how, when and to what extent information about them is shared or communicated with others whereas security refers to freedom from doubt/risk during the service delivery process, *interdependence i.e.* indicates if two or more persons e.g. between the customer and the bank, want to achieve their objectives, in such a scenario they have to consider each other *and benevolence i.e.* it is the belief of the customer that the bank cares about and is motivated to act in one's interest, may infuse a positive feeling in the mind of its customers because this is what they expect from their bank in today's fiercely competitive global scenario.

Technology

Banking sector requires sound and effective technological requirements in meeting and/or exceeding the expectations of its customers. Dimensions such as *technological infrastructure, knowledge management and dissemination system and information analysis system i.e. data mining tools to analyze the patterns and other important information* are some of the parameters which today's customer expect from their banks. Apart from this, use of various analytical tools like cause and effect analysis for prompt/timely exploration of probable causes of problems and barriers to success, and the customers feeling about latest technology in services being used, also play a lead role in enhancing the customers expectations of their bank.

Personalization

This factor comprises of dimensions such as *collaboration in product design* and *customer life time value identification* i.e. it is the measure of expected future value of profit to a business derived from customer relationships from the current time to some future point, has a positive impact on the customers' perceptions about the services which they receive from their bank.

Market Orientation

Banks customers rely heavily upon the reputation of their banking organization while choosing it as their banking service provider. Some of the dimensions upon which the customers usually rely when reputation is the deciding factor are—*competitor orientation* coupled with *brand/market image* may tilt the balance in favor of a particular banking organization in the eyes of its customers.

CONCLUSION

Around the globe various standard methods are employed to rank the companies within an industry and identify the industry leaders from getting responses from all the companies and distributing weights to the criteria on which responses are received. For example

Interbrand uses discounted values and Fortune Magazine uses company revenue to rank the companies. The approaches used by these companies to rank the companies is very robust and already in practice. But there is no such measure available in the Indian banking industry that capture the behaviour of the customers and assign more importance to those factors on which customers give more emphasize. The outcome of the research work in terms of CRM Index is an innovative tool which forms the cornerstones for the CRM strategies for the Indian banking sector by laying down the importance of the various factors and indicators as being perceived by the existing customers of the Indian banks. Banking customer's behaviour and preferences can be captured in various geographies that will be of great help and will give the multinational banks the new insights and the areas to work upon and will be result in the fruitful outcomes.

The proposed CRM Index indicates the importance of empirically validated CRM factors/indicators being perceived by the customers as well banking service providers. The gaps have been identified between the perspectives of customers and banking service providers. Academically this study gives an holistic value of CRM in Indian banking sector by analyzing the service providers as well as customers point of view and finally resulted into the CRM index which can be used as an strategic tool for capturing the customers preferences from time to time and designing and implementing newer marketing strategies for effective customer relationship management. Managerially the proposed index will serve as a step by step guideline for the banking organizations to check and measure the effectiveness of their CRM initiatives from time to time. For customers of different banking organizations it can be used as a instrument to give their opinions about the CRM practices. Taking the customers views through the index the banking organizations can devise and follow appropriate CRM strategies with more inclination towards favourable indicators or the factors carrying maximum weightage as shown in the results whereas putting less emphasis on factors/indicators having less weightage. As the customers preferences are captured through the proposed index which is of paramount importance in the current business scenario. The factors weightage along with the conclusion drawn can serve as the proper guidelines to keep in mind while devising CRM strategies so as to achieve the competitive advantage as well as the maximum benefits by satisfying the needs of the customers in an efficient and effective manner.

The proposed CRM index can also be used as a tool for differentiation as it takes care of both the perspectives customers as well as service providers thereby creating a balancing situation between the two and can serve as the foundation for better and effective CRM practices leading to win-win situation for all the stakeholders of the business organizations. This will ultimately have a positive impact on Indian economy as the banking system serves as a backbone. Novelty of this work lies in the fact that considering the views of customers as well as service providers of different banks all across India and proposing a comprehensive index for better implementation of CRM in banking sector. The proposed CRM index can serve as a diagnostic tool to identifying the problem areas as well as exploring new business opportunities in a much better way than even before.

LIMITATIONS AND FUTURE RESEARCH LINES

The sample sizes itself were relatively small, which is one of the limitations of this study. Large and more diversified samples can be taken for the further enhancement as well as validation of this research work. The applicability, validation and generalizability of the proposed index can be done by replicating this study in CRM aspects of other business segments at a national level.

REFERENCES

Agariya, A.K. and Singh, D. (2011a). CRM In Banking: One Size Doesn't Fit All. *AIMA Journal of Management and Research, 5*(2), 1–25.

Agariya, A.K. and Singh, D. (2011 b). What Really Defines Relationship Marketing? A Review of Definitions, General and Sector-Specific Defining Constructs. *Journal of Relationship Marketing, 10*(4), 203–237.

Anderson, J.C. and Gerbing, D.W. (1988). Structural equation modelling in practice: A review and recommended two-step approach. *Psychological Bulletin*, 103, 411–423.

Asmild, M., Paradi, J.C., Reese, D.N. and Tam, F. (2007). Measuring overall efficiency and effectiveness using DEA. *European Journal of Operational Research*, 178(1), 305–21.

Avlonitis, G. and Gounaris, S. (1999). Marketing orientation and its determinants: an empirical analysis. *European Journal of Marketing*, 33(11/12), 385–402.

Barnabas Nattuvathuckal and Mekoth Nandakumar (2010). Autonomy, market orientation and performance in Indian retail banking. *Asia Pacific Journal of Marketing and Logistics, 22*(3), 330–350.

Berger Sven, C. (2009). Self-service technology for sales purposes in branch banking. *International Journal of Bank Marketing*, 27(7), 488–505.

Berry, L.L. and Parasuraman, A. (1991). *Marketing Services.* New York: Free Press.

Berry, L.L., Shostack, G.L. and Upah, G.D. (Eds) (1983). *Emerging Perceptions on Service Marketing.* Chicago, IL: American Marketing Association.

Bitner, M.J., Booms, B.H. and Tetreault, M.S. (1990). The service encounter: Diagnosing favourable and unfavourable incidents. *Journal of Marketing,* 54, 71–84.

Brige, A. (2006). Building relationship with customers by using technological solutions in commercial banks of Latvia. *Baltic Journal of Management*, 1(1), 24–33.

Byrne, B.M. (2001). *Structural Equation Modelling with AMOS: Basic Concepts, Applications and Programming.* Mahwah, NJ: Lawrence Erlbaum Associates.

Carmines, E.G. and Zeller, R.A. (1988). *Reliability and Validity Assessment.* Beverly Hills, CA: Sage.

Carter, L. and Gray, D. (2007). Relational competence, internal market orientation and employee performance. *The Marketing Review*, 7(4), 385–400.

Collie, T. and Sparks, B.A. (1999). Perceptions of key success factors and key success inhibitors in Australian restaurant and catering business operations. Australian *Journal of Hospitality Management*, 6(2), 23–33.

Das, K., Parmar Jitesh, and Sadanand V.K. (2009). Customer Relationship Management (CRM) Best Practices and Customer Loyalty A Study of Indian Retail Banking Sector. *European Journal of Social Sciences*, 11(1), 61–85.

Day, G.S. (2000). Managing market relationships. *Journal of the Academy of Marketing Science*, 28(1), 24–30.

Debnath, R.M. and Shankar, R. (2008). Measuring performance of Indian banks: an application of data envelopment analysis. *International Journal of Business Performance Management*, 10 (1), 57–85.

Deshpande, R., Farley, J. and Webster, F. (1993). Corporate culture, customer orientation and innovativeness in Japanese firms: a quadrand analysis. *Journal of Marketing*, *57*(January), 23–37.

Doyle, P. and Wong, V. (1998). Marketing and competitive performance: an empirical study. *European Journal of Marketing*, 32(5/6), 514–35.

Fornell, C. and Larcker, D.F. (1981). Evaluating structural equation models with unobservable variables and measure. *Journal of Marketing Research,* 18, 39–50.

Fournier S., Dobscha S and Mick D.G. (1998). Preventing the premature death·of relationship marketing. *Harvard Business Review*, 76(1), 42–51.

Ganguli S. and Roy S.K. (2011). Generic technology-based service quality dimensions in banking: Impact on customer satisfaction and loyalty. *International Journal of Bank Marketing*, 29(2), 168–189.

Harris, L. (2000). The organisational barriers to developing market orientation. *European Journal of Marketing*, *34*(5/6), 598–624.

Harris, L. (2001). Market orientation and performance: objective and subjective empirical evidence from UK companies. *Journal of Management Studies*, *38*(1), 17–43.

Howcraft, B. and Durkin, M. (2003). Effective marketing management in financial services context. *Journal of Marketing Management*, 19, 911–14.

Jaworski, B. and Kohli, A. (1993). Market orientation: antecedents and consequences. *Journal of Marketing*, 57(July), 53–70.

Kamath G. Barathi (2007). The intellectual capital performance of Indian banking sector. *Journal of Intellectual Capital*, 8(1), 96–123.

Kumar, K., Subramanian, R. and Yauger, C. (1998). Examining the market orientation performance relationship: a context specific study. *Journal of Management*, 24(2), 201–233.

Kumar, S. and Gulati, R. (2010). Measuring efficiency, effectiveness and performance of Indian public sector banks. *Journal of Productivity and Performance Management*, 59(1), 51–74.

Malhotra Pooja and Singh Balwinder (2010). An analysis of Internet banking offerings and its determinants in India. *Internet Research,* 20(1), 87–106.

Megicks Philip, Mishra Atul and Lean Jonathan (2005). Enhancing microfinance outreach through market-oriented new service development in Indian regional rural banks. *International Journal of Bank Marketing*, 23(1), 107–125.

Mouzas, S. (2006). Efficiency versus effectiveness in business networks. *Journal of Business Research*, 59(10/11), 1124–32.

Narver, John C. and Stanley F. Slater (1990). The Effect of a Market Orientation on Business Profitability. *Journal of Marketing*, 54(October), 20–35.

Pelham, A. (1999). Influence of environment, strategy, and market orientation on performance in small manufacturing firms. *Journal of Business Research*, 45, 33–46.

Ram Mohan, T.T. and Ray, S. (2004). Productivity growth and efficiency in Indian banking: a comparison of public, private, and foreign banks. Working Paper, University of Connecticut, Storrs, CT.

Reisinger, Y. (2000). Unique characteristics of tourism, hospitality and leisure services. In Kandampully, J., Mok, C. and Sparks, B., *Service Quality Management in Hospitality, Tourism and Leisure*, New York, NY: Haworth Hospitality Press.

Rowley, J. (2005). Building Brand Webs: Customer Relationship Management through the Tesco Clubcard Loyalty Scheme. *International Journal of Retail and Distribution Management*, 33(3), 194–206.

Sanjeev, G.M. (2006). Does banks' size matter in India. *Journal of Services Research, 6*(2), 135–44.

Sathye, M. (2003). Efficiency of banks in a developing economy: the case of India. *European Journal of Operational Research*, 148(3), 662–71.

Sensarma, R. (2006). Are foreign banks always the best? Comparison of state-owned, private and foreign banks in India. *Economic Modelling*, 23(4), 717–35.

Shanmugam, K.R. and Das, A. (2004). Efficiency of Indian commercial banks during the reform period. *Applied Financial Economics*, 14(9), 681–686.

Siguaw, J. and Diamantopoulos, A. (1995). Measuring market orientation: some evidence on Narver and Slater's three-component scale. *Journal of Strategic Marketing*, 3, 77–88.

Sin, Leo Y.M., Tse, Alan C.B. and Yim Frederick H.K. (2005). CRM: Conceptualisation and scale development. *European Journal of Marketing*, 39(11/12), 1264–1290.

Sobti, R. (2003). *Banking and Financial Services in India: Marketing Redefined.* New Delhi: New Century Publications.

Straughan, R.D. and Cooper, M.J. (2002). Managing internal markets: a conceptual framework adapted from SERVQUAL. *The Marketing Review*, 2, 253–65.

Member Satisfaction in Urban Co-operative Banks: Definition and Preliminary Scale Determination

Jacob George and Roji George
Saintgits Institute of Management, Kottayam, Kerala

ABSTRACT: *This paper applies Barton's (1989) conceptualization of member roles to develop a member satisfaction scale for urban cooperative banks. The study constructs a valid and reliable scale of member satisfaction and goes on to test the relationship between member satisfaction and members' trust of top management in urban cooperative banks in a developing nation. We conducted survey at 10 urban cooperative banks and got 103 usable responses. We used principle axis factoring with oblique rotation to analyze data. The scale was tested for its dimensionality, reliability, and various validities. The findings show a positive association between member satisfaction and cognitive trust of members on the top management of the urban cooperative banks. Organizational performance of banks is usually measured using financial statements. Member satisfaction gives a new perspective to organizational success and helps us to evaluate a co-operative bank in a more transparent way.*

Keywords: Member Satisfaction, Urban Cooperative Banks, Members' Trust, Scale Construction, India.

INTRODUCTION

Member Organizations (MOs) are organizations where socially significant goals are also pursued by its members apart from normal economic goals. Membership is considered more important than capital. Cooperatives are member organizations with the following four critical principles (International Cooperative Alliance (ICA) Congress, 1966).

1. Voluntary and open membership.
2. Democratic control (one member, one vote).
3. Limited interest on share capital (members' capital deployed should be paid fixed, limited interest).
4. Patronage dividend (Surplus should be distributed in proportion to usage).

Cooperative Banks are different from other cooperatives in that the members are both the suppliers and buyers of the banks' facilities where as in other types of cooperatives they are beneficiaries, either as suppliers or customers with public as the business counterpart. That is, they are purchasing and marketing cooperatives at the same time (Dakurah *et al.*, 2005). So it makes the study of co-operative banks as a true representative of a member organization with clear cut principles and self-contained transactions very much relevant.

Cooperative banks of India were constituted under Co-operative Societies Act 1912. Under Reforms Act 1919 cooperation became a state subject. Kerala is a small state in southern India. The Kerala Co-operative Societies Act of 1969 came into force with effect from 15.5.1969 in order to enact a uniform law on cooperation applicable throughout the State. Consequent to its introduction, Societies with unlimited liability ceased to exist and societies with limited liability came into existence. The ICA Cooperative Congress, 1995 revised the critical principles to some extent. But, the Kerala Cooperative Societies Act, 1969 has essentially retained the older principles. Also, organization and control came under the Registrar of Cooperative, who is a state employee heading the Department of Cooperation. The Reserve Bank of India (RBI) exercises control in Urban Cooperatives Banks (UCBs), a special type of cooperative bank, through the Banking Regulation Act, 1949 and 1969 (AACB).

The Cooperative Banks of India have been vested with the vital role of extending credit facility to the weaker segments of the population by the state. As far as UCBs are concerned, its members are mainly in the priority sector defined as owners of small scale and cottage industries, small traders, self employed people, professionals and the weaker sections of the urban community like dalits, women, handicapped etc. Thus one of the primary goals of a Cooperative Bank in India is to provide cheap and easy credit to its members. In the quest for bank performance and protection to depositors, is it possible to lose focus on this goal and dissatisfy the members? UCBs are a type of cooperative banks in India with primary membership. So retention of cooperative nature in this category assumes importance.

RBI itself has identified the preservation of the cooperative nature as crucial to UCBs according to Madhav Rao Committee Report (1999). It was implicitly acknowledged that it is impossible to satisfy members without retaining this nature. In other words, emphasis on performance, depositor protection and financial system stability may result in UCBs succeeding as banks but losing their social commitment as part of the larger cooperative movement. This may even eventually transform the average successful UCB to another commercial bank.

This may result in the relative deprival of credit to the priority sector which has lower creditworthiness compared to the corporate world. An illustration of this phenomenon is follows. It was earlier mandatory for UCBs to have 60% of net bank credit to priority sector. The weaker sections get 25% of this priority sector lending. From 2010 onwards, by a circular of the RBI, priority sector gets only 40% on par with commercial banks. And correspondingly the weaker sections get underrepresented.

Reserve Bank of India (RBI) has been closely monitoring the bank performance all these years using objective parameters. It has basically been concentrating on the CAMELS rating to evaluate the performance of the UCBs, right from the time the Report of the Working Committee on the Rating system for Urban Cooperative Banks (2002).

However it has not looked into measuring a critical, but invisible, parameter which has a sustained effect on the long-term success of any UCB. That is the satisfaction level of the members of the Cooperative Banks. State Governments which also share responsibility for the UCBs have also not studied Member Satisfaction to the best of the knowledge of the researcher.

This article has been divided into four sections. After the introductory session, session 2 deals with the objectives and methodology. Third is the analysis and discussions. Last is the concluding session.

No much literature was observed to offer a definition on Member Satisfaction in member organizations even though it is mentioned in innumerable articles. Customer Satisfaction of organizations is measured by the American Customer Satisfaction Index (ACSI) (Fornell, *et al.,* 1996). No comparable index or scale has been developed for Member Satisfaction in member organizations to the best of the knowledge of the researchers. The three roles that the cooperative members have, as owner, controller and user/beneficiary (Barton, 1989), are taken as the basis of a construct development for Member Satisfaction. Osterberg and Nilsson (2009) found members' willingness to participate in co-operative governance to be the single most important explanation for Member Satisfaction. As a beneficiary, the crucial issue in member satisfaction is whether one chooses a member organization or an investment oriented firm to gain one's benefits (Bhuyan, 2007).

Operationally, Member Satisfaction is defined as the feeling that a member in a member organization experiences when his social and economic needs, rights, duties and responsibilities that he expected to fulfill when he joined the organization are completely met.

Members are key stakeholders in Cooperative Banking and stakeholder satisfaction leads to good organizational performance according to Donaldson and Preston (1995). So it is expected that, since high level in Member Satisfaction leads to good Organizational Performance, Member Satisfaction should be measured and understood.

Gap in the research is that no scientifically validated and reliable scale has been developed to measure Member Satisfaction in Cooperative Banks and hence the organizational success of the Cooperative Banks is not reported in a balanced way.

OBJECTIVES AND METHODOLOGY

So, the objective of the study was to develop a scale to measure Member Satisfaction in Cooperative Banks. Member satisfaction is best captured by a subjective assessment of the perception of the members' role satisfaction. The member's three roles as an owner, controller (voter and board member) and as beneficiary are taken into consideration and the members are assessed for their satisfaction level through questionnaire interview. The subjective assessment can be done through a measure best called the member satisfaction scale.

As indicated earlier, as population for this study, UCBs of Kerala were taken. UCBs of Kerala are stand alone banks which function along the lines of commercial banks and compete with them. There are 60 urban cooperative banks in Kerala according to the list published by Reserve Bank of India. As mentioned earlier, these are under the Banking Regulation Act, 1949 of Reserve Bank of India as far as their banking operations are considered. They report to the Cooperative Registrar of Kerala State under the Kerala Cooperative Societies Act, 1969 as far as the administration as a cooperative is considered. Thus the administrative and banking issues are factored out. Above all, most of the UCBs are healthy and running successfully. So there is a high degree of homogeneity among the UCBs of Southern Kerala which permits comparison among them.

We hypothesized member satisfaction scale as a one-dimensional construct made up of three equally important reflective components: ownership role, controllership role and beneficiary role.

There were three stages in the development of the scale. They are described below:

First step was the item generation where a small group of professionals with long work experience in senior managerial positions at various Kerala UCBs were asked to list the activities, practices and behaviors that reflected a member's roles as owner, controller and beneficiary in a cooperative. This was in addition to the list that the author had developed based on study and observation of UCBs. The intention in generating a large list of items was to ensure a sufficient breadth of content and an adequate pool of items within each of the theoretical components (Clark and Watson, 1995).

This step was successfully completed with the help of retired General Managers (GMs) of various Urban Cooperative Banks of Kerala. Six ex-GMs with an average work experience of 20.2 years as GMs were interviewed. They generated 63 questions concerned with the member's role as an owner, 79 as a controller and 85 as beneficiary, totaling to 227 questions.

Second step was the rigorous editing done by the researcher to eliminate ambiguous, repetitive and loaded questions. Double barreled questions were split into separate questions.

This step was satisfactorily done by the researchers, by which we cut down the number of questions concerned with the member's role as an owner to 49, as a controller to 52, as a beneficiary to 58, totaling to 159 questions.

The third and last step was an academic rating where a small group of academicians with background in cooperatives are to rate the items based on their suitability to be included in the final list. If the question was very suitable to be included in the final questionnaire it was given a rating of 5. If it was very little suitable it was given a rating of 1. If the question was of intermediate quality, scores of 4, 3, or 2 were given depending on the degree of suitability in the descending order of suitability. Those items which were scored 3 or less by at least two members were rejected.

This step was successfully completed with the help of five experienced senior academicians from the area of cooperation in India with an average academic experience of 26.6 years. The number of questions pertaining to owner was cut down to 13, controller to 13 and beneficiary to 19, totaling to 45 questions.

Then, in stage 2, a pilot study was conducted with at least 10 participants in which a questionnaire having the short-listed member satisfaction questions in Likert scale was used. Participants indicated their agreement or disagreement about the satisfaction of the bank on a five-point scale. At this point, questions which the interviewees indicated as confusing, ambiguous, irrelevant or otherwise difficult to answer were deleted. At the end of the pilot study we had the set of questions needed for the first stage in scale determination.

This stage was successfully completed with the help of Changanacherry Cooperative Urban Cooperative Bank members. Twelve of them were interviewed and the questions on owner were cut down to 8, controller to 9 and beneficiary to 16, totaling to 33 questions.

As stage 3, a preliminary survey was conducted where the data collection and analysis was done as follows. It was an exploratory study. The study explored whether Member Satisfaction can be measured scientifically. Exploratory Factor Analysis was done on the data collected and the scale was tested for Content, Construct and Nomological Validity. The scale was also tested for reliability. Scope was confined to the Urban Cooperative Banks of Southern Kerala (Ernakulam, Alappuzha, Idukki, Kottayam, Pathanamthitta, Kollam, and Thiruvananthapuram) and to the members having operating account in urban cooperative banks and who were eligible to vote the Board of Directors to power.

The questionnaire had 33 items, as mentioned earlier, investigating member satisfaction construct in Likert scale. Participants agreed or disagreed with the statements on a five-point scale. The questionnaire to measure cognitive trust of the directors' board and the top management were also handed over to the members.

Participants were drawn from 10 Urban Cooperative Banks of southern Kerala, with at least one bank from each district of Southern Kerala. We distributed the questionnaires to

50 members in each bank totaling to 500 participants who had full membership in these banks. Participants were sent a covering letter, the questionnaire and a self-addressed stamped return envelope. The covering letter explained the importance of the study, but did not disclose the constructs so as not to influence the judgments of the participants. To reduce the impact of social desirability, we promised to keep their responses confidential (Heneman, 1974; Podsakoff, MacKenzie, Lee and Podsakoff, 2003).

We received 113 replies. However, we discarded 10 replies because the participants had ticked in the same column for all the 33 items implying that they had not bothered to understand the questionnaire. In other words, the standard deviation was zero for those participants. We were left with 103 usable responses. We considered a sample size of more than 100 respondents adequate for a preliminary scale in accordance with Netemeyer, Bearden and Sharma (2003).

For nomological validity, the following existing theoretical finding was tested. Members' Satisfaction with the Cooperative as a trading partner and as a member organization is significantly related to members' trust in the board of directors and in the management (Nilsson *et al.,* 2009). A validated scale of the cognitive trust of the directors' board and top management was used as a proxy (Hansen *et al.,* 2002). It was included in the questionnaire for nomological validity testing.

ANALYSIS AND DISCUSSIONS

Only 3% of the total data points were missing completely at random. Roth, Switzer and Switzer (1999) recommended using either the regression technique or the technique of using a person's mean response for other items on a scale to impute values to missing data. We explored the statistical properties, such as kurtosis, skewness, and standard deviation of all the scale items. Following (Clark and Watson, 1995) we deleted 3 items from the beneficiary role because they showed a highly skewed score distribution. Two items from ownership role, one item from controllership role and one item from beneficiary role were deleted because their mean-to-standard deviation ratio were less than three which indicated inadequate variability and inability of the items to discriminate at different points along the continuum.

We had hypothesized that member satisfaction was a one-dimensional construct with three correlated components. We used exploratory factor analysis (EFA) to analyze the data. Our a priori decision rule specified retention of only those items that had achieved higher than 0.32 loadings on one of the factors and less than 0.32 cross loadings on the rest. Following Conway and Huff's (2003) recommendation for high quality EFA decisions, we used the principal axis factoring (PAF) with the oblique rotation (Promax) technique to produce a simple factor structure. Oblique rotation permits factors to demonstrate

Table 1: Factor Structure of the Member Satisfaction Scale (MSS)

Scale Item	*Item Code*	*Factor 1 (BR*)*	*Factor 2 (CR**)*	*Factor 3 (OR***)*
I feel confident about the well being of the institution.	OR2			0.630
I get due recognition from the board of directors as an owner.	OR3			0.365
I am satisfied with the bank's financial dealings.	OR4			0.428
The price of share is very reasonable.	OR6	0.696		
I am aware of my responsibilities as an owner.	OR8			0.507
I do not see any obstruction in exercising my right to elect the board of directors.	CR2		0.563	
My right to know about the working of the bank is recognized by the bank management.	CR4		0.434	
The bank is helped by the good management of the General Manager.	CR5		0.895	
The bank is helped by the proper governance of the Board of Directors.	CR6		0.816	
Interference by political parties does not affect the free choice of voters.	CR7		0.379	
I am encouraged to bring to attention the best practices of other competing banks.	CR9		0.395	
I get all the benefits that should be available to a member of a cooperative bank.	BR1	0.651		
The bank gives better terms for loans compared to competing banks.	BR2	0.594		
The bank staff is very polite and cordial in their behavior.	BR3	0.602		
I feel no discrimination in securing loans.	BR4	0.658		
Modern day technology is used to ensure better service to members at the bank.	BR5	0.610		
The bank staff gives me excellent service.	BR8	0.810		
The bank management is more approachable than that of the competing banks.	BR9	0.378		
Loan procedure is simple.	BR10	0.761		
Loans are sanctioned without undue delay.	BR12	0.481		
The Loan procedure is explained to member's satisfaction at the time he applies for a loan.	BR13	0.642		
Bank charges reasonable service fees.	BR15	0.582		

Note: *= Beneficiary Role Sub Scale; **= Controllership Role Sub Scale; ***= Ownership Role Sub Scale.

correlation, which is desirable in the construction of a scale because would normally have a certain amount of overlap among them (Conway and Huffcutt, 2003). The scree plot yielded three factors and a sharp elbow afterwards, which supported our hypothesis about the construct dimensionality. These four factors extracted 42.145% variance. Barlett's test of Sphericity was highly significant at $p < 0.0001$. The KMO statistic was 0.758, above 0.7 being considered adequate for an exploratory scale. Refer to Table 1 for the factor structure of our scale with 22 items. For the sake of simplicity, we call this scale as MSS. It may be noted that one item, OR6, originally thought to be in the Ownership Role subscale, was found to be aligned with the Beneficiary Role subscale. So, OR6 is grouped with BR Subscale in the final scale.

SCALE RELIABILITY

Member Satisfaction Scale (MMS)

To test whether the scale is internally consistent, we calculated the coefficient alphas for the overall member satisfaction scale and its three subscales. Table 2 contains the various psychometric properties of the scales.

The composite MMS and its subscales except the ownership role subscale, achieve coefficient alpha values adequately greater than 0.7, indicative of good internal consistency (Nunnally, 1978). We would have liked a higher coefficient alpha value, at least 0.7, for the ownership role. However, we believe that a relatively larger sample would have achieved that.

The MMS achieves a coefficient of 0.87 and a value greater than 0.32 for inter-item correlations. Robinson, Shaver and Wrightsman (1991) consider a coefficient alpha greater than 0.8 and an average inter-correlation greater than 0.3 as exemplary.

Cognitive Trust of the Members of the Co-op Management

Hansen, Morrow and Batista (2002) have provided a comprehensive measure of Cognitive Trust of the Members of the Co-op Management. For the purpose of this research we have adopted their measure of Cognitive Trust for Co-operatives. The Scale achieved a Coefficient Alpha of 0.852 which is above the required minimum of 0.7.

Table 2: Reliability and other Psychometric Properties of MMS

Scale Item	*Mean*	*Standard Deviation*	*Standard Error*	*Corrected Item-Total Correlation*	*Alpha, if Item Deleted*	*Coefficient Alpha of Scale*
OR2	4.4757	0.95840	0.09443	0.396	0.435	0.556
OR3	4.0196	1.14348	1.14348	0.360	0.485	
OR4	4.7282	0.62926	0.06200	0.333	0.507	
OR8	4.5562	0.80690	0.07951	0.321	0.501	
CR2	4.6092	0.82059	0.08086	0.487	0.721	0.754
CR4	4.4292	0.97196	0.09577	0.528	0.709	
CR5	4.6639	0.70540	0.06951	0.543	0.714	
CR6	4.5187	0.75335	0.07423	0.494	0.722	
CR7	3.9682	1.22767	0.12097	0.455	0.743	
CR9	3.9459	1.03699	0.10218	0.543	0.705	
OR6	4.4222	0.75121	0.07402	0.597	0.861	0.873
BR1	3.8932	1.25957	0.12411	0.574	0.866	
BR2	3.8253	1.18643	0.11690	0.560	0.866	
BR3	4.7904	0.49334	0.04861	0.478	0.869	
BR4	4.5609	0.81475	0.8028	0.646	0.858	
BR5	4.2693	1.03142	0.10163	0.597	0.861	
BR8	4.6155	0.68552	0.06755	0.629	0.860	
BR9	4.5543	0.76996	0.07587	0.515	0.866	
BR10	4.3357	0.87396	0.08611	0.739	0.852	
BR12	4.6384	0.65419	0.06446	0.531	0.865	
BR13	4.6117	0.73074	0.07200	0.597	0.862	
BR15	4.4000	0.86850	0.86850	0.485	0.868	

Coefficient Alpha of MMS = 0.874.

SCALE VALIDITY

Validity cannot be measured directly but can be inferred from the behaviour of a measure's scores in some kind of a theoretically meaningful way.

Content Validity

Content Validity refers to the extent to which the items of a scale represent some theoretical domain of interest. The content validity of our scale is reflected in the quality of the procedures followed in developing the scale. At every stage of development, we systematically tried to build content validity by strictly adhering to the procedures prescribed in the literature on scale development (Churchill, 1979; Netemeyer, Bearden and Sharma, 2003). We requested 10 General Managers from various Urban Cooperative Banks to review our final list of scale items. They found the items quite relevant to and adequate for the construct.

Construct Validity

To collect evidence of construct validity, we analyzed the pattern of correlations between the member satisfaction scale and its three components. We had hypothesized that member satisfaction scale was a one-dimensional construct with three correlated components. The factor analysis with oblique rotation yielded the three factors solution, which supports our hypothesis. Refer to Table 3 for correlation between the factors.

Table 3: Factor Correlations

	MSS	*OR*	*CR*	*BR*
MSS	1.000			
OR	0.306	1.000		
CR	0.866**	0.283**	1.000	
BR	0.910**	0.062	0.652**	1.000

**Correlation is significant at the 0.01 level (2-tailed).

We had expected that each of the components will have significant loadings on the member satisfaction construct. The results in Table 3 show that two components have highly significant loading, above 0.8, and one slightly below the required 0.5 loading at 0.3 which indicates the existence of a higher order construct (Clark and Watson, 1995). The three components share significant correlations with each other, except for the ownership role and beneficiary role pair. In addition, the high values of corrected item-total correlations and coefficient alpha attained by the MSS (refer to Table 2) indicate convergent validity. Thus we find support for the hypnotized structure of the member satisfaction scale.

Nomological Validity

In a nomological validity test, a law-like relationship, derived from a certain theory, is put to test. A construct must fit into a relevant network of theoretically meaningful constructs, or nomological net, as referred to by Cronbach and Meehl (1955).

Nilsson, Kihlen and Norell (2009) have suggested a strong positive relationship between member satisfaction and member's trust in the board of directors and in the management. This is supported by an earlier research by Gray and Kraenzle (1998) who found that members' participation is positively correlated to a number of variables including satisfaction with the management. In Hansen, Morrow and Batista (2002) we find that there are two types of trust, cognitive trust and affective trust. Cognitive trust is indicated as that based on the individual's making judgment based on information stored from past experiences whereas affective trust is indicated as that based on one's feelings that reflect the individual's experience with the group and group members. It is shown that in co-ops that offer relatively more complex services, members have a strong incentive to rationally evaluate (cognitive) the skills and abilities of the management in carrying out those services. So, here, in urban cooperative banks, when we consider the trust, we mean the cognitive trust.

This relationship is tested by putting forward the following hypothesis:

1. Member Satisfaction is positively associated with cognitive trust of the members of the co-op management.

To establish nomological validity, our measure of member satisfaction must show a significant and positive association with the cognitive trust of the members of the co-op management. The result of the regression analysis, as given by Table 4, shows evidence of nomological validity for the MSS.

Table 4: Results of Regression Analysis

Independent Variable (X) = (Member Satisfaction)
Dependant Variable (Y) = (Cognitive trust of Cooperative Management)
Y = 2.988*** + 0.327*X
Standard Error = 0.69750
R Square = 0.048

*** Correlation is significant at the 0.001 level.

* Correlation is significant at 0.1 level.

The result shows the significant and positive association of member satisfaction with cognitive trust. The result provides evidence of the nomological validity of the scale.

FINDINGS AND CONCLUSION

The research aims to know whether member satisfaction can be scientifically measured and also how to measure it. The regular monitoring of Member Satisfaction Level according to a standard questionnaire with some key questions can bring to focus the unfulfilled needs of the members of UCB. It is hoped that this will lead UCBs to organizational success, which is genuinely aligned to both bank's financial performance and member satisfaction.

The main benefit visualized is a testing of a scientifically validated member satisfaction scale which can be applied for measuring the success of the organization. The basic premise here is that organizational performance should not be limited to the measurement of CAMELS rating. A scientifically validated scale can be effectively used to administer annual member satisfaction survey. RBI can better assess current bank performance including an assessment of the level of member satisfaction, predict in a better way future performance and also gain inputs to formulate future policy on Urban Cooperative Banks. Urban Cooperative Banks can self-monitor their cooperative goals in a meaningful manner and gain a better balance between economic and social goals. They can also more meaningfully work at improving the relationship between the members and the management. The members can express their satisfaction/ dissatisfaction in an effective way through these annual surveys. The government can Identify which all of the social responsibilities of the UCBs are fulfilled and intervene in a more meaningful manner in their functioning. The society stands to gain through the development of more trusting and reciprocating transactions among its members.

The main limitations and future research directions are as follows. First our ownership role subscale achieved only 0.556 coefficient alpha value whereas we would have liked it to reach 0.7. However developing a scale is a long and iterative process, and given the preliminary nature of the scale, we consider it adequate. We believe that a larger sample and a confirmatory scale analysis would achieve the required coefficient alpha value for the subscale. Second, we covered only the seven southern districts of Kerala. It is because, an exhaustive coverage of all the 60 urban cooperative banks of Kerala, licensed by the Reserve Bank of India, would have been impossible under the time and resource constraints we had. However, the seven districts, we consider, were sufficiently divergent and representative of the state.

Future researchers may test the validity of the scale for Primary Agricultural Credit Societies, the main rural banks of India with primary membership. Researchers may also test empirically if there is any significant relationship between member satisfaction and organizational success.

REFERENCES

Barton, D. (1989). What is a Cooperative? *Cooperatives in Agriculture,* Prentice-Hall, Englewood Cliffs.

Berrone, P., Surroca J. and Tribo J.A. (2007). Corporate Ethical Identity as a determinant of Firm performance: A test of the mediating role of Stakeholder Satisfaction, *Journal of Business Ethics,* Springer, Vol. 76(1), 35–53.

Bhuyan, Sanjib (2007). The "People" factor in Cooperatives: an analysis of Members' attitudes and behavior, *Canadian Journal of Agricultural Economics,* Vol. 55, 275–298.

Churchill, G. (1979). A Paradigm for developing better Measures of Marketing Concepts, *Journal of Marketing Research,* Vol. 16(16), 64–73.

Clark, L. and Watson, D. (1995). Constructing Validity: Basic Issues in Objective Scale Development, *Psychological Assessment,* Vol. 7(3), 309–319.

Conway, J. and Huffcutt, A. (2003). A review and Evaluation of Exploratory Factor Analysis: Practices in Organizational Research, *Organizational Research Methods,* Vol. 6(2) 147–168.

Cronbach, L. and Meehl, P. (1955). Construct Validity in Psychological Tests, *Psychological Bulletin,* Vol. 52(4), 281–302.

Dakurah, Henry A., Goddard, E. and Osuteye, N. (2005). Attitudes towards and satisfaction with Credit Unions in Alberta. A regression and Scale Analysis, Draft *Paper presented at Canadian Agricultural Economics Association Annual Meeting*, San Francisco, CA.

Donaldson, Thomas and Preston Lee, E. (1995). The Stakeholder theory of the Corporation: Concepts, Evidence, and Implications, *Academy of Management Review,* Vol. 20(1), 65–91.

Fornell, C., Johnson, M.D., Anderson, E.W., Cha, J. and Bryant, B.E. (1996). The American Customer Satisfaction Index: Nature, Purpose, and Findings, *Journal of Marketing,* Vol. 60(4), 7–18.

Gray, T.W. and Kraenzle, C.A. (1998). Member Participation in Agricultural Cooperatives: A regression and Scale Analysis, *RBS Research Report 165,* Washington DC: US Department of Agriculture, Rural Business-Cooperative Service.

Hansen, M.H., Morrow, J.L. and Batista, J.C. (2002). The impact of Trust on Cooperative Membership retention, Performance and Satisfaction: an exploratory study, *International Food and Agribusiness Management Review,* Vol. 5, 41–59.

Heneman, H. (1974). Comparisons of Self and Superior Ratings of Managerial Performance, *Journal of Applied Psychology,* Vol. 59(5), 638–642.

ICA Cooperative Congress Report, 1966.

Madhav Rao Committee Report, 1999.

Netemeyer, R., Bearden, W. and Sharma, S. (2003). Scaling Procedures: Issues and Applications, *Thousand Oaks: Sage Publications.*

Nilsson, J., Kihlen, A. and Norell, L. (2009). Are traditional Cooperatives an endangered species? About shrinking Satisfaction, Involvement and Trust, *International Food and Agribusiness Management Review,* Vol. 12(4), 103–123.

Nunnally, J. (1978). Psychometric Theory, 2nd ed., *New York: McGraw-Hill.*

Podsakoff, P., MacKenzie, S., Lee, J. and Podsakoff, N. (2003). Common Method Biases in Behavioral Research: A Critical Review of the Literature and Recommended Remedies, *Journal of Applied Psychology,* Vol. 88 (5), 879–903.

Report of the Working Committee on the Rating system for Urban Cooperative Banks, Reserve Bank of India (2002).

Robinson, J., Shaver, P. and Wrightsman, L. (1991). Criteria for Scale Selection and Evaluation, ed., Measure of Personality and social Psychological Attitudes*, San Diego, CA: Academic Press.*

Roth, P., Switzer, F. and Switzer, D. (1999). Missing Data in Multiple Item Scales: A Monte Carlo Analysis of Missing Data Techniques, *Organizational Research Methods,* Vol. 2(3), 211–232.

Role of CRM in Banks

R.C. Bhatnagar and Rajesh Verma

Amity School of Insurance, Banking and Actuarial Science, Amity University, U.P

ABSTRACT: *Today's customers buying decisions are not based simply on the quality of the product alone but with the service relationship they expect post sales from the company. Banking industry has gone through many changes, Private Organization to Nationalization and now new Generation Banks joining hands with the entry of more International players. All would be accepting Deposits and giving Advances and rendering services to a larger and ever growing number of clients with an ever expanding Basket of Products. .Globalization and Technology innovations are going to open new vistas albeit with more competition. In this new era companies including Banks are focusing on managing Customer Relationships in order to efficiently maximize Revenues. Today marketing is not just Developing, Delivering and Selling; it is actually Developing and Maintaining Long Term Relationships with customers which will come with good CRM. Relationship marketing is becoming more and more important in BFSI. Business Managers need to look at areas where opportunities lie, because industry consolidation, virtual delivery channels and thė ability to move money around with a click of a mouse are making it easier for customers to switch banks, added to this is the possibility of Account Portability, In this situation Customer Relationship Management (CRM) is the key to success for developing business in Banks.*

Keywords: Relationship Marketing, CRM, Role and Importance of CRM in Retaining Customers and Maximizing Revenues.

> *"You cannot tailor-make the situations in life but you can tailor-make the attitudes to fit those situations."*
>
> —***Zig Ziglar***

INTRODUCTION

The new millennium has exposed the entire Banking System to new challenges of Competition and Struggle for survival. The era of liberalization, deregulation, globalization and privatization has let loose a close race for internecine competition in the banking industry. In India, the wave starting from deregulation in early 1990s has created heightened competition and greater challenges for banks and other financial intermediaries. The cross-border flows and entry of new players and products have forced banks to adjust the product-mix and undertake rapid changes in their processes and operations to remain competitive. The deepening of technology has facilitated better tracking and fulfillment of commitments, provided multiple delivery channels for customers and faster resolution of miscoordinations. Unlike in the past, the banks today are both, market driven and market responsive. One of the major concerns of every bank's CEO is how to increase or at least maintain the market share in every line of business against the backdrop of heightened competition. With the entry of new players and multiple channels, customers (both Corporate and Retail) have become more discerning and less "loyal" to banks. This makes it imperative that banks provide best possible products and services to ensure Customer Delight. To address the challenge of retention of customers, there have been active efforts in the banking circles to switch over to customer-centric business model. The success of such a model depends upon the approach adopted by banks with respect to customer data management and customer relationship management.

Over the years, Indian banks have expanded in large geographic and functional areas to meet the developmental needs both in India and abroad. They have been procuring and managing a world of information about customers—their profiles, location, and personal details etc.

They have to have a close relationship with their customers with good knowledge of their needs, requirements and cash positions. Though this offers them a unique advantage, they face a fundamental challenge i.e during the initial period of planned economic development; the bank products were bought in India and not sold.

What our banks, especially those in the public sector lack are the marketing attitude. Marketing is a customer-oriented operation. What is needed is the effort on their part to improve their service image and exploit their large customer information data base effectively to communicate product availability. Achieving high revenue requires leveraging of existing customer database to gain a deeper insight into the relationship the customers have with the institution, and improving customer service-related processes so that the services are quick, error free and convenient for the customers. Customers have become demanding and loyalties are becoming diffused. There are multiple choices, the market share per bank has reduced with demand for flexibility and customization. Customer retention calls for Customized and hassle free, flawless service delivery. Furthermore, banks need to have very strong in-house research and market intelligence units in order to face the future challenges of competition, especially customer retention. Only this is likely to help Banks to achieve higher revenue with improved loyalty; Marketing is a question of demand (customers) and supply (financial products and services, customer services through various delivery channels). Both demand and supply have to be understood in the context of geographic locations and competitor analysis to undertake focused marketing (advertising) efforts. Focusing on region-specific campaigns rather than national media campaigns would be a better strategy for a diverse country like India, and CRM is an effective tool for this. It costs 6 times more to attract a new customer than it does to keep an old one. According to Market Line Associates, the top 20% of typical bank customers produce as much as 50% of overall profits, while the bottom 20% drain about 50% from bank's bottom line and the revenues from the rest just meeting their expenses. In another study by BCG, it is reported that 20% of a bank's customers account for 80% of the business and the other 80% account for the balance 20% of the business. The buzz words are CAPTURE and RETAIN !

CUSTOMER RELATIONSHIP MANAGEMENT: THE CONCEPT

Customer Relationship Management is the establishment, development, maintenance and optimization of long-term mutually valuable relationships between consumers and the organizations. Successful customer relationship management focuses on understanding the needs and desires of the customers and is achieved by placing these needs at the heart of the business by integrating them with the organization's strategy, people, technology and business processes. Data warehousing and Data mining are the two important tools to start the CRM in Banks. CRM should also be used for customer education in the form of seminars, meetings, demonstrations, group interaction, electronic mails and provision of literature on line. The process of customer education should be institutionalized in every bank.

THE EMERGING OPPORTUNITIES FOR INDIAN BANKS

In 2008, India crossed the twin landmarks of a trillion dollar GDP and $1000 per capita income. While it took 60 years after independence to cross the first trillion dollar of GDP, the next trillion is likely to be crossed by 2012 and double again to 4 trillion in the next 4–5 years. Following factors will be driving the change over next two decades:

1. Ours is a young country and will see a sharp rise in its working age population
2. More Indians will get rich within one generation.

According to McKinsey, India will witness a rapid growth of its middle class with a disposable income from 20 to 90,000 rupees a year from about 50 million at present(5% of the population) to about 583 million(41% of the population) by 2025. This large workforce will drive consumption and investment demand in the economy. The demand for financial services will increase and the Banking and Financial Sector will have a key role in intermediating Savings and Investments from large number growing incomes which will fuel growth.

BCG has also pointed out large number of opportunities in Banking Sector:

1. The total mortgages in the books of banks have grown from 1.5 % to 10% of total Bank advances. The ratio of total mortgages outstanding to the GDP is expected to reach 20% by 2020. The outstanding mortgages are expected to cross INR 40 trillion by 2020 from the present level of INR 4.9 trillion. This will be higher than the entire loan book of the Banking Industry placed at INR 30 trillion in 2009.
2. By 2020 the top 5% households residing in metros and Tier I cities will account for 30% of the total disposable income. These people will ask for Wealth Management advisors.
3. The middle class those with annual household income of INR 90,000 TO INR 200,000 per annum will be the single largest group of customers. Banks will need low cost business models, smaller cost effective branches and extensive use of technology to service their needs.
4. There will be a requirement of 40000–50000 additional branches and 160,000 to 190,000 ATMs in the coming years.
5. Banks will have to encourage the use of alternate channels. Presently only 9% of consumers use Internet and Call Centers for accessing Banking Services compared to 63% in USA. Deutsche Bank has assessed that by 2020, 60% of the European Union will migrate to Online Banking. In India presently Internet and Mobile Banking is low but it will get revolutionized over the next few years. Even if 25–30% of mobile users with activated 3G/GPRS start using Mobile Money and Wallet etc, it would mean 250–300 million new customers for the banking industry .
6. Banks in India offer on an average 2.2 products per customer which is significantly low compared to the global benchmark of 6 products per customer.
7. Financial Inclusion will bring the banking habits within the reach of larger percentage of population.
8. Customer diversity and individualism will pervade their buying behavior.
9. Youthful customers are restless, technology savvy; believe in researching and negotiating for the best deals.
10. Long established life patterns on jobs, marriage and the social Value systems are changing fast.
11. Loyalty is likely to be at a discount for the service providers including banks.

In such a scenario customers decisions are going to be more complex and demanding. They will expect and demand low prices basic services but will be ready to pay more for Customized Products and services.

ROLE OF CRM IN BANKS

At the heart of a perfect CRM strategy is the creation of mutual values for all the parties involved in the business process. It is about creating a sustainable competitive advantage by being the best at Understanding, Developing, Communicating, and Delivering to the existing customer relationships, in addition to creating and keeping new customers. So the concept of product life cycle is giving way to the concept of customer life cycle focusing on the development of products and services that anticipate the future need of the existing customers and creating additional services that extend existing customer relationships beyond transactions. CRM is a comprehensive approach for creating, maintaining and expanding customer relationship. It provides seamless co-ordination between customer service, marketing, information technology and other customer related functions. It integrates people, process and technology to maximize relationships with all the customers. It does not aim to build closer relationship with all customers, but it recommends that organizations take initiative to identify the most valuable customers by looking for their life time value. CRM means building an interdependent relationship with the customer in whom each relies on the other for business solutions and successes. From the Bank's point of view, it is the management process or approach of acquiring, retaining and growing with the customers. Bank of India's "Relationship Beyond Banking..." says it all beautifully.

THE INDIAN BANKING SECTOR AND CRM

The economic reforms initiated by the Government of India roughly about a decade ago have changed the landscape of several sectors of the Indian economy. The Indian banking sector is no exception. The economic reforms have also generated new and powerful customers (huge Indian middle class) and new mix of players (public sector units, private banks, and foreign banks). The emerging competition has generated new expectations from the existing and the new customers. The new rules of competition require recognition of the importance of consumers and the necessity to address the needs through innovative products supported by new technology. Perceptions and expectations of the customers have undergone a sea change, with the innovative and modern banking services offered to the customers.

This necessitates banks to include a customer-oriented approach whereby they build, maintain and manage longstanding relationships with their profitable customers in order to gain sustainable competitive edge.

NEED OF CRM IN THE BANKING INDUSTRY

A Relationship-based Marketing approach has the following benefits.

Over time, retail bank customers tend to increase their holding of the other products from across the range of financial products/services available.

Long-term Customers are More Likely to Become a Referral Source

The longer a relationship continues; the better a bank can understand the customer and his/her needs and preferences, and so greater the opportunity to tailor products and services and cross-sell the product/service range.

Customers in long-term relationships are more comfortable with the service, the organization, methods and procedures. This helps reduce operating cost and costs arising out of customer errors.

Intense Competition

There is intense competition among the Private Sector Banks, Public Sector Banks and Foreign Banks and they are all taking steps to attract and retain the customers. New technologies, research facilities, globalization of services, the flood of new products and the concept of all the facilities under one roof to provide better customer service leading to customer delight.

Well Informed Customers

The Customers in Banking Industry today are well informed. With the introduction of new technology, the world has shrunk. Thus, if a Bank wants to have more customers, it must develop a good sustainable relationship with its present customers and try to nurture the same in the future, generation after generation.

Decline in Brand Loyalty

In the present scenario, brand loyalty is on decline. The customers are switching over to avail the better facilities from other banks. Newer and Superior Products and Services are being introduced continuously in the financial market. Thus, the banks need to upgrade their products, achieve Customer Delight and create bonds of Trust through empathy and care for customer needs and regular communications. With the help of CRM, strong customer loyalty and a good image for the organization can be developed.

Improved Customer Retention

In the intensely competitive banking industry, retention of existing customers is vital, which can be achieved through the process of CRM.

With increased number of banks, products and services and practically nil switching costs, customers are switching banks whenever they find better services and products. Banks are finding it tough to get new customers, and more importantly, retain existing customers.

According to a research by Reichheld and Sasser in the Harvard Business Review, 5% increase in customer retention can increase profitability by 35% in banking business, 50% in insurance and brokerage, and 125% in the consumer credit card market. Therefore, banks are now stressing on retaining customers and increasing market share. According to the research conducted by Technical Assistance Research Project (TARP) in Washington D.C. in late 1980s, "It Costs Five Times More to Acquire a Customer than to retain a Customer".

In other words the emerging opportunities and the need for a strong CRM approach are already felt by the banks in India since last 2–3 years. A search is already on for a comprehensive solution that can convert the ever growing amount of available data into useful and actionable Business Opportunities since this goldmine of information if used effectively can be a good source of new business growth and additional revenues for the banks. Moreover the quantity and quality of Data that Banks are able to gather about the customers has increased and improved dramatically thanks to technology. Greater automations in Banking Processes, an increase in points of data capture and more customer transactions undertaken via service channels have enriched the same.

THE WAY FORWARD

Data warehousing and Data mining with the help of strong CRM software will provide the edge to banks in their efforts to gain a higher market share of customers and retain them. An analysis of the available data on the following lines will help the banks in better strategy planning both for acquisition and retention of customers:

- Profile, taste and preferences, attitude of the customer and purchasing behavior since he started dealing with the Banks (Useful for Cross sale of the products and services)
- What transactions does a customer do before shifting to a competitor (for better retention of customers?)
- Which products are often purchased together by the customers of which particular profile (to improve target marketing?)
- What patterns in Credit transactions lead to frauds ?(to detect and deter frauds as part of effective preventive vigilance)
- What is the profile of a high risk borrower?(to prevent defaults and bad loans for better NPA management)
- What services and benefits would current customers desire? (to increase customer retention and loyalty)
- Who are the customers getting what type of services ?(to identify opportunities for cross sell) in Credit transactions
- Who are the customers who are availing limited services specially the Online products? (to improve the percentage of such customers in the total customers)

- Which geographical areas have potential for which particular products? (to innovate and improve the basket of products)
- Study the expectations of the customers (to help innovate products, processes and procedures to raise the level of customer satisfaction and achieve CUSTOMER DELIGHT!).

CONCLUSION

CRM in banking industry entirely differs from other sectors, because banking industry is purely related to financial services, which needs to create the trust among the people. Establishing customer care support during on and off official hours, making timely information about interest payments, maturity of time deposit, issuing credit and debit cum ATM card, creating awareness regarding online and e-banking, adopting mobile request etc are required to nurture a long lasting relationship with customers. The CRM broadly means capture and retention of customers. However, the two things that would make a difference for a bank, so far as he clients go, would be (i) the innovation in products which invariably would have to anticipate the needs of the people, and (ii) the attitude of the banks employees towards clients only a few of whom will be net high worth.

Also, appropriately a discussion of the issues in CRM has to be situated in the context of the country under consideration. Requirements of a country like Sweden which is socially homogeneous and has by and large relatively small variations of income will be very different from a country of wide variety of every conceivable kind. This in our context would include two things: (i) a closer understanding of the people to be served—besides region specific demographic factors like needs and preferences of the people, this would include income distribution in the society; (ii) A survey of all kinds of banking services that have made their way to the region. This is necessary to take a measure of the competition besides the tasks that remain to be taken up. This would mean not only the mix of public sector, private sector and foreign banks, but a whole host of others e.g. cooperative banks, rural banks, sector-specific banks, micro-loan facilities and other formal and informal avenues to meet financial needs of the people. Clearly a society as diverse and iniquitous as India would have to be imaginatively segmented for anticipation of needs of customers and for devising solutions to meet them The task becomes highly complex when one considers that probably 50% of the population is out side the pale of market economy and another thirty percent may be hard stretched to make the two ends meet. Another 15% would be accounted for in the ₹ 50,000 to 5, 00,000 pa category. The banks have to decide which segment(s) they would like to serve. Would they like to confine themselves to the customary top 5% of the pyramid or they could spot gold in the middle and the bottom of the pile and devise ways to mine it. Identifying the target segment(s) makes thing much easier. Public sector banks are in an unenviable position here as they have to cater to most segments according to what the government dictates; they would, by their nature, continue to tormented between conflicting demands and obligations.

For reorienting an institution for service and efficiency, one needs—besides clarity of objectives, and efficient systems and procedures—effective training on two fronts: (a) inculcating a genuine, helpful service-attitude in the employees and officers; (b) training of customers including guidance at the premises of the bank itself. While reorientation training for employees have been taken up routinely, often through short-term programmes, it is not clear if it is followed to monitor effectiveness of such programmes in changing the attitudes of employees at different levels. Speaking of the public sector banks which cater to an overwhelmingly large number of common people, it is felt that though there is an improvement in the in the general attitude of the people in the bank's employ, it is evident to a more marked degree at the officers level than in the behavior of persons at the counter. This would point to the need of a more sincere and effective way to gauge consumer satisfaction.

Which takes one to a greater need for research in Indian banking industry—about demographic variations, about customer preferences, about limitations the customers face, about the fluid policy framework and its impact on customer behaviour, *et al.* and generating Indian data and Indian solutions. Basing discussion of Indian scene on the data from the US or the European societies and markets could not be of much use in the Indian context.

The present day CRM also includes developing customer base. The bank has to pay adequate attention to increase customer base by all means. It is possible if the Customer Service is at a satisfactory level, the existing clients can recommend others to have banking connection with the bank he is operating with. Hence asking reference from the existing customers can develop their client base. A satisfied customer works wonders for getting more and more clients. He is the true brand ambassador for every institution. Thus the customer base gets increased with the help of marketing and referrals. Further if these improved numbers of customers are served with a SMILE backed by a 24x7 Customer Care support System, the profitability is bound to increase. Hence the banks have to innovative and implement CRM practices to CAPUTURE and RETAIN the customers. One must remember that the adoption of most advanced software on CRM will deliver only if it is backed by a committed and passionate human ware to capture and retain the customer who truly is the purpose of any business.

There has been a shift from bank centric activities to customer centric activities for marketing of products and services. The private sector banks in India deployed many innovative strategies to attract new customers and to retain existing customers. CRM in public sector is still in evolutionary stage. They have also started taking ideas from customers to improve their services and empower the customers in many ways. The use of CRM in banking has gained importance with the aggressive strategies for customer acquisition and retention being employed by the bank in today's competitive milieu. This has resulted in the adoption of various CRM initiatives by the banks.

Recent initiatives like establishing Future Branches, Loan Factory, Branches for Gen-next, Retail Banking Outlets, opening of Ultra Small Branches in remote areas, providing road side Service Kiosks and offerings to open accounts online etc are just the beginning of a new era in the Indian Banking, a result of CRM studies in Public and Private sector banks . Few days back a Public Sector Bank announced starting a Product Innovation Cell (Agriculture). Objectives are to improve its market share in these products and finance the progressive farmers under Investment credit. It won't be surprising if banks open self service branches in foreseeable future where drafts or Letters of Credit are generated by the customers themselves On line (like generating a boarding pass on the airport) with digitalized signatures !!!

Thus it can be seen that implementation of CRM will only help Banks to increase their sales effectiveness, help enhance customer satisfaction, enhance customer retention, streamline Business Systems and Procedures identify and resolve bottlenecks, all directly contributing to increased revenues.

But one must remember that CRM is not software, it is a business philosophy, and it is a strategy. In brief it is strategy software which is going to be the way of life in Banking Sector over the next few years. In the words of Mahatma Gandhi:

> *"Consciously or unconsciously, every one of us does offer some service or another. If we cultivate the habit of doing this service deliberately, our desire for service will steadily grow stronger, and it will make not only for our own happiness, but that of the world at large. ...."*

REFERENCES

Blattberg, R.C. and Deighton, J. (1996). Managing marketing by the customer equity criterion. *Harvard Business Review*, Jul–Aug, 74, 136– 44.

Berry, Leonard (1995). Relationship marketing of services-growing interest, emerging perspectives. *Journal of the Academy of Marketing Science*, 23(4), 236–245.

Cronbach, L.J. (1951). Coefficient alpha and the internal structures of tests. *Psychometrika*, 16(3), 297–333.

Crosby, L. and Johnson, S. (2004). The three Ms of customer loyalty. Marketing Management, July/August, 12–13.

Dick, A.S. and Basu, K. (1994). Customer loyalty: Toward an integrated conceptual framework. *Journal of the Academy of Marketing Science,* 22 (Spring), 99–113.

Dwyer, F.R., Paul H.S. and Sejo, Oh. (1987). Developing buyer-seller relationships. Journal of Marketing, 51, 11–27.

Dyche, J. (2001). The CRM handbook: A business guide to customer relationship management. Addison-Wesley Pub Co. Fallat, F., and Ancarali, F. (2008). Yield management, dynamic pricing and CRM in telecommunications. *Journal of Service Marketing*, 22, 465–478.

Finnegan, D., and Willcocks, L. (2007). Implementing CRM: From technology to knowledge. Chichester, West-Sussex: John Wiley and Sons.

Gustafsson, A., Johnson, M. and Roos, I. (2005). The effects of customer satisfaction, relationship commitment dimensions, and triggers on customer retention. Journal of Marketing, 69, 2–10.

Chen, I.J. and Popovich, K. (2003). Understanding customer relationship management (CRM): People, process and technology. *Business Process Management Journal*, 9, 672–688.

Jain, A.K., Pinson, C. and Malhotra, N.K. (1987). Customer loyalty as a construct in the marketing of banking services. *International Journal of Bank Marketing,* 5(3), 49–72.

Kumar, V. and Reinartz, W. (2006). Customer relationship management: A database approach. NewYork: John Wiley and Sons Inc.

Majumdar, A. (2005). A model for customer loyalty for retail stores inside shopping malls—An Indian perspective. *Journal of Services Research,*Special Issue, December, 47–64.

Zineldin, M. (2006). The royalty of loyalty: CRM, quality and retention. Journal of Consumer Marketing, 23, 430–437.

Rangarajan, C., The Indian Banking System-Challenges Ahead, Bancon, November 2011, Chennai, BCG report on "Indian Banking 2020" September 2010.

http://www.crmnext.com/us/academy/crmchallenges.pdf

Chakarborty, K.C., "Why it is a Defining Decade for Indian Banking" Bancon, November 2011, Chennai.

CRM in Banking: Issues and Challenges

Sarita Bhatnagar

*National Institute of Bank Management, NIBM, NIBM Campus
Kondhwe Khurd, Pune*

ABSTRACT: *Bank Marketing has evolved from Transactional to Relationship Marketing. Customer acquisition, customer satisfaction, customer retention, all is acquiring the focal point of planning and marketing strategies in Banking. Enabled by CBS and operating in a multichannel, hi-tech environment many Indian Banks have adopted the concept of Customer Relationship Management with intent to generate better understanding of the customer and maintain long term mutually beneficial relationship with the customer. CRM is a strategic initiative which has organization wide implications. In Indian Banking sector CRM is still at a nascent stage. Avery small proportion of its potential has been utilized. Also implementation wise it has been implemented on a limited scale. The paper proposes to analyze the issues and challenges pertaining to the CRM in Indian Banking Sector. Although the CRM software may be owned and customer centric initiatives be communicated, the successful implementation seems to be a scenario not evident in near future in most Banks. Implementation rests on four pillars of People, Process, Data and Technology. A coordination of all these and transformation to CRM System is a huge Challenge and encompasses multidimensional problems. An overview of these problems and issues will be provided and analyzed.*

INTRODUCTION

A global survey conducted by the IBM Institute for Business and Value and part of IBM Business Consulting Service's three part series "Doing CRM Right" claims that only 15% of current CRM projects are fully successful, but that the success rate can be improved to as high as 80% through proper business process methodology and prioritization. One of the main reasons for CRM failure is the lack of understanding about the true meaning and implication of practices for managing relationships with customers.

Deloitte Consulting found that 70% firms found little or no improvement through CRM implementation. The reasons are many: The CRM system was poorly designed, it became too expensive, users didn't make much use of it or report much benefit, and collaborators ignored the system.

Indian banking system is witnessing the adoption of CRM Systems for greater competitiveness. Although the type and range of CRM enabling technologies differ from Bank to Bank, the ultimate goal is higher customer focus. Technology has successfully initiated this journey towards customer centricity, but there are large number of issues and challenges to adoption and implementation of CRM. The true potential of CRM still remains to be explored in its true sense. The paper attempts to identify these issues in the light of information about how CRM has been utilized by some leading players in International and National Banking Scenario.

CRM DEFINED

CRM is a sound business strategy to identify the Bank's most profitable customers and prospects, and devotes time and attention to expanding account relationships with those customers through individualised marketing, repricing, discretionary decision making and customised service – all delivered through various sales channels that the bank uses.

CRM is the practice of analysing and utilising marketing databases and leveraging commmunication technologies to determine corporate practices and methods that will maximize the lifetime value of each individual customer to the firm (Kumar and Reinartz, 2006).

> *"CRM is a comprehensive strategy and process of acquiring, retaining and partnering with selective customers to create superior value for company and the customer."*
>
> **—*Jagdish Sheth and Atul Parvatiyar***

Paul Greenberg, the Author of CRM at the Speed of Light, has his own classic definition about CRM:

> *"CRM is philosophy and a business strategy, supported by a system and a technology, designed to improve human interactions in a business environment. It is also a continuing business initiative that demands a dynamic, ongoing strategy of customer engagement".*

Whilst Scott Hornstein, the Principal of Hornstein Associates, defines CRM as:

> *"CRM is the delivery of customer care as a strategic product, with measurement and reward focused on generating happier customers that stay longer and buy more".*

- *From a strategic standpoint*, CRM mobilizes resources around customer relationships rather than product groups and fosters activities that maximize the value of lifetime relationships.

- *From an operational standpoint,* CRM links business processes across the supply chain from back-office functions through all customer contact channels ("touch points"), enabling continuity and consistency across a customer relationship.
- *From an analytical standpoint,* CRM provides a host of resources that enable banks to fully understand customer segments, assess and maximize lifetime value of each customer, model "what-if" scenarios, predict customer behaviors, and design and track effective marketing campaigns.

CRM: Pay Offs to Banks

- Restoring the personal-service connotation that was previously removed.
- Fostering greater long-term loyalty through relationship building.
- Maximizing lifetime value of each customer through cross-selling.
- Enabling immediate action to retain the most valuable customers.
- Identifying high-risk customers and adjusting service accordingly.
- Enabling the bank to fulfill customer needs at the right time with the right offer.
- Increasing the rate of return on marketing initiatives.
- Efficient fraud detection.

Review of Literature

Berry (1983) recommended the following five strategies for practicing relationship marketing:

1. Developing a core service around which to build a customer relationship,
2. Customizing the relationship to the individual customer,
3. Augmenting the core service with extra benefits,
4. Pricing services to encourage customer loyalty,
5. Marketing to employees so that they will perform well for customers.

Gartner's Research shows that less than10% of Banks have a single integrated view of their customers and those that do are just beginning to leverage their investments to improve customer loyalty and profitability. Payne's[1] study summarises the barriers to CRM implementation as: Lack of skills; Poor Data quality; Failure to understand the business benefits; Functional Boundaries; Lack of leadership and management involvement; and inadequate measurement systems.

Several authors (Boulding, Staelin, Ehretand Johnson, 2005; Newwell, 2003; Ngai, 2005; Payne, 2006) point out some problems that lead to CRM failure such as: Lack of skills in

[1]Roy, S.K. (2008). ICFAI Journal of Management Research, Vol. 7.

building and using the new IT based CRM systems; Inadequate investments, as many projects dramatically exceed their planned cost and sometimes even their scope; poor data quality and quantity, mainly for companies that are at early stage of CRM development; Lack of leadership and top management involvement; inadequate measurement systems (sometimes organizations do not exactly know what they want from a CRM operation); cultural problems; alignment of organisational vision, mission, technology and goals is an important CRM adoption issue; employee resistance to CRM.

Wharton's George Day concludes that one of the reasons many CRM failures occurs is that companies concentrate on customer contact processes without making corresponding changes in internal structures and systems.

Mishra H. in IBA special Report on 'Operational Business Intelligence in Banking' Nov 2007 notes that information needs of banking are unique. There is a large variety of Banking services and this variety has given rise to multiplicity of technology solutions in banking. No single software solution today can satisfy even the transaction processing requirements of a large bank. Ramchandra SJ suggests CRM implementation requires revolutionary changes in the entire organization, top management support and long term view.

Managing individual customer relationships has a profound effect on enhancing long-term customer loyalty, thereby increasing the enterprise's long-term profitability. Relationship strategies, for example, have a substantial effect on customer retention in the financial services sector. A study conducted in 2000 by Peppers and Rogers Group (with Roper Starch Worldwide) found that only 1 percent of consumers who rate their financial services provider high on relationship management say they are likely to switch away products. One-fourth of consumers (26 percent) who rate their primary financial services provider as low on rclationship management attributes say they are likely to switch away one or more products during the next 12 months. The financial implications of these findings are staggering using a conservative average annual profitability per household for U.S. retail banks of $100, a reduction in attrition of 9 percentage points by providing excellent customer relationship management (e.g., recognizing returning customers, anticipating their needs, etc.), that institution with an average household profitability of $500, the increase in profitability climbs to $900,000.

CRM: Global Scenario

Wachovia Bank

Wachovia Bank uses customer transaction data to support modeling processes that evaluates each branch's current and long term profitability. In Atanta, Bank's largest market, significant performance improvements were attained when it used the outputs of modeling process as a basis to decide which of its 96 branches to close and which location to open new ones.

Royal Bank of Canada

RBC is Considered Canada's largest bank when measured in terms of assets and market capitalization with $270 Billion in assets, 23 Million retail accounts, 700 Products, 58,000 Employees and 10 Million personal, commercial, corporate, and public sector customers served in North America and much of the world. RBC Royal Bank (personal and commercial retail banking) comprised of 1,300 branches, 4,800 ABM's, 87,250 proprietary POS terminals, 900+ mobile sales staff, 1.4 million online banking customers and 2 million telephone banking customers with 300 offices in 30 countries

RBC developed superior computing and database power, along with sophisticated statistical programs, to analyze customer information and test specific actions it should take with specific customers. Once profitability and lifetime value was determined, these measures were included when determining customer decisions. For RBC this meant: Customized Marketing Campaign, Establishing Service Levels, and Product Design and Pricing.Customer profitability was a determinant used for segmenting and targeting.The CRM system used customer profitability and future potential calculations to give pricing parameters to account managers to determine how to price products depending on the customer. RBC also determined a set of customer treatment strategies using the customer segment categories. A customer's category would determine the length of wait and type of customer service representative the customer talks to. To learn the most about its customers, RBC has undertaken an intense ongoing statistical analysis of them. It is developing and refining the prototype for an algorithm to model the long-term lifetime values of its individual customers. Part of this effort includes a "client potential" model that measures how "growable" certain kinds of customers are to the bank. It also analyzes a customer's vulnerability to attrition and tries to flag the most vulnerable before they defect, in order to take preventive action in a focused effective way.

BNP Paribas

BNP Paribas became one of world's most admired Banking brands, leader in European Financial Services Sector which operates in more than 85 countries and over 100,000 employees. The business challenges were:

Restructuring its services around customers to achieve ever-increasing satisfaction levels and to create a fully integrated customer experience across all channels, using technology fusion as the foundation for future success and enhanced revenue streams, CRM enabled integrated multichannel retail banking platform providing consistent customer interactions across channels. It enabled Back office process engineering. Also Integration of Banks database of 6 million retail clients was done, with daily reporting of events leading to daily updation of customer profiles. Results were that: More than 300 million discrete customer contacts, Management of 4.3 billion individual transactions, peaking at 800 per second, over a single infrastructure, Improvement in customer service, Customer relationship centers handling more than 2 million calls and 3.7 million appointments booked by electronic appointment system.

Wells Fargo

Wells Fargo is one of the largest Internet Banking entities in the world. It is recognized as industry leader in US for alternative delivery strategies of banking Services

The goal of CRM is providing "Every channel our customers want, every product our customers need, anytime our customers choose". The focus is on Innovation efforts in customized service, speed and Convenience. One of its main concerns is that of servicing its high net worth customers by better integration of customer information and service applications and to assist representatives of customer sales and services to easily provide a one – stop – shop for any banking service or transaction.

Capital One

Capital One is reaping the rewards of full-fledged Customer Value Management. It uses customer value in its segmentation process as well as its behavioral indicators, offering open data access to its front line with a uniform and holistic view of its customer data. Capital one was also one of the first players in the industry to conduct offer prioritization based on expected increase in customer value (across value drivers), using propensity models for cross-selling to maximize the value of customers it had acquired. It also analyzes client purchase patterns and dates to infer its risk and propensity to buy specific products. As a result, it is able to target tailored customer offers (over 3,000 credit card variations) to over 100,000 segments. It also conducts highly flexible test-and-learn campaigns at a rate of more than 65,000 tests a year. These efforts are given top-priority support by the organization via elements such as a unique relational database management system, specific customer acquisition targets for employees at all levels, and an extra bonus to staff who sell higher-yielding products.

CRM: Indian Scenario

YES Bank

Yes Bank adopted Collaborative CRM which has two logical separation models: a pre-acquisition and a post-acquisition service cycle for customers. The customer information captured in the YCCRM is mapped to blog-like entries made by employees. These entries include ideas, suggestions and perceptions of the sales representatives. The sales and product teams can then analyze this information and figure out related business opportunities. Such information can also be leveraged to customize existing products or conceive new products altogether. Through YCCRM, officers are provided with a template where they can fill details (other than the standard keywords) noted during their interaction with the customer. Typically, sales staff interacts with customers over the phone, jotting down the most important parts of their conversation on little pieces of paper. This information is filled on a separate form. Sales representatives can now upload or download scribbled information from their phones to the main CRM System. As a sales representative, part of the job includes being constantly on the field, which leaves them little time to fill in their reports. As a result, it is not always possible to feed detail of their interaction with customers on the day they meet them. YCCRM provides an additional tab of source date (the date mentioned as the source date) when they meet the customer and the system date when it is registered in the system .The integrated and personalized dashboard with an activities planner enables the smooth functioning of a sales representative. And its social value-based relationship management helps in cross-selling. There has been a drastic improvement in customer acquisition after sales leads were passed on via discussion boards. "There is servicing of 10 lakh leads and around 5 lakh service requests per year. Customer service has improved by 60 per cent and turnaround time for its processes by almost 70 per cent. The repository also enables geography wise customer segmentation to plan a promotional campaign better. Customers can directly send their feedback or use blogs to interact with us. Same time it will provide us with a new set of opportunities in understanding the customer.

Punjab National Bank

Moving ahead of CBS, PNB deployed CRM software Customer First which comprises of modules for Business prospect management, Lead Management, activity management, Product management, complaint management and business intelligence reporting. The pay offs to PNB are in terms of increased customer base, cross selling, sales force optimization, efficient lead management and higher productivity. It has helped increase PNB's customer base from 5.81 crore (as on March 2010) to more than 6.5 crore. In 2009–10, the Bank generated 61243 Leads, out of which 353,250 leads were converted amounting to Rs. 788 crore of Business.

ICICI Bank

In ICICI, the situation before CRM implementation was marked by waiting line, high cost per transaction and scenarios like call centres providing only account information.

ICICI adopted an enterprise CRM strategy. Nycamp consulting Group prepared a detailed and comprehensive CRM action plan. ICICI identified five functional areas which when integrated will give Bank its CRM Business transformation map. Core areas of business transformation were – Business focus, organization structure, Business matrix, marketing focus and Technology. ICICI ensured that all the functional areas like Strategy Development, Value Creation Process, Multichannel Integration Process, Information Management Process and Performance Assessment Process should be integrated for implementation of CRM. The payoffs were: Lower total cost of ownership, efficient management of volume growth, greater responsiveness to market needs, improved operations, decrease in operational costs, reduction in turnaround time, and integrated platform for all applications of the Bank. This technology platform had several benefits: A decreased need for data management as data is now taken from a central system; up to date information appearing on the screen of the employee to improve performance and higher degree of coordination and services; All customer contact points are now coordinated.

SBI

SBI has presence in 32 countries with more than 13 crore customers and over 13,800 branches and 5 associate banks. The business data of SBI spreads over several domestic and international source systems such as Core Banking, Trade finance, Treasury, ATMs, Internet Banking etc. The top management didn't have a mechanism of having a consolidated view of business across all functions of the bank on a real time basis. To overcome this challenge the Bank decided to employ, a Business Intelligence system which integrated data from nearly 15 source systems (with nearly 70 databases) to form a single enterprise data warehouse logical model. The system has empowered the decision makers to have actionable data leading to faster decision making based on latest information. The system generates 248 reports daily for the top management and each of the branches have access to reports generated particularly for them. Dash board covering the key focus areas is available to the top management with the ability to drill down to each individual branch in each of the matrix being tracked. With the help of campaign management solution bank has managed to successfully execute 71 campaigns targeting 4.88 million customers.

CRM Issues and Challenges

The previous section described the various forms in which CRM was adopted and utilized, and in each case the pay offs have been worth while. This cannot be considered as the complete picture of CRM implementation. Many banks are still struggling to make proper use of this very useful mechanism. However, the adoption and utilization is dependent on a number of factors and impediments. Broadly the issues are pertaining to:

People, Processes, Data and Technology. Also a major drawback is the general perception of CRM being a Technology imperative. There is a great need to understand that technology is only the enabler to CRM. In the real sense it is an organization wide strategy. The success of this depends on a careful integration of Organization's goals, structure, systems, processes and resources. In the following section, we will examine these issues

CRM: Technology Issues

Technology Component of a Total CRM Strategy

The technology component of CRM offers banks a comprehensive understanding of its customers through data analysis and predictive modeling, to support sales and marketing Strategies. It enables:

- *Single customer view*—A managed and integrated view of the customer, drawn from all contact points and product purchases, enables financial institutions to better understand customers and therefore serve them more effectively.
- *Predictions for profit*—Banks can accurately predict which products and services will appeal to an existing customer, and which they are most likely to purchase.
- *Customer lifetime value*—Banks can calculate the probable profitability of a customer over their lifetime, ensuring that they don't alienate low-value customers with high-value potential.
- *Personalized services*—Businesses can segment the market into specific target groups by demographics or purchase types. With a closer understanding of customers by small segments, banks can adopt individual marketing approaches rather than relatively ineffective mass marketing.

The following are the impediments to CRM implementation in context of technology:

(a) *Misconception about role of technology:* Most officers perceive technology as a limited to record of information and transaction. The use of technology in further sophisticated information processing and dissemination is not done.

(b) *Lack of Integration:* There are multiple channels and multiple technologies in use simultaneously in customer interface, service and sales. The integration of this complex system of technologies is a challenge.

(c) *Empowerment to frontline staff:* A Frontline staff has customer profile and data. Most of them have no motivation to further process these and make full utilization of these to provide better services and proactive selling effort. They are neither trained to use customer analytics nor to customize the Banks offering.

(d) *Underutilization:* The single integrated view of customer, past transactions preferred mode of business are known, but no mechanism is in place to utilize this with aid of software like lead management and activity management for higher effectiveness in sales and service.

Data Issues

The core of a successful CRM decision support system is a multidimensional data warehouse that:

- Integrates raw input from multiple sources and platforms, such as credit card, mortgage, insurance and savings account systems.
- Integrates input from multiple contact point systems, such as ATMs, branch visits, Internet and call center transactions.
- Integrates with popular back-office systems (financial transaction processing, for example) and front-office systems (such as sales force automation).
- Transforms this raw data into cleansed, validated and structured information.

The issues related to data are:

(a) *Fragmented data:* Banks have multiple repositories of data accumulated across various channels. Systematically collecting and organizing this huge data is big challenge.

(b) *Legacy systems:* Historical data collected from legacy systems tend not to have been collected in any standard form.

(c) *Quality of data:* As huge amount of data has to be cleaned and a lot of missing data has to be identified and included. This process has to be carried out across branches which in addition to their core tasks have this work.

(d) *Lack of understanding, skill and initiative to manage and utilize data:* Employees expected to organize and systematically manage data may not dot efficiently because of the lack of understanding of the strategic perspective of this activity. They also lack the necessary infrastructure and skill to complete this task.

People Issues

(a) Lack of knowledge and skills in converting data to customer knowledge.

(b) Lack of motivation for utilizing the potential of CRM solution.

(c) Inadequate performance management parameters.

(d) *Less or insufficient decision making authority:* In order to use CRM concept towards customer centricity, sufficient decision making power is required to provide customized, responsive and proactive services.

(e) *Training:* Staff lacks training in IT, its applications, the complete use of software and its applications as well as marketing skills, analytical skills, uses of customer information and service skills for implementation CRM.

Process Issues

As CRM is an organization wide strategy the entire processes need to be aligned appropriately. Some important process issues are:

(a) *Change in Culture:* The CRM implementation demands a change in organizational culture in terms of vision, mission, philosophy, and shared values. This encompasses a fundamental change in the organizational practices and employee behavior.

(b) *Breaking the Silos:* CRM can not succeed in Silò structure of departments. It demands integration and collaboration of all departments on a continuous basis. So, Breaking of silos prevalent in traditional organization structure is a challenge.

(c) *Change in Structure and Systems:* CRM success lies in ownership of CRM by all departments with Marketing in the strategic role of combining efforts in all these towards better customer service. This basic structural change from product centric organization to customer centric organization faces impediments in terms of role conflicts, ambigiuty, resistance and attitudinal impediments.

(d) *Demand for More Proactiveness and Flexibility:* The former strict hierarchical and rigid structure has to be transformed to flexible, responsive and proactive structure. This demands top management support, proper training and efficient follow up systems. In addition to behavioral issues the full utilization of CRM benefits cannot be attained unless this is enabled.

CONCLUSION

Customers have grown to expect comprehensive financial services from a single point of contact. They are attracted by many new products and services that non-banking institutions have been offering. The challenge for banks is to package these products and services and deliver them through convenient, user-friendly channels. Only by integrating people, processes, and technology across business lines will banks be able to forge a portfolio of virtual banking services based on the priorities of specific customer market segments.

Consumer centric practices will be at the nucleus of functioning and business plans of Banks in the next decade. The banking sector will increasingly move towards a CRM banking where the banks will have to develop and service products suited at different phases of a customer's life. The true potential of CRM will be realized only when the CRM will get buy in from all stakeholders viz. IT, Marketing, Operations and Top Management. With this integrated effort and supporting structures and processes, a culture revolving around customer centricity will enable banks to leverage on this asset. We can enumerate certain fundamental strategies for successful CRM in Banking:

1. An organizational transformation from product centricity to customer centricity.
2. CRM led and supported by top management.

3. Development and adoption of processes and procedures to enable and use CRM.
4. Provision of infrastructural support for CRM implementation at all levels.
5. Regular follow up of implementation and communication to stakeholders.
6. Performance evaluation and incentives linked to adoption and implementation of CRM procedures.
7. Ownership of CRM by marketing Department with IT Department in an enabling role
8. Development of Marketing organization structure which can strategically align all the related activities throughout the towards customer focus with CRM as a key initiative.
9. A continuous effort of awareness, training and information sharing should be oriented towards generating understanding, applications, technological aspects and marketing imperative, should be carried out.

REFERENCES

Gordan 1, "Best Practices: Customer Relationship Management", Ivey Business Journal (November–December 2002).

Onut, Erdem I. "Customer Relationship Management in Banking Sector and A Model Design for Banking Performance Enhancement".

Coltman, T., "Can Superior CRM Capabilities Improve Performance in Banking", *Journal of Financial Services Marketing*, Vol. 12, 2 (2007).

Nielsen, S. and Hathi, N. 'CRM: Untapped Engine for Growth', Investment Advisor (August 2011).

Gartner Research (2001). "CRM at Work: Eight Characteristics of CRM Winners"

Mukherjee, K., "Using CRM Effectively" TMTC Journal (Vol. 8, No. 2) December 2010, pp. 59–65.

Khirallah K., "CRM Case Study: The Analytics that power CRM at Royal Bank, Tover Group Research Note (2001).

Brown, A. and Meesha, G. (2002). "Performance Driven CRM" PWC Consulting, John Wily and Sons Canada Ltd.

Kale, Sudhir, "CRM Failure and the Seven Deadly Sins", Marketing Management, Sept–Oct. 2004, Vol. 12, Issue 5, pp. 42–46.

Payne, Adrian and Frow, Peannie (2005). "A Strategic Framework for Customer Relationship Management", *Journal of Marketing,* Oct. 2005, Vol. 69, Issue 4, pp. 167–176.

Pepper, Don and Rogers Martha, "Hail to the Customer", Sales and Marketing Management, Vol. 157, Issue 10, 2005.

Part–III

Challenges Relating to Financial Inclusion, HR and Other Issues

Financial Inclusion—An Inter-State Analysis of Credit and Deposit Penetration in India

Sandhya M. Das, U.S. Mishra and N. Vijayamohanan Pillai

Centre for Development Studies (JNU), Prasanthnagar, Ulloor, Thiruvananthapuram, Kerala

ABSTRACT: *This paper attempts to capture the inclusiveness in distribution of the two basic financial services namely, deposit and credit, at the sub-national level, by measuring the temporal changes in their penetration during three time-points viz., 1999–2000, 2004–05 and 2009–10 using the state-wise data on distribution of deposit and credit accounts, published by the Reserve Bank of India in the Basic Statistical Returns of Scheduled Commercial Banks in India. We compute a set of nine standard indicators to assess the relative performance of States/Union Territories in usage of these services and employ the quintile income statistic to demonstrate the correlation between inclusiveness in distribution of financial services and growth in terms of per capita income. The study concludes that as greater accessibility of financial services is a pre-requisite for inclusive growth, financial sector reforms that promote broader access to these services and building inclusive financial systems that focus on equalizing opportunities and reducing inequalities hold the key for development.*

Keywords: Financial Inclusion, Deposit, Credit.

INTRODUCTION

The last two decades witnessed steady progress in achieving socio-economic development and strengthening collaborative relationships among governments, social institutions and civil society worldwide. Nonetheless, inequality and exclusion persist, with many societies experiencing negative social conditions, such as widening disparities and marginalization of certain groups and communities. Recognising the need to make growth more inclusive in terms of reaching out to the hitherto unreached vulnerable sections of the population, the Approach Paper to the Eleventh Five Year Plan (2007–12) of India adopted faster and more inclusive growth as its central theme.

Recent literature recognises the fact that financial market imperfections, which limit access to finance, play an important role in perpetuating inequalities. Financial inclusion represents one aspect of inclusive growth as it offers incremental and complementary solutions to tackle poverty, promote inclusive development and address the Millennium Development Goals (MDGs). Cross-country studies illustrate that countries with low levels of income inequality tend to have lower levels of financial exclusion and *vice versa.* In Sweden and Canada, two and three percent of adults respectively lacked an account in 2000; in Portugal this was about 17 per cent (Kempson 2006). On the contrary, more than 90 per cent of the adults lacked a bank account in low-income countries like Burundi, Congo, Ethiopia, Madagascar and Cambodia (Financial Access Database 2009). Both theoretical and empirical literature reveal a contemporaneous correlation between financial sector development and economic growth (eg. McKinnon 1973, Shaw 1973, King and Levine 1993). The direction of causality is, however, still a debatable issue.

FINANCIAL INCLUSION—A PERSPECTIVE

The objective of financial inclusion is to expand the scope of activities of the organised financial system, including within its gamut, people with low incomes, thereby lifting them out of poverty through graduated credit and alleviating risks through other financial services like savings, payments, remittance facilities and insurance. It implies an absence of obstacles to the use of these services, whether the obstacles are price or non-price barriers to finance. In India, although a slew of measures spanning from the strengthening of co-operatives, nationalisation of banks and establishment of Regional Rural Banks (RRBs) to the microfinance movement, have been implemented from time to time to increase the outreach of banking services in the country, the low levels of financial penetration and deepening in India compared to that in other countries raised concerns for inclusive growth. The extent of exclusion has been brought out by data from certain sources like the All India Debt and Investment Survey (AIDIS) of the National Sample Survey Organisation (NSSO – 59th Round, 2002–03), Basic Statistical Returns (BSR) of the Reserve Bank of India (RBI), Data of Centre for Monitoring Indian Economy (CMIE) etc. The NSSO data revealed that 45.9 million farmer households in the country, i.e., 51.4 per cent of the nearly 89.3 million farmer households of India do not access credit either from institutional or non-institutional sources. More importantly, only 27 per cent of the total farm households are indebted to formal sources; of them one-third also borrow from informal sources (NSSO 2005). There also exist regions where more than 95 per cent of the farm households do not get credit from any sources. Thus, in addition to the fact that exclusion itself is large, it also varies widely across regions, social groups and asset holdings. *The poorer the group, the greater is the exclusion.*

It is in this backdrop that the Reserve Bank of India (RBI) made an explicit announcement in its Annual Policy Statement for the year 2005–06, for putting the financial inclusion process into mission mode. Subsequently, the Government of India constituted a

Committee on Financial Inclusion under the chairmanship of Dr. C. Rangarajan. The Committee on Financial Inclusion (GoI, 2008: 2) defined financial inclusion broadly as the "process of ensuring access to financial services and timely and adequate credit where needed by vulnerable groups such as weaker sections and low income groups at an affordable cost". The Indian policy approach towards financial inclusion since the early 2000s has been focussed on ensuring inclusion at the individual and household level. The first step in this direction has been the scheme of "no-frills accounts" (no pre-condition, low minimum balance maintenance), initiated by the RBI in 2005 to provide an easy savings facility together with an entry into the formal banking system.

Through this paper, we attempt to capture the inclusive focus of these policies by measuring the temporal changes in the penetration of the two most basic financial services namely, deposit and credit, at the sub-national level, over the last decade (1999–2000 to 2009–10) using the data published by the RBI in the BSR of scheduled commercial banks. The rest of the paper is organized in three sections. First section briefly enumerates the data and methods employed in the paper. In the next section we examine the inclusiveness of finance in terms of distribution of number and value of deposit accounts, credit accounts and the changes in Credit-Deposit Ratio across space and time. Last section concludes with challenges and policy implications.

DATA AND METHODS

We employ data on state-wise distribution of number and value of total deposit accounts, number of credit accounts and amount of credit outstanding in respect of scheduled commercial banks in India during three time-points viz., 1999–2000, 2004–05 and 2009–10. Inter-temporal changes in the distribution of these financial services have been analysed and correlations drawn in comparison with the per capita state domestic product of States and UTs. Availability and use of credit and deposit services, being a continuous variable, the most appropriate way for a comparative analysis of performance of states is by ranking them and drawing correlations with relevant growth and development parameters. However, this method suffers from the limitation of being order-specific and hence cannot explain the underlying distributional aspects. Therefore, with a view to capturing the inclusiveness in terms of distribution of financial services at the sub-national level, the paper further examines the feasibility of employing the "quintile income" statistic or the income of the poorest 20% of the population, a concept advanced by Kaushik Basu (2001, 2006) and suggested for wider policy applications in inclusive development by Subramanian (2010, 2011).

We compute a set of nine different standard indicators measuring the extent of financial penetration in terms of usage of two important aspects of finance viz., deposit and credit,

Table 1: Descriptive Statistics of Various Parameters showing Deposit and Credit Penetration Across States/Union Territories in India

Year/ Summary Statistic	*Average Deposit Size (₹)*	*Per Capita Deposit (₹)*	*No. of Deposit a/c per 1000 Adults*	*Deposit-Income Ratio*	*Average Credit Size*	*Per Capita Credit o/s (₹)*	*No. of Credit a/c per 1000 Adults*	*Credit - Income Ratio*	*Credit-Deposit Ratio*	*p.c NSDP at Factor Cost Current Prices (₹) (base 1999–2000)*
1999–2000										
Mean	21350	19480	816	0.83	87835	9056	84	0.37	38	18611
Minimum	7623	2938	191	0.22	9429	981	22	0.07	7	5786
Maximum	53599	101298	2758	2.58	566839	83070	240	1.87	89	44502
Median	18952	12608	665	0.71	48392	3828	72	0.25	34	15159
Skewness	1.49	2.68	1.85	2.06	3.04	3.42	1.27	2.59	0.84	1.52
Kurtosis	5.50	9.08	5.72	7.01	12.37	13.91	4.67	9.21	2.98	4.72
Coefficient of Varn.	0.44	1.24	0.74	0.63	1.28	1.91	0.57	1.11	0.57	0.49
2004–05										
Mean	39094	35131	777	1.06	160681	18662	94	0.55	46	27414
Minimum	21194	5794	167	0.35	29422	2151	29	0.12	10	7449
Maximum	117368	223465	2643	4.10	915095	161435	262	2.56	101	79562
Median	32672	22750	660	0.89	104228	8304	72	0.41	44	22953
Skewness	2.41	3.05	2.16	2.98	3.14	3.43	1.20	2.56	0.77	1.85
Kurtosis	9.77	11.67	7.50	13.37	12.27	13.72	3.71	9.00	3.13	6.45
Coefficient of Varn.	0.48	1.32	0.73	0.65	1.16	1.84	0.60	0.98	0.48	0.56
2009–10										
Mean	61403	83907	1166	1.42	334759	54784	138.09	0.86	54	50403
Minimum	30200	14441	341	0.57	70829	4943	29.00	0.24	7	15475
Maximum	168824	514742	3442	4.97	2377630	559216	373.00	4.33	131	129228
Median	49723	54144	1049	1.10	192103	23331	100.00	0.62	52	43617
Skewness	1.99	2.98	1.94	2.50	3.61	3.76	1.30	2.90	0.92	1.36
Kurtosis	6.48	11.17	6.33	9.75	16.19	16.42	3.73	10.66	3.67	4.49
Coefficient of Varn.	0.52	1.28	0.62	0.63	1.30	1.99	0.66	1.06	0.51	0.54

Table 2: Spearman's Rank Correlation Coefficient

year = 1999–2000 *no. of observations =29*

Parameter	*Average Deposit Size*	*Per Capita Deposit*	*No of deposit a/c per 1000 adults*	*Deposit-Income Ratio*	*Average Credit Size*	*Per Capita Credit o/s*	*No of credit a/c per 1000 adults*	*Credit - Income Ratio*	*Credit-Deposit Ratio*	*Per Capita income*
Average Deposit Size	1.0000									
Per Capita Deposit	0.6621*	1.0000								
No of deposit a/c per 1000 adults	0.2860	0.858*	1.0000							
Deposit-Income Ratio	0.4852*	0.7754*	0.6484*	1.0000						
Average Credit Size	0.4941*	0.7734*	0.7183*	0.5956*	1.0000					
Per Capita Credit o/s	0.4015*	0.8271*	0.8309*	0.6581*	0.8921*	1.0000				
No of credit a/c per 1000 adults	0.0005	0.4795*	0.6573*	0.3307	0.3218	0.6609*	1.0000			
Credit - Income Ratio	0.2344	0.6451*	0.6764*	0.6889*	0.8026*	0.9219*	0.6096*	1.0000		
Credit-Deposit Ratio	–0.0367	0.2850	0.3864*	0.1815	0.6373*	0.7308*	0.5326*	0.8034*	1.0000	
Per Capita income	0.6842*	0.8424*	0.7407*	0.3897*	0.6700*	0.7138*	0.4938*	0.4378*	0.2737	1.0000

(cond...)

(Table 2 cond...)

year = 2004–05 *no. of observations = 31*

Parameter	*Average Deposit Size*	*Per Capita Deposit*	*No. of Deposit a/c per 1000 Adults*	*Deposit-Income Ratio*	*Average Credit Size*	*Per Capita Credit o/s*	*No. of Credit a/c per 1000 adults*	*Credit - Income Ratio*	*Credit-Deposit Ratio*	*Per Capita Income*
Average Deposit Size	1.0000									
Per Capita Deposit	0.5755*	1.0000								
No of deposit a/c per 1000 adults	0.1848	0.8790*	1.0000							
Deposit-Income Ratio	0.3535*	0.7485*	0.6827*	1.0000						
Average Credit Size	0.6177*	0.7170*	0.5762*	0.5431*	1.0000					
Per Capita Credit o/s	0.3757*	0.8490*	0.8589*	0.6271*	0.7313*	1.0000				
No of credit a/c per 1000 adults	0.0385	0.6461*	0.7592*	0.4489*	0.2293	0.7766*	1.0000			
Credit -Income Ratio	0.1579	0.6031*	0.6516*	0.6796*	0.5973*	0.8491*	0.6688*	1.0000		
Credit-Deposit Ratio	–0.0561	0.1861	0.2956	0.1461	0.3438	0.6158*	0.5446*	0.7774*	1.0000	
Per Capita income	0.5363*	0.8622*	0.7903*	0.3823*	0.6525*	0.7951*	0.6328*	0.4008*	0.1979	1.0000

(cond...)

(Table 2 cond...)

year = 2009–10 *no. of observations = 31*

Parameter	*Average Deposit Size*	*Per Capita Deposit*	*No. of Deposit a/c per 1000 adults*	*Deposit-Income Ratio*	*Average Credit Size*	*Per Capita Credit o/s*	*No of credit a/c per 1000 adults*	*Credit - Income Ratio*	*Credit-Deposit Ratio*	*Per Capita income*
Average Deposit Size	1.0000									
Per Capita Deposit	0.7786*	1.0000								
No of deposit a/c per 1000 adults	0.3520	0.8270*	1.0000							
Deposit-Income Ratio	0.4893*	0.6442*	0.5542*	1.0000						
Average Credit Size	0.5899*	0.6347*	0.5032*	0.3785*	1.0000					
Per Capita Credit o/s	0.5609*	0.8476*	0.8024*	0.4186*	0.7274*	1.0000				
No of credit a/c per 1000 adults	0.3165	0.6901*	0.7211*	0.3283	0.1985	0.7676	1.0000			
Credit -Income Ratio	0.2709	0.5855*	0.6442*	0.4935*	0.6359*	0.8245*	0.6358*	1.0000		
Credit-Deposit Ratio	0.0520	0.2186	0.2957	–0.1072	0.4939*	0.6370*	0.4590*	0.7254*	1.0000	
Per Capita income	0.7032*	0.8742*	0.7411*	0.2913	0.6319*	0.8540*	0.6675*	0.4480*	0.3731*	1.0000

for all the 35 States/Union Territories during the three time-points. The indicators included average deposit size, per capita deposit, number of deposit accounts per 1000 adults, Deposit to Income Ratio, average credit size, per capita credit, number of credit accounts per 1000 adults, Credit to Income Ratio and Credit—Deposit Ratio. Higher values of each of these measures indicate better performance of states in usage of services. The States/UTs were then divided into quintiles based on these indicators (separately) and matched with the quintile classification of States/UTs obtained on the basis of per capita Net State Domestic Product (NSDP) to demonstrate the correlation between inclusiveness of finance and growth in terms of per capita income. As a test of inclusiveness, the normalized gap between the value of the indicator obtained for each of the States/UTs and the best performing State/UT has been computed. A reduction in the distance from the best performing State/UT over the reference period implies that the State in question is treading towards the path of inclusion and *vice versa*.

ANALYSIS

States/UTs in India differ widely in terms of the usage of financial services, as they do in the distribution of key socio-economic variables, as indicated by the high coefficient of variation for almost all indicators. The patterns of change in the indicators are also quite diverse over time in different States/UTs. The Spearman's rank correlation coefficient computed separately for the three time-points showed that all the indicators are positively correlated with each other as well as with per capita income. We examine the patterns of distribution of deposit and credit and the extent of inclusiveness obtained in the states in the following sub-sections.

Deposit

The most basic indicator for measuring the usage of financial services is the number of deposit accounts per 1000 adults (CGAP 2009). However, indicators like average deposit size, per capita deposit and Deposit to Income ratio also convey different notions of deposit penetration in terms of usage. The data on these four deposit indicators for all the States/UTs for the three time-points are presented in Appendix I. The number of deposit accounts per 1000 adults varied from 191 (Manipur) to 2758 (Chandigarh) during 1999–2000, whereas it increased to a range of 341 (Manipur) to 3442 (Delhi) during the year 2009–10. During the ten-year period the average for the country grew from 629 to 950 accounts per 1000 adults. All States/UTs except Bihar and Lakshadweep have shown considerable improvement in terms of this indicator in absolute terms during the ten-year period. This becomes more evident from the fact that while every adult individual had more than one deposit account in only six States/UTs during 1999–2000, it was so in 18 States/UTs during 2009–10. Also, a higher proportion of the population (more than

50 percentage) had no contact with and no access to the formal financial system in 11 States/UTs during 1999–2000, whereas, there were only two states (Manipur and Nagaland) in this category during 2009–10.

The all-India average deposit size showed a more than three-fold increase from ₹ 20,000 to ₹ 62,000, while per capita deposit increased from ₹ 13,000 to ₹ 59,000 during the reference period. The Deposit-Income Ratio (DIR) at the all-India level increased from 79 to 132 per cent during the same period. Delhi and Chandigarh invariably occupied the top-most positions in terms of per capita deposit and DIR throughout the period. In the case of average deposit size, Maharashtra ranked second during 2004–05 and 2009–10. The very high levels of these indicators in these three States/UT could be due to the presence of huge amounts of industrial or corporate deposits. The yawning gap between the lowest and highest DIR (22 to 258 per cent in 1999–2000 and from 57 to 497 per cent in 2009–10) stands testimony to the growing disparity and inequality in income between the low and high income states.

Further, looking at the relative performance of States/UTs in terms of growth of number of deposit accounts during the ten-year period by comparing with the levels exhibited by the highest ranking state, one can find that the normalized distance from the best performing state has reduced in the case of most of the states/UTs, with pronounced effects observed in Delhi, Andhra Pradesh, Dadra and Nagar Haveli, Jharkhand and Uttarakhand, implying higher growth (Table 3). On the contrary, the gap actually increased in the case of Bihar, Madhya Pradesh, Lakshadweep, Meghalaya, Punjab, Uttar Pradesh and Chandigarh, signifying either a slower or a negative growth. This implies that the growth in number of deposit accounts has plateaued in the case of high income states whereas it has further deteriorated in the case of low income states. Assam and Manipur, with already less number of deposit accounts, showed static growth in terms of this indicator, as revealed by the constant gap from the top-most state, consistently retaining their positions in the bottom quintiles of income and reinforcing their inherent weaknesses. The growth in other indicators of deposit usage, viz., average deposit size and per capita deposit, was rather slow in most of the states when compared to that of the best performing states (Delhi, Chandigarh), as shown by larger distances during the terminal year vis-a-vis base year, the only exception being Lakshadweep and Maharashtra. The DIR increased substantially for all the States/UTs except Bihar where it declined. The deterioration in growth of deposit indicators, observed in the three states of Uttar Pradesh, Madhya Pradesh and Bihar, could be partially ascribed to the bifurcation of these states, as the new states carved out of them, viz., Chattisgarh, Jharkhand and Uttarakhand show a higher growth in these parameters.

Table 3: State-wise Normalised Distance of Various Deposit Indicators from the Best Performing State State-wise (1999–2000, 2004–05 and 2009–10)

Sl. No.	*State/Union Territory*	*No of deposit a/c per 1000 adults*			*Average Deposit Size (Rs.)*			*Per Capita Deposit (Rs.)*		
		1999–2000	*2004–05*	*2009–10*	*1999–2000*	*2004–05*	*2009–10*	*1999–2000*	*2004–05*	*2009–10*
1.	Andaman and Nicobar	0.80	0.79	0.77	0.74	0.79	0.80	0.89	0.90	0.91
2.	Andhra Pradesh	0.85	0.78	0.73	0.83	0.96	0.95	0.94	0.94	0.94
3.	Arunachal Pradesh	0.90	0.91	0.87	0.75	0.79	0.72	0.94	0.95	0.93
4.	Assam	0.89	0.89	0.89	0.93	0.98	0.95	0.98	0.98	0.98
5.	Bihar	0.87	0.92	0.95	0.85	1.00	0.97	0.95	0.99	0.99
6.	Chandigarh	0.00	0.02	0.09	0.37	0.49	0.24	0.00	0.19	0.18
7.	Chhattisgarh*		0.92	0.91		0.88	0.86		0.97	0.97
8.	Dadra and Nagar Haveli	0.90	0.80	0.74	0.57	0.89	0.94	0.91	0.93	0.94
9.	Daman and Diu	0.67	0.64	0.65	0.48	0.69	0.79	0.70	0.78	0.86
10.	Delhi	0.35	0.30	0.00	0.00	0.00	0.14	0.01	0.00	0.00
11.	Goa	0.19	0.00	0.11	0.54	0.78	0.59	0.36	0.51	0.49
12.	Gujarat	0.83	0.79	0.79	0.66	0.82	0.83	0.88	0.90	0.92
13.	Haryana	0.76	0.74	0.72	0.81	0.90	0.81	0.90	0.91	0.89
14.	Himachal Pradesh	0.71	0.68	0.70	0.82	0.92	0.90	0.88	0.90	0.91
15.	Jammu and Kashmir	0.79	0.77	0.77	0.75	0.89	0.92	0.89	0.92	0.94
16.	Jharkhand*	1.07	0.87	0.72		0.90	0.89		0.95	0.92
17.	Karnataka	0.79	0.75	0.73	0.78	0.84	0.79	0.90	0.90	0.89
18.	Kerala	0.73	0.63	0.71	0.75	0.94	0.86	0.86	0.89	0.91
19.	Lakshadweep	0.27	0.81	0.75	1.00	0.85	0.57	0.87	0.92	0.83
20.	Madhya Pradesh	0.86	0.88	0.89	0.83	0.95	0.94	0.95	0.97	0.97
21.	Maharashtra	0.82	0.77	0.80	0.40	0.44	0.00	0.79	0.78	0.71
22.	Manipur	1.00	1.00	1.00	0.83	0.86	0.91	1.00	1.00	1.00
23.	Meghalaya	0.88	0.89	0.91	0.69	0.73	0.68	0.92	0.93	0.94
24.	Mizoram	0.99	0.96	0.94	0.63	0.72	0.78	0.97	0.97	0.96

Sl. No.	*State/Union Territory*	*No of deposit a/c per 1000 adults*			*Average Deposit Size (Rs.)*			*Per Capita Deposit (Rs.)*		
		1999–2000	*2004–05*	*2009–10*	*1999–2000*	*2004–05*	*2009–10*	*1999–2000*	*2004–05*	*2009–10*
25.	Nagaland	0.98	0.98	0.97	0.58	0.73	0.67	0.96	0.98	0.96
26.	Orissa	0.93	0.90	0.88	0.87	0.96	0.92	0.98	0.98	0.97
27.	Puducherry	0.71	0.65	0.64	0.70	0.86	0.88	0.83	0.86	0.89
28.	Punjab	0.61	0.60	0.63	0.73	0.88	0.87	0.79	0.85	0.89
29.	Rajasthan	0.89	0.87	0.88	0.84	0.98	0.95	0.96	0.97	0.98
30.	Sikkim	0.93	0.86	0.82	0.36	0.51	0.56	0.89	0.87	0.87
31.	Tamil Nadu	0.80	0.78	0.74	0.78	0.89	0.87	0.90	0.92	0.92
32.	Tripura	0.89	0.89	0.85	0.89	0.94	0.93	0.97	0.97	0.97
33.	Uttar Pradesh	0.81	0.82	0.82	0.89	1.00	1.00	0.94	0.97	0.97
34.	Uttarakhand*		0.70	0.48		0.83	0.82		0.87	0.82
35.	West Bengal	0.81	0.82	0.84	0.80	0.88	0.83	0.92	0.94	0.94
36.	All India	0.83	0.80	0.80	0.73	0.83	0.77	0.90	0.91	0.91

Formula for Normalisation: Normalised distance = (M – Xi)/(M – m), where, M – maximum value of the indicator, m – minimum value of the indicator and Xi - value of the indicator for the ith State/UT.

Best Performing State/UT:

No of deposit a/c per 1000 adults - Chandigarh (1999–2000), Goa (2004–05) and Delhi (2009–10).

Average Deposit Size– Delhi. Per Capita Deposit (Rs.)- Chandigarh (1999–2000); Delhi (2004–05 and 2009–10).

Note: *These three states were constituted during 2000–2001.

The quintile classification of the states on the basis of these indicators showed that states like Punjab, Delhi, Chandigarh, Goa and Daman and Diu have consistently maintained their position in the top-most quintile (Q5) throughout the ten year period. The three newly formed states, viz., Chattisgarh, Uttarakhand and Jharkhand made significant improvements by moving to the upper quintiles in terms of the number of deposit accounts and per capita deposit. This could be due to new capital infusion and thrust for rapid infrastructure development received from the Centre as well as the newly formed State Governments in the wake of creation of these States. Kerala and Himachal Pradesh showed deterioration in their relative positions in the quintile classification based on number of deposit accounts as they were relegated to the fourth quintile from the topmost one during the period, despite a slight improvement in the indicator in absolute terms. The most pertinent observation that emerges is that the low-income states and the North-Eastern states (except Sikkim) have consistently remained in the bottom quintiles throughout the reference period, indicating a clear example of path dependence. The middle income states also occupied corresponding middle positions in terms of the indicators measuring deposit usage also. This may be better demonstrated by a matching of the quintile classification of the States obtained with respect to the different deposit indicators with that of per capita income (Table 4). The crowding of States/UTs along the diagonal from top-left to the bottom-right shows that the States/UTs belonging to a particular quintile in terms of per capita income also fall in the same quintile grouping in terms of the indicator considered, with only a few variations. Besides this, one can also observe a higher concentration of States/UTs along the diagonal with the passage of time. Thus, one can infer that the higher the per capita income of the states/UT, the higher the usage of deposit services.

Table 4: Matrix Showing Matching of Quintile Distribution of States/UTs for Per Capita Income and Per Capita Deposit

Per Capita Income	*Per Capita Deposit*				
	Q1	*Q2*	*Q3*	*Q4*	*Q5*
(a) 1999–2000					
Q1	Orissa, Assam	Bihar, UP			
Q2	Manipur	Rajasthan, MP, Arunachal Pradesh		J&K	
Q3	Nagaland, Tripura	AP	Meghalaya, WB	Sikkim,	
Q4	Mizoram		Tamil Nadu, Karnataka,	Gujarat, HP, Kerala	Maharashtra
Q5			Haryana	A&N islands,	Puducherry, Punjab, Delhi, Goa, Chandigarh
(b) 2009–10					
Q1	Bihar, MP, UP, Assam, Manipur	J&K	Jharkhand		
Q2	Rajasthan, Orissa	Chattisgarh, Tripura, Mizoram, Nagaland	Meghalaya, West Bengal		
Q3		Andhra Pradesh	Arunachal Pradesh, HP	Sikkim, Karnataka, Kerala	Uttarakhand
Q4			Gujarat, Tamil Nadu	Punjab, A&N Islands,	Maharashtra
Q5				Puducherry, Haryana	Delhi, Goa, Chandigarh,

Source: Analysis based on data from RBI and CSO, GoI.

Note: Three UTs viz., Dadra and Nagar Haveli, Daman and Diu and Lakshadweep have been excluded from this part of the analysis as data on per capita income is not available for these UTs.

Credit

The number of borrowers and value of credit outstanding are the most appropriate and easily available measure of the use of finance, though the institutional data available from the regulators does not reflect the presence of multiple accounts. The penetration of loans as measured by the number of bank loans per 1000 adults varies widely across regions and is closely correlated with economic development. Recent research by various agencies including the Consultative Group for Assisting the Poor has found that developed economies have the largest number of loans per 1000 adults (CGAP, 2009). In India, the growth in credit penetration was rather dismal compared to that of deposits during the reference period. It was relatively slow upto 2004–05 and gathered momentum only during the latter half of the decade when there was a rapid growth, coinciding with the policy announcements for greater outreach of banking services since 2005. Also the beneficial impact of measures like SHG Bank Linkage Programme (SBLP) since 1992, Kisan Credit Card (KCC) Scheme since 1998 and doubling of credit under the Farm Credit Package of 2004–05 were realised during this period. Although there has been a massive increase in the credit flow from commercial banks and RRBs, the credit penetration in India in terms of number of credit accounts continued to be abysmally low at 153 per 1000 adults during 2009–10, even after a nearly two-fold growth from the level of 83 during the year 1999–2000 (Appendix II). The highest credit penetration was observed in Chandigarh (373), Tamil Nadu (369), Maharashtra (337) Puducherry (278), Kerala (245), Andhra Pradesh (241) and Karnataka (213) in the descending order of number of credit accounts per 1000 adults during 2009–10. These States/UTs represent the group of high income states and the four Southern states which fall under the middle income category. Only a handful of states/UTs (8 out of 35) had a credit penetration consistently above the all-India average during all the three time-points. At the lower end were Daman and Diu, Dadra and Nagar Haveli, Manipur, Chattisgarh, West Bengal, Bihar, Meghalaya and Arunachal Pradesh with less than 10 per cent of the adults availing credit facility from scheduled commercial banks.

An analysis of the performance of the States/UTs in terms of the normalized distance from the best performing State/UT (Table 5) revealed that Tamil Nadu reduced the distance completely, exhibiting the highest growth in number of credit accounts per 1000 adults and ranked first during 2004–05 (262) and second during 2009–10 (369) after Chandigarh (373). Maharashtra and Puducherry also showed tremendous improvement with drastic reduction in the distance and a more than two-fold increase in the number of credit users. At the other extreme, West Bengal, Tripura and Bihar drifted further away from Chandigarh, deteriorating drastically in terms of increasing the outreach of credit during the period. Although, on the positive side, Punjab, Uttar Pradesh, Orissa, Madhya Pradesh, Himachal Pradesh and Arunachal Pradesh showed improvement in credit

Table 5: State-Wise Normalised Distance of Various Credit Indicators and CD Ratio from the Best Performing State (1999–2000, 2004–05 and 2009–10)

Sl.No.	State/Union Territory	No of credit a/c per 1000 adults			Average Credit Size (₹)			Per Capita Credit (₹)			Credit Income Ratio			Credit Deposit Ratio		
		1999–00	2004–05	2009–10	1999–00	2004–05	2009–10	1999–00	2004–05	2009–10	1999–00	2004–05	2009–10	1999–00	2004–05	2009–10
1.	Andaman and Nicobar	0.87	0.85	0.80	0.93	0.90	0.93	0.98	0.97	0.97	0.99	0.96	0.97	0.89	0.81	0.76
2.	Andhra Pradesh	0.50	0.38	0.38	0.94	0.94	0.95	0.94	0.93	0.93	0.83	0.81	0.82	0.30	0.29	0.21
3.	Arunachal Pradesh	0.82	0.92	0.86	0.98	0.95	0.95	1.00	0.99	0.98	0.99	0.98	0.98	0.90	0.87	0.84
4.	Assam	0.89	0.92	0.86	0.95	0.95	0.98	0.99	0.99	0.99	0.96	0.96	0.97	0.70	0.72	0.75
5.	Bihar	0.78	0.91	0.88	0.97	0.99	1.00	0.99	1.00	1.00	0.87	0.93	0.98	0.82	0.80	0.82
6.	Chandigarh	0.00	0.25	0.00	0.39	0.14	0.38	0.00	0.00	0.00	0.00	0.22	0.00	0.08	0.13	0.00
7.	Chhattisgarh*		0.92	0.90		0.92	0.92		0.98	0.98	1.04	0.93	0.95		0.63	0.64
8.	Dadra and Nagar Haveli	1.00	0.99	0.96	0.83	0.78	0.75	0.98	0.97	0.96					0.73	0.57
9.	Daman and Diu	0.90	0.95	1.00	0.80	0.87	0.78	0,95	0.97	0.98				0.90	0.98	0.90
10.	Delhi	0.61	0.47	0.61	0.00	0.00	0.00	0.27	0.14	0.32	0.17	0.00	0.15	0.35	0.42	0.46
11.	Goa	0.51	0.53	0.47	0.80	0.80	0.88	0.82	0.84	0.88	0.83	0.88	0.91	0.80	0.83	0.85
12.	Gujarat	0.82	0.86	0.83	0.81	0.81	0.86	0.93	0.94	0.95	0.83	0.87	0.91	0.49	0.60	0.53
13.	Haryana	0.73	0.77	0.73	0.89	0.85	0.88	0.95	0.93	0.93	0.91	0.91	0.92	0.57	0.54	0.55
14.	Himachal Pradesh	0.71	0.73	0.74	0.94	0.91	0.94	0.97	0.95	0.97	0.94	0.92	0.94	0.80	0.71	0.72
15.	Jammu and Kashmir	0.88	0.88	0.86	0.85	0.82	0.92	0.96	0.94	0.97	0.85	0.82	0.88	0.68	0.60	0.68
16.	Jharkhand*		0.85	0.72	1.02	0.95	0.96	1.01	0.98	0.97	1.04	0.93	0.88		0.78	0.78
17.	Karnataka	0.44	0.31	0.47	0.91	0.91	0.92	0.91	0.88	0.91	0.78	0.70	0.77	0.31	0.30	0.43
18.	Kerala	0.40	0.30	0.37	0.93	0.94	0.96	0.93	0.91	0.94	0.84	0.83	0.88	0.58	0.51	0.55

Sl.No.	State/Union Territory	No of credit a/c per 1000 adults			Average Credit Size (₹)			Per Capita Credit (₹)			Credit Income Ratio			Credit Deposit Ratio		
		1999–00	2004–05	2009–10	1999–00	2004–05	2009–10	1999–00	2004–05	2009–10	1999–00	2004–05	2009–10	1999–00	2004–05	2009–10
19.	Lakshadweep	0.87	0.87	0.81	0.97	0.99	1.00	1.00	1.00	1.00				1.00	1.00	1.00
20.	Madhya Pradesh	0.77	0.83	0.82	0.92	0.92	0.95	0.96	0.97	0.98	0.86	0.86	0.90	0.49	0.51	0.57
21.	Maharashtra	0.76	0.55	0.10	0.53	0.60	0.86	0.77	0.69	0.77	0.55	0.39	0.57	0.03	0.07	0.39
22.	Manipur	0.95	1.00	0.95	0.96	0.94	0.97	1.00	1.00	1.00	0.99	0.99	1.00	0.63	0.64	0.72
23.	Meghalaya	0.82	0.86	0.86	0.97	0.87	0.96	0.99	0.96	0.99	0.97	0.87	0.98	0.89	0.63	0.85
24.	Mizoram	0.91	0.86	0.79	0.96	0.92	0.96	1.00	0.98	0.98	0.99	0.94	0.96	0.81	0.58	0.63
25.	Nagaland	0.98	0.99	0.86	0.95	0.95	0.97	1.00	1.00	0.99	1.00	1.00		0.90	0.86	0.81
26.	Orissa	0.65	0.70	0.73	0.98	0.96	0.97	0.99	0.97	0.98	0.92	0.89	0.93	0.58	0.43	0.62
27.	Puducherry	0.49	0.48	0.28	0.93	0.93	0.97	0.93	0.93	0.94	0.92	0.92	0.93	0.68	0.69	0.60
28.	Punjab	0.66	0.71	0.73	0.84	0.81	0.85	0.90	0.89	0.92	0.83	0.81	0.86	0.61	0.56	0.48
29.	Rajasthan	0.81	0.82	0.81	0.92	0.91	0.92	0.97	0.96	0.97	0.90	0.85	0.88	0.52	0.35	0.35
30.	Sikkim	0.88	0.78	0.76	0.94	0.89	0.92	0.99	0.95	0.95	0.96	0.87	0.89	0.91	0.78	0.76
31.	Tamil Nadu	0.53	0.00	0.01	0.86	0.93	0.96	0.88	0.87	0.90	0.73	0.71	0.79	0.00	0.00	0.14
32.	Tripura	0.33	0.63	0.70	1.00	1.00	1.00	0.99	0.99	0.99	0.98	0.99	0.99	0.78	0.79	0.81
33.	Uttar Pradesh	0.80	0.81	0.84	0.95	0.96	0.97	0.98	0.98	0.99	0.90	0.89	0.93	0.74	0.69	0.71
34.	Uttarakhand*		0.72	0.51		0.93	0.95		0.96	0.94		0.90	0.89		0.84	0.79
35.	West Bengal	0.75	0.84	0.89	0.89	0.86	0.85	0.95	0.95	0.96	0.86	0.86	0.89	0.53	0.53	0.56
36.	All India	0.72	0.66	0.64	0.87	0.86	0.91	0.93	0.91	0.93	0.79	0.76	0.83	0.40	0.38	0.48

Note:

* These three states were constituted during 2000–2001.

Best Performing State/UT:

No of credit a/c per 1000 adults and Credit-Income Ratio - Chandigarh; Average Credit Size –Delhi

Per Capita Credit – Chandigarh (1999–2000 and 2009–10); Delhi (2004–05)

CD Ratio-Tamil Nadu (1999 2000 and 2004–05); Chandigarh (2009–10)

penetration, it is disheartening to note that the progress achieved in terms of inclusiveness was negligible as the growth rates were actually decelerating compared to the benchmark, as revealed by the increasing distances during the period. This points to the increasing inability of the low-income customers who form a large part of the population particularly in poorer and rural regions to access institutional finance.

The quintile classification of states/UTs based on the ascending order of the three indicators of credit penetration viz., number of credit accounts per 1000 adults, average credit size and per capita credit almost corresponds to that obtained in terms of per capita income (Table 6). There were however a few exceptions. Tripura, Jharkhand and Orissa which belonged to the lowest quintiles (bottom two quintiles) in terms of income, per capita credit and average credit size fell in the fourth quintile of number of credit accounts per 1000 adults during 2009–10. This could be explained by the fact that there are a large number of states/UTs with very low number of credit accounts and hence spread over the bottom four quintiles and hence a huge gap between the average for the topmost quintile and the rest of the quintiles. Delhi, Chandigarh, Goa, Puducherry and Maharashtra which possessed the highest per capita income also had their positions in the top two quintiles in terms of the three indicators of credit usage. The case of Delhi is, however, contrary to the expectations with a lower number of credit accounts (162), compared to Chandigarh (373) during 2009–10. On the other hand, Delhi topped in terms of average credit size with a whopping ₹ 23.77 lakh per account, signifying that majority of the accounts are high valued, mostly representing corporate credit. The above distribution which clearly shows a higher concentration and penetration of credit services in the high income States/UTs, implies that at the sub-national level, the inclusive policies have not found much favour with poorer states. Again, at the intra-sub-national level, even in richer states, the outreach is concentrated among the large borrowers and businesses, which is evident from the lower share of both the number and value of small borrower accounts in better performing regions like Delhi, Chandigarh, Maharashtra, Gujarat and Punjab. Lastly, a matching of the quintile distribution of States/UTs obtained for credit parameters with that of per capita income also reveals trends similar to that obtained with deposit parameters.

Thus, there is no doubt that, in the current growth process, the gains from growth are much more unevenly distributed, marginalizing people across space and sectors. Though two major changes viz., greater financial deepening (which drives demand) and the advent of technology (which drives distribution of services) have taken place during the process of transition from growth to inclusive growth, the fact remains that we do not yet have effective instruments to address the issue of inequality of opportunities. The results obtained while juxtaposing the quintile income classification of states with their performance in the inclusiveness of banking conform to earlier studies (eg. Kurian 2001).

Credit-Deposit Ratio

The CD ratio of scheduled commercial banks shows wide variation among states, with an all-India average of 72 during 2009–10, representing an improvement from the level of 56 in 1999–2000 and 66 in 2004–05 (Appendix II). Across the states, the CD ratio spanned from as high as 131 in Chandigarh to as low as 7 in Lakshadweep during 2009–10. Excluding the Union Territories from the analysis, this ranges between 114 in Tamil Nadu and 26 in Goa and Meghalaya during the year 2009–10. This wide variation can be ascribed to the uneven economic development and diverse nature of political economy of Indian States/UTs. On the positive side, the CD ratio has improved in almost all the States/UTs, with the exception of Maharashtra and Meghalaya, through the 2000s. Among the North-Eastern States, Sikkim and Mizoram exhibited good progress in achieving higher levels of CD ratio during the decade. In addition to the three Southern states (Tamil Nadu, Andhra Pradesh and Karnataka), Chandigarh, Rajasthan and Punjab registered tremendous positive change. Kerala and West Bengal showed only modest increases in the ratio, which reached a level just above 60 during 2009–10. An unwelcome development in this regard is the decline in the ratio in three states viz., Maharashtra, Meghalaya and Orissa during the year 2009–10 as against the levels attained during 2004–05.

A look at the temporal changes in the classification of States/UTs according to CD ratio during the reference period (Table 7) revealed that the number of States/UTs with CD ratio above the all-India average did not change much, with the figure at six during both 1999–2000 and 2004–05 and eight during 2009–10. Further, only six States/UTs, viz., Tamil Nadu (89), Maharashtra (86), Chandigarh (82), Andhra Pradesh (64) and Karnataka (63) and Delhi (61) registered a CD ratio of more than 60 (national benchmark) during 1999–2000. During the year 2009–10, this group expanded to 13 States/UTs, with the addition of Gujarat, Haryana, Kerala, Madhya Pradesh, Punjab, Rajasthan and West Bengal. The number of States with a CD ratio of less than 40, which stood at 18 during 1999–2000, declined at a rather slow pace to the level of 16 and 13 respectively during 2004–05 and 2009–10. This clearly indicates that much of the improvement in the all India average CD ratio comes from the progress achieved by a handful of more developed States/UTs. It also shows that credit disbursement in less developed States is far lower as compared to that in advanced States.

Further, there existed wide state to state variations in the pace of reduction of gap from the highest CD ratio (Table 5). During the reference period, the CD ratio of 13 States/UTs experienced a drift further away from that of the State/UT with the highest CD ratio, as can be seen from an increase in the normalized distance from the latter, implying a slower growth vis-à-vis the highest. Majority of these States/UTs belonged to the low-income and less developed category (Assam, Bihar, Chattisgarh, Madhya Pradesh, Manipur,

Orissa, Tripura and West Bengal), the exceptions being Delhi, Goa, Gujarat, Karnataka and Maharashtra. The performance of these 13 States/UTs in terms of reducing the distance from the all-India average CD ratio showed diverse patterns with some states reducing the distance, thereby approaching the average and the others experiencing an increase in distance from the average during the first half of the decade followed by an decrease in distance during the second half of the decade or vice versa. Jammu and Kashmir and Jharkhand are the states whose relative position remained constant throughout the decade with reference to the State/UT with highest CD ratio, in spite of an improvement over the initial level.

CHALLENGES FOR POLICY AND CONCLUSION

The results of this analysis showed that the use of finance too shows disquieting trends in tandem with that of income. Also, most of the improvement in various parameters is observed in a few high income states. This is in agreement with the finding of earlier studies that the level of financial inclusion inevitably rise in response to prosperity and declining inequalities (eg. Sarma 2008). Any region that excludes a majority of its population from the formal financial system cannot be optimally employing its human resources. Eventually, economic growth would be lower than what it could have been if a larger majority is drawn into the formal financial system. This constitutes the logical core of the more modern idea that access to formal financial services be made universal rather than confining it to be need-based. The presence of a large segment of financially excluded population can be viewed as a form of market failure where commercial providers do not supply those whose effective demand is judged inadequate. However, the institutional data is insufficient to exemplify this conditionality.

The factors responsible for the observed patterns in distribution of deposit and credit across the states becomes evident only with an analysis of the determinants of access to and use of financial services, which is beyond the scope of the present paper. However, a survey of existing literature on the possible causes of financial exclusion offers possible explanations. A recent study in the Indian context has shown that the access to financial services and its usage are not strictly correlated (Kamath *et al.,* 2010). The interplay of a host of factors ranging from market, institutional, cultural, social and personal to government policies (Kempson *et al.,* 2000) has been identified to cause financial exclusion. Though these multiple factors leading to exclusion are not directly related to income, low income is associated with financial exclusion, as seen from the profile of distribution of deposit and credit across the Indian States/UTs grouped according to quintile income. This is so because low income groups are least likely to have a bank account, which in turn is considered the starting point for accessing other important financial services. Low-income implies a lack of effective demand for financial services.

This could, however, be interpreted as a failure of supply and the limitations of the current service provision to become inclusive and responsive to the needs of low-income groups. An underlying argument in this direction is that the financial services sector has been showing a trend of shifting away from providing basic deposit and credit products towards 'growth-orientated investment related products' (Kempson *et al.,* 2000:16–17; Rogaly and Fisher 1999:4). This is evident from the retreat of financial service providers from the already deprived and low income States/UTs to better performing and higher income ones, which also happen to be generally more endowed in terms of natural resources, infrastructure and investment climate.

The banking system in India witnessed some revolutionary changes during the late sixties, with the introduction of social control over commercial banks 1968, followed by the nationalisation of major commercial banks in 1969 and 1980. This marked a paradigm shift as the over-arching objective of nationalisation of banks was to take banking to the masses. Consequently, the nationalised banks explicitly set quantitative targets to expand their network in rural and semi-urban areas and to direct credit to priority sectors. The expansion of rural branches continued to be encouraged on the premise that the scheduled commercial banks had a role to play in the process of institutionalisation of rural savings and rural credit. The number of offices of scheduled commercial banks increased from 8187 in 1969 to 67030 as at the end of March 2000 and further to 86960 as at the end of March 2010 (BSR, RBI). The average population per branch office declined from 64000 to 8895 during the same period. However, the bulk of this expansion took place prior to the economic reforms of the 1990s, after which the explicit policy of spread of branch network in rural areas was given up by the RBI. This left out certain under-banked states such as Bihar, Assam, Madhya Pradesh, Uttar Pradesh, Chattisgarh, West Bengal and most of the North Eastern States, where the average population per branch office continued to be very high in the range of 10000 to 23000 compared to the national average and that of highly banked states of Chandigarh (2264), Goa (2443), Punjab (5162) during 2009–10. The number of offices per lakh population in these under-banked states was less than ten during 2009–10 as against the highest of 44 in Chandigarh.

The SHG-Bank Linkage Programme (SBLP) evolved as a corporate strategy in 1992 under the aegis of the National Bank for Agriculture and Rural Development (NABARD), in order to bridge the rural-urban divide in access to financial services. The growth of the microfinance sector in India since 1995–96 has been quite impressive and hence SBLP is widely recognized as an effective and sustainable model for financial inclusion. Nonetheless, a vast majority in the rural areas of these states remained untouched, as evident from the geographically skewed distribution of microfinance, with a higher concentration in the Southern and Western States. Inadequate banking infrastructure is therefore a cause of concern while pushing the agenda for financial inclusion in the low-income states, the remedy for which lies in the adoption of cost-effective expansion of financial services through more recourse to branchless banking involving business correspondents and technology options. The unique problems plaguing the regions with low CD ratios have to be identified for expanding banking facilities and formulating area-specific action plans for accelerated financial deepening.

Qualitative factors like cultural identification, participation and awareness also play an equally important role as that of proximity and appropriate range of services in influencing the access of low income population to the formal financial system. Lastly, credit alone may not help improve the income and productive capacity of the poor as the credit absorptive capacity depends upon various factors such as policy environment, infrastructure and supply chain facility. The factors associated with the political economy of growth and the growth in public investment have a strong impact on shaping opportunities and creating an enabling environment for expanding the level of output of the economy. The differences in these aspects and their implications for the regional economies of India can provide alternative explanations for the widening regional inequalities. Enhancing the economic opportunities in backward areas depends on the initial asset endowments, market conditions, quality of institutions and development interventions. The rising inter-state disparities in both per capita income and infrastructure over the past 25 years confirm the role of infrastructure on growth of output and income. The appalling inter-state disparities in access to and use of banking services could therefore be seen as part of the vicious cycle of decelerating public investment, poor quality of institutions and reduced efficiency of public goods and infrastructure, which together act as barriers for the disadvantaged and low-income groups to access different kinds of services. Inclusive measures have to be 'self-generating', rather than 'policy-driven' and programmes for inclusion have to be designed in a 'proactive' rather than 'reactive' framework (Drabu 2009: 49). To summarise, greater accessibility and availability of financial services is a pre-requisite for inclusive income growth. Therefore, financial sector reforms that promote broader access to financial services and focus on equalizing opportunities hold the key for development.

REFERENCES

Basu, K. (2001). 'On the Goals of Development' In Meier, G.M. and Stiglitz, J.E. (Eds.) *Frontiers of Development Economics: the Future in Perspective.* Oxford University Press, New York.

Basu, K. (2006). 'Globalisation, Poverty and Inequality: What is the Relationship? What can be Done?' *World Development,* 34(8): 1361–73.

Consultative Group to Assist the Poor (CGAP) (2009). *Measuring Access to Financial Services to the Poor.* Consultative Group to Assist the Poor and The World Bank, Washington DC.

Drabu, H.A. (2009). 'Economics and Inclusion' in Kochhar, S. *et al.* (Ed.) *Financial Inclusion*, Academic Foundation, New Delhi, pp. 47–51.

Financial Access Database (2009). International Monetary Fund.

Government of India (2008). 'Report of the Committee on Financial Inclusion' (Chairman: Dr. C. Rangarajan), Ministry of Finance, Government of India, New Delhi.

Kamath, R., Mukherji, A. and Sandstrom, M. (2010). 'Accessing Institutional Finance: A Demand Side Story for Rural India'. *Economic and Political Weekly.* XLV(37). September 11–17, pp. 56–62.

Kempson, E. (2006). 'Policy level Response to Financial Exclusion in Developed Economies: Lessons for Developing Countries'. Paper presented at the conference, *Access to Finance: Building Inclusive Financial Systems*, World Bank, Washington DC.

Kempson, E., Claire, W., Caskey, J. and Collard, S. (2000). 'In or Out? Financial Exclusion: A Literature and Research Review.' Financial Services Authority, London.

King, R.G. and Levine, R. (1993). 'Finance and Growth: Schumpeter might be right'. *Quarterly Journal of Economics,* Vol. 108, pp. 717–37.

Kurian, N.J. (2001). *A Note on Socio-Demographic Disparities among Major Indian States,* Planning Commission, New Delhi.

McKinnon, R.I. (1973). *Money and Capital in Economic Development.* The Brookings Institution, Washington.

National Sample Survey Organisation (NSSO) (2005). 'Situation Assessment Survey of Farmers-Indebtedness of Farmer Households: NSS 59th Round (January–December 2003)'. *National Sample Survey Organisation Report No. 498 (59/33/1),* NSSO, Ministry of Statistics and Programme Implementation, Government of India, New Delhi.

Rajan, R. and Luigi Z. (2003). *Saving Capitalism from the Capitalists: Unleashing the Power of Financial Markets to Create Wealth and Spread Opportunity.* New York: Crown Business.

Reserve Bank of India (various years). *Basic Statistical Return of Scheduled Commercial Banks.* Reserve Bank of India, Mumbai.

______ *Database of Indian Economy*, http://dbie.rbi.org.in

Rogaly, B. and Fisher, T. (1999). 'Introduction', in B. Rogaly, T. Fisher and E. Mayo (Eds.), *Poverty, Social Exclusion and Microfinance in Britain*, Oxford: Oxfam Publishing.

Sarma, M. (2008). 'Index of Financial Inclusion'. *Working Paper No. 215.* Indian Council for Research on International Economic Relations.

Shaw, E.S. (1973). *Financial Deepening in Economic Development.* Oxford University Press, New York.

Subramanian, S. (2010). 'Identifying the Income-Poor: Some Controversies in India and Elsewhere'. *Discussion Paper No. 46, Poverty, Equity and Growth.* November. Courant Research Centre, Gottingen.

Subramanian, S. (2011). 'Inclusive Development and the Quintile Income Statistic'. *Economic and Political Weekly.* Vol. XLVI (4), pp. 69–72.

APPENDICES

Appendix Table 1: State-wise Distribution of Deposit of Scheduled Commercial Banks in India (1999–2000, 2004–05 and 2009–10)

Sl. No.	*State/Union Territory*	*No. of Deposit Accounts per 1000 adults*			*Average Deposit Size (₹)*			*Per Capita Deposit (₹)*			*Deposit –Income Ratio*		
		1999–2000	*2004–05*	*2009–10*	*1999–2000*	*2004–05*	*2009–10*	*1999–2000*	*2004–05*	*2009–10*	*1999–00*	*2004–05*	*2009–10*
1.	Andaman and Nicobar	698	694	1049	19720	41021	58238	13765	28479	61064	0.57	0.82	0.97
2.	Andhra Pradesh	582	721	1176	15660	25348	37414	9114	18264	44009	0.59	0.76	0.91
3.	Arunachal Pradesh	441	402	739	19028	41251	69116	8384	16585	51111	0.60	0.75	1.22
4.	Assam	477	435	686	10898	23160	37225	5195	10084	25533	0.42	0.60	0.93
5.	Bihar	534	366	503	14519	21203	33877	7748	7753	17036	1.34	1.04	1.10
6.	Chandigarh	2758	2592	3154	36725	70052	135257	101298	181549	426570	2.28	2.28	3.30
7.	Chhattisgarh*		355	612		32573	49423		11562	30252		0.68	0.87
8.	Dadra and Nagar Haveli	442	660	1161	27394	31637	38722	12112	20892	44966	na	na	na
9.	Daman and Diu	1047	1049	1422	31383	50875	59451	32845	53380	84524	na	na	na
10.	Delhi	1871	1904	3442	53599	117368	149542	100283	223465	514742	2.58	4.10	4.97
11.	Goa	2266	2643	3111	28910	42252	86722	65516	111666	269836	1.55	1.69	2.35
12.	Gujarat	624	699	996	23273	38278	54345	14522	26764	54144	0.77	0.93	0.94
13.	Haryana	799	822	1202	16163	30690	57089	12922	25230	68620	0.56	0.67	0.87
14.	Himachal Pradesh	941	965	1286	15999	28942	44719	15060	27936	57490	0.72	0.90	1.19
15.	Jammu and Kashmir	724	741	1052	18914	31879	41326	13688	23630	43481	0.99	1.22	1.57
16.	Jharkhand*		500	1211		31185	45216		15600	54773		1.00	2.12
17.	Karnataka	728	780	1193	17845	36225	59368	12994	28258	70821	0.74	1.14	1.51
18.	Kerala	880	1078	1244	18990	26682	49723	16716	28752	61850	0.86	0.99	1.15
19.	Lakshadweep	2075	638	1129	7623	35807	89263	15820	22858	100773	na	na	na
20.	Madhya Pradesh	538	456	695	15442	26387	39053	8306	12040	27128	0.67	0.83	1.06
21.	Maharashtra	659	730	946	35311	74757	168824	23256	54602	159713	1.01	1.69	2.39

Sl. No.	*State/Union Territory*	*No. of Deposit Accounts per 1000 adults*			*Average Deposit Size (₹)*			*Per Capita Deposit (₹)*			*Deposit –Income Ratio*		
		1999–2000	*2004–05*	*2009–10*	*1999–2000*	*2004–05*	*2009–10*	*1999–2000*	*2004–05*	*2009–10*	*1999–00*	*2004–05*	*2009–10*
22.	Manipur	191	167	341	15371	34700	42377	2938	5794	14441	0.22	0.35	0.57
23.	Meghalaya	494	434	613	21751	47496	74563	10736	20619	45700	0.75	0.97	1.21
24.	Mizoram	229	258	533	24751	48307	60197	5677	12479	32087	0.35	0.56	0.77
25.	Nagaland	238	222	438	26833	47311	76559	6393	10496	33562	0.45	0.52	na
26.	Orissa	383	416	709	13729	24628	41976	5254	10251	29771	0.49	0.63	0.95
27.	Puducherry	937	1026	1466	21342	34683	46964	19989	35577	68828	0.66	0.82	0.93
28.	Punjab	1188	1155	1483	20063	32672	48415	23834	37748	71777	0.93	1.14	1.15
29.	Rajasthan	477	498	716	15072	23391	36888	7194	11640	26405	0.53	0.69	0.85
30.	Sikkim	364	505	887	37094	67912	90590	13513	34322	80361	0.91	1.44	1.84
31.	Tamil Nadu	700	718	1140	17569	31668	48129	12293	22750	54855	0.63	0.83	0.96
32.	Tripura	481	449	794	12742	26569	39383	6131	11920	31267	0.43	0.52	0.93
33.	Uttar Pradesh	677	603	894	12676	21194	30200	8578	12789	26990	0.88	1.05	1.23
34.	Uttarakhand*		901	1949		37856	54706		34124	106595		1.48	2.05
35.	West Bengal	671	610	842	16817	32318	54236	11292	19724	45653	0.71	0.87	1.10
36.	All India	629	653	950	19898	37422	62066	12520	24442	58963	0.79	1.05	1.32

Source: BSR, RBI.

Note: * These three states were constituted during 2000–2001.

Appendix Table 2: State-wise Distribution of Credit and CD Ratio of Scheduled Commercial Banks in India (1999–2000, 2004–05 and 2009–10)

State/Union Territory	*No. of Credit Accounts per 1000 Adults*			*Average Credit Size (₹)*			*Per Capita Credit (₹)*			*Credit-Income Ratio*			*CD Ratio*		
	1999–00	*2004–05*	*2009–10*	*1999–2000*	*2004–05*	*2009–10*	*1999–2000*	*2004–05*	*2009–10*	*1999–00*	*2004–05*	*2009–10*	*1999–00*	*2004–05*	*2009–10*
Andaman and Nicobar	50	65	98	46290	117004	226715	2307	28479	22313	0.10	0.22	0.35	17	27	37
Andhra Pradesh	130	175	241	45157	78275	192103	5854	18264	46273	0.38	0.57	0.96	64	75	105
Arunachal Pradesh	61	48	77	21580	75973	183311	1314	16585	14078	0.09	0.16	0.34	16	22	28
Assam	45	49	78	37108	72830	123101	1662	10084	9650	0.14	0.21	0.35	32	35	38
Bihar	71	51	70	24634	42347	70829	1740	7753	4943	0.30	0.29	0.32	22	28	29
Chandigarh	240	204	373	346715	789976	1501061	83070	181549	559216	1.87	2.03	4.33	82	89	131
Chhattisgarh*		48	63		104228	249509		11562	15814		0.30	0.45		44	52
Dadra and Nagar Haveli	22	33	42	104500	222458	642344	2277	20892	26961	na	na	na	na	35	60
Daman and Diu	43	42	29	119858	146959	582540	5163	53380	17042	na	na	na	16	12	20
Delhi	107	152	162	566839	915095	2377630	60692	223465	384047	1.56	2.56	3.71	61	62	75
Goa	128	138	211	121767	203622	339012	15600	111666	71429	0.37	0.42	0.62	24	25	26
Gujarat	61	63	88	116178	197278	401194	7116	26764	35347	0.38	0.43	0.61	49	46	65
Haryana	80	82	121	68292	158137	358414	5473	25230	43456	0.24	0.34	0.55	42	51	63
Himachal Pradesh	86	92	118	41690	110172	206080	3577	27936	24281	0.17	0.33	0.50	24	36	42
Jammu and Kashmir	48	58	77	95803	190072	261070	4580	23630	20164	0.33	0.57	0.73	33	47	46
Jharkhand*		64	125		72393	154386		15600	19231		0.30	0.75		30	35
Karnataka	144	191	213	57146	109413	258420	8230	28258	54948	0.47	0.84	1.17	63	74	78
Kerala	152	193	245	45690	81564	159646	6942	28752	39042	0.36	0.54	0.72	42	55	63

State/Union Territory	*No. of Credit Accounts per 1000 Adults*			*Average Credit Size (₹)*			*Per Capita Credit (₹)*			*Credit-Income Ratio*			*CD Ratio*		
	1999–00	*2004–05*	*2009–10*	*1999–2000*	*2004–05*	*2009–10*	*1999–2000*	*2004–05*	*2009–10*	*1999–00*	*2004–05*	*2009–10*	*1999–00*	*2004–05*	*2009–10*
Lakshadweep	49	59	94	23814	37184	78050	1178	22858	7343	na	na	na	7	10	7
Madhya Pradesh	72	68	90	56377	96173	183350	4078	12040	16439	0.33	0.45	0.64	49	55	61
Maharashtra	74	135	337	272268	384427	393502	20091	54602	132457	0.87	1.60	1.98	86	95	83
Manipur	32	29	47	34144	83699	130490	1100	5794	6073	0.08	0.15	0.24	37	42	42
Meghalaya	61	62	77	28543	145181	151767	1750	20619	11707	0.12	0.42	0.31	16	44	26
Mizoram	41	61	100	32033	98188	170146	1321	12479	17066	0.08	0.27	0.41	23	48	53
Nagaland	27	32	79	36364	75042	129502	981	10496	10171	0.07	0.12	na	15	23	30
Orissa	98	99	121	22289	63641	133392	2182	10251	16189	0.21	0.39	0.52	42	62	54
Puducherry	133	150	278	50493	90960	141663	6722	35577	39386	0.22	0.31	0.53	34	38	57
Punjab	96	97	121	97924	195429	424683	9384	37748	51330	0.37	0.57	0.83	39	50	72
Rajasthan	63	72	93	53048	111097	250683	3360	11640	23331	0.25	0.47	0.75	47	69	88
Sikkim	49	81	113	41906	125491	265150	2040	34322	29911	0.14	0.43	0.69	15	29	37
Tamil Nadu	124	262	369	87511	87909	169329	10891	22750	62447	0.56	0.84	1.09	89	101	114
Tripura	167	116	133	9429	29422	72125	1576	11920	9614	0.11	0.15	0.29	26	29	31
Uttar Pradesh	65	73	84	37357	66276	138902	2419	12789	11680	0.25	0.40	0.53	28	38	43
Uttarakhand*		94	198		88694	181633		34124	35959		0.36	0.69		24	34
West Bengal	76	66	68	67958	157234	414818	5136	19724	28097	0.32	0.46	0.68	45	52	62
All India	83	108	153	84628	149379	276699	7015	24442	42440	0.44	0.70	0.95	56	66	72

Source and note: Ibid.

Financial Inclusion under MGNREGA: Achievements and Challenges

P. Leelavathi, K. Hanumantha Rao, G. Rajani Kanth and C. Dheeraja

Centre for Wage Employment and Poverty Alleviation,
National Institute of Rural Development, Hyderabad

ABSTRACT: *Since nationalisation of banks, there has been increased flow of credit to rural areas, agriculture and even to the poorer sections. However, the NSSO survey on situation analysis of farmers (2003) highlighted two stark realities-nearly 51 per cent of the Indian farmers had no access to credit and a sizeable proportion of them could not receive any credit support from the formal financial institutions. Dr. Rangarajan Committee on Financial Inclusion (2008) has suggested a National Rural Financial Inclusion Plan (NRFIP) to provide financial services to all rural households by 2015. The National Rural Employment Guarantee Act (NREGA) of 2005, the major flagship programme of the Ministry of Rural development (MoRD) is another public intervention aiming at linking the rural poor with banks and post offices through payment of wages. The scale of its operations both in terms of number of households covered and availability of funds, assumes significance for the financial inclusion of the poor. The purport of the paper is to highlight the contribution of the MGNREGA in formalising the link between the rural poor and also the opportunity for the banks to market their products given the vast size of the new clientele group. The studies of NIRD in the five states—Chattisgarh, Gujarat, Orissa, Rajasthan and Uttar Pradesh, have come out with interesting findings dealing with the aspects such as satisfaction of the poor with the formal association with the banks, attitude of bankers, the utility of IT applications to reach the poor in under banked areas and the demand for other financial services. The paper also highlights some of the opportunities and challenges for an effective financial inclusion envisaged by the banking sector and MoRD.*

INTRODUCTION

Since independence, India has been launching several reforms to make growth process rapid and socially inclusive. Improved access of the poor to credit is one of the avowed objectives of financial sector reforms. The Nationalisation of Banks in 1969 can be construed as one of the major initiatives of the state in this direction. The introduction of

Poverty Alleviation schemes in late 70s more so Integrated Rural Development Programme (IRDP) is another historical milestone in linking bank credit with self employment Programmes. The SHG-Bank Linkage Scheme of NABARD has opened up new vistas in the sphere of credit flow to the poor. To strengthen the process further, the self-employment oriented poverty reduction programme has been restructured and Swarnjayanti Gram Swarojgar Yojana (SGSY) came into being in 1999. However, the National Sample Survey Organisation's study on the situation analysis of farmers (2003) has come out with startling findings which include: about 51.4 per cent of the farmers were having no access to credit and most of the indebted farmers were having limited access to institutional finance. The Government of India has launched a massive 'rights' based wage employment programme known as "National Rural Employment Guarantee Act (NREGA), 2005" to ensure livelihood security to the poor. Under this Act, it is made mandatory to make wage payments through a network of banks and post offices to all the workers in 2008. The scale of funds and coverage of rural households made NREGA as the largest wage employment programme in the world and its pace financial inclusion surpassed the outreach formal financial institutions. The Rangarajan Committee on Financial Inclusion (2008) made several valuable suggestions to address the supply side as well as demand side problems. It recommended a National Rural Financial Inclusion Plan (NRFIP) to include all rural households under comprehensive financial services by 2015.

In this context, the paper attempts to make an assessment of the effectiveness of financial inclusion under the MGNREGA in five selected states of India.

OBJECTIVES

The specific objectives of the study are:

- to what extent MGNREGA could link the poor with formal financial institutions with special reference to public sector banks; and
- to document the benefits realised by the poor from financial inclusion and their perceptions.

The study also attempted to examine the special efforts made by the banks to improve the access of the rural poor to quality credit.

The information on the progress made by MGNREGA under financial Inclusion both in terms of number of accounts and amount disbursed towards wage payment for workers was taken from the MIS data of the Ministry of Rural Development (MoRD) to examine the first objective. The approaches followed for financial inclusion by the states of Chhattisgarh, Gujarat, Orissa, Rajasthan and Uttar Pradesh was discussed in brief. The second objective was studied with the help of data collected from a sample of MGNREGA worker households drawn from the five states indicated above.

PROFILE OF THE SAMPLE STATES

Chhattisgarh

The economy of Chhattisgarh heavily depends on agriculture. In spite of its abundant natural resources and manpower pool, Chhattisgarh remains a poverty stricken and socially backward region. One third of Chhattisgarh's population is of tribes, mostly in the thickly forested areas. The access to banks and financial inclusion is one of the biggest problems because of its geographical remoteness.

Gujarat

Gujarat is one of the most prosperous states of the country owing to its booming economy and industry. The state provides about 19.8% of the country's total industrial output and is the most industrialized state of the country. The rural economy of Gujarat is diversified but levels of poverty in rural areas remained 39 per cent in 2004–05.

Orissa

Orissa is primarily an agrarian economy having nearly 30% contribution to the Net State Domestic product (NSDP) with 73 percent of the work force engaged in this sector. The cropped area is about 87.46 lakh hectares out of which 18.79 lakh hectares are irrigated. Orissa is predominantly a tribal state with 62 tribal communities and with a total population of 8.14 million (Census of India 2001). Out of them, 11 tribal communities have been identified as primitive. Orissa's economy has a contrasting scenario. Despite of vast land, forest and mineral resources it hasn't made significant stride. It is one of the backward states with high levels of poverty.

Rajasthan

Owning 11% of the India's total geographical area, Rajasthan is the largest state in the country. In the west, Rajasthan is relatively dry and infertile; this area includes some of the Desert areas. The decline in poverty level has been significant during the recent decades. Also, the MGNREGS (Mahatma Gandhi National Rural Employment Guarantee Scheme) has fared well in the state in the initial years pumping in a lot of money in rural areas.

U.P

The status of human development in U.P continues to be far from satisfactory. It ranked at 13th position in terms of Human Development Index (HDI). It is lagging behind in terms of the major indicators of social development (Literacy rate in U.P 56.3 percent) and health indicators like life expectancy, infant mortality rate, etc. Economically also

Uttar Pradesh is among the most backward States of India, characterized by the pre-dominance of the agricultural sector with heavy dependence on Monsoon, high percentage of marginal and small land holdings, high population pressure, small manufacturing sector, structural deficiencies in infrastructure, glaring regional imbalances. Poverty levels are relatively high in Uttar Pradesh.

In each of the five states, one backward and one developed district were randomly selected. Further, from each selected district, one developed and one interior block with more SC and ST population having sizeable number of SB accounts were randomly chosen. From each block, two gram panchayats were selected based on a number of factors like distance from block headquarters, level of development, size of SC&ST population and MGNREGA SB accounts. From each sample GP, 30 workers were selected from the list of workers who participated in MGNREGA during 2008–09. In all six states, 10 districts, 20 blocks, 40 gram panchayats and 1200 worker households constitute the sample. The survey was conducted in 2010 and the reference years for the data collection were 2008–09 and 2009–10. The details are presented in Annexure–A.

RESULTS

The term financial inclusion concerns with the process of establishing formal link between the people and formal financial agencies so that the former can access the various products offered by the latter. Financial Inclusion is the process of ensuring access to financial services and timely and adequate credit where needed by the vulnerable groups such as weaker sections and low income groups at an affordable cost (Rangarajan, 2008). Under MGNREGA, the financial inclusion has been envisaged to make the whole wage payment process transparent and to prevent embezzlement of funds by eliminating the role of intermediaries. It also provides opportunities to the poor to develop savings habit and access other financial services.

Since amending the Act to make wage payments through financial agencies mandatory in 2008, the number of savings bank (SB) accounts has gone up remarkably. An estimated 12.36 crore households were registered with MGNREGA and about 9.12 crore accounts have been opened during 2011–12. Of these, nearly 3.41 crore SB accounts were opened by the banks. However, 4.44 crore SB accounts were active and were in operation benefiting an estimated 4.98 crore worker households during 2011–12. Since over 90 per cent of the MGNREGA worker households are poor, one can infer that a sizeable proportion of rural poor households have been linked to either banks or post offices. Further, the share of SC and ST in the total MGNREGA worker households (41 per cent) is higher than their share in population (25 per cent) indicating the 'social inclusion' orientation of the MGNREGA.

The Table 1 provides the status of financial inclusion under MGNREGA as on March 2012 with reference to banks. All 361 banks, including public and private banks have been

Table 1: Financial Inclusion under MGNREGA: Contribution of Banks (2011–12)

S. No.	*State*	*No. of Active Bank Accounts*	*Percentage of Bank Accounts in Total Accounts*	*Amount of Wages Disbursed through Bank Accounts (Rs. in lakhs)*	*Percentage of Amount Disbursed through Banks in Total Amount disbursed (Rs. in lakhs)*
1.	AP	652930	16.23	34341	24.11
2.	Arunachal Pradesh	797	25.09	44	94.56
3.	Assam	543608	41.68	18333	44.53
4.	Bihar	54935	3.15	2761	3.33
5.	Chhattisgarh	1287387	29.43	40307	32.65
6.	Goa*	10450	100.00	469	100.00
7.	Gujarat	235588	21.38	7397	22.14
8.	Haryana*	244128	88.31	14832	89.31
9.	HP*	236610	85.53	14542	86.69
10.	J and K*	239924	90.84	11301	90.97
11.	Jharkhand	174272	9.24	6045	8.79
12.	Karnataka	1194376	65.69	76336	63.60
13.	Kerala*	1093985	88.43	75078	89.13
14.	MP	1543870	64.72	60018	66.93
15.	Maharashtra	270783	14.91	10266	11.78
16.	Manipur	19610	14.33	0	0.00
17.	Meghalaya	75136	66.47	0	0.00
18.	Mizoram	19394	18.19	2515	26.99
19.	Nagaland*	95603	100.00	INA	INA
20.	Odisha	811778	48.32	24821	47.49
21.	Punjab	123533	58.07	4640	61.80
22.	Rajasthan	2590278	50.61	100334	53.65
23.	Sikkim	33086	58.49	2196	62.09
24.	Tamil Nadu	478604	99.89	0	0.00
25.	Tripura	418419	69.50	40282	71.31
26.	UP*	7182000	87.97	275817	89.18
27.	Uttarakhand	142979	54.73	6550	54.46
28.	West Bengal	1762982	36.25	59542	38.26
29.	Andaman And Nicobar*	4678	95.43	254	96.61
30.	Lakshadweep	128	3.51	7	3.86
31.	Puducherry	12398	99.94	289	99.96
	Total	21554249	48.51	889316	51.90

*State/UT with good participation of banks.

actively associated with MGNREGA under the financial inclusion. The total active SB accounts of MGNREGA workers with banks were 2.15 crores accounting for almost 51.5 per cent of the total MGNREGA SB accounts. The prominence of banks is more evident in the states and UTs of Goa, Haryana, HP, Kerala, Nagaland, UP, Andaman and Nicobar and Puducherry. During the year 2011–12, the banks have disbursed wages equivalent to ₹ 8893.16 crore and the percentage share of banks in total wage transactions was 51.90.

The average amount transacted by the banks per SB account was ₹ 4126 during this year.

From Table 2, it is evident that a large proportion of sample households belong to SC and ST. Illiterates account for 68–69 per cent among the sample respondents in the states of Rajasthan and Uttar Pradesh, while the percentage of illiterates hover around 44–55 in the other states. The landless constitute about one-fourth of the sample households in Gujarat and one-third in the states of Chhattisgarh and Rajasthan. In the backward states of Uttar Pradesh and Orissa their representation is very high (46–50 per cent). The share of marginal and small farm households was significant in all the five states. It is interesting to note that about 15 per cent of the sample workers are medium and large farmers in Chhattisgarh which only indicates the low productivity of lands of these farming communities.

Table 2: Socio-Economic Profiles of the Sample Workers

(%)

	Chhattisgarh	*Gujarat*	*Orissa*	*Rajasthan*	*U.P*
Caste					
SC and ST	60.8	74.2	81.2	85.2	62.8
OBC and Minorities	28.3	25.8	8.8	13.2	30.6
Others	10.8	–	10.0	1.6	6.6
Literacy					
Illiterates	43.8	55.0	50.8	67.6	69.4
Landholding					
Landless	33.3	25.0	46.3	36.0	49.6
Marginal and Small	51.3	73.8	52.4	62.4	49.6
Medium and Large	15.4	1.3	1.3	1.6	0.8
Worker per Household	1.44	0.75	0.89	1.08	1.36

In most of the states, the opening of Savings Bank accounts has been done in a mission mode and in some states like Gujarat the Programme Officer (PO) has taken lead. The details of opening of account with the financial institutions by the sample workers are presented in Table 3. In Rajasthan about 40 per cent of the sample workers informed that the SB accounts were opened in the village itself. In other four states, the venue was Bank or post office. The officials and elected representatives of PRIs at GP level played the facilitating role in the opening of SB accounts.

Table 3: Details of Opening of SB Accounts—Responses of Sample Workers

(%)

	Chhattisgarh	*Gujarat*	*Orissa*	*Rajasthan*	*U.P*
Opening Accounts-Place					
In the village	26.3	7.9	18.3	39.6	1.7
At the Bank/PO	70.8	90.0	76.3	54.8	95.9
At Block level	3.0	2.1	5.4	5.6	1.2
Account opening mela	–		–	–	1.2
Facilitating Agency					
GRS	10.8	10.0	42.5	48.8	64.0
GP Secretary	36.7	10.8	28.8	18.0	16.1
GP Sarpanch/Ward Member	32.5	17.1	22.1	18.4	11.6
SHG Member	–	–	–	–	2.1
Mate	–	–	–	14.8	
Education Youth	–	–	–	–	5.4
Programme Officer	5.0	47.5	2.1	–	
Other account holder	1.3	–	4.6	–	0.8
Not aware	13.8	14.6	–	–	–

In financial inclusion process, the main issues are: whether the workers are able to operate the SB accounts; what are the transaction costs incurred? Whether workers are confident of operating on their own? And what is frequency of transactions made? The data in Table 4 reveal that a very high proportion of workers are operating the accounts for withdrawal of wages on their own. It varied from 52 per cent (Rajasthan) to 83 per cent (Orissa). Some of the sample respondents (14–17 per cent) from Rajasthan and Gujarat are also seeking the help of other family members in operating the account.

The GP officials, Sarpanch or Members of GP are also helping the workers in this regard and such cases are reported in Chhattisgarh, Gujarat and Orissa. Only in Rajasthan, about 31 per cent informed that they are dependent on outsiders for withdrawal of wages from the financial institution.

The workers have to incur costs towards travel, board and lodging for withdrawal of wage earnings if these institutions are far away from the village. About 95 per cent in Gujarat and 61 per cent in Rajasthan from among the sample households reported incurring of transaction cost. On an average it was about ₹ 50 – ₹ 58 in the states of Chhattisgarh,

Gujarat and Orissa. In the other states, the sample workers incurred about ₹ 72 – ₹ 88 per transaction.

The number of transactions has increased considerably in 17–18 per cent of the sample households of Orissa. For a considerable proportion of sample workers (over 56 per cent) in Gujarat, Orissa and Rajasthan, the number of transactions have gone up moderately.

Due to the establishment of formal linkage with financial institutions, a very few sample households have been able to access to other services of the financial institutions (see Table 5). UP is laggard in this respect. So, it is clear that banks have yet to establish better links with the worker community.

Table 4: Operating the SB Accounts—Responses of Sample Workers

(%)

	Chhattisgarh	*Gujarat*	*Orissa*	*Rajasthan*	*U.P*
Operating SB Account					
Self	62.9	72.5	82.9	52.0	74.8
Other Family Members	3.8	14.2	4.2	16.8	5.8
GP Functionary	16.3	–	–	–	17.4
GP Sarpanch/Member	12.9	13.3	11.2	–	–
Other co worker	–	–	–	–	2.1
Any Other Person	4.2	–	1.7	31.2	–
Transaction cost					
Reporting (%)	27.92	95.00	12.08	61.20	36.36
Average Amount per worker (Rs)	50.45	56.05	58.10	71.82	87.73
Confident of operating SB Account					
Now it self	10.0	7.5	36.7	12.0	21.9
After 6 months	6.7	10.0	12.5	7.6	8.7
After one year	4.6	8.8	4.6	3.6	5.0
After two years	0.8	1.3	4.6	5.2	2.9
Can not say	22.1	32.5		28.4	7.0
Never	36.7	36.7	45.5	10.4	54.5
Number of transactions					
Increased	2.9	–	17.1	9.2	6.2
Moderately increased	12.1	20.9	56.7	60.0	32.2
No change	60.0	61.9	26.2	30.8	33.1
NA	25.0	17.2	–	–	28.5

Table 5: Accessing other Financial Services by the Sample Workers

(%)

	Chhattisgarh	Gujarat	Orissa	Rajasthan	U.P
Accessing other Financial Services					
SHG	0.8	3.3	14.6	8.4	–
SGSY loan	–	0.8	–	–	–
Crop loan	1.6	0.8	6.3	3.2	–
Bore well loan	–	–	0.8	–	–
Personal loan	–	0.4	–	–	–
IAY benefit	1.2	5.0	–	0.8	–
Social security pension	2.0	0.4	–	1.2	–
Watershed	–	–	0.4	–	–

After formal financial inclusion, about 80 per cent of the sample households of Gujarat reported no dependency on money lenders and other informal credit providers (Table 6). In other states, a very few proportion of households are in such stage. However, substantial percentage of sample households (68–72 per cent) in Rajasthan and UP informed that their dependency on informal credit institutions has been reduced.

Table 6: Dependency on Informal Sources of Credit—Responses of the Sample Workers

(%)

	Chhattisgarh	Gujarat	Orissa	Rajasthan	U.P
Dependency on Informal Sources of Credit					
No dependency	12.9	80.4	8.8	2.0	1.7
Reduced dependency	16.7	13.3	28.8	67.6	46.7
Same as previous	52.9	4.6	62.5	30.4	13.2
Cannot say	17.5	1.7	–	–	38.4

SPECIAL INITIATIVES OF THE BANKS

The financial inclusion has become a mandate for all the banks and every bank has to attempt to achieve the set targets under financial inclusion plan approved by the Reserve Bank of India. To expedite the process banks have been advised to adopt service area approach and also Business Correspondent (BC) model. As per the RBI policy (2010), the banks are allowed to engage companies other than non banking financial institutions as Business correspondents. The banks have been entering into agreements with telecom providers, technology solutions providers and financial payment systems to deliver the financial services effectively. About 73,000 villages with population more than 2000 as per 2001 census have been provided with new bank branches which will serve the adjacent areas. Banks will open branches in under banked districts under the service area inhabitations with populations of more than 5000 by Sept. 2012. The common service centres (CSCs) have been entrusted the responsibility of credit delivery through BC model. The pilot projects of BC-CSC model for delivery of financial services have been proved to be successful. About 42230 CSCs will be engaged by various banks to achieve the objective of financial inclusion. The 'Swabhiman' Scheme (2011) launched by the government aimed at extending the banking facility to all by providing loans and other credit facilities at subsidised rates. It set a target of 50 million households to be reached by March, 2012.

The sample workers in the five studies, except those who have as membership in self help groups, are new to financial inclusion process. Most of the illiterate households could not learn much from mission mode approach followed for opening of SB accounts by the banks and others. However, some of them are confident of operating the SB accounts on their own in the near future. As per the perceptions of workers, the financial inclusion is benefical to them and they have more confidence in the banking system.

There has been reluctance on the part of most of the bank managers to cover the huge number of MGNREGA workers under financial inclusion due to lack of financial literacy on the part of the workers. Lack of automation in RRBs and cooperatives also added to the problems of management of large number of SB accounts and timely delivery of services (payment of wages). Bankers perceive that the absence incentive structure is another deficiency in HR policy.

OPPORTUNITIES AND CHALLENGES

The inclusive and rapid growth of economy and also rise in wages has led to more cash flow and monetary transactions in the rural areas. The rural labour markets are also rapidly experiencing changes and the focus is more on development of skills and quality of employment to alleviate the poverty. With the increasing concern of the state to expand social safety nets to the poor, more so insurance, the financial institutions have to play a more positive and welfare oriented role. To fulfil the social responsibility of banks, the bankers should view financial inclusion under MGNREGA as an opportunity. The 'interest' benefit from MGNREGA funds can be used by the banks to evolve an incentive structure. Further payment of ₹ 80 per active account of MGNREGA workers per year is a good incentive for the bank staff. The increasing number of CBOs/SHGs in rural areas is another welcome sign who can be used as conduits. The BC model and IT applications can reduce the transaction cost. The 'MGNREGA accounts' is an untapped market for the various products of the banking sector.

CONCLUDING REMARKS

For sustainable and inclusive growth, access to quality credit more so from formal financial institutions for all (rural) households is one of the pre-requisites. The banking sector has taken several measures to reach the rural farm and non-farm households during the last four decades. Despite these efforts, nearly half of the farm households did not have access to the institutional credit while most of the these were denied access to formal credit institutions. The Rangarajan Committee recommendations on the financial inclusion and MGNREGA's objective of providing link between the rural poor and financial institutions paved way for improved access to credit to all the households. However, MGNREGA's experience reveals that the rural poor in many states are not able to access other financial services from the banks. It also highlighted the need for banks to take additional efforts to develop and nurture friendly relations with the rural poor. This helps the latter to get into more number and variety of transactions which are beneficial to both the parties. Bankers should also attempt to convert some of the challenges into opportunities through IT and non-IT based interventions.

REFERENCES

Government of India (2008). Report of the Committee on Financial Inclusion Reserve Bank of India.

Government of India (2011). Delivering Financial Inclusion Services to Rural Citizens through the common service centres, Ministry of information Technology.

NIRD (2011). Financial Inclusion through NREGA, study in Six States (mimeo).

Reserve Bank of India (2010–11). Annual Policy Statement.

ANNEXURE–A

Details of the Sample Units in the Five States

State	*Districts*	*Blocks*
Chhattisgarh	Bilaspur	Masturi
		Gourela
	Surguja	Ambikapur
		Odigi
Gujarat	Dahod	Devgarh
		Garhbada
	Sabarkantha	Himmatnagar
		Khedbrahma
Orissa	Mayurbanj	Saraskana
		Baripada
	Bargarh	Bhatli
		Bargarh
Rajasthan	Alwar	Umrain
		Rainy
	Dungarpur	Bitchuwada
		Simulawada
UP	Sitapur	Khairabad
		Rampur Mathura
	Fathepur	Bhitaura
		Dhata

Financial Inclusion Strategies: An Overview

T. Soumya Krishna and Sai Satish Peri

Department of Banking, Insurance & Financial Services,
Institute of Public Enterprise, Hyderabad

INTRODUCTION

In our Indian economy, there are many financial services which have been provided to the people under the poverty line, but many of them are not aware of these services. Hence in order to make people aware of all these services, financial inclusion has been introduced.

Financial Inclusion was first started by the former UN Secretary-General Kofi Annan on 29 December 2003. In India The Reserve Bank of India (RBI) set up the Khan Commission in 2004 to look into financial inclusion and the recommendations of the commission were incorporated into the mid-term review of the policy (2005–06). In India, financial inclusion first featured in 2005, when it was introduced by K C Chakraborthy, the chairman of Indian Bank. Mangalam Village became the first village in India where all households were provided with banking facilities.

Global initiatives other than United Nations in this perspective are:

The United Kingdom was one of the first countries to realize the importance of financial inclusion. It published its strategy of financial inclusion in its report Promoting Financial Inclusion which was published alongside the Pre-Budget Report of 2004.

In 1997, banks and regulators in Brazil created a network of "correspondents bancarios" or "banking correspondents", small outlets with extended working hours that offered basic banking services.

The Financial Sector Charter in South Africa led to the establishment of the 'Mzansi' account; a National no frills Bank Account (NBA). In its first year of operation itself, it garnered nearly 2 million accounts.

A sophisticated example of global payments network operating via postal banks is the Singapore Post which regards payments and remittance services, an important catalyst for enhancing financial inclusion.

In 2004, BSP, the central bank of Philippines sanctioned two e-money products. The first was 'Smart Money', product of a major commercial bank and the second was 'G-cash', a non-bank product whose provider was ultimately licensed as a remittance agent. The impact of these e-money products has been substantial. Some 8 million people use one or other of the two products, while the numbers of banks involved has grown rapidly.

The significance of financial inclusion (FI) is growing in India, given the gaps that exist for the people belonging to underprivileged groups of both urban and rural areas. A large part of the country does not have access to the formalized basic banking and financial services. This has resulted into the creation of a huge group of financially excluded citizens across India. Such exclusion cripples the development and slows down the economic growth of any country.

Policymakers in India have been focusing on this gap to address the issues and challenges of financial exclusion in the country and urging mainstream banks to cater to these financially excluded regions to pace up sustainable and inclusive growth initiatives. Other parties who are also contributing to this drive of curbing the evils of financial exclusion include government agencies, post offices, non-banking financial institutes, various types of urban, rural and district cooperative banks and societies, micro finance institutions, self-help groups and many non-government organizations, some of whom have been catering to this financially excluded populace since long. However, given the current context of such financial exclusion, the social context and the awareness of the target group, banks and other financial institutions are expected to start providing the most basic banking services to bridge the gaps and pull off the financial inclusion plan. These services include providing a bank account to the rural people, and making accessible basic financial services such as savings, credit, remittances etc., albeit given the constraints of accessibility to these areas along with profitability challenges that the mainstream banks face in these areas.

The definitional emphasis of financial inclusion varies across countries and geographies, depending on the level of social, economic and financial development; the structure of stake holding in the financial sector; socioeconomic characteristics of the financially excluded segments; and also the extent of the recognition of the problem by authorities or governments.

The Report of the Committee on Financial Inclusion in India (Chairman: C Rangarajan) (2008) defines financial inclusion as the "process of ensuring access to financial services and timely and adequate credit where needed by vulnerable groups such as weaker sections and low income groups at an affordable cost".

SCOPE OF FINANCIAL INCLUSION

Through voluntary effort by the banking community itself for evolving various strategies, in order to bring within the ambit of the banking sector the large strata of society.

Internationally, financial exclusion has been viewed in a much wider perspective. Merely having a bank account is not regarded as an accurate indicator of financial inclusion. Rather, its scope is considered to be quite large and ranges from empowerment of people through schemes of financial literacy/education to ensuring their participation in institutional credit, insurance cover and remittance services. The scope of financial inclusion is much broader and hence, it is considered to be critical for achieving inclusive and sustainable growth in the country.

BENEFITS OF FINANCIAL INCLUSION

Improvements in access to financial institutions accrue several benefits to the consumer, regulator and the economy alike. Establishment of an account relationship can pave the way for the customer to avail the benefits of a variety of financial products. The bank accounts can also be used for multiple purposes, such as, making small value remittances at low cost and making purchases on credit. Furthermore, the regulator benefits, as the audit trail is available and transactions are conducted transparently in a medium that can be monitored.

The economy benefits, as greater financial resources become transparently available for efficient intermediation and allocation, for uses that have the highest returns. Promoting financial inclusion can also help in the regeneration of local areas if money saved by increased access to financial services can be re-invested in the community. Inclusive finance—safe savings, appropriately designed loans for poor and low income households and for micro, small and medium sized enterprises, and appropriate insurance and payments services—can help people help themselves to increase incomes, acquire capital, manage risk, and work their way out of poverty. Increasing the inclusiveness of financial sectors, fuelled by domestic savings to the greatest extent possible, will, over time, bolster the poorer segments of the population as well as those segments of the economy that most affect the lives of poor people.

Holding a bank account itself confers a sense of identity, status and empowerment and provides access to the national payment system. Therefore, having a bank account becomes a very important aspect of financial inclusion. While financial inclusion, in the narrow sense, may be achieved to some extent by offering a single financial service/product, the objective of "comprehensive financial inclusion" would be to provide a holistic set of services encompassing all of the above.

INITIATIVES FOR PROMOTING FINANCIAL INCLUSION 1991–2005

With the onset of economic reforms in the beginning of the 1990s, a strong and resilient financial sector was considered necessary for accelerating the growth momentum in the country and also for expanding the coverage of financial services in a sustainable manner. Accordingly, the financial sector reform process placed more emphasis on creating a strong, vibrant and competitive banking system. A high-powered Committee on the Financial System (CFS) was constituted by the Government of India in August 1991 to examine all aspects relating to the structure, organization, functions and procedures of the financial system (Chairman: Shri M. Narasimham).

The main issues faced in this phase were:

1. Increase the flow of credit to agriculture and SMEs
2. Strengthen the urban cooperative banks and resolve the issue of dual control and
3. Bring a large segment of excluded population within the fold of the banking sector.

Credit to the SME and agriculture sectors decelerated in the 1990s and early years of the current decade. Given the significance of both the sectors, concerted efforts were made by the Government and the Reserve Bank to increase the flow of credit to these sectors. The restructuring of RRBs by merging them sponsor bank wise at the state level was done to make them larger and stronger to serve as a better instrument of rural credit delivery.

An important step to bring financially excluded people within the fold of formal financial sector was the promotion of microfinance in India. The SHG bank linkage programme was launched by NABARD in 1992, with policy support from the Reserve Bank, to facilitate collective decision making by the poor and provide 'door step' banking. Banks, as wholesalers of credit, were to provide the resources, while the NGOs were to act as agencies to organize the poor, build their capacities and facilitate the process of empowering them.

INITIATIVES FOR PROMOTING FINANCIAL INCLUSION – 2005 ONWARDS

The objective of bringing financially excluded people within the fold of the banking sector received renewed emphasis in 2005–06 as the term 'financial inclusion' was explicitly used for the first time in the Annual Policy Statement for 2005–06. It observed that there were legitimate concerns in regard to the banking practices that tended to exclude rather than attract vast sections of population, in particular pensioners, self-employed and those employed in the unorganized sector.

It also indicated that the Reserve Bank would:

1. Implement policies to encourage banks which provide extensive services, while disincentivising those which were not responsive to the banking needs of the community, including the underprivileged.

2. The nature, scope and cost of services would be monitored to assess whether there was any denial, implicit or explicit, of basic banking services to the common person, and
3. Banks urged to review their existing practices to align them with the objective of financial inclusion.

The recent approach focuses on financial inclusion on the individual and household level. The important difference in the recent focus on financial inclusion is the adoption of market oriented approach that recognizes the importance of business consideration of banks and other financial institutions for the long-term sustainability of the process.

USE OF INTERMEDIARIES AS AGENTS

With the objective of ensuring greater financial inclusion and increasing the outreach of the banking sector, banks have been allowed to use the services of NGOs/SHGs, MFIs and other civil society organizations as intermediaries in providing financial and banking services through the use of business facilitator and correspondent models. The BC model allows banks to do 'cash in/cash-out' transactions at a location much closer to the rural habitation, thus addressing the last mile problem. Banks are also entering into agreements with India Post for using the vast network of post offices as business correspondents, thereby increasing their outreach and leveraging on the postman's intimate knowledge of the local population.

FINANCIAL LITERACY AND CREDIT COUNSELING

Recognizing that lack of awareness is a major factor for financial exclusion, the Reserve Bank has taken a number of measures towards imparting financial literacy and promotion of credit counseling services. The Reserve Bank has undertaken a project titled "Project Financial Literacy" to disseminate information regarding the central bank and general banking concepts to various target groups, including, school and college going children, women, rural and urban poor, defense personnel and senior citizens. It would be disseminated to the target audience with the help of, among others, banks, local government machinery, schools/colleges using pamphlets, brochures, films, as also, the Reserve Bank's website. The Reserve Bank has also created a link on its web site 'For the Common Person' to give him the ease of access to information, in Hindi, English and 11 regional languages (Assamese, Bengali, Gujarati, Kannada, Malayalam, Marathi, Oriya, Punjabi, Tamil, Telugu and Urdu). A 'Financial Education' site link on the Reserve Bank's website was launched on November 14, 2007, mainly aimed at teaching basics of banking, finance and central banking to children in different age groups. The comic books format has been used to explain the complexities of banking, finance and central banking in a simple and interesting way for children.

In May 2007, convener banks of the SLBCs/UTLBCs were advised to set up, on a pilot basis, a Financial Literacy and Credit Counseling Centre (FLCC) in any one district in the State/Union Territory coming under their jurisdiction. The objectives of the FLCCs are to provide free financial literacy/education and credit counseling—educating people in rural and urban areas with regard to various financial products and services available, providing face-to face financial counseling services and formulating debt restructuring plans for borrowers in distress and recommending the same to formal financial institutions for consideration. FLCCs should not, however, act as investment advice centers. In rural areas, the centers could concentrate on financial literacy and counseling for farming communities and those engaged in allied activities while the centers in metro/urban areas could focus on individuals with over dues in credit cards, personal loans, housing loans, etc. Among others so far, banks have reported setting up or proposing to set up 123 credit counseling centers in various states of the country.

In order to implement all the above mentioned things, two particulár models have been introduced, Business correspondent model and Business facilitator model. The following are the two models that have been introduced.

Use of Business Facilitators and Correspondents

With the objective of ensuring greater financial inclusion and increasing the outreach of the banking sector, it has been decided in public interest to enable banks to use the services of Non-Governmental Organizations/Self Help Groups (NGOs/SHGs), Micro Finance Institutions (MFIs) and other Civil Society Organizations (CSOs) as intermediaries in providing financial and banking services through the use of Business Facilitator and Correspondent models as indicated below.

Business Facilitator Model: Eligible Entities and Scope of Activities

Under the 'Business Facilitator'; model, banks may use intermediaries, such as, NGOs/ Farmers' Clubs, cooperatives, community based organizations, IT enabled rural outlets of corporate entities, Post Offices, insurance agents, well-functioning Panchayats, Village Knowledge Centers, Agri Clinics/Agri Business Centers, Krishi Vigyan Kendras and KVIC/KVIB units, depending on the comfort level of the bank, for providing facilitation services.

Such services may include:

1. Identification of borrowers and fitment of activities;
2. Collection and preliminary processing of loan applications including verification of primary information/data;

3. Creating awareness about savings and other products and education and advice on managing money and debt counseling;
4. Processing and submission of applications to banks;
5. Promotion and nurturing Self Help Groups/Joint Liability Groups;
6. Post-sanction monitoring;
7. Monitoring and handholding of Self Help Groups/Joint Liability Groups/Credit Groups/others; and
8. Follow-up for recovery.

As these services are not intended to involve the conduct of banking business by Business Facilitators, no approval is required from RBI for using the above intermediaries for facilitation of the services indicated above.

The Business Correspondent model allows non-financial service providers to provide financial services (savings accounts, money transfer etc.) on a small scale basis (maximum limits imposed). The money is still held at a financial institution, however is serviced by the BC.

Financial inclusion has been a focus of attention in recent times. However, the facts above reveal the real and somewhat uncomfortable picture. The increase in the number of branches has not answered the needs of the farmers; and reaching the unbanked population to enable inclusive growth is a serious problem today. Branchless banking could be the big step towards providing easy financial access to the poor people and achieving financial inclusion.

Business Correspondent Model

Branchless banking is the concept of providing banking services outside the conventional bank branches by either using information and communication technology services or third party organizations (commonly referred to as 'Business Correspondents').

The business correspondent (BC) model allows the bank to use third party financial institutions to handle account opening, transaction management, and other financial services. Regulations from RBI emphasize that transactions should be visible in the bank's books within 24 hours. Such a compulsion has encouraged the use of smart cards and mobile technology by the BCs (for e.g. pilot projects by Corporation Bank). They use a biometric scanner cum identifier (for e.g. fingerprint or voice recognition), a mobile, and a printer to process the payments. The biometric device is used for the identification and authentication of the beneficiary. Once authenticated, the Radio Frequency Identification Device (RFID) chip embedded in the card gets charged. This chip communicates with the mobile device, and the necessary transaction forms are made available in the mobile.

The BC selects the relevant option and feeds the transaction amount and sends a message to the back-end server. The server authenticates the message, processes the transaction, and sends an update back to the mobile, which in turn writes back to the card. When the card is brought close to the printer, a transaction report is printed. This technology can also be used to conduct other financial activities like fixed deposits, loan disbursement, and insurance.

Business Correspondent Model: Eligible Entities and Scope of Activities

Under the 'Business Correspondent' Model, NGOs/MFIs set up under Societies/Trust Acts, Societies registered under Mutually Aided Cooperative Societies Acts or the Cooperative Societies Acts of States, section 25 companies, registered NBFCs not accepting public deposits and Post Offices may act as Business Correspondents. Banks may conduct thorough due diligence on such entities keeping in view the indicative parameters given in Annex 3.2 of the Report of the Intern available to examine issues relating to Rural Credit and Micro-Finance (July 2005). In engaging such intermediaries as Business Correspondents, banks should ensure that they are well established, enjoying good reputation and having the confidence of the local people. Banks may give wide publicity in the locality about the intermediary engaged by them as Business Correspondent and take measures to avoid being misrepresented.

In addition to activities listed under the Business Facilitator Model, the scope of activities to be undertaken by the Business Correspondents will include:

- Creating awareness about savings and other products and education and advice on managing money and debt counselling.
- Identification of potential customers
- Collection and preliminary processing of various forms for deposits including verification of primary information/data
- Filling of applications/account opening forms including nomination clause and submission to the Bank.
- KYC will also be completed by the BCs.
- Opening of no frill deposit accounts and other products as permitted from time to time by leveraging technology.
- Collection and payment of small value deposits and withdrawals; Min: nil; Max: ₹ 2000 to ₹ 5000 per transaction depending on the technology service provider.
- Receipt and delivery of small value remittances/other payment instruments, as per FI Plan of respective Banks.
- In respect of all such transactions, the BC/his agent will be authorized to accept/deliver cash either at his place of work or at any convenient location subject to the ceilings per customer.

- Furnishing of minimum account statements and other account information, for a period of 3 months.
- Any other service on behalf of the Bank, duly authorized by the appropriate authority.
- The activities undertaken by the Business Correspondents would be within the normal course of the Bank's banking business, but conducted through and by the entities at places other than the Bank's premises.
- In respect of all such transactions, the BC/his/her agent will be authorized to accept/deliver cash either at his place of work or at any convenient location subject to the ceilings per day/per customer as laid down. The Business Correspondents will be linked to a nearby branch (base Branch).
- Cross-selling of other financial products like insurance/mutual fund products/pension products/any other third party product, as and when they are assigned to do so.
- In case duly appointed sub-agents of BCs, BCs to take care of reputational risks involved.

The activities to be undertaken by the Business Correspondents would be within the normal course of the bank's banking business, but conducted through the entities indicated above at places other than the bank premises. Accordingly, in furtherance of the objective of increasing the outreach of the banks for micro-finance, in public interest, the Reserve Bank hereby permits banks to formulate a scheme for using the entities indicated abovc. Correspondents Banks should ensure that the scheme formulated and implemented is in strict compliance with the objectives and parameters laid down in this circular.

Role of a Business Facilitator/Business Correspondent

1. He/she is an intermediary between the Bank and the villagers.
2. He/she is an intermediary and confidant of the bank. He/she gathers information on the prospective borrower's:
    - Name
    - Address
    - Family size
    - Family details
    - Details of the economic and income earning activity pursued by the members of the household
    - Land Holding including its size and pattern and its whereabouts
    - Crop cultivated and the cropping pattern followed
    - Cash Flow Pattern
    - Annual Net Income of the household
    - Spending Pattern of the household.

The information so gathered is used for drawing the Borrower's Profile which in turn helps the bank to take appropriate credit decisions.

3. He/she is an information assimilator. Using the information he/she has gathered, it is possible to prepare a Cash-Flow Statement and prepare the farmer's Cash Budget.
4. This follows customer counseling on the financial needs and how can it be met and customer education on the products and services available from the bank.
5. He/she should give to the farmers and others complete, factual and truthful information on the bank on various products and other aspects.
6. He/she should not overlook or hide any vital and material information to the customer.
7. He/she should protect and respect the privacy of the customer.
8. He/she should not compromise his/her personal interest to that of the Bank.
9. He/she should treat all customers alike and with no disparity and with respect and dignity. He/she should not differentiate the customers' one against the other and should not hurt any caste or communal feelings.

The bank is using the BC for the purpose of financial inclusion. Each BC or its agent is attached to a particular branch of the bank which is mostly networked under the CBS scheme. There are about 500 branches which are outside the CBS but under a computerized environment called Total bank mechanization. Branches under TBA are also connected to bank's data center at Mumbai through a separate server at the data center. The transactions recorded in the CBS system are also recorded in this particular server before they are merged with the main server at the data centre. This server maintains the details of all individual accounts including those covered under this financial inclusion unlike some other banks which permit the individual accounts to be maintained by the BC and a consolidated account of the BC is maintained by the bank. This method—of maintaining individual accounts by the bank in its books of account instead of through a consolidated account of the BC—will facilitate the customer to access his/her account through a different BC in case of a need or an emergency.

The selection and enlistment of BC or its agents is undertaken by the Zonal Managers.

The operational procedure is summarized below:

- Each branch is authorized to have two or three BCs. Higher number of BCs can be entertained as there is no specific restriction on the number of BCs.
- Each BC is allowed an overdraft of ₹ 10,000.
- The transaction limit per BC per day is ₹ 10,000. As regards the customer, while the minimum amount of the transaction is ₹ 10, the maximum amount that can be withdrawn is ₹ 5000. There is no ceiling for the amounts deposited.
- Currently, the ceiling for the cash carrying by the BC is kept at ₹ 10,000. If the BC arranges for transit insurance this can be enhanced.

- The BC can scan up to 6 finger prints of each customer. Each hand held device can store finger prints of 100 customers (600 images). After the same are transported to the server of the bank the device will be free again for further storing.

The BC idea came from Brazil where retail vendors, lottery outlets and post offices double as bank branches. An estimated US$ one billion in transactions were processed with point-of-sale (POS) devices such as biometric or smart card readers through Brazil's 90,000 agents in 2005 and a total of about 12 million accounts were opened across the network in only three years.

INITIATIVES TAKEN BY CERTAIN BANKS

Andhra Bank

These are certain measures Andhra Bank has taken regarding Financial Inclusion:

- Use of Intermediaries
- Opening of No Frills Accounts
- General Purpose Credit Cards
- Strengthening of SHGs
- Debt Swapping
- Use of Smart Card Technology for Payment
- Old Age Pensions and Wages Under REGP (Rural Employment Guarantee Programme)
- Use of Technology in Financial Inclusion.

Future Initiatives

1. To extend the smart card scheme to all our lead districts viz. Srikakulam, Guntur, East Godavari, West Godavari, Ganjam and Gajapathi districts in First Phase and to cover the remaining districts in Andhra Pradesh by March 2009.
2. To give loans through smart cards to the farmers and other weaker sections.
3. To install more biometric ATMs in rural and semi urban areas.
4. To open exclusive Micro Finance branches.
5. To introduce "Mobile" bio-metric ATMs.
6. To open Financial Literacy centers in all six Lead Districts by March 2008.
7. To finance more number of Urban Self Help Groups.
8. To implement total financial inclusion project in selected slums in urban areas.
9. To cover all SHGs under Micro Insurance by March 2009.
10. To cover all Tenant Farmers in service area of the bank through Joint Liability Groups (JLGs)/Rythu Mithra Groups (RMGs in AP).
11. To develop 'Model' villages in each of 22 districts in Andhra Pradesh.

Syndicate Bank

Initiatives taken by syndicate bank:

- Exclusive department for Financial Inclusion
- Special Financial Inclusion plan
- Opening of Branches in the allotted FI Villages having a population of above 2000
- Engaging BCs and CSPs
- Training initiatives
- Initiatives in providing Financial Literacy
- Financial Inclusion Resource Centers
- Recording of Transaction on Smart Cards
- Engaging BC Supervisors on Contract Basis
- Assigning weightage in officers Annual Performance appraisal reports for implementation of Financial Inclusion.

The Bank was able to extend banking network to remote and far flug villages allotted to the Bank by engaging BCs and CSPs appointed by the TSPs. In all, 1219 villages allotted to the bank with population of over 2000 were covered by BCs and CSPs.

Indian Overseas Bank

Steps to ensure Financial Inclusion by Indian Overseas Bank:

- Opening No-frills SB accounts.
- Issuing General Purpose Credit Cards.
- Granting Overdraft facilities in SB accounts.
- Providing banking services at the door step of villagers through Smart Cards.
- Providing Banking outlet in un-banked villages.
- Providing easy access to banking at the door step promotes savings.
- As customers do not visit branch, branches with large number of Savings bank a/cs, pension a/cs, insurance a/cs can be served in a better way.
- Growing branch Business with new customer base.
- Easy recovery from the villages.
- Providing online transactions to ensure hassle free accounting.
- Marketing bank products.
- Engagement of Business Correspondents (BC)/Business Facilitators (BF).

Indian Overseas Bank decided to extend banking services to the allotted villages through Smart Card Banking with the use of Business Correspondents (BC).

State Bank of India

Following are certain initiatives taken by the State Bank of India:

- Issuance of financial products and services on cards.
- KYC of customers (or assignment of role to a suitable entity like an NGO/MFI/Village Panchayat/Government body, etc).
- Settlement of transactions.
- Bring Business Facilitators/Business Correspondents.
- Publish tariff table for various banking related services at the Customer Service Outlets.
- Maintain fingerprint and photograph databases of customers.
- Maintain customer credit rating bureau.
- Promotional activities and customer awareness programs.

Having twin objective of ensuring greater financial inclusion and increasing the outreach of the bank through biometric authentication with the help of the laptop connected to the bank branch. SBI were successful in providing comprehensive financial services to the under privileged encompassing saving, credit, remittance, insurance, mutual funds and pension funds in cost effective manner particularly in unbanked areas. In order to help the people under financial inclusion plan SBI has improved process efficiencies and reduced transaction costs by providing linkages between the existing network of their Branches and the informal and formal agencies engaged with the poor, by adopting technology based solutions. Hence by implementing the above mentioned objectives SBI has been able to run the transactions well and implement the business correspondent model under financial inclusion plan in an effective and efficient manner.

Limitations of Financial Inclusion

- Scaling up of activities
- Transaction cost too high
- Appropriate business model yet to evolve
- BC model too restrictive
- Limitation of cash delivery points
- Lack of Interest/Involvement of Big Technology Players.

CONCLUSION

All the activities under Financial Inclusion have been running smoothly with certain limitations. In order to reduce these limitations, The Reserve Bank of India recently made certain statements.

It says that:

- The 'Basic Savings Bank Deposit Account' should be considered a normal banking service available to all.
- The account shall not have the requirement of any minimum balance.
- The services available in the account will include deposit and withdrawal of cash at bank branch as well as ATMs; receipt/credit of money through electronic payment channels or by means of deposit/collection of cheques drawn by Central/State Government agencies and departments.
- While there will be no limit on the number of deposits that can be made in a month, account holders will be allowed a maximum of four withdrawals in a month, including ATM withdrawals.
- Facility of ATM card or ATM-cum-Debit Card.

The above facilities would be provided without any charges.

Financial Inclusion: Microfinance Institutions as Extended Arms of Banks

A. Sridhar Raj

Institute of Public Enterprise, Hyderabad

ABSTRACT: *The role of microfinance institutions has been commended due to their role in filling up the vacuum of financial exclusion which has been the result of policy and institutional flaws over a period of time. The role of banks in enabling the poor to access financial products and services has not been fulfilled due to institutional and operational bottlenecks resulting in the exclusion of a large mass of the people from benefitting from economic growth and development. Efforts towards the same direction met with little success and inspired by the Bangladesh experiment, the microfinance was seen as potential tool for financial inclusion of poorer sections of the society. The paper focuses on how microfinance institutions can not only enable the poor to access financial products and services but also create financial awareness, all of which supplement the efforts of the banks towards financial inclusion.*

Keywords: Financial Inclusion, Microfinance, Banks, Women Empowerment, SHGs.

> *Microfinance is an important plank in the agenda for financial inclusion—*
> *Malegam Committee.*

INTRODUCTION

Finance has always been at the core of innumerable debates and discussions which range from economic growth on the one hand to social development on the other raising the questions of ways and means of ameliorating the living conditions of the poor and downtrodden sections of the society. In fact, almost all the governments across the world have utilized the financial models, tools and institutions to reduce skewed growth and development and provide decent standards of living for the people. The role of governments under such circumstances becomes *tight rope walking*, balancing the interests of multiple stakeholders and taking everybody in the its stride towards development and the exclusion of any section of the social system may become perilous for the government itself as the excluded stakeholders may destabilize the existing governance system either peacefully or violently.

Therefore, the government is morally responsible for the inclusion of as many stakeholders as possible in the process of growth and development and such an inclusion is possible by regulating the economic activities through legislations duly passed by the representative bodies and the same getting executed by the operational bodies. In a country like India, inclusion assumes all the more importance as growth and development led disproportionate accumulation of wealth in the hands of a few in a few pockets of the country which can be counted on fingers. The vast majority has been deprived of the fruits of planned development with the help of state regulation of economic activities and through public sector enterprises. In a democratic set up, it becomes imperative that such a vast majority cannot be excluded from prosperity and opulence for a long time; hence, attempts towards integrating them into the mainstream is the bounden duty of the government.

FINANCIAL INCLUSION: THE NEED OF THE HOUR

Any system which keeps majority at bay is prone to suffer from not only limitations is also considered as non-holistic as majority is out of the system and financial system is not an exception. The focus on development through various financial policies, programmes, strategies, tools and institutions can hit a roadblock in a country like India where majority belongs to poor and very poor sections by any standards. In fact, their poverty is attributed to *general exclusion* from growth and development and more so is the result of *financial exclusion.*

Such exclusion is the result of consistent and continuous policies and programmes of the government which have neglected the rural lot and women in the process of economic growth and development. However, the error of exclusion has come under focus wherein the government has over a period of time started taking measures which paved the way for the inclusion of more and poor and downtrodden sections of the society into the mainstream. One such policy was nationalization of banks through which the government wanted to push the agenda of growth and development on the one hand and also include the majority in the fold of development.

Therefore, banks have been given a social, economic and development agenda and the broader objective of such was to *inclusion* in the process of economic growth and development. The credit facilities to the industries, enterprises, etc., were meant to spur economic growth and various financial products – loans, insurance, etc., were meant to enable the people to have access to the benefits of economic growth and development. Therefore, right from day one, the focus of banks was not only to provide financial services to the people but also provide services to those who have been deprived of access to financial services.

The Report of the Committee on Financial Inclusion by NABARD defined financial inclusion as the process of ensuring access to financial services and timely and adequate credit where needed by vulnerable groups such as weaker sections and low income groups at an affordable cost. Further financial inclusion refers to all those process and practices which enable lower income people to avail financial services, including credit, at an affordable cost so that they not only increase their earnings over a period of time but also move up in the socio-economic hierarchy.

The people who are living at the lower rungs of the society, particularly in rural areas, do not have access to financial products and services, thereby get deprived of the those services which could have significantly raised their income levels and standard of living as well. Financial inclusion refers to providing financial products such as bank accounts, savings prodcuts, and remittance and payment services to the disadvantaged sections of the society. (Economic Times, 29th May 2012) Financial inclusion is providing financial services at an affordable cost to the vast sections of disadvantaged and low-income groups (Teki and Mishra, 2012).

BANKS AND FINANCIAL INCLUSION

According to the Annual Report 2011 of Reserve Bank of India, the banking sector is a key driver of inclusive growth and the banks along with other financial institutions are expected to play an important role in enabling the poor in accessing the financial services. The Business Correspondents Model of reaching out to the remote areas is a significant development and marks a new development in financial inclusion due to its no-frills and simple model of providing financial services to the poor in rural areas. Besides, the Reserve Bank of India also suggested the banks to devise strategies for financial inclusion by taking into consideration various issues haunting the rural and unorganized sector. Fortunately, banks have been doing well towards financial inclusion by supporting various stakeholders in rural areas—farmers, artisans, entrepreneurs, women, etc.

The commercial banks have reached to the SHGs through SHG-Bank Linkage Programme through which 15.95 lakh SHGs have been covered by March 2007. This programme played a key role in the process of financial inclusion of women in particular who are a part of SHGs. When Regional Rural Banks (RRBs) were established in the year 1975 there was an air of hope and optimism that they would cater to the credit needs of the farmers. As the focus of RRBs was to rural areas, they gradually spread in to remote parts where the commercial banks did not make much headway in the past as the former accounts for 37% of total offices all scheduled commercial banks in rural areas.

(Table 1) This itself is indicative of the fact they have made inroads into the deep pockets of rural India and are well entrenched to play a critical role in financial inclusion.

Table 1: Offices of Scheduled Commercial Banks (2005)

Bank Group	*Rural Offices*		*Semi-urban Offices*		*Urban/metro Offices*		*Total*	
	No.	*% of Total*	*No.*	*% of Total*	*No.*	*% of Total*	*No.*	*% of Total*
RRBs	11824	37	2284	15	537	2	14645	21
SCBs other than RRBs	20143	63	13335	85	21846	98	55324	79
	31967	100	15619	100	22383	100	69969	100

Source: Report of the Committee on Financial Inclusion, NABARD.

Therefore, the mandate given to the RRBs for financial inclusion can yield results as they are spread across the rural areas which are in desperate need for financial access of products and services. According to the Report of the Committee on Financial Inclusion, NABARD microfinance services provided through SHG-Bank Linkage has so far been the most successful initiative in financial inclusion.

The SHG-Bank Linkage Programme is a boon in disguise as 90% of its members are women and the programme has been successful in providing loans to women, who hitherto were not able to secure the same from any organized sources. Various reports indicate that RRBs have been linked to almost one third of SHGs and through such linkage they have provided loans to various sections constituting one third of the total loans provided by other banks. Therefore, commercial banks in general and RRBs in particular are positioned to play an important role in financial inclusion of poor and very poor sections of the society.

As the Government of India is gearing to provide the benefits under various welfare schemes through electronic transfers, particularly all cash payments above Rs. 1000, the role of financial inclusion of the poorer sections of the society becomes an important dimension of banking. Therefore, the role of banks in the process of financial inclusion has been made clear by mandating them to offer at least one bank account to every family in rural areas.

MICROFINANCE INSTITUTIONS AND FINANCIAL INCLUSION

The role of commercial banks has been limited in the process of financial inclusion of the poor and downtrodden sections of the society who have been deprived of access to financial products and financial services. Therefore, the role of RRBs and Business

Correspondents has become important in the recent past as the push for financial inclusion has become an important agenda for the government. However, even such changes too could not bring lead to financial inclusion of certain sections of the society, which paved the way for the emergence and spread of Microfinance Institutions.

Microfinance Institutions (MFIs) provide small loans to mostly rural poor for either starting entrepreneurial activity or expanding the present economic activity with a view to increase income levels and also break the cycle of poverty. The loans provided by MFIs do not have any collateral security and repayment is done in either weekly or fortnightly installments by the clients. In spite of colossal efforts to reach out to the unbanked in rural areas through various programmes and strategies, commercial banks and RRBs stopped at certain point of time which created a huge vacuum in providing financial products and services.

The MFIs are uniquely placed in limited geographical zones wherein they know how to make deep inroads into hinterland and provide necessary financial services to the people, who hitherto had been deprived of access to such services. MFIs reach out to the poor and provide loans aimed at promoting, expanding or diversifying economic and entrepreneurial activities. Such activities not only supplement the existing income of the people but also provide an opportunity to them to upgrade their business activities with the hassle-less loans from MFIs.

The Report of the Committee on Financial Inclusion, NABARD observed that MFIs can play a significant role in facilitating inclusion as they understand the markets and people better and also enjoy higher acceptability amongst the people in rural areas. Therefore, the Committee suggested that MFIs with their accountable and transparent practices can play a major role in providing financial services which eventually leads to financial inclusion of the poor in rural areas. The Impact Assessment Study report by SIDBI in the year 2008 "Assessing Development Impact of Micro Finance Programmes" studied different MFI models—Grameen, SHG and IB/SS. Table 2 shows the main findings of the study.

In a nutshell, the study found that micro finance has helped in increasing the main source of income among the poor household, facilitating in increasing the size of the activity, helping the borrowers children in reaching out to schools, promoting the people to the immediate next level of category in terms of poverty, expansion of coverage of life insurance, participation of women in meetings and other activities, etc. In the words of the Report, " Positive economic impact of micro finance was observed in terms of increased income, diversification of household activities and reduced dependence on the single main occupation of the household, larger employment opportunities—particularly for women, increased number of earning members per household, improvement in their dietary habits, general improvement in their quality of life, including housing conditions and education of children, particularly of girl child. Reduced dependence on the moneylender, however, can be considered to be a net gain of the micro finance movement (Impact Assessment Study report by SIDBI, 2008).

Table 2: Impact Assessment Study Report by SIDBI

Sl. No.	*Assumptions of the Study*	*Findings of the Study*
1.	Micro Finance as a strategy for the extension of financial services to the poor.	Very poor category is still deprived of the loans and women clientele group is covered exhaustively
2.	Increase in access to micro finance	Access to micro credit has improved for clients
3.	Micro Finance increases enterprise activities	Start of new enterprises or expansion of the existing enterprises.
4.	Improvement in income	Asset acquisition, children education, diversification of livelihood, etc.
5.	Capacity building to manage risks	Income enhancement and risk mitigation
6.	Women empowerment	Increase in savings and also income generating avenues for women
7.	Overall improvement in socio-economic status	Increase in household income and improvement in the pattern of food consumption

Source: The Impact Assessment Study report by SIDBI in the year 2008.

The Nair Committee (2012) found that small and marginal farmers who constitute more than 80 per cent of total farmer households in the country face exclusion from the formal financial channels. The committee also observed that the country's vision is universal financial access through affirmative financial inclusion of the marginalized sections of the society. The committee felt that the loans provided by banks directly and through SHG/JLG mechanism will be eligible to be classified as priority sector advances and this is where the role of MFIs comes into picture in enabling the people to access financial services.

The committee also stated that bank credit to Micro Finance Institutions extended for on-lending to individuals and also to members of SHGs/JLGs are eligible for categorization as priority sector advance under respective categories, viz., agriculture, micro and small enterprise, and micro credit. Even the Malegam Committee Report also suggested that the advances received by the MFIs should be treated as "priority sector lending" status but such funds should comply with the regulation. The committee was aware of the fact that due to high demand for the capital in rural areas, the MFIs have mushroomed with the help of private equity and as the latter expects profits, the focus of MFIs.

Therefore, the role of MFIs in financial inclusion cannot be overlooked due to certain hiccups which happened due to overzealous MFIs in states like Andhra Pradesh. The unethical ways and means of MFIs in Andhra Pradesh cannot absolve them from their highhandedness in the collection of dues from the customers. However, that does not mean that the entire sector is to be painted with black as they can contribute in the process of extending financial services deep into the rural areas. The commercial banks have their limitations—structure, manpower, cost, etc, and therefore, the MFIs with their flexible operations are in a better position to reach the unbanked and under-banked in rural areas; hence can act as extended arms of banks in financial inclusion. Given the post-regulation scenario (with the Government of India introducing Micro Finance Institutions (Development and Regulation) Bill 2012), the role of MFIs can be game changer in rural areas in financial inclusion.

There is a stupendous increase in terms of reaching out to the clients of MFIs like Equitas and Sahayata which have grown at 2700% and 2870% from March 2008 to March 2010. (The SIDBI Study on Interest Rates and Costs of Microfinance Institutions in the year 2011) MFIs have proved conclusively that they can cater to the needs of the lowest rungs of the society which itself is a big accomplishment. The World Bank has recognized the importance of micro finance as a tool for financial inclusion towards sustainable efforts of poverty eradication. The World Bank came up with a project, "Scaling up Sustainable and Responsible Microfinance Project" in the year 2010 and the main objective of the project was to scale up access to sustainable microfinance services to the financially excluded in under-served areas of India.

Financial Literacy

The biggest contribution of MFIs can come from spreading financial literacy among the rural people as that itself would act as a catalyst for financial inclusion. People in rural areas are not well aware of the services that are offered by the banks and other financial institutions (both public and private) and if one were to take into account the operations of MFIs, it can be stated that people have become aware of various terms pertaining to financial services. This itself can be a good beginning and MFIs can take such a literacy campaign further if given a right opportunity.

Access to Financial Services

The role of commercial banks has been limited to urban and industrial areas where their services have been effectively used by the customers of all types. The RRBs too have done their bit in spreading the banking services in rural areas but suffer from certain limitations—they cannot cater to the poorer segments of the society, cannot provide small and tiny loans, etc. Although efforts have been made by banks with Business

Correspondent model, it is too early to expect quick results. Therefore, MFIs with the structured network is in a better position to penetrate deep into rural areas and offer financial services. They can offer credit which is small without any collateral, which is not possible for commercial banks.

Access to Credit for Income Generation

MFIs offer loans to activities like—animal husbandry, opening of kirana shops, fishing, vegetable shops, telephone booths, etc. All such activities have led to increased income to the customers of MFIs. The best part was that these customers have been able to repay their loans on time and also secure loans again and again. Therefore, MFIs have been able to help the people in rural areas to increase their income levels, albeit marginally.

Women Empowerment

The biggest success of MFIs is reaching out the women who have never made into economic activities for various reasons. In all the models, of microfinance, over 90% of customers are women which is a pointer to the fact that women have become enough matured to take their own decisions with regard to investment patterns for the family and income generation activities. Frequent discussions among the group members and with the MFI agents have not only helped them in increasing their awareness but also feel confident about their social and economic positions.

Inclusive Growth

Under the Unique Identification Project (UID), the Government of India is planning to transfer the benefits to the poor in rural areas through financial institutions, particularly banks. With their increased awareness, the customers are now in a position to access banks and also avail financial services from them. Though such a transformation could be attributed to various institutions like SHGs, the role of MFIs also cannot be overlooked as they too have done their bit in spreading the net of financial services which is gradually leading to inclusive growth.

Technology

Technology can be effectively used by the MFIs to deliver and process loans as is happening with Business Correspondent Model. The banks are reaching out the poor and inaccessible areas with help of Business Correspondents and are providing various financial services and for MFIs with such a network and good returns, implanting technology in its processes which can mitigate the discretionary powers of the collection agents can be a great succor. MFIs have been successful in reaching out to the poor and downtrodden sections of the society and have been successful in spreading financial awareness and arming with technology, they can minimize the costs of operation and thereby pass on such benefits to the clients.

CONCLUSION

All said and done, the role of MFIs has come under scanner given their high-handed tactics in recovering loans and also driving the poor towards financial debt, occasionally leading to suicides (as happened in some parts of Andhra Pradesh). The SIDBI Study on Interest Rates and Costs of of Microfinance Institutions in the year 2011 found that some MFIs have been charging costly insurance pre mium which is finally borne by the clients. The intervention of the Government of India to regulate the MFIs could be watershed in the process of financial inclusion as the MFIs will have a regulator so that microfinance does not become either a *customer killer or get killed* by governments at the state level. Given the large number of people who do not have access to financial products and services, the MFIs, under the watchful eye of the Reserve Bank of India holds the promise of becoming *Extended Arms of Banks* in the process of financial inclusion, besides other institutions like commercial banks, RRBs, Business Correspondents, etc. MFIs need to be given another opportunity to clean their records and history to become a genuine agent of provider of financial services to the poor and downtrodden sections towards the larger goal of financial inclusion.

NOTES

1. The Government of Andhra Pradesh curtailed the activities of MFIs through an Ordinance—Andhra Pradesh Micro Finance Institutions (Regulation of Money Lending) Rules 2010 suspecting the role of MFIs in the suicide of the borrowers.
2. The Government of India has introduced the Bill—Micro-finance Institutions (Development and Regulation) Bill 2012 in Parliament wherein the focus is to regulate the affairs of the MFIs and also protect the clients from high interest rates.

REFERENCES

Andhra Pradesh Micro Finance Institutions (Regulation of Money Lending) Rules 2010.

Annual Report of Reserve Bank of India, 2011.

Assessing Development Impact of Micro Finance Programmes, SIDBI, 2008.

Every Family to have Bank Account in Inclusion Push, Economic Times, 29th May 2012, p. 11.

Micro Finance Institutions (Development and Regulation) Bill 2012.

Report of the Committee on Financial Inclusion, NABARD, 2008.

Report of the Committee to Re-Examine the Existing Classification and Suggest Revised Guidelines with Regard to Priority Sector Lending Classification and Related Issues, 2012.

Report of the Sub-Committee of the Central Board of Directors of Reserve Bank of India to Study Issues and Concerns in the MFI Sector, 2011.

Scaling up Sustainable and Responsible Microfinance Project, World Bank, 2010.

Study on Interest Rates and Costs of Microfinance Institutions, SIDBI, 2011.

Teki, S. and Mishra, R.K. (2012). Microfinance and Financial Inclusion, Academic Foundation, New Delhi.

A Comparison of Indian Public and Private Sector Banks Based on Banking Service Quality Model

Mihir Dash and Garima Saxena[1]

Quantitative Techniques School of Business, Alliance University

[1]Banking and Finance School of Business, Alliance University

INTRODUCTION

Indian banks are amongst the most technologically advanced in the world, with vast networks of branches empowered by strong banking systems, and their product and channel distribution capabilities are on par with those of the leading banks in the world. With the economy in overdrive and buoyancy in consumption and investment demand, nine Indian banks, led by HDFC Bank and ICICI Bank, have made it to the top fifty Asian banks list in the Asian Bankers-300 report. Simultaneously, the State Bank of India has become the top loan manager in the Asia-Pacific region in 2007, according to UK-based Project Finance International (PFI).

The Indian banking system was heavily dominated by nationalised commercial banks until globalisation. The financial regulation and credit controls imposed by the government created a system in which competition was very less. A more competitive banking environment has gradually been achieved through the deregulation measures and permission granted to many private and foreign banks into the Indian banking industry. These changes have also caused a compression of profits and a re-orientation of banking strategy towards quality service provision. The introduction of new private sector banks and foreign banks has decreased margins and revenues to banks. As a result of the heightened competition, bank service quality has become an increasingly important factor in determining market shares and profitability in banking sector. With a high potential in the Indian banking industry, all leading banks are differentiating themselves based on service quality offering.

Service quality has been described as a measure of matching the customer expectations with the degree of service delivery, and is measured with comparing customers' expectations and perceptions of the services extended by the organisation. For this purpose, perceptions are expressed as consumer's attitude about the service received and expectation as consumer's requirements. Thus, the knowledge about customer's expectations and perceptions is important to service marketers to attain sustainable competitive advantage by maintaining service quality.

The sustainable competitive position in service industry emphasizes the importance of quality of customer service, which has the impact of the technology advancement and LPG namely, liberalization, privatization and globalisation. Thus, assessing customer service quality in service industries such as banks, hospitals, library, telecommunications and insurance is very important in determining the standard expected from the industry.

To attain this sustainable competitive advantage, service industries face a unique challenge of meeting the needs of the customers regularly and continuously. Though mechanised form of activity has its own impact on service delivery performance, many service industries still remain to be manual because there exists no equivalent substitute for personal interaction between employees of service industry and customers.

Only through excellent customer service, an organisation can consistently exceed customer expectations. Excellent customer service and thereby the effectiveness of service delivery process has been identified to influence the overall customer satisfaction. In order to achieve this customer satisfaction, therefore, every service organisation must understand and improve service delivery process and implement valid and reliable service performance measures to measure the same.

LITERATURE REVIEW

The five basic dimensions of service quality in a wide range of service e contexts have been identified in the pioneering research of Parasuraman *et al.* (1987), through the SERVQUAL model. The five dimensions defined in their research are considered the drivers of service quality, representing how consumers organise information about service quality in their minds.

Reliability is defined as the ability to perform the promised service dependably and accurately. In the broadest sense, reliability means that the company delivers on its promises—promises about delivery, service provision, problem resolution, and pricing. Customers want to do business with companies that keep their promises about the service outcomes and core service attributes. Of the five dimensions suggested, reliability has been consistently shown to be the most important determinant of perceptions of service quality among U.S. customers.

Responsiveness is the willingness to help customers and to provide prompt service. This dimension emphasizes attentiveness and promptness in dealing with customer requests, questions, complaints and problems. Responsiveness is communicated to customers by the length of time they have to wait for assistance, answers to questions, or attention to problems. Responsiveness also captures the notion of flexibility and ability to customise the service to customer needs.

To excel on the dimension of responsiveness, a company must view the process of service delivery and the handling of requests from the customer's point of view rather than from the company's point of view.

Assurance is defined as employees' knowledge and courtesy and the ability of the firm and its employees to inspire trust and confidence. This dimension is likely to be particularly important for services that customers perceive as high risk or for services of which they feel uncertain about their ability to evaluate outcomes—for example, banking, insurance, brokerage, medical and legal services.

Empathy is defined as the caring, individualized attention that the firm provides its customers. The essence of empathy is conveying, through personalised or customised service, that customers are unique and special and that their needs are understood. Customers want to feel understood by and important to firms that provide service to them. Personnel at small service firms often know customers by name and build relationships that reflect their personal knowledge of customer requirements and preferences. When such a small firm competes with larger firms, the ability to be empathetic may give the small firm a clear advantage.

Tangibles are defined as the appearance of physical facilities, equipment, personnel, and communication materials. Tangibles provide physical representations or images of the service that customers, particularly new customers, will use to evaluate quality. Service industries that emphasize tangibles in their strategies include hospitality services in which the customer visits the customer visits the establishment to receive the service, such as restaurants and hotels, retail stores, and entertainment companies.

The service-gap model is one of the most important concepts in the understanding of the key concepts, strategies, and decisions in services marketing and is widely used to guide the service provided to customers.

The customer gap is the difference between customer expectations and perceptions (i.e. between expected service and perceived service). Customer expectations are standards or reference points that customers bring into the service experience, whereas customer perceptions are subjective assessments of actual service experiences. Customer expectations often consist of what a customer believes should or will happen.

Closing the gap between what customers expect and what they perceive is critical to delivering quality service; it forms the basis for the gaps model. Because customer satisfaction and customer focus are so critical to competitiveness of firms, any company interested in delivering quality service must begin with a clear understanding of its customers.

To close the all–important customer gap, the gaps model suggests that four other gaps—the provider gaps—need to be closed. These gaps occur within the organisation providing the service and include:

The first provider gap is the difference between customer expectations of service and company understanding of those expectations. A primary cause in many firms for not meeting customers' expectations is that the firm lacks accurate understanding of exactly what those expectations are.

Accurate perceptions of customers' expectations are necessary, but not sufficient, for delivering superior quality service. Another prerequisite is the presence of service designs and performance standards that reflect those accurate perceptions. A recurring theme in service companies is the difficulty experienced in translating customer expectations into service quality specifications that employees can understand and execute. These problems are reflected in the second provider gap, the difference between company understanding of customer expectations and development of customer—driven service designs and standards. Customer—driven standards are different from the conventional performance standards that companies establish for service in that they are based on pivotal customer requirements that are visible to and measured by customers.

The third provider gap is the discrepancy between development of customer—driven service standards and actual service performance by company employees. Even when guidelines exist for performing services well and treating customers correctly, high—quality service performance is not a certainty. Standards must be backed by appropriate resources (people, systems and technology) and also must be enforced to be effective—that is, employees must be measured and compensated on the basis of performance along those standards. When the level of service delivery falls short of the standards, it falls short of what customers expect as well. Narrowing gap 3—by ensuring that all the resources needed to achieve the standards are in place—reduces the customer gap.

The fourth provider gap illustrates the difference between service delivery and the service provider's external communications. Promises made by a service company through is media advertising, sales force, and other communications may potentially raise customer expectations, the standards against which customers assess service quality. The discrepancy between actual and promised service therefore has an adverse effect on the customer gap. Broken promises can occur for many reasons: overpromising in advertising or personal selling, inadequate coordination between operations and marketing, and differences in policies and procedures across service outlets.

The full conceptual model explained in the earlier points conveys a clear message to managers who wish to improve their quality of service. The key to closing the customer gap is to close provider gap 1 through 4 and keep them closed. To the extent that one or more of provider gaps 1 through 4 exist, customers perceive service quality shortfalls. The gap model serves as a framework for service organisations attempting to improve quality service and services marketing.

A new scale for measuring the service quality, specifically in retail banking was developed by Bahia and Nantel (2000). This new scale popularly known as Banking Service Quality (BSQ) is a further modification and extension of the SERVQUAL scale developed by Parsuraman *et al.* (1985). BSQ in addition to the dimensions as proposed by Parsuraman *et al.* (1985) includes other dimensions such as courtesy and access (Carman, 1990), and items representing the various marketing mix elements like product/service, place, process, participants, physical surroundings, price and promotion (Booms and Bitner, 1981).

The BSQ includes thirty-one items under seven dimensions which describe the service quality relevant to the banking sector. These dimensions are: *effectiveness* (recognition of regular clients, knowledge of the clients on a personal basis, valorisation of the clients by personnel, confidentiality, and confidence); *access* (waiting is not too long, queues that move rapidly, sufficient number of open tellers, and no delays); *price* (reasonable fees for the administration of the accounts, balance amount from which service charges begin, good explanation of service charges begin, keeping the client informed every time a better solution appears for a problem, and the bank contacts the clients every time it is useful); *tangibles* (decoration of facilities, efficacious work environment, cleanliness of facilities); *service portfolio* (complete gamut of services, the range of services is consistent with the latest innovation in banking services, and modern equipment); *reliability* (absence of error in service delivery, precision of filling systems, no contradiction between decisions of personnel and management, delivery when promised, precision of account statements, and well-trained personnel); and *assurance* (feeling of security, good reputation, sufficient number of ATMs per branch, indication (communication) of quality, and no interruption of service).

The Banking Service Quality model therefore provides an extended number of dimensions over which a retail bank's perceived service quality can be judged. These dimensions can be used to then apply the concept of Gaps Model to bring about a comparison between the expectation of the customers of the service quality on a particular dimension and the existing quality of the service on that dimension. Therefore the gap between the two can be studied in detail with the help of these dimensions provided.

There are very few studies that have been conducted to identify the important dimensions of service quality in banking sector.

Amudha and Vijaya Banu (2007) studied the quality of services offered by ICICI Bank, Tiruchirapalli District and identified the gaps were in the services in all five dimensions of service quality, the overall weighted SERVQUAL score being –1.92. They suggested that ICICI Bank Ltd. should take steps to close the gaps by establishing a service quality information system.

Kamble (2008) suggested the use of the BSQ instrument as a measure of bank service quality. He found that there was a significant difference in the perception of service quality of public and private sector banks. Private banks were perceived better on the dimensions of effectiveness, access, and tangibles, whereas the public sector banks are perceived better on the dimensions of price and reliability. The results have significant implications in developing operational, marketing and human resource strategies in private and public sector banks based on the identified dimensions of service quality in banks.

Vanniarajan and Naina Mohammed (2009) found that customers' perceptions of service quality provided in the Indian banking industry were consistently lower than their expectations. From the result of gap analysis, they concluded that the service quality gap and delivery gap were the main reasons contributing to the service quality shortfalls in the Indian banking industry.

DATA AND METHODOLOGY

In the light of recent meltdown of the financial system in various developed economies, the reverberations are also expected to be seen for the developing economies. In the wake of such events, every bank is struggling to maintain the sense of reliability and assurance in their customers. Service quality in such an environment becomes imperative to retain customers and enhance their trust in them. The present study undertakes an analysis of the perception of customers towards banking service quality using the BSQ model, in particular comparing the perceptions of service quality of Indian public and private/foreign sector banks. The data for the study was collected from a sample of one hundred customers of Indian banks using a structured questionnaire (viz. the BSQ scale). A Likert scale was used, with '1' representing "strongly agree," '2' representing "agree," '3' representing "neither agree nor disagree," '4' representing "disagree," and '5' representing "strongly disagree."

ANALYSIS AND INTERPRETATION

The descriptive statistics of the expectations and perceptions of the respondents towards different aspects of banking service quality is shown in Table 1.

Table 1: Expectations and Perceptions of Banking Service Quality

	Expectations		*Perceptions*		*t-Test*	
	Mean	*Std. Dev.*	*Mean*	*Std. Dev.*	t_{cal}	*p-Value*
Bank enjoys good reputation in the market	1.4000	0.7910	2.1300	1.1950	–12.5360	0.0000
Bank is financially dependable and money is safe	1.4000	0.7250	2.2900	1.1750	–12.5610	0.0000
Bank does not make its clients wait too long before an employee is available to serve	1.4100	0.7260	2.4000	1.1280	–14.8490	0.0000
Bank has queues that move rapidly	1.4200	0.7680	2.4300	1.0180	–9.5140	0.0000
Bank delivers the service as and when it has been promised	1.4200	0.8190	2.4900	1.0100	–10.1030	0.0000
Bank maintains strict confidentiality of client's personal details	1.4300	0.7280	2.6200	1.1700	–14.4080	0.0000
Bank provides great value to its clients	1.4500	0.6420	2.6300	1.1600	–13.3430	0.0000
Bank has sufficient number of ATMs available	1.4600	0.7970	2.6700	1.1810	–10.6210	0.0000
Bank's personnel are well trained	1.4700	0.7450	2.6900	1.1250	–12.4860	0.0000
Bank's facilities cleanliness is well maintained	1.4700	0.6580	2.6900	1.1870	–10.6810	0.0000
Bank recognises regular clients	1.5000	0.6890	2.7300	1.0900	–13.9650	0.0000
Bank provides service without delay due to bureaucratic factors	1.5100	0.7980	2.7300	0.9410	–13.5190	0.0000
Bank provides good explanation of the service fees charged	1.5300	0.7840	2.8300	1.1460	–14.5740	0.0000
Bank's range of services is consistent with the latest innovation in banking services	1.5500	0.8210	2.8500	1.0090	–12.5000	0.0000
Bank charges service charges from a reasonable balance amount in the account	1.5600	0.8080	2.8600	1.1890	–8.4260	0.0000
Bank's range of services is complete	1.5600	0.9350	2.8800	1.0080	–11.2030	0.0000
Bank's quality of communication to clients is good	1.5600	0.7010	2.9400	1.2130	–9.4250	0.0000
Bank has adopted modern equipment in its operations	1.5700	0.9240	2.9400	0.7630	–7.8260	0.0000
Bank's account statement provided to clients has good precision level	1.5700	0.8440	2.9800	1.1280	–8.9330	0.0000
Bank's interior and exterior facilities are attractive	1.5800	0.8060	2.9800	1.0630	–7.5790	0.0000
Bank's employees instil confidence in its clients	1.5900	0.7260	3.0000	1.0050	–11.5490	0.0000

	Expectations		*Perceptions*		*t-Test*	
	Mean	*Std. Dev.*	*Mean*	*Std. Dev.*	t_{cal}	*p-Value*
Bank keeps the clients informed every time any changes are made in the service fees charged	1.6000	0.8160	3.0300	1.0100	–6.1200	0.0000
Bank has good knowledge of the clients on a personal value	1.6100	0.6650	3.1400	0.9320	–11.6460	0.0000
Bank charges reasonable fees for the administration of the client's accounts	1.6100	0.8270	3.1500	1.0580	–8.8100	0.0000
Bank has an efficient work environment	1.6200	0.8380	3.1500	0.9890	–7.1800	0.0000
Bank has sufficient number of open tellers	1.6300	0.8610	3.1500	0.7830	–11.0100	0.0000
Bank provides interruption-free service to its clients	1.6300	0.8610	3.1600	1.1350	–7.1320	0.0000
Bank delivers error-free service to its clients	1.6500	0.9030	3.1800	1.1320	–7.2350	0.0000
Bank's contacts are useful and informative	1.6800	0.7230	3.2600	0.9910	–10.2270	0.0000
Bank's clients do not experience contradiction between decisions of lower level personnel and management	1.9100	0.7400	3.2900	1.1040	–11.8420	0.0000
Bank's filling systems have good precision level	2.1100	0.9840	3.3000	1.0960	–13.8910	0.0000

It was found that the expectations of quality were very high on each of the aspects of banking service quality, ranging in mean value between 1.00 and 2.00. It was found that the most important aspects of banking service quality were: good reputation, security/safety, waiting is not too long, queues that move rapidly, and the delivery of service as and when promised. The expectation and perception of the respondents towards different aspects of banking service quality were found to be similarly-ordered, and were highly correlated. Further, it was found that there were statistically significant differences in the expectation and perception of each aspect of banking service quality.

The mean values of the different dimensions of banking service quality for public and private/foreign banks is shown in Table 2.

The mean expectations of quality for each of the dimensions of BSQ were found to be not significantly different, but among the dimensions, "assurance" was found to have highest expectation. This dimension includes the following variables: feeling of security, good reputation, sufficient number of ATMs per branch, indication (communication) of quality, and no interruption of service.

Table 2: Tests of Equality of Mean Values of Banking Service Quality Dimensions for Public and Private/Foreign Banks

	Public Banks		*Private/Foreign Banks*		*Overall*		*Difference in Expectation*		*Difference in Perception*	
	Expectation	*Perception*	*Expectation*	*Perception*	*Expectation*	*Perception*	*Fcal*	*p-value*	*Fcal*	*p-value*
Access	1.4611	2.6578	1.5182	2.9455	1.4900	2.6420	0.2190	0.6410	6.8900	0.0050
Price	1.5956	3.3333	1.5964	2.9545	1.4925	3.1250	0.0001	0.9950	2.1690	0.0720
Tangibles and Service Portfolio	1.5519	2.9956	1.5636	3.1927	1.5160	2.8160	0.0080	0.9280	7.1130	0.0045
Reliability	1.6852	2.8963	1.6909	2.4909	1.5583	2.6733	0.0020	0.9640	3.8650	0.0260
Assurance	1.5022	2.7407	1.4800	2.9758	1.5960	3.1040	0.0350	0.8520	4.8190	0.0155
Effectiveness	1.4667	2.4622	1.5564	2.7891	1.6883	2.8700	0.9290	0.3380	4.4800	0.0185

On the other hand, it was found that there is a significant gap between expectations and perceptions on each of the dimensions of banking service quality. The gap between these expectations and perceptions of the respondents shows the extent to which improvements can be made by Indian banks to satisfy customers better. It was found that the largest gap between expectations and perceptions were for the dimensions of "access" and "price." Further, it was found that the gaps between expectations and perceptions on each of the dimensions of banking service quality existed for public and private/foreign banks alike. It was found that there was no significant difference in expectations of different dimensions of banking service quality for public and private/foreign banks. However, it was found that there were significant differences in the perceptions of banking service quality between public and private/foreign banks: public banks were perceived to have better access, tangibles and service portfolio, assurance, and effectiveness than private/foreign banks, while private/foreign banks were perceived to be better than public banks in terms of price and reliability.

DISCUSSION

The analysis shows that there is a significant difference between the expectations and the perceptions of banking service quality of the respondents for all of the variables under the Banking Service Quality (BSQ) model.

It was found that the mean ratings for the expectations and the perceptions for the following variables were close:

- the bank maintains strict confidentiality of client's personal details
- the bank's filling system have good precision level

- the bank's account statement provided to clients have good precision level
- the bank is financially dependable and money is safe
- the bank enjoys good reputation in the market.

This is also identified with the fact that Indian banks have fared well even in these difficult times. This is probably one of the reasons that most customers feel that Indian banks are financially dependable and enjoy a good reputation in the market.

For all other variables the mean expectation of quality is much higher than the perception of quality of the banks. Some of the variables that are important to customers were found to be:

- the bank does not make its clients wait too long before an employee is available to serve
- the bank has queues that move rapidly
- the bank provides good explanation of the service fees charged
- the bank keeps the clients informed every time any charges are made in the service fees charged
- the bank has good knowledge of the clients on a personal level.

In particular, the variables for "assurance" were found to be fundamentally very important for customers and therefore it becomes essential for the banks to improve their perceived existing quality. There is a wide gap between the expectations and perceptions of assurance which should be minimised as soon as possible.

For almost for all variables under the BSQ model, there is a great scope for Indian banks to improve the perceptions of quality of service of the customers against their expectations. With the increasing expectations of the customers important that the gap between the expectation and the customer perceived is minimised as soon as possible.

In the times of crisis like this for the financial services industry, customer orientation has become a very important factor. Therefore, it is not only enough to provide all services but is important to meet the customer's expectation for each of the dimensions of banking service quality, in order to achieve sustainable competitive advantage.

It was found that public banks fared better overall than private/foreign banks in terms of perceptions of banking service quality. This can be explained partially by the experience with private/foreign banks worldwide. With the sudden collapse of some of the oldest and most well-established international banks and the onset of the global financial meltdown, customers have become more cautious about private/foreign banks. At the same time the trust level on public banks have increased. Therefore, private/foreign banks would have to concentrate on meeting customer expectations better.

The study shows that there is a gap between the expectations of the customers and their perceptions of banking service quality which needs to be addressed by marketers so that the customers can be satisfied better. This would imply making their entire range of services more accessible, reliable; give a feeling of assurance and making it available at a reasonable price.

With the financial service industry witnessing a tough time after the breakdown of US financial system, retaining and maintaining the trust of customers in your organisation has become even more. Public banks have to tighten their belts and be ready to capitalise the opportunity and win as many customers as possible. At the same time private/foreign banks would need to become even more cautious and customer oriented than before to attract new customers and retain their existing ones. They would have to build a very strong trust system in their organisation which would make their customers stick to them rather than shift to other players.

In short, serving the customers of Indian banks would require improving every dimension of banking service (effectiveness, access, price, tangibles and service portfolio, reliability and assurance) and aiming to reach the customer's expectations more and more.

The study has some limitations which should be addressed in subsequent research. The sample used for the study is very small, so that the results may be indicative only. The study is based on customer perceptions, and thus does not take the perspectives of the employees or management of the banks into consideration. Also, the study considers only the factors pertaining to the service quality of the banks and does not put any light on the technical factors of the bank. Many a time customer's choice of banks would also depend on the technical factors pertaining to the bank under consideration. There is much scope for further research into banking service quality to confirm and extend the results of the present study.

REFERENCES

Amudha, R. and Vijaya Banu, C. (2007). "Service quality in Banking with special reference to ICICI Bank Ltd., Tiruchirapalli District," *Asia-Pacific Business Review*, Volume III, Number 2, July–December 2007.

Kamble, S. (2008). "An assessment of service quality in Indian Retail Banks," *Global Mnagament Review*, Volume 2, Issue 4, August 2008.

Parasuraman, A., Berry, L.L. and Zeithaml, V.A. (1985). "A Conceptual Model of Service Quality and Its Implications for Future Research," *Journal of Marketing*, 49/4.

Vanniarajan, T. and Naina Mohammed, K. (2009). "Service Quality Gap Analysis in Indian Banking Industry: A Perspective from customer and officials," *PES Business Review*, Vol. 4, Issue 1, Jan 2009.

Impact of Exchange Rate on Foreign Exchange Reserves of Indian Banking Industry

G. Sabitha

Dr. B.R. Ambedkar Institute of Management and Technology, Hyderabad

ABSTRACT: *Foreign exchange operations that are unsterilized will cause an expansion or contraction in the amount of domestic currency in circulation, and hence directly affect monetary policy and inflation. The quantity of foreign exchange reserves can change as a central bank implements monetary policy. A central bank that implements a fixed exchange rate policy may face a situation where supply and demand would tend to push the value of the currency lower or higher.*

The data in foreign exchange reserves comprising foreign currency assets (FCA), gold and Special Drawing Rights (SDRs). The foreign exchange reserves were not dwindling at a fast rate, in order to be able to prevent the rupee from falling sharply; the forex reserves should be used. This paper discusses the impact of Foreign exchange rate on Forex reserves of Indian Banking Industry and its movement in the foreign exchange reserves year after year.

Keywords: FCA, SDRs, Foreign Exchange Reserves.

INTRODUCTION

There has been a very rapid rise since the early 1990s in foreign reserves held by developing countries like India. These reserves have climbed to almost 30 percent of developing countries' GDP and 8 months of imports. Assuming reasonable spreads between the yield on reserve assets and the cost of foreign borrowing, the income loss to these countries amounts to close to 1 percent of GDP. The standard approach for measuring international reserves takes into account the unencumbered international reserve assets of the monetary authority; however, the foreign currency and the securities held by the public including the banks and corporate bodies are not accounted for in the definition of official holdings of international reserves.

The exchange rate policy in India is not guided by a fixed or pre-announced target or band; rather, it is determined by the demand and supply in the foreign exchange market.

However, the objective of exchange rate policy has been to retain the flexibility to intervene in the foreign exchange market if the capital inflows are lumpy and volatile or if they disrupt the macroeconomic situation.

MANAGEMENT OF FOREIGN EXCHANGE RESERVES

The guiding objectives of foreign exchange reserves management in India are safety, liquidity and returns in line with the general international practices in this regard. The level of foreign exchange reserves has traditionally been the outcome of the Reserve Bank's intervention in the foreign exchange market to contain excessive exchange rate volatility and valuation changes due to movement in prices of securities and of the US dollar against other currencies. Moreover, the reserves which are built up mostly out of the volatile capital flows do not represent surplus earnings through trade like in the case of some other countries and they are required to be held as buffer during periods of sudden stops and reversal in capital flows.

OBJECTIVES OF THE STUDY

The main objective of the study is to analyze the Impact of Exchange Rate on Foreign exchange reserves of Indian Banking Industry, the other objectives are:

- To analyze the movement in foreign exchange reserves
- To explore the Sources of variation in foreign exchange reserves
- To study relationship between foreign exchange reserves and GDP.

METHODOLOGY

The present study is of analytical in nature and makes use of secondary data. The relevant secondary data are collected from various publications of Government of India, Ministry of Finance, Department of Economic Affairs, Economic Division, India, Reserve bank of India reports and World Investment Report Published by UNCTAD etc.

ANALYSIS AND DISCUSSION

Analysis of Exchange Rate Indicators

With adequate foreign exchange reserves, India remains capable of handling any pressures emanating from the external sector in the near term. However, from a medium to long term perspective, it is important to improve resilience of external account by pursuing policies that shift the composition of capital flows so as to reduce dependence on its volatile components. Augmenting FDI further could bring about a better balance between different components of capital flows and reduce the possibility of volatile currency movements and any pressure on reserves in the face of contagion risks.

The exchange rate regime has evolved towards greater flexibility as a conscious policy choice, but this has been calibrated to the changing structure and dynamics of the economy without loss of monetary policy independence. Policies had supported this move over a period of time, *inter alia*, by capacity building to withstand volatility and shocks. It has increasingly allowed exchange rate to serve as a buffer, depreciating to help the economy when it was weak and appreciating to reduce excess demand when it was strong. In the past two years, there has been no significant foreign exchange market intervention. The small increase in the Reserve Bank's foreign exchange reserves mainly reflects various accruals, interest earnings and valuation changes. Increased exchange rate flexibility has also minimized the danger that foreign inflows would be attracted by "one-way bets" on appreciation, or that domestic firms would borrow excessively from abroad without hedging their exposure.

Table 1: Exchange Rate Indicators

Item	*Average 1990–91 to 1999–2000*	*Average 1999–2000 to 2009–10*	*Average 2003–04 to 2007–08*	*2008–09*	*2009–10*	*2010–11*
(a) Exchange Rate (Rupee/US Dollar) End of Period	34.1	45.4	43.1	50.9	45.1	44.6
Average	32.7	45.6	44.1	45.9	47.4	45.6
(b) 36 - Currency REER (Percentage Change)	–0.04	0.4	1	–9.9	–3.1	7.7
(c) 36 - Currency NEER (Percentage Change)	–1.3	–0.3	0.5	–10.9	–2.6	2.9
(d) 6 - Currency REER (Percentage Change)	0.4	1.5	2.5	–9.3	–0.3	13.1
(e) 6 - Currency NEER (Percentage Change)	–4	–1.4	0.4	–13.6	–3.7	5.7

Source: RBI Annual Report.

India resorted to capital control in the year 2010–11, The country hardly intervened through purchase/sale of foreign currency or active capital account management. The rupee dollar exchange rate showed two-way movement in the range of `44.03–47.58 per US dollar. The rupee appreciated by least of 4.0 per cent on an average basis against the US dollar during the year 2010–11, depreciated slightly between the years 2004 and 2008. Highest appreciation occupied in the year 2008–09 nearly 12.5%.

On an average basis, the 6-currency real effective exchange rate (REER) appreciated by 13.1 per cent in 2010–11, the 36 currency REER by 4.5 per cent and the 36 currency REER by 7.7 per cent. The 6-currency index showed the maximum appreciation compared to other indices reflecting higher inflation differential with the country. The 36-currency REER is lowest during the year 2008–09. 36 currency NEER and 6-currency NEER also got higher percentage change in the year 2008–09.

MOVEMENT OF FOREIGN EXCHANGE RESERVES

Several investors view the valuation in the Indian stock market as attractive on an expected future earnings basis. Interest differentials are likely to remain large and alluring to debt flows. With India's growth prospects still broadly intact, its attractiveness as an investment destination may increase. In the short run, if commodity prices soften and global crisis remains contained, the resultant benefit it may have in lowering inflation, fiscal and current account deficits could attract fresh investments. Therefore, the possibility of lumpy capital inflows cannot be ruled out. Over the course, capital flows could remain volatile and may depend on how trade and capital flows, as also other macro-economic parameters, respond endogenously to exchange rate movements (Tables 2&3).

Table 2: Percentage Change in Movement in Foreign Exchange Reserves (in SDR mn)

Year	*Total Foreign Exchange Reserves (in SDR mn)*	*Movement in Foreign Exchange Reserves (in SDR mn)*	*% Change in Movement*
2001	34,034	5,306	1.40
2002	43,876	9,842	0.85
2003	55,394	11,518	0.17
2004	76,298	20,904	0.81
2005	93,666	17,368	–0.17
2006	105,231	11,565	–0.33
2007	131,890	26,659	1.31
2008	188,339	56,449	1.12
2009	168,544	–19,795	–1.35
2010	183,803	15,259	–1.77
2011	192,254	8,451	–0.45

In the year 2001, the movement of foreign exchange reserves secured higher percentage of change i.e. 1.4%. less in the year 2005. The percentage change in the movement is even negative in the years 2005, 2006, 2009, 2010 and 2011.

Table 3: Movement in Foreign Exchange Reserves from the year 2001–2011

Year	*Foreign Exchange Reserves (in Crores)*					*Foreign Exchange Reserves (US $ mn))*					*Total Foreign Exchange Reserves (in SDR mn)*	*Movement in Foreign Exchange Reserves (in SDR mn)*
	SDRs	*Gold*	*Foreign Currency Assets*	*Reserve Tranche Position in IMF*	*Total*	*SDRs*	*Gold*	*Foreign Currency Assets*	*Reserve Tranche Position in IMF*	*Total*		
2001	11	12,711	1,84,482	2,873	2,00,077	2	2,725	39,554	616	42,897	34,034	5,306
2002	50	14,868	2,49,118	2,977	2,67,013	10	3,047	51,049	610	54,716	43,876	9,842
2003	19	16,785	3,41,476	3,190	3,61,470	4	3,534	71,890	672	76,100	55,394	11,518
2004	10	18,216	4,66,215	5,688	4,90,129	2	4,198	107,448	1,311	112,959	76,298	20,904
2005	20	19,686	5,93,121	6,289	6,19,116	5	4,500	135,571	1,438	141,514	93,666	17,368
2006	12	25,674	6,47,327	3,374	6,76,387	3	5,755	145,108	756	151,622	105,231	11,565
2007	8	29,573	8,36,597	2,044	8,68,222	2	6,784	191,924	469	199,179	131,890	26,659
2008	74	40,124	11,96,023	1,744	12,37,965	18	10,039	299,230	436	309,723	188,339	56,449
2009	6	48,793	12,30,066	5,000	12,83,865	1	9,577	241,426	981	251,985	168,544	–19,795
2010	22,596	81,188	11,49,650	6,231	12,59,665	5,006	17,986	254,685	1,380	279,057	183,803	15,259
2011	20,401	1,02,572	12,24,883	13,158	13,61,013	4,569	22,972	274,330	2,947	304,818	192,254	8,451

Source: RBI report-2011.

SOURCES OF VARIATION IN FOREIGN EXCHANGE RESERVES

The flows of foreign exchange reserves in BOP statistics, however, exclude variation in gold and valuation changes in FCA and SDRs. While most of the components such as exports, imports, foreign direct investment, portfolio investment, external assistance, external commercial borrowings, etc. are self-explanatory, a few other items, i.e., investment income, banking capital and 'other capital' needs further elaboration. Banking capital comprises assets and liabilities of authorized dealers, NRI deposits and movement in balance of foreign central banks and international institutions like, World Bank, IDA, ADB, IFC, etc. maintained with RBI. 'Other Capital' is a residual item and broadly includes delayed exports receipts, funds raised and held abroad by Indian corporate, India's subscriptions to international institutions, quota payments to IMF (Table 4).

Table 4: Sources of Variation in Foreign Exchange Reserves

Item	*Average 1990–91 to 1999–2000*	*Average 1999–2000 to 2009–10*	*Average 2003–04 to 2007–08*	*2008–09*	*2009–10*	*2010–11*
Current Account Balance (US$ billion)	–4.4	–8.3	–4.7	–27.9	–38.4	–44.3
Net Invisibles	6	44.2	45.8	91.6	80	86.2
of which: Services	1.3	21.5	23.4	53.9	35.7	47.7
Private Transfers	7.8	27.9	27.6	44.6	52.1	53.4
Investment Income	–3.5	–5	–4.9	–6.6	–7.2	–13.9
Net Capital Flows (US$ billion)	7.7	31	44.4	6.8	53.4	59.7
of which: FDI to India	1.6	16.3	15.3	37.7	33.1	23.4
FIIs	1.3	7.1	10.6	–15	29	29.4
NRI Deposits	1.3	2.5	2	4.3	2.9	3.2
Reserve Changes (BoP basis) (US $ billion) (Increase/Decrease)	–3.3	–22.9	–40.3	20.1	–13.4	–13.1
External Debt Indicators						
(a) External Debt Stock (US$ billion)	93	157	156	224.5	261	305.9
(b) Debt-GDP Ratio (%)	29	19	17.7	20.5	18	17.3
(c) Import cover of Reserves (in Months)	6.5	12.5	14	9.8	11.1	9.6
(d) Short-term Debt to Total Debt (%)	6	11.8	13.6	19.3	20	21.2
(e) Debt Service Ratio (%)	24.9	8.8	8.3	4.4	5.5	4.2
(f) Reserves to Debt (%)	23	96	114.2	112.2	106.9	99.6

Source: Ministry of Finance, Department of Economic Affairs. Economic Division. INDIA and RBI Report.

FOREIGN RESERVES AS A SHARE OF GDP

The massive increase in developing countries' foreign exchange reserves in recent years. Reserves have risen from a range of 6–8 percent of GDP during the 1970s and 1980s to almost 50 percent of GDP by 2011. Reserves begin to trend sharply up just around 1990, the year that is commonly identified with the onset of the era of financial globalization. There is no similar jump in the reserves held by industrial countries, which have remained roughly steady at below 5 percent of GDP since the 1950s.

Prior to the era of financial globalization, countries held reserves mainly to manage foreign exchange demand and supply arising from current account transactions. The traditional rule of thumb for Central Banks was that they should hold a quantity of foreign exchange reserves equivalent to three months of imports. Therefore at least part of the increase in reserves may be due to the increased commercial openness of developing countries. But, the increase in reserves is equally evident when looked at in relation to imports (Tables 5&6).

Table 5: GDP and Total Foreign Exchange Reserves

Year	*GDP*	*Total Foreign Exchange Reserves*
2004–05	14653	93,666
2005–06	24584	105,231
2006–07	56390	131,890
2007–08	98642	188,339
2008–09	142829	168,544
2009–10	123120	183,803
2010–11	88520	192,254

Source: World report.

Table 6: Ratio of Export Plus Imports of Goods to GDP

Year	*Export Plus Imports of Goods/GDP*	*Export Plus Imports of Goods and Services/GDP*
Average 1990–91 to 1999–2000	18.8	22.9
Average 1999–2000 to 2009–10	29.5	39.2
Average 2003–04 to 2007–08	30.4	40.8
2008–09	41	54
2009–10	35	46.3
2010–11	36.5	49

Source: RBI Report and World Bank Report.

Ratio of Export plus Imports of Goods to GDP is increasing from year to year in an average of 50% in each 10 years period. In this same line it is recorded 36.55 by the year 2010–11. There was a decline in the year 2009–10 from the year 2008–09.

CONCLUSION

Exchange rate policy is guided by the need to reduce excess volatility, prevent the emergence of destabilizing speculative activities, help maintain an adequate level of reserves and develop an orderly foreign exchange market, and is not governed by any predetermined target/band.

India's foreign exchange reserves falling largely due to suspected sale of dollars. The RBI is not providing any reasons for the change in foreign currency assets. It said the assets expressed in US dollar terms included the effect of appreciation or depreciation of non-US currencies such as the pound sterling, euro and yen held in reserve. However, the RBI is understood to have sold dollars from the reserves to curb the slide in the value of rupee.

REFERENCES

Allen, L. and Rai, A. (1996). Operational Efficiency in Banking: An International Comparison, *Journal of Banking and Finance*, Vol. 20, No. 4, May, pp. 655–72.

Kose, A. Ayhan, Eswar Prasad, Kenneth Rogoff and Shang-Jin Wei (2009). "Financial Globalisation and Economic Policies", IZA Discussion Paper No. 4037.

Cameron, R. (ed.) (1991). *International banking,* 1870–1914, Oxford University Press, New York.

Reports by Government of India, Ministry of Finance, Department of Economic Affairs, Economic Division, India.

Indian Banking Association, Report on Banking Industry vision 2011.

Chartered Financial Analyst, Indian Banking 2005 special, The ICFAI university Press, No. (2005).

World Investment Report Published by UNCTAD etc.

Should Not the Public Sector Banks have a More Positive HR Orientation? A Preliminary Inquiry

Anand Saxena and Ashis Taru Deb[1]

Department of Commerce, Deen Dayal Upadhyaya College, University of Delhi

[1]Department of Economics, College of Vocational Studies, University of Delhi

ABSTRACT: *On the basis of the evidence of U-shaped curve of employment data of Public Sector Banks in the post-VRS (Voluntary Retirement Scheme) period, the study posits that there could be something amiss about the strategy of induced separation of manpower via the VRS. That such a conduct should be observed at a time when the industry was poised for growth is seen to have implications for HR orientation of the PSBs. While the scheme was given for uniform implementation across all the public sector banks, the study notes that the individual banks missed the opportunity of strategic behaviour, more so when the human resources are believed to be the prominent differentiators of organisational performance. Thus, it makes a case for better HRM orientation.*

Keywords: HRM, Banks.

INTRODUCTION

The structure of the Indian banking industry, like most other sectors of the economy, seems to have come full circle. In the colonial era it was characterised by laissez faire. Nineteen seventies comprised the era of nationalisation. The present era is characterised by privatisation and deregulation of the industry. Consequently, in this era, one has witnessed facilitation of entry into the industry of foreign and private banks. In fact, we might as well have business house owned/controlled banks. Entry of the private and foreign controlled banks has meant competition for the public sector banks necessitating emphasis on efficiency, service quality, product and technological innovation etc. Not only are they required to compete with the private sector/foreign banks, there now is inter se competition between the public sector banks as well and these banks can no longer be considered as acting in unison and following similar strategies. It may be noted that public sector enterprises in India were generally envisaged to implement the will of the welfare state. Thus, they were mandated, inter alia, to be creators of employment opportunities and aspire to become the model employers. Such an HR orientation was inevitable in view of the exploitative HR practices of the laissez faire regime of the pre-independence era characterised by lack of job security, insufficient remuneration, poor working conditions and conditions of employment tilted in favour of the employers. HR orientation of the banks toward employment creation and staff welfare since nationalization would, thus, be only natural. Now that the PSBs are managing the transition toward free-market competition it raises an important research question as to what implications has this coming of full circle of the changing structure of Indian banking industry had for the HR practices in public sector banks? The salience of this research question has only been amplified with PSB's experience with the Voluntary Retirement Scheme that had the intended objective of improving the efficiency of performance but resulted in the serious crunch of human resources in several cases.

The purpose of the present paper is to examine whether there has been a shift in the HR orientation of the PSBs since privatization and deregulation of the industry. More importantly, and in view of the growing inter se competition among themselves, whether there is a variation as regards their HR orientation.

Rest of the paper is organised as follows. In Section II, we develop the rationale of the study, state its objectives and spell out the hypotheses. We review the extant literature on the subject in Section III. Section IV is devoted to an elaboration of the methodological issues including the unit of analysis, period of the study, sample description, operational definitions of the terms and their empirical measures as well as the model specifications. In Section V we present the results. Section VI contains our concluding observations and implications of the study.

RATIONALE, OBJECTIVES AND HYPOTHESES

Rationale

The impetus for the study came from the recent reports that public sector banks are on a hiring spree and not so distant reports about the implementation of the voluntary retirement scheme (VRS) in these banks. In an evaluation of the scheme, Jain and Shukla (2002) cite "a candid notice asking customers to bear with the inconvenience caused by the voluntary retirement scheme (VRS)," disgruntled employees and dissatisfied managements suggestive of the necessity of examining the HR related practices of the PSBs in the last decade or so. Could the situation turn so drastically that in the space of 10 years we witness a wave of retrenchment via voluntary retirement followed by a counter wave of hiring? Could these developments be attributable to a grand design of the reform of public sector banks or could one conjecture that there was something amiss about the policy at the first place? What could be relative pay-offs of training, development and education of the existing human resources for organizational adaptation vis-à-vis the strategy of getting rid of the deadwood and inducting the fresh blood? In retrospect, does the stated overstaffing in PSBs merely represent the liability of a welfare state of employment creation and staff welfare and was therefore devoid of any strategic considerations? Do all the PSBs follow an identical HR policy or do the individual banks try to differentiate on this count?

Objectives

The specific objectives of the paper are as follows:

1. To see if there is a trend of retrenchment and subsequent hiring, considering the PSBs as a unit, i.e. taking all the public sector banks together; and
2. To decompose the trend across individual banks so discern typological differences if any.

Hypotheses

It may be recalled that pursuant to the findings of overstaffing to the extent of 35% by the Federation of the Indian Chambers of Commerce and Industry (FICCI) and 30% overstaffing by the Ministry of Finance, Government of India (Kumar, 2010) industry- wide VRS was implemented by 26 of the 27 PSBs from 2000. The scheme was envisaged to assist banks to effect induced separation of excess human resources and thereby their optimal use, achieve a balanced age and skills profile in tune with their business strategies (banknetindia, 2012). If the retrenchment of employees via VRS were inadequately founded in the sectoral strategy, then the behaviour of the number of employees on rolls should exhibit a secularly downward sloping curve. Conversely, if there was something amiss about the strategy of retrenchment via VRS, the series of employee data of the sector should exhibit a U-shaped curve implying course correction. Thus, the first hypothesis is stated as under:

(H1): The behaviour of the number of employees on roll of the public sector banks as a whole is descriptive of a downward curve.

The deregulation and liberalisation of banking industry meant that PSBs would be competing not only with the private/foreign banks but also with each other. In other words, there would be an opportunity for strategic behaviour for the individual PSBs. In such a scenario it is quite likely that different PSBs would follow distinguishable HR practices. Indeed, the decentralization of recruitment by taking it out of the purview of the Banking Sector Recruitment Board (BSRB), had the intention of liberalisation of PR practices in the sector so that the individual banks could follow the policies that suited best to their respective situation. The fact that Corporation Bank refused to exercise VRS at that point and was actually hiring 200-odd new employees (highlights the opportunity for strategic behaviour in HR at bank level. Thus, the second hypothesis of the study is articulated as under:

(H2): There is no variation in the behaviour of the number of employees on roll of the individual public sector banks.

We seek to fit a quadratic trend to employment data over time. The equation to be fitted is:

$$Y = a + bt + ct^2$$

where 'Y' stands for employment and 't' stands for time.

We test a pair of null hypothesis and conduct one-tail test in both the cases of linear and quadratic trend, see Table 1.

Table 1: Hypotheses of the Study

Coefficients	*Hypotheses*	
	Null Hypotheses	*Alternative Hypotheses*
Linear trend	H_O: b=0	H_A: b < 0
Quadratic trend	H_O: c =0	H_A: c >0

We do not expect both the null hypothesis to be rejected in all the cases. For example, each coefficient may turn out to be either insignificant or positive-and-significant or negative-and-significant. One can anticipate as many as nine scenarios, albeit we would be interested in two scenarios in particular:

1. 'b' is negative-and-significant and 'c' is insignificant showing a fall in employment over time in the post VRS phase.
2. 'b' is negative-and-significant and 'c' is positive-and-significant showing a U-shaped behaviour of employment over time.

However, there could be other possibilities as well.

REVIEW OF LITERATURE

The extant literature on HR practices in PSBs since liberalisation is scant but growing. See Table 2. The studies reviewed here could be categorised into those pertaining to (a) The impact of VRS/Organizational Down/Right Sizing on organizational performance; and, (b) Psychological reaction to and causes of opting for/not opting for VRS. While the salient findings of these studies are summarized in Table 2, it would be appropriate to take stock of these in somewhat greater detail, more so in regard to the underlying theoretical currents and empirical evidence from elsewhere.

Organisational Downsizing

Cameron (1994) defines organizational downsizing as "a set of activities, undertaken on the part of the management of an organization and designed to improve organizational efficiency, productivity, and/or competitiveness. It represents a strategy implemented by managers that affects (a) the size of the firm's workforce, (b) the costs, and (c) the work processes... Four major attributes of downsizing help define it and identify its commonality or distinctiveness from other related concepts. They relate to *intent* [purposiveness], *personnel* [personnel reduction], *efficiency* [cutting costs, enhancing organizational performance and bolstering competitiveness] *and work processes* [redesigning, restructuring]."

There are several studies that pertain to organizational consequences of downsizing strategy. Much of the literature in this regard remains skeptical about the efficacy of the exercise in realizing the intended outcomes. For example Cameron (*ibid*) reports a survey by a consulting firm that found that of the 1005 firms downsizing between 1986–1991, only 46 per cent actually reduced costs, only 32 per cent increased profits, only 22 percent actually increased productivity, and only 17 per cent actually reduced bureaucracy although each of these goals was intended.

In Indian context, the findings of D' Souza (2002) seem to suggest that productivity gains are possible despite growth in employment as happened in cased of private sector/foreign banks. This could be possible via product diversification, market development and improving service quality, i.e. enlarging the numerator of the productivity ratio. It's a question worth considering therefore, as to whether or not it was desirable and feasible to examine the issue of improvements in the numerator rather than reducing the denominator alone?

Psychological Reactions/Perceptions

Laying-off of personnel is the most common aspect of downsizing strategy (McClune *et al.*, 1988). As such, downsizing has psychological implications for the persons eased out as well as those remaining in the organisations. In an extensive review of literature, Kozlowski *et al.* (1993) note that the researchers have investigated several aspects of individual perceptions about and psychological reactions to lay-offs and job loss, viz., financial well-being, health, personal attitudes, personal/family/social relationships etc.

In their study of the reasons for voluntary retirement, Suri and Poonam (2003) find that reasons for opting for voluntary retirement were different from those for not opting for

Table 2: Studies on Changing Paradigm of HR Practices in PSBs since Liberalisation

Author/s	*Title*	*Year*	*Nature of Study*	*Model/ Methodology*	*Key Findings/Conclusions*	*Remarks*
Jain and Shukla	A Not So Golden Handshake	2002	Theoretical	None	VRS consequences: manpower shortages; disgruntled employees; management dissatisfaction with the resultant efficiency	–
Pramod Kumar	Impact on Indian Banking Systems through V.R.S.	2010	Theoretical	None	VRS key to reducing staff cost and weeding out inefficiencies	–
Errol D'Souza	Employment and Human Resource Practices in Public Sector Banks in the Nineties Paper	2002	Empirical	Comparative Ratios	Superior performance of Private and Foreign Banks related to their HR practices .	–
Vivek S. Sachan	Organizational Downsizing and Its Impact on Performance of Indian Public Sector Banks	2011	Empirical	Correlation between manpower and various measures of bank performance	VRS increases financial performance of public Sector Banks.	Bank performance is subject to the influence of a host of factors, which if not controlled could mask the correct assessment of the impact of VRS/downsizing on bank performance.

Author/s	*Title*	*Year*	*Nature of Study*	*Model/ Methodology*	*Key Findings/Conclusions*	*Remarks*
Narayan Kayarkatte	Impact of Voluntary Retirement Scheme (VRS 2000) on the Employee Beneficiaries of Public Sector Banks	2011	Empirical	Perceptual Survey CMO (Context Mechanism, Outcome) Model of impact assessment	Of the 445 persons who availed of VRS and responded to the surve, majority regretted that their decision was not well considered and was an unwise decision	–
R.K. Suri and Poonam	An Analysis of The Reasons for Voluntary Retirement	2003	Empirical	Perceptual Survey	Transfer of self or spouse was reported as the top reason for opting for VRS. On the other hand, lack of alternative employment was cited as the top reason for not opting for the VRS.	–
Navdeep Kaur	Voluntary Retirement Scheme in Public Sector Banks—A Comparative Study of Punjab & Sind Bank and State Bank of India	2007	Empirical	Perceptual Survey of the employees of SBI and Punjab and Sindh Bank	Majority of the responding employees of the Punjab and Sind Bank felt that the introduction of the VRS was not a step in the right direction, whereas nearly 60% of the SBI employees approved of the VRS scheme.	–
Anonymou s	HRM In Indian Banking Industry: A Comparative Study Of SBI and HDFC	2011	Empirical	Case Method	VRS in SBI linked to computerization. Whereas HDFC kept hiring for an effective combination of human resource and technology in disseminating their banking functions	–

voluntary retirement. Their finding that transfer of self or spouse was the top reason for the persons opting for retirement seems to be suggestive of the 'compulsory' content of the scheme of voluntary retirement scheme. The study of Narayan Kayarkatte (2011) shows that majority of over 400 responding persons who had opted for the VRS regretted that their decision was not well considered. Hardships associated with premature retirement underline the limitations of the strategy from the point of view of the employees. Demps and Baker (2009) evaluate ethical integrity of firm downsizing from the perspectives of (a) selection—the decision to downsize; (b) communication—the criteria according to which employees are selected for downsizing; (c) transition and transfer—opportunities for transfer within the organization; (d) process—the way in which employees are "let go"; (e) the rebuilding of morale among remaining employees; and (f) pastoral/spiritual reality—visibility of leadership after downsizing for support purposes. They find particular difficulties in regard to the last three aspects of downsizing.

In the case of voluntary retirement one may argue that the decision is left to the discretion of the employees who would be "rational" in the exercise of the option and hence the management might feel relived of the burden of the ethical dilemmas associated with 'selection' and 'communication.' Indeed while discussing the implementation of the VRS scheme in PSBs, it is often stated that it was opted for by those who in management's contemplation, were not the indented beneficiaries (or targets) of the scheme. That is officers rather than clerks and subordinates. We would like to contest this on the grounds of information asymmetry between the proposers and acceptors of the VRS, 'bounded rationality' and the uncertainty of organizational outcomes of the voluntary action of the employees, whereas the proposal of the VRS at the first place would be governed by the strategic imperatives.

METHODOLOGICAL ISSUES

Sample Description

The study examines the employment behaviour of all the Public Sector Banks rather than any representational sample thereof as in case of case method or comparative studies.

Unit of Analysis

Basic unit of analysis is the individual public sector banks, albeit we do consider the pattern of change in employment in PSBs as a whole.

Period of the Study

We cover the employment and other relevant data for the period 1998–2011. The choice of the period corresponds to the post-VRS period as the PSBs were required to complete the process within a 7-month window closing on March 2001. This means that the study also makes use of the control period of two years prior to 2000–01.

Operational definitions of the terms and their empirical measures.

HR Orientation: We refer to the change in the size of the employment as a measure of HRM orientation of the firm. For a HR oriented firm rather than inducing separation via VRS would strive to retain its manpower by reallocation, retraining and reframing of incentives.

Model Specifications

We rely on quadratic function regression model whereby we regress the time series of independent variable 'number of employees' over the years 't' 1998 (=1) – 2011 (=14) and 't^2' to see whether the behaviour of the time series of 'number of employees' corresponds to a U-shaped curve. The presence of a U-shaped curve is taken to be indicative of course correction from the employee separation induced by the VRS and therefore the inappropriateness of the strategy of VRS.

RESULTS

PSBs as a Whole

It may be noted that the Ministry of Finance approved of the scheme of VRS to be implemented uniformly across all the public sector banks. If the premises of such a recommendation were correct, then, the time series of employment in the PSB's as a whole should exhibit a secular, linear downward trend. In other words, the regression of employment data in respect of PSBs as a whole should return the coeeficient of 't' i.e. 'b' as negative-and-significant and the coefficient of 't^2 ' i.e.'c' as insignificant showing a fall in employment over time in the post VRS phase. However, that was not the case. See Table 3.

A U-shaped behaviour of the data of aggregate employment of the PSBs as a whole is evident from the regression output shown in Table 4.1 with 'b' turning out to be significantly negative and 'c' significantly positive. We consider this as sufficient evidence to suggest that there was something amiss about the regulatory intent of induced separation of manpower via the VRS. One could argue that the U-shaped curve of employment data with respect to time could be attributable the challenging conditions of the industry in pre-VRS and favourable conditions in the post-VRS periods. We chose to apply a log linear trend to the number of branches of all the PSBs taken together to map the industry prospects in terms of growth rate. See, Table 4.

Table 3: Trend of Aggregate Employment in PSBs as a Whole

Regression Statistics					
Multiple R	0.97				
R Square	0.93				
Adjusted R Square	0.92				
Standard Error	17782.15				
Observations	14.00				
ANOVA					
	df	*SS*	*MS*	*F*	*Significance F*
Regression	2.00	47729871295.88	23864935647.94	75.47	0.00
Residual	11.00	3478251980.48	316204725.50		
Total	13.00	51208123276.36			
	Coefficients	*Standard Error*	*t Stat*	*P-value*	
Intercept	945466.21	16568.26	57.06	0.00	
b	–41664.69	5081.53	–8.20	0.00	
c	1928.62	329.53	5.85	0.00	

Table 4: Growth Rate of Total Number of Branches in PSBs as a Whole

Regression Statistics					
Multiple R	0.93				
R Square	0.87				
Adjusted R Square	0.86				
Standard Error	0.02				
Observations	14.00				
ANOVA					
	df	*SS*	*MS*	*F*	*Significance F*
Regression	1.00	0.02	0.02	77.96	0.00
Residual	12.00	0.00	0.00		
Total	13.00	0.02			
	Coefficients	*Standard Error*	*t Stat*	*P-value*	
Intercept	4.63	0.01	517.63	0.00	
b	0.01	0.00	8.83	0.00	

Presence of a significantly positive coefficient of the log-transformed series of the data in respect of the number of branches (Table 4) is indicative of the fact that the PSBs, in fact, were experiencing growth. Manpower retrenchment in the wake of the prospects of growth seems quite paradoxical.

How was the situation at the bank-level? Lets turn to bank level analysis.

Bank-Level Analysis

Whilst, the VRS scheme was offered uniformly to all the 27 PSBs, adoption thereof was left to the voluntary discretion of the respective banks. Twenty-six of the 27 banks seem to be in agreement with the Ministry of Finance's assessment of overstaffing and adopted the scheme, while the Corporation Bank chose otherwise. Whose decision should one consider strategic? Of the complying 26 banks or that of the outlier corporation bank? Lets have a look at the data (Table 5).

Table 5: Nature of Trend of Employment in Respective PSBs

S. No.	*Name of the Bank*	*Coefficient of Linear Trend*	*t-Stat*	*Coefficients of Quadratic Trend*	*t-Stat*
1.	Allahabad Bank	–1133.61	–8.61[a]	67.72	7.94[a]
2.	Andhra Bank	–574.25	–3.75[a]	37.26	3.76[a]
3.	Bank of Baroda	–2080.28	–4.13[a]	–2080.28	–4.13[a]
4.	Bank of India	2681.50	–5.27[a]	110.63	3.36[a]
5.	Bank of Maharashtra	–685.51	–6.02[a]	32.06	4.34[a]
6.	Canara Bank	–1766.72	–3.95[a]	58.04	2.00[b]
7.	Central Bank of India	–2145.76	–3.40[a]	55.32	1.35[c]
8.	Corporation Bank	–109.33	–1.13[#]	25.77	4.10[a]
9.	Dena Bank	–1365.89	–6.72[a]	66.61	5.05[a]
10.	Indian Bank	–1248.51	–5.90[a]	44.97	3.28[a]
11.	Indian Overseas Bank	–1442.90	–7.05[a]	83.12	6.26[a]
12.	Oriental Bank of Commerce	–325.50	–2.64[b]	30.91	3.86[a]
13.	Punjab and Sind Bank	–543.09	–4.14[a]	15.94	1.87[b]
14.	Punjab National Bank	–2034.36	–4.15[a]	81.11	2.55[b]
15.	State Bank of Bikaner and Jaipur	–646.92	–5.92[a]	23.87	3.37[a]
16.	State Bank of Hyderabad	–443.70	–4.18[a]	22.60	3.28[a]
17.	State Bank of India	–13516.14	–5.18[a]	714.05	4.22[a]

S. No.	Name of the Bank	Coefficient of Linear Trend	t-Stat	Coefficients of Quadratic Trend	t-Stat
18.	State Bank of Mysore	–529.63	–5.87[a]	27.93	4.77[a]
19.	State Bank of Patiala	–624.59	–6.67[a]	35.79	5.89[a]
20.	State Bank of Travancore	–445.74	–4.66[a]	22.14	3.57[a]
21.	State Bank of Indore	–71.56	–1.93[b]	1.88	0.73[#]
22.	State Bank of Saurashtra	–173.58	–2.49[b]	5.30	0.94[#]
23.	Syndicate Bank	–3180.83	–8.93[a]	155.63	6.74[a]
24.	UCO Bank	–1982.06	–7.57[a]	83.11	4.89[a]
25.	Union Bank Of India	–1829.86	–6.95[a]	116.09	6.80[a]
26.	United Bank Of India	–971.05	–6.18[a]	27.68	2.72[b]
27.	Vijaya Bank	–837.46	–5.69[a]	40.16	4.21[a]

Notes:

[a,b,c] Refer to 1%; 5%; and 10% levels of significance respectively.

[#] Denotes insignificance.

U-shaped behaviour of employment data is confirmed in 24 of the 27 cases, compelling us to accept the null hypothesis of strategic behaviour of individual public sector banks. Apparently, these banks chose to follow the line of the Ministry of Finance. Lets examine the exceptions. Corporation Bank is an expected exception as it chose not to adopt VRS. Not only is the coefficient of the linear trend insignificant (albeit negative implying natural rate of separation) but also the coefficient of the quadratic trend significantly positive. This implies that the Corporation Bank continued to expand workforce whereas its counterparts retired the employees. The absence of the reversal of the trend of employment data in case of State Bank of Indore and State Bank of Saurashtra suggests that they rightly chose to take recourse to downsizing as a means of salvaging corporate performance.

CONCLUDING OBSERVATIONS AND IMPLICATIONS

Presence of the U-shaped curve of employment data in respect of PSBs as a whole as well as 24/27 individual banks implies the desirability and feasibility of a more positive HR orientation of PSBs. This becomes all the more expedient in view of the fact that the inefficiencies of the PSBs that were stated to be the driver of the VRS could not have arisen all of a sudden. Rather these should be traceable to a long drawn, gradual process and the context of a controlled economy. The malice was instutionalised, it would be improper to address it with a conduct variable such as the VRS. There is a need to embark upon an institution-wide transformation process of which the human resources would be an integral part rather than an easily dispensable resource. The process has to be rooted strongly in the fundamental banking theory. The history of PSBs does not assure much as to whether these banks indeed conformed to the banking theory that justifies the existence of a bank as a financial intermediary vis-à-vis direct finance on the basis of their basic functions, that is attending to the three basic problems of information asymmetry, namely ex-ante, interim and ex-post information asymmetry, over an individual lender. Literature already has taken explicit note of the failure of the India PSBs on these three counts (Biswas and Deb, 2004).

Instead, they served more the imperatives of state directed development process. Till the initiation of reforms in 1992, Indian PSBs, had been operating not as an independent organization, but as if a subsidiary to the government with the objective of meeting the financial requirements of the state. They operated under the strict guidelines of the RBI, which were all encompassing. Although most of their deposit came from the private sector, i.e., households, a major part of their lending was confined to the government, and they also made substantial investment in government bills/securities. The developmental policies of the state-requiring mobilisation of a large sum of money made the state a major customer of the PSBs. RBI acted as the mediator between the state and PSBs more or less determining the amount/share of the deposit to be allocated to the state and the private sectors. With frequent intervals, RBI changed CRR, SLR, and shares of loans to priority sector and other sectors, and the banks gradually learnt to adjust receiving deposits, lending and making investments accordingly. Through division of labour in the branches, banks were able to routinise things. Under this system, there was very limited scope for making profitable innovations in terms of both organisational changes and seeking new sources of fund and new avenues of investments/lending. Once RBI fixed the share of loans and the rate of interest to particular sectors, banks became constrained not to discriminate among borrowers of a limited number. For a long period, real interest rates were negative for many of these loans; obviously, vested interest, political and local intervention would creep in, in order to extract surplus in the system (i.e., difference between the opportunity costs and actual cost of borrowing). Since it was not mandatory on the part of the banks to declare NPA or recover loans, and since, RBI was happy so long as the banks were able to finance state expenditure, a laxity crept into the banking sector. This happened particularly for the kind of private sector lending mentioned above and, in general, profit earning/meeting the interests of the depositors became the secondary objective of the banks. Often the non-intended borrowers received the loans, and even for the case of some target borrowers, the influential brokers who arranged the loans would take away a sizeable amount of the loan disbursed. The borrowers would not be able to repay the loans; even if they could, they would not be interested in doing so. The broker had to manipulate the system in such a way that the bank could not penalise the borrowers. On the contrary, the bank granted fresh loans to the defaulters so that the debt would roll on (known as ever-greening of accounts). Thus a new institution which is degenerative of the bank evolved. The institution involved a nexus of some personnel of banks, brokers, and borrowers, that would siphon off public money through manipulating banking machinery, state machinery, mobilising political and local forces.

It is difficult to provide any direct quantitative estimate of mal-functioning of PSBs during the pre-reform period. However, an attempt may be made to provide an indirect estimate. It is known that interest was added to income on accrual and not on the basis of realization basis, which renders figures on spread and consequently profitability disconnected from the real story. There was no concept of non- performing asset, let alone measurement. There was a concept of a "loan account not working satisfactorily". However, such information was neither reported in the public domain, nor used very seriously by PSBs to their benefit in a regime, where they were not subjected market discipline and competition. The data on NPAs was first reported in 1996. It appears that the NPAs of PSBs during the pre-reform period were higher than 1996. In 1992–93, pursuant to the Narasimham Committee Report (1991), several prudential norms relating to asset-classification and income-recognition were implemented. To the complete dismay of RBI, as many as twelve banks reported losses during 1992–93 as opposed to just one during 1991–92. The net profit to total assets plummeted to 0.28 to –0.99 over just one year.

The purpose of providing the historical narrative on the deterioration of the performance of the PSBs is to reiterate the fact that it has occurred over a long period of time and is attributable to varied forces relating to the state, the market and the society. Strangely enough the case for the VRS was stated only in terms of the problem of overstaffing. Secondly, the fact that the PSBs had to embark upon a hiring spree soon thereafter (i.e. the VRS) also underlines the need for a better HR orientation of the PSB banks. This need has been recently emphasized by the Commitee on HR issues of Public Sector Banks (Khandelwal Committee, 2010).

"Post liberalisation and pursuant to the banking reforms PSBs, have caught up with retail revolution and many other customer-centric innovations. In the matter of technology, almost all PSBs have networked their branches, rolled out core banking, set up a vast network of ATMs and enlarged the basket of offerings to the customer. They have also adjusted to the new prudential norms, improved their financials as also productivity and efficiency. Many PSBs have changed their business models and are repositioning their key branches as sales and service outlets. Integration of PSBs with other major segments of finance, notably the security markets and international markets, has been a hallmark. PSBs have also grown in terms of market capitalization even during the times of global meltdown... In spite of very many positives, PSBs today need to evolve institutional mechanism for sustained human capital management." (p.x)

The PSBs certainly need to strengthen their HR orientation.

REFERENCES

Anand, A. (2000). "Banking Sector Employment in India: Emerging Trends and Pattern", *Indian Journal of Labour Economics*, 43(4), pp. 1001–1012.

Biswas, P and Deb, A.T. (2004). "Determinants of NPAs in the Public Sector Banks," *ICFAI Journal of Bank Management,* 3(3): 15–45.

Cameron, Kim S. (1994). "Strategies for Successful Downsizing," *Human Resource Management: Summer,* 33(2).

Commitee on HR issues of Public Sector Banks (Khandelwal Committee, 2010), New Delhi: Ministry of Finance, government of India.

Demps II, Julius and Baker, Erica (2009). "Evaluating Ethical Integrity: Organizational Downsizing in Northeast Florida during an Economic Recession," A Paper presented at AABRI Conference Orlando, 24–26 September.

D'Souza, E. (2002). "Employment and Human Resource Practices in Public Sector Banks in the Nineties," in Shuji Uchikawa (Ed.). *Labour Market and Institution in India: 1990s and Beyond.* Japan: Institute of Developing Economies.

Hanson, James A. (2004). "Public Sector Banks and Their Transformation." Paper presented at 6th Annual Financial Markets and Development Conference, Washington D.C.: World Bank, April 26–27.

http://www.banknetindia.com/banking/vrs.htm, 19 January 2012 7:41:19 PM

IBA (1999). "Database on Indian Banking 1987–98", Economics Department, Indian

Banks' Association, Mumbai, December.

IBA (2000). "Indian Banking Year Book, 1999", Indian Banks' Association, Mumbai.

IBA (2001). "Performance Highlights of Banks 1999–2000", Economics Department, Indian Banks' Association, Mumbai, February.

Jain, Shweta and Gauri Shukla (2002). "A Not So Golden Handshake," *The Business Standard*, 8th February.

Kaur, Navdeep (2007). "Voluntary Retirement Scheme in Public Sector Banks—A Comparative Study of Punjab and Sind Bank and State Bank of India," *Indian Management Studies Journal,* 11: 129–40.

Kayarkatte, Narayan (2011). "Impact of Voluntary Retirement Scheme (VRS 2000) on the Employee Beneficiaries of Public Sector Banks," A Paper Presented at the Eighth AIMS International Conference on Management, Ahmedabad: IIM, 1–4 January.

Kozlowski, S.W.J., Chao, G.T., Smith, E.M. and Hedlund, J. (1993). "Organizational Downsizing: Strategies, Interventions and Research Implications." *International Review of Industrial and Organizational Psychology.* New York: Wiley.

Kumar, Pramod (2010). "Impact on Indian Banking Systems through V.R.S.", *International Referred Research Journal,* 1 (8): 28–30.

Mankidy, J. (2000). "Human Resource Management in Banks: Need for a Paradigm

Shift", *Prajnan*, Vol. XXVIII, No. 4, 357–372.

McCLune, J.T., Beatty, R.W. and Montagno, R.V. (1988). "Downsizing: Practices in Manufacturing Firms," *Human Resource Management Journal,* 27, 145–161.

Sachan, Vivek Singh (2011). "Organizational Downsizing and Its Impact on Performance of Public Sector Banks," *VSRD-IJBMR*, Vol. 1 (8), 2011, 525–534.

Uppal, R.K. (2011). "E-Age Technology–New Face of Indian Banking Industry: Emerging Challenges and New Potentials," *Journal of Social and Development Sciences*, 1 (3) April, 115–129.

Varkkey, B. and Mankidy, A. (1995). "Human Resources Management in Banking Industry: A Historical Perspective", *National Institute of Bank Management*, March, Pune.

Verma, M.S. (1999). "Report of the Working Group on Restructuring Weak Public Sector Banks", RBI, Mumbai.

Financial Inclusion: Strategies and Challenges

P. Tejaswi and D. Snadeep Babu

PGDM-BIF, IPE

ABSTRACT: *In the past few years we have seen different definitions of financial inclusion and various initiatives taken by Government and the concerned organizations, but there is a need to move from definitions and initiatives, and employ different strategies to improve from the current situation. This paper emphasizes on the strategies that could be used to move from the scenario where 60% of the population does not have a bank account and 90% do not get loans and where financial literacy is a major concern. Added to this situation there are various other factors that need high priority such as effectiveness and usage of technology in the process. There is excessive reliance on the MFI's and as far as the government is concerned, it seems to think financial inclusion is ensuring that everyone has a bank account. Whether the accounts have any money or in what way those accounts will help the holders of accounts, is not its concern. It must not stop there, but where exactly should we be going? These are the various aspects the paper proposes to discuss, classify the challenges and come to a conclusion where in we are in position to know what needs and what should be done.*

Objectives of the Article

- Highlight the issue of financial exclusion
- RBI initiatives and guidelines
- Challenges faced in financial inclusion in India
- Further suggestions.

INTRODUCTION

What is Financial Inclusion: Financial inclusion is delivery of banking services at an affordable cost to the vast sections of the disadvantaged and the low income groups.

> *"The process of ensuring access to appropriate financial products and services needed by vulnerable groups such as weaker sections and low income groups at an affordable cost in a fair and transparent manner by mainstream Institutional players."*
>
> ***—Dr. C. Rangarajan***

INDIAN SCENARIO

Bank nationalization in India has marked a paradigm shift in the focus of banking as it was intended to shift the focus from "Class Banking" to "Mass Banking". The rationale for creating Regional Rural Banks was also to take banking services to the poor. The average population for branch office has been decreased from 64,000 to 16,000 in the past three decades. However there are certain unbanked states such as Bihar, Orissa, Rajasthan, Chhattisgarh, Jharkhand and a large number of north eastern states where average population per branch office continues to be quite high compared to the national average. As you would be aware, the new branch authorization policy of RBI encourages banks to open their branches in these under banked areas.

One of the benchmarks employed to assess the degree of reach of financial services to the population of the country, is the quantum of deposit accounts (CASA accounts) held in a ratio to the adult population. In the Indian context taking into account the Census of 2001 the ratio of deposit accounts to the total adult population was only 59%. Within the country, there is a wide range of variation across states. For instance, the ratio for the state of Kerala is as high as 89% while Bihar is marked by a low coverage of 33%. Compared to the developed world, the coverage of our financial services is quite low. For instance, as per a recent study conducted by the British Bankers Association 94% of the population of UK has either current or savings bank account.

Reasons for Financial Exclusion

- Remote, hilly and sparsely populated areas with poor infrastructure and difficult physical access.

Fig. 1

- Lack of awareness, low income, social exclusion, illiteracy.
- Distance from bank branch, branch timings, cumbersome documentation/procedures, unsuitable products, language, staff attitude are common reasons.
- Ease of availability of informal credit.
- KYC—documentary proof of address/identity.

HISTORY OF STRATEGIES FOR INCLUSIVE GROWTH

Phase I (1960–1980)

- Social control of Banks – (1960)
- Nationalisation of Banks – (1969)
- Setting up of Regional Rural Banks – (1975)
- Priority sector lending stipulation by RBI – (1972)
- Lead Bank scheme – (1969)

Phase II (1980–2005)

- Integrated Rural Development programme/SGSY promoted by government of India.
- Microfinance programme – SHG – Bank linkage facilitated by NABARD.

Phase III (2005 onwards)

- Development of MFIs.
- Financial Inclusion in a "MISSION" mode.

MICROFINANCE

Of the different models for delivery of microfinance, the SHG-Bank Linkage Programme has emerged as the major micro-finance programme in the country. It is being implemented by commercial banks, RRBs and cooperative banks. As on March 31, 2008 3.6 million SHGs had outstanding bank loans of ₹ 17000 crore, an increase of 25 per cent over March 31, 2007 in respect of number of SHGs credit linked. As at end-March 2008, SHGs had 5 million savings accounts with banks for ₹ 3785 crore.

Based on the findings of a joint study conducted by the Reserve Bank along with a few major banks, the banks were advised in November 2006 to encourage microfinance institutions (MFIs) assisted by them to:

1. Focus on unbanked and under banked areas;
2. Desist from multiple lending;
3. Engage in capacity building and empowerment of the groups; and
4. Follow practices that maintain the cohesiveness of the groups.

This led to banks financing NGOs/MFIs for on-lending under micro-finance. As on March 31, 2007, the number of MFIs that had outstanding bank loans was 550 amounting to ₹ 1585 crore. Recognising the potential of microfinance to positively influence the development of the poor, the Reserve Bank has advised commercial banks that micro credit should cover not only consumption and production loans for various farm and non-farm activities of the poor, but also include their other credit needs such as housing and shelter improvements. A Micro Financial Sector (Development and Regulation) Bill, 2007, which envisages the regulation of the sector, is currently under consideration of the Parliament.

'NO-FRILLS' ACCOUNTS

The Reserve Bank reiterated the concerns of financial inclusion in its Midterm. Review of Annual Policy Statement for 2005–06. All banks were advised in November 2005 to make available a basic banking 'no-frills' account either with 'nil' or very low minimum balances as well as charges that would make such accounts accessible to vast sections of population. The nature and number of transactions in such accounts could be restricted, but made known to the customer in advance in a transparent manner. All banks were also advised to give wide publicity to the facility of such a 'no-frills' account including on their web sites indicating the facilities and charges in a transparent manner. Significant progress has been made in this regard, and till now, banks have opened more than 15 million no-frills accounts in the country.

As announced in the Annual Policy Statement for the year 2008–09, and in order to give further impetus to financial inclusion, banks were advised in May 2008 to classify overdrafts up to ₹ 25000 (per account) granted against 'no-frills' accounts in rural and semi urban areas as indirect finance to the agriculture sector under priority sector with immediate effect.

RELAXATION OF KYC NORMS

The Reserve Bank in its Annual Policy Statement for 2005–06, emphasised that banks should empower depositors by providing wider access and better quality of banking services. Furthermore, banks were advised in August 2005 to ensure that customers belonging to poor sections of the society are not kept away from banking system, on account of difficulties in meeting the KYC requirements for opening bank account. The KYC procedure for opening accounts was simplified further for persons who intend to keep balances not exceeding ₹ 50000 in all their accounts taken together and the total credit in all the accounts taken together is not expected to exceed ₹ 1 lakh in a year. The customer is allowed to exceed the threshold limit only after the full compliance with the KYC norms. Based on feedback received on the extant KYC/AML/CFT regime, relevant guidelines were revised on February 18, 2008.

These guidelines include among others:

1. in case of close relatives who find it difficult to furnish documents relating to place of residence while opening accounts, banks can obtain an identity document and a utility bill of the relative with whom the prospective customer is living, along with a declaration from the relative that the said person (prospective customer) wanting to open an account is a relative and is staying with him/her. Banks can also use any supplementary evidence such as a letter received through post for further verification of the address;
2. banks have been advised to keep in mind the spirit of the instructions and avoid undue hardships to individuals who are otherwise classified as low risk customers;
3. banks should review the risk categorization of customers at a periodicity of not less than once in six months.

KISAN CREDIT CARDS

The KCC scheme enabling farmers to purchase agricultural inputs and draw cash for their production needs was further extended by providing personal accident insurance coverage on an ongoing basis at competitive rates/terms, thus safeguarding the interest of the KCC holders. Banks have been given the discretion to approach either any general insurance company which is a member of GIPSA (General Insurer's [Public sector] Association of India) or any private sector general insurance company, to take advantage of the competitive offers. However, the banks have been advised that they may, while negotiating with the insurers, keep in mind the guiding principles of Personal Accident Insurance Scheme (PAIS), especially the aspects such as premium sharing formula and coverage. This "add on" benefit is expected to bring in an increasing number of farmers under the KCC fold, thereby leading to complete coverage. The cumulative number of KCCs issued by public sector banks aggregated 31.22 million (provisional) up to March 31, 2008 involving an amount of ₹ 1.54 crore.

GENERAL PURPOSE CREDIT CARDS

With a view to providing credit card like facilities in the rural areas, with limited point-of sale (POS) and limited ATM facilities, the Reserve Bank advised all scheduled commercial banks, including RRBs, in December 2005 to introduce a General Credit Card (GCC) facility without insistence on collateral or purpose, with a revolving credit limit up to ₹ 25000 based on the assessment of income and cash flow of the household to enable hassle free access to credit to rural and semi-urban households. The Reserve Bank also advised banks to classify fifty per cent of the credit outstanding under loans for general purposes under General Credit Cards (GCC), as indirect finance to agriculture under priority sector. The Reserve Bank further advised banks in May 2008 to classify

100 per cent of the credit outstanding under GCCs as indirect finance to agriculture sector under the priority sector with immediate effect.

USE OF INTERMEDIARIES AS AGENTS

With the objective of ensuring greater financial inclusion and increasing the outreach of the banking sector, banks have been allowed to use the services of NGOs/SHGs, MFIs and other civil society organizations as intermediaries in providing financial and banking services through the use of business facilitator and correspondent models. The BC model allows banks to do 'cash in/cash-out' transactions at a location much closer to the rural habitation, thus addressing the last mile problem. Banks are also entering into agreements with India Post for using the vast network of post offices as business correspondents, thereby increasing their outreach and leveraging on the postman's intimate knowledge of the local population.

Banks have also been permitted to engage retired bank employees, ex-servicemen and retired government employees as BCs with effect from April 24, 2008, in addition to the entities already permitted, subject to appropriate due diligence. While appointing such individuals as BCs, the Reserve Bank advised banks to ensure that these individuals are permanent residents of the area in which they propose to operate as BCs and also institute additional safeguards as may be considered appropriate to minimize agency risk. With a view to ensuring adequate supervision over the operations and activities of the BCs, the Reserve Bank advised banks that every BC should be attached to and be under the oversight of a specific bank branch to be designated as the base branch. The distance between the place of business of a BC and the base branch, ordinarily, should not exceed 15 kms. (further extended to 30 kms from April 2009) in rural, semi-urban and urban areas. In metropolitan centers, the distance could be up to 5 kms. However, in case a need is felt to relax the distance criterion, the matter can be referred to the District Consultative Committee (DCC) of the district concerned for approval.

THE BUSINESS CORRESPONDENT MODEL: ANDHRA PRADESH CASE STUDY

The Rural Development Department of Government of Andhra Pradesh launched a pilot project in six *Mandals* of Warangal District for payment of Social Security Pensions (SSP) and National Rural Employment Guarantee Scheme (NREGS) benefits to the beneficiaries. The pilot programme involved six banks *viz.*, State Bank of India, Union Bank of India, State Bank of Hyderabad, Andhra Bank, A.P. Grameena Vikas Bank and Axis Bank. The benefits are paid to the villagers by the business correspondents of banks at the habitation level in the villages. The Rural Development Department, Government of Andhra

Pradesh, played a very active role in the project and has financed a major portion of the cost of the cards and the devices. The project was coordinated by the Reserve Bank with the Regional Director, Hyderabad being the Convenor of the Steering Group for the project. The Institute for Development and Research in Banking Technology (IDRBT) was given the role of providing the management information systems (MIS) to the Government in the required format. In the second phase, the project will be scaled up to 50,000 villagers. The State proposes to scale up the efforts to the entire State in due course. The Andhra Pradesh Government also proposes to issue smart cards to all the SHG members in the State.

The project involves payment of SSP and NREGS benefits through BCs with the use of smart card and mobile technology. The BC uses a fingerprint scanner cum identifier, a mobile and a printer to process the payments. The beneficiaries hold smart cards with their photographs and images of their fingerprints pre-loaded at the time of their enrolment. The photograph and fingerprint are used for identification and authentication of the beneficiary. Once authenticated, the radio frequency identification device (RFID) chip embedded in the card gets charged.

When the card with charged chip is brought close to the mobile phone, message templates for deposit, withdrawal and balance enquiry are generated in the mobile. The BC needs to select the relevant option and feed the amount of transaction through the mobile keypads and send the message to the back-end server. The server authenticates the message, processes the transaction and sends an update back to the mobile, which, in turn, writes back to the card. When the card is brought close to the printer, transaction report is printed in triplicate. The BC carries cash physically for making payments to the beneficiary. Thus, in effect, each BC carries a pocket ATM to the village in which it operates. The technology holds potential for whole range of activities that banks can conduct through BCs and this includes other products like fixed deposits, various loans, insurance, among others. The mobiles connect to a central data base server of the banks. The application has an off-line model also, which enables its operation in remote areas where there is no connectivity. Presently, the SSP and NREGS benefits are being paid through post offices which are given a commission of 2 per cent. The State Government, for the initial pilot covering six mandals, agreed to pay ₹ 90 per smart card, ₹ 10,000 per hand held device and 2 per cent commission on transactions.

The Government agreed to meet a part of the infrastructure costs to kick start the project. For the scaled up project, it is expected that the 2 per cent commission on turnover will be maintained and banks will fund the infrastructure. However, the model may have to be different in States with lesser turnover, as fixed cost per village is almost the same. The banks pay ₹ 1,000 to the village organization member in the village who is the representative of the BC of the bank.

The cost of cards is a one-time exercise and enrolment of beneficiaries also involves an expense of ₹ 50 per person in addition to the card cost. The advantages to the bank are that the cost of transactions is reduced and there is scope for other services like crop loans, access to cheap savings in villages and microinsurance, among others. The State Government can make all its payments through this mechanism. This would include salaries, pensions and contractor payments. The model ensures cost savings in the payment delivery mechanism and payments can be made centrally from the district or the State headquarters. An added benefit is that several bogus beneficiaries have been weeded out because of bio-metric identification and the State Government is expecting to save substantial amount on that account. The model adopted for the project involves selection of technology and technology vendor by the bank; appointment of a BC; finalizing the operating procedures with respect to transactions entered between bank and BCs such as movement of cash, crediting beneficiary accounts, payment of fee/commission and control mechanism. Other aspects of the model are enrolment and collection of critical data about the beneficiaries and issue of cards to them, training and sensitizing the beneficiaries and meeting operational needs through ongoing support in servicing of instruments, constant monitoring and periodic evaluation of the project for improvement.

If we look at the recent statistics till 2008 given below (Table 1).

Table 1

State	Current Accounts	Savings Accounts	Adult Population	Total no. of account	No. of acc per 100 of Population.
Northern Region	4215701	52416125	67822312	56631826	84
North-Eastern Region	476603	6891081	19708982	7367684	37
Eastern Region	1814219	47876140	122136133	49690359	41
Central Region	2202217	64254189	129316677	66456406	51
Western Region	3178102	49525101	86182206	52703203	61
Southern Region	4666014	83386898	135574225	88052912	65
ALL - INDIA	16552856	304349534	541031553	320902390	59

Above Table 1 tells us that for every 100 people only 59 people have accounts. This clearly paves the way for new initiatives and strategies.

CHALLENGES

Its always about the people, as they are an integral part of the system who cannot be neglected one bit. Rules and protocols change but do these changes make a significant impact on the people involved in the process, so as to utilize the new opportunities better, now that depends on the level of awareness and education its always how to manage the behavior of the people who are a part of the system. If we look at the Indian population its as follows.

India's small towns are making their presence felt in the nation's economic landscape. It is not just the FMCG or consumer durable companies or car makers, but also a slew of banking and financial services companies that are ramping up their operations.

Over the last couple of years, these small cities and towns have shown an increasing appetite for financial products. But financial inclusion can't ever succeed without financial literacy. If people are not aware about basic financial planning and lack the skills to save and invest, can they mitigate economic hardships that come their way. This lack in skill will impact the long-term strategy of companies to develop rural markets.

Financial literacy must be the centrepiece of financial inclusion. From a survey recently conducted to gauge the strengths and weaknesses of financial education worldwide, and to find solutions to challenges that exist. Among 28 countries surveyed across the world, India stands at 22nd spot, clearly indicating the work that lies ahead.

While urban areas are perceived to be high on financial literacy, this may not necessarily be the case. Financial literacy is also dependent on spread of the banking network. Only 40 per cent of India's total population has access to formal banking channels, and the problem is acute when one looks at the villages, where only 5 per cent have a proper established branches. This explains why financial literacy levels in rural India are poor.

ISSUES IN LITERACY

The Government and the RBI have been working towards bringing the country's hitherto unbanked regions and population into the fold of formal banking system. While improving penetration is one pillar of this strategy, the other key component is making India financially literate.

And while progress has been made, there is more to be done. The principal reason for improving financial literacy is the impact it has on financial inclusion and stability a branch with all the financial offerings could be established, but that alone can't bring a customer on board unless the customer is educated on the financial front. Higher degree of awareness and understanding about banking and financial products is the first step towards creating demand and increasing adoption.

The issue of financial literacy is not as simple as it sounds. It requires an understanding of the information gap across consumer segments, banked and unbanked, and crafting communication strategies that address the unique needs of specific segments.

It would be wrong to assume that a consumer living in a metropolitan city is financially literate because he is surrounded by a variety of financial institutions offering a plethora of choices. Maybe she invests in traditional banking instruments like savings and fixed deposits, but can be educated on managing his/her consumption better or investing in equity markets.

Indians are known to be great savers, something that is reflected in the overall domestic savings rate which stands at a healthy 31 per cent. However, this figure has dropped over the last couple of years, which is in part due to higher consumption expenditure by households, especially in urban areas. Also, a study reveals that Indians do not have more than three months of savings, in case they face an emergency.

TARGETING CONSUMERS

At the other end of the spectrum are those who haven't had any exposure to formal banking. An RBI study of financial literacy and credit counseling centers reveals low awareness levels about existence of such centers. The content distributed at these centers goes little beyond the bank's publicity material.

So while at one end there is an urgent need to spread the network to educate citizens, it is equally important to ensure that the information shared by such centers is neutral and in a language that the average person can understand.

This brings us back to target consumer segmentation, and the need to match skills to be imparted with the population category. We need to create an army of financial literacy trainers, well equipped to educate people on money management.

There is also a greater understanding in India as well as around the globe of weaving financial planning skills in school education. A survey reveals that the worldwide average age of introducing financial literacy to children is 11.3 years. It is heartening to note that the central bank is engaging with school boards to introduce these concepts in the curriculum.

TECHNOLOGY SKILLS

Going forward, technology will play a key role in promoting financial inclusion and financial literacy. According to research by Sumit Agarwal, senior financial economist with the Federal Reserve Bank of Chicago and a visiting professor at the Indian School of Business, Internet-savvy Indians are 20 per cent more financially literate than Americans and on par with Europeans. Real time information, updates on products and norms, better financial management and investment decision making can be enabled through safe and secure technology platforms.

The choices made by a financially aware consumer will help develop products that are relevant and lead to financial innovation. We need to develop a scalable and multi-pronged approach towards financial literacy. This requires time, planning and collaboration among various stakeholders.

Financial literacy is about changing behavior, and this is the right time to sow the seeds of change.

SUGGESTIONS

Once the unbanked are bought into the banking model, a whole range of financial services can be delivered through self-service technology, with minimal need for person to person interaction.

Self-service technologies are the foremost sustainable and scalable solutions because they offer multiple products and services from the same platform/device, at lower costs, ease-of-use, higher levels of availability and accessibility.

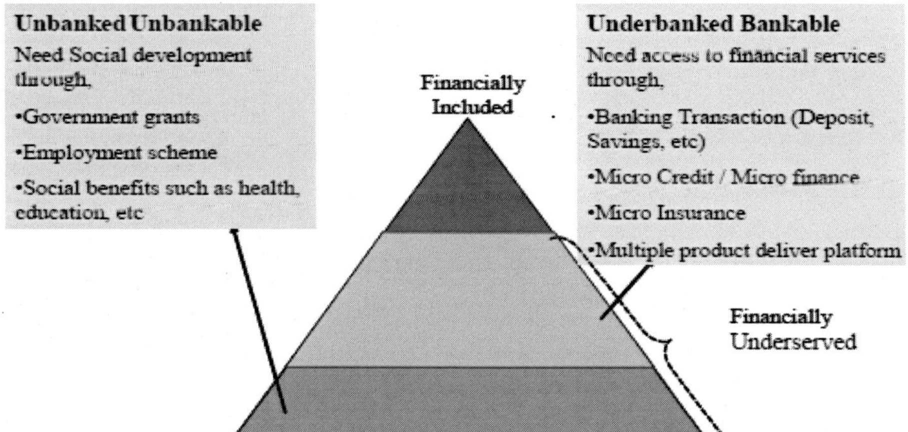

Fig. 2

To increase the adoption and usage, enabling technologies must be integrated into self-service systems, such as biometric readers, multi-lingual software, interactive voice response services, and graphical user interfaces, helping to reach out to the millions of illiterate and semi-literate people in geographically and linguistically diverse regions.

Together, policy makers, financial institutions and technology providers can establish a collaborative business model to profitably address the social, moral and economic imperative to bring financial and information services to the masses.

Added to the above other measures that can be taken are as follows:

Giving a Saving cum Overdraft account. Banks provide an account or a Branch service but due to the dire poverty of the people the bank is not used at all or used by very few people.

RBI has already made it possible in 2005 that a over draft account can be created but its acceptance by most of the banks is very low.

Creating No-Frill account itself is not financial inclusion. When a transaction takes place In that No-Frill account then the financial inclusion takes place. So Banks should concentrate mainly on enabling the banking transactions in terms of Savings, in terms of loans and in terms of remittances as all the three are prerequisite for any modern economy.

So it is evident that transaction in the bank account proves whether the person or the individual is a productive asset to the society or not.

Another research says that financial exclusion could lead to social exclusion.

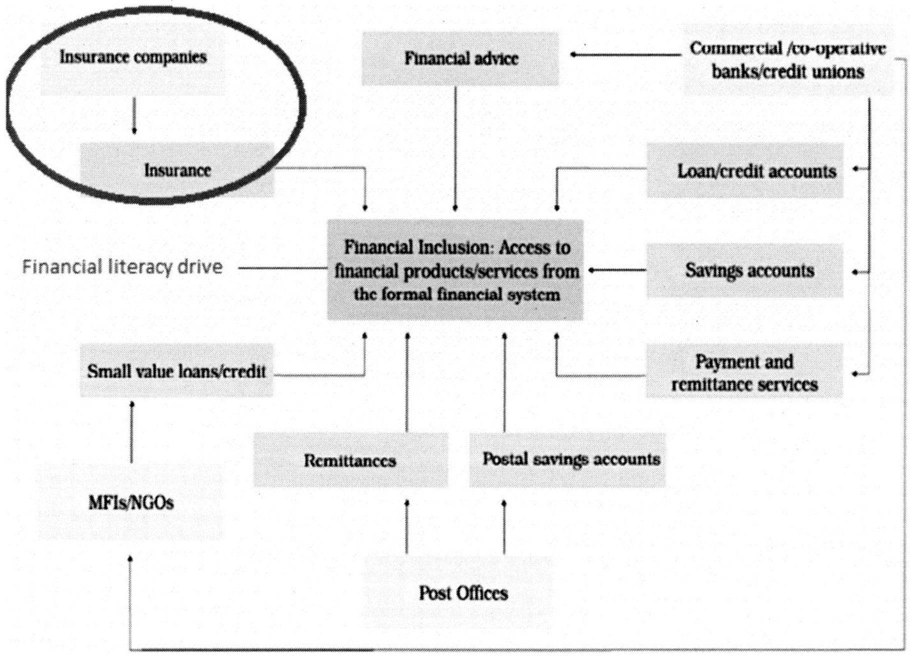

Fig. 3

The above Figure 3 is shows the structure of financial inclusion with the medications that could possibly suit the current situation, these modifications are shown in red. If we consider the circled portion i.e. of insurance sector which needs more attention and innovation as it is a important part of financial inclusion. Also a lot of emphasis should be laid on financial literacy. This shall certainly be rewarding for all the parties involved.

CONCLUSION

Banks need to redesign their business strategies to incorporate self plans to promote financial inclusion of low income group treating it both a business opportunity as well as a corporate social responsibility. They have to make use of all available resources including technology and expertise available with them as well as the MFI's and the NGO's. It may appear in the first instance that taking banking to the sections constituting "the bottom of the pyramid", may not be profitable but it should always be remembered that even relatively low margins on high volumes can be a very profitable proposition. Financial inclusion can emerge as a very profitable business.

The current approach to financial inclusion is unidirectional this should change to a multi dimensional growth that shall facilitate balanced growth throughout the country.

BIBLIOGRAPHY

Chakravarthy, K.C. (2011). (T.O. India, Interviewer).

India, G.O. (2007, Feb.). Budget 2007–2008, *Budget.*

RBI (2008). *Bussiness Correspondent Model: AP Case Study.* Retrieved from RBI.

RBI (2008). Financial Inclusion. *Report on Currency and Finance.*

Sangwan, S. (2008). *Financial Inclusion and Self-help Groups.*

An Assessment on the Online Interface Accessibility of the Public Bank Websites for VIPs (Visually Impaired Persons)

G. Vinod Kumar, S.S. Maniraja, S. Victor Anandkumar, Pravin Cumar, Alfred John S. and T. Sivakumar

Department of Management Studies,
Pondicherry Central University, Puducherry

ABSTRACT

Objective: *To assess the websites of the Public banks (India) for potential accessibility issues confronting visually impaired customers.*

Methodology: *It is a descriptive study based on primary data. The research relied on passive primary data collected by using the Web Accessibility Evaluation Tool (WAVE). The data were obtained through observation of Websites. The study adopted inclusive criteria of 23 Public banks for the assessment.*

Findings

Practical Implications: *This paper will reveal the significance of critical variables and its influence on the accessibility of the websites through which the usability of the online banking opportunity for VIPs can be understood.*

Contribution to the Literature: *Research on banking sector is becoming very common among Indian publications. Many researchers have been conducted in the area of extended channel options of banks in India. With the poor literature support there is very little scope for conducting research amongst VIPs (visually challenged persons) in the area of banking. This paper with the design to assess the web accessibility of public banks in India will offer literature support as well as scope to conduct further research amongst VIPs.*

Keywords: Website Accessibility, Inclusive Banking, Visually Impaired Customers, User Interface Design.

INTRODUCTION

The banking industry in India has transformed into a most promising and competitive market in the global stage. Thanks to the recent technological developments that has made the banking operations and process user friendly. The foreign players and their technological interferences have played a vital role in the growth of Indian banking industry and its expanding potential for Indian public to consume banking. The beginning of this century witnessed huge demand for plastic banking mode as the card culture amongst the Indian customers increased at study rate. The popularity of the credit and debit cards transactions also made way for internet banking. E banking had become a critical channel option for the bankers to offer their range of products and services as it helped the customers to consume the banking services anywhere, anytime without commuting to branch (Christopher, G.C. Mike, L. Visit and W. Amy, 2006). The Online banking option becomes very common in Indian market with higher younger generation population in India that was receptive to newer technologies. Online banking facility also helps the banks to extend its services through mobile using its internet banking platform. The market now is experiencing a change in banking consumption with new channel in the form of Mobile banking coming into existence. With higher rate of younger generation population and improved education standard the e-banking usage rate is definitely looking good when comparing with the traditional branch banking culture. Apart from normal customers there is a possibility for e-banking process to become an effective tool for the visually challenged customer segment as it can offer support through technology that can simplify and make it user-friendly. But the most important question to be posed is, if the bank websites are usable or accessible for the VIPs. This paper will assess the online accessibility of the Public banks websites for VIPs.

LITERAUTRE REVIEW

Visually Challenged Customers and Banking Industry in India

The Indian banking industry was one of those sectors that played a vital role in the Indian economic growth. The globalization of services gave the momentum to the Indian banking industry through its most effective technology and innovative process that helped the banks to reduce the cost and serve the customers better. The banks in India were ignorant about the needs of the visually challenged customer segment until 2008. In the year 2008 Reserve bank of India issued guidelines that insisted banks to provide accessibility to VC customers as it if offered to normal persons (RBI, 2008). The information published by the Confederation of the Indian Industry highlights some of the guidelines issued by the RBI that suggest banks to install ATMs along with Braille keys to enable easy operations for VC segment and also reports the suggestions offered by IBA to its member banks to offer facilities and guidance to the VC segment on using the Opening and Operation of

Independent Accounts Standard Banking service like ATMs, Debit and Credit Cards, Cheque book (CII, 2010).

Website Accessibility and Visually Challenged Persons

Web The Web is an important do-it-yourself tool for people with special needs, since they can retrieve various kinds of information by themselves through the Web and thereby reduce their dependency on others. For example, the visually impaired people can easily access the Web using screen reader or non-visual browsers such as voice browsers. However, the Web is becoming more difficult for blind users as more visual content, such as image links, is being used in websites. They pose serious accessibility issues which if not addressed could result in visually impaired users getting annoyed at wasted time and effort, to having to abandon a task or ask for sighted help. Special-needs persons are a rapidly growing segment of customers. India is now home to the world's largest number of blind people. Of the 37 million people across the globe who are blind, over 15 million are from India (Times of India, 2007). With sizable population and growing potential to consume banking services, the visually impaired customer segment needs to be concentrated by banks (Vinod Kumar *et al.*, 2012). In particular, blind people who have mobility problems may successfully utilize on-line banking services. Unfortunately these websites have complex layouts, crowded with active elements that are often difficult to navigate via screen reader. Indeed, it has been acknowledged that blind people face the serious problem that reading certain Web pages is quite difficult (Theofanos and Redish, 2003; Takagi *et al.*, 2004; Fukuda *et al.*, 2005; Leporini and Paterno, 2008; Buzzi *et al.*, 2009).

The challenge to online customer interface designers and developers is to create transaction-enabled websites that are not only visually attractive, but are also accessible and friendly to visually-impaired people. Various studies have studied the usability/accessibility of e.Commerce systems and include a general discussion on accessibility (Vinod Kumar and Victor Anandkumar, 2012), but research on visually impaired persons and their access of bank websites is hitherto unexplored.

The evolution of core banking solutions and the rapid growth of online banking have fuelled a great diffusion of transaction-enabled websites. Usability is a key factor in the success of such websites. The term *usability* is precisely defined by the International Organization for Standardization in the ISO 9241, a multi-part standard covering a number of aspects for people working with computers: 'the extent to which a product or website can be used by specified users to achieve specified goals with effectiveness, efficiency and satisfaction in a specified context of use'(ISO, 1998). Many factors can impact the experience at the online customer interface (such as a website), such as rapidity of finding the desired information, efficiency and security when carrying out the transaction, reliability of the delivery service behind the website and so on (Buzzi *et al.*, 2009). They also researched on Usability and Accessibility of eBay for visually impaired persons and found that restructuring the web page in logical sections can provide blind users with a page overview. They also offered to understand that important guideline for simplifying user navigation is related to the logical partitioning of content (Buzzi *et al.*, 2009). Lazar *et al.* surveyed 175 Web masters' accessibility knowledge and perceptions and Knight surveyed and interviewed 117 designers, information officers and accessibility advocates about attitudes and knowledge regarding accessibility; these exploratory results are relevant and discussed in terms of possible reasons for not ensuring accessibility.

RESEARCH OBJECTIVES

The purpose of this research is to assess the websites of the Indian banks for potential accessibility issues confronting visually impaired customers. This study attempts to categorize the accessibility issues in terms of the seriousness of the impediments they pose and also look for a difference, if any, between the websites of public and private Indian banks in terms of the website accessibility.

RESEARCH METHODOLOGY

This is a descriptive study to assess the website accessibility of the Indian banks using passive primary data collected by using the Web Accessibility Evaluation Tool (WAVE), provided by Web AIM. It brings to light the different website accessibility issues faced by visually-impaired customers. WAVE is a web accessibility tool that can greatly assist in the evaluation of web content. Rather than providing a complex technical report, WAVE shows the original web page with embedded icons and indicators that reveal the accessibility of that page. These accessibility assessment icons are observed and collected as passive primary data. Observational studies can provide rich data and insights into the nature of the phenomena observed. The data obtained through observation of events as they normally occur are generally more reliable and free from respondent bias (Sekaran, 2003). WAVE is developed and made available as a free community service by Web AIM. The objects of this study were the websites of public sector banks (shown in Table 1) in India. The bank websites were studied during Q2, 2012.

A total 23 Public sector bank websites were considered for the study. Each site was examined in detail by posting its Uniform Resource Locator (URL) in the WAVE tool. The WAVE tool provides an output consisting of the accessibility issues related to a particular URL and these issues were classified as Errors, Alerts and Accessibility features (WAVE, 2012) based on the severity of the issues:

- Errors represent the presence of those issues which will almost certainly hamper accessibility of the website by a visually impaired customer.

- Alerts represent the presence of those issues which may or may not hamper accessibility, but typically indicate an area where accessibility is often an issue or where it may be made better. They should each be checked for possible impact.
- Accessibility Features are those issues for which the author should check for accuracy.

Table 1: List of Indian Public Sector Banking Websites Taken for the Study

1 www.onlinesbi.com	2 www.sbbjonline.com
3 www.onlinesbh.com	4 www.onlinesbm.com
5 www.onlinesbp.com	6 www.sbtonline.in
7 www.allbankonline.in	8 www.andhrabank.in
9 www.bankofbaroda.com	10 www.bankofindia.com
11 www.mahaconnect.in	12 www.centralbank.net.in
13 www.corpbank.com	14 www.inet.idbibank.co.in
15 www.indianbank.net.in	16 www.obconline.co.in
17 www.netpnb.com	18 www.syndicatebank.in
19 www.ucoebanking.com	20 www.unitedbankofindia.com
21 www.unionbankonline.co.in	22 www.canarabank.in
23 www.vijayabank.com	

In the Errors, Features, and Alerts View, WAVE first inserts a summary report of the errors found in the page, along with any icons that apply to the page itself. Figure 1 shows a sample summary report consisting of the total accessibility errors.

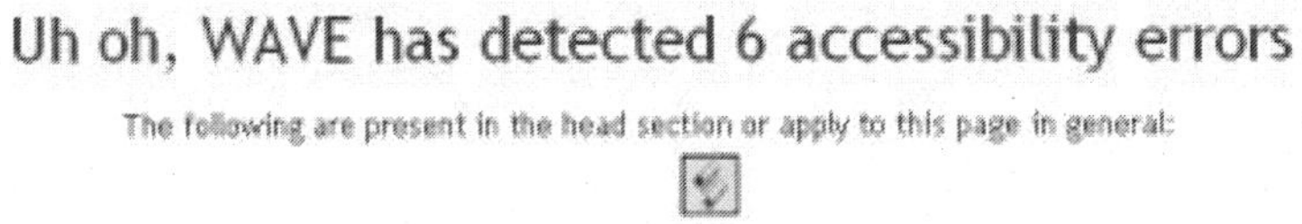

Fig. 1: Summary Report Consisting of Total Accessibility Errors

The summary is useful for reporting purposes, but the most useful feedback occurs below this area, in the main part of the WAVE report. In the main part of the errors, features, and alerts view, WAVE inserts informative, colour-coded icons and commentary alongside the webpage content. These icons and commentary highlight the accessibility issues on the webpage and provide guidance to customer interface designers and developers. In the screenshot below (Figure1), red and yellow icons in the context of the web page, represent accessibility errors and alerts, respectively (Wave, 2012).

KEY FINDINGS

Table 2 show the accessibility issues of the Indian public sector banks' websites. Among the 23 public sector banks whose websites were considered for the study, only

Table 2: Public Sector Banks Accessibility Issues

Bank Name	*Webpage Link*	*Number of Errors*	*Number of Alerts*	*Number of Accessibility Features*
State Bank of India	https://www.onlinesbi.com	0	31	6
State Bank of Bikaner and Jaipur	https://www.sbbjonline.com	0	34	10
State Bank of Hyderabad	https://www.onlinesbh.com	0	29	9
State Bank of Mysore	https://www.onlinesbm.com	0	30	8
State Bank of Patiala	https://www.onlinesbp.com	0	31	8
State Bank of Travancore	https://www.sbtonline.in/	0	34	9
Allahabad Bank	https://www.allbankonline.in	38	11	0
Andhra Bank	http://andhrabank.in/english/Retail.aspx	9	93	56
Bank of Baroda	http://www.bankofbaroda.com	53	29	8
Bank of India	http://www.bankofindia.com	2	67	18
Bank of Maharashtra	www.mahaconnect.in/jsp/index.html	0	39	4
Canara Bank	www.canarabank.in/English/Scripts/Home.aspx	37	30	10
Central Bank of India	https://www.centralbank.net.in	27	2	2
Corporation Bank	http://www.corpbank.com	30	48	46
IDBI Bank	http://www.idbi.com	22	38	21
Indian Bank	www.indianbank.net.in	5	15	2
Oriental Bank of Commerce	https://www.obconline.co.in	1	2	1
Punjab National Bank	http://www.netpnb.com/index.html	29	20	1
Syndicate Bank	http://www.syndicatebank.in	78	66	5
UCO Bank	http://www.ucobank.com	31	50	60
United Bank of India	www.unitedbankofindia.com English/HomePage.aspx	2	48	11
Union Bank of India	http://www.unionbankonline.co.in	5	58	1
Vijaya Bank	http://vijayabank.com/vijaya/vijaya	18	16	20

7 banks, namely State Bank of India, State Bank of Bikaner and Jaipur, State Bank of Hyderabad, State Bank of Mysore, State Bank of Patiala, State Bank of Travancore and Bank of Maharashtra had their websites without any accessibility errors. Banks like Bank of Baroda and Syndicate Bank showed the highest number of errors. Errors pose a serious threat as far as the accessibility by a visually impaired customer is concerned.

The Alerts are tolerable and they may or may not be accessibility issues, but typically indicate an area where accessibility is often an issue or where it may be made better. They should each be checked for possible issues. Amongst the Public sector Banks, Andhra Bank and Syndicate Bank recorded high alerts and amongst the private sector banks Kotak Mahindra Bank and Federal Bank recorded very high Alerts.

CONCLUSION

Inclusive Banking is the delivery of financial services at affordable costs to sections of disadvantaged and low income segments of society (Wikipedia). The Reserve Bank of India has issued guidelines to make banking facilities easily accessible to visually impaired customers. The guidelines advice the banks to offer all the services and facilities to this customer segment as they offer to the normal customers and thereby making inclusive banking mandatory for the Indian banks (RBI, 2008). Of all the services and facilities, online and mobile banking solutions provide the greatest challenge to the service providers (Vinod Kumar and Victor Anandkumar, 2012).

Online Banking services are provided by Banks to cover all the parts of the country and include all people. But the study showed that the websites of most of these Banks have accessibility issues – both real and possible (in the form of alerts). Among the Public sector banks whose websites were studied, seven of them were without any accessibility errors. All other banks had accessibility issues. And surprisingly all the private sector banks had accessibility errors. As a result, there is no difference between website accessibility of public and private sector banks.

In order to ensure inclusive banking, the websites of the banks should comply with the following:

- *Appropriate alternative text:* Appropriate alternative text must be used in place of images, image links, image maps, and image buttons.
- *Form labels:* Websites must have descriptive and informative form labels. They must ensure that all necessary information for completing that form element is available within the label.
- *Tables and table headers:* Every Table should have a very clear and informative header.
- *Logical heading structure:* All the headings must be ordered in a logical way.

- Descriptive and informative page titles.
- *Assistive Technology Compatibility:* Visually impaired customers use screen readers or other assistive technologies to access content through various senses or to modify content to be best perceivable to them. Therefore the Bank's websites should be compatible with these assistive technologies.
- Periodic reviews of their websites must be made for accessibility by visually challenged people.
- All the accessibility features should be periodically checked for accuracy.

REFERENCES

Buzzi, Maria Claudia, Buzzi, Marina, Leporini, Barbara and Akhter, Fahim (2009). Usability and Accessibility of eBay by Screen Reader, in A. Holzinger and K. Miesenberger (Eds.): Usability Symposium 2009, Lecture Notes in Computer Science 5889, pp. 500–510, Springer-Verlag Berlin Heidelberg.

Buzzi, Marina, Leporini, Barbara and Akhter, Fahim (2009). Usability and Accessibility of eBay by Screen Reader, Springer-Verlag Berlin Heidelberg, USAB 2009, LNCS 5889, pp. 500–510.

Christopher, G.C. Mike, L. Visit and Amy, W. (2006). A Logit Analysis of Electronic Banking in New Zealand. *International Journal of Bank Market*, 24: 360–383.

Fukuda, K., Saito, S., Takagi, H. and Asakawa, C. (2005). Proposing new metrics to evaluate web usability for the blind. In: CHI 2005 on Human factors in computing systems, pp. 1387–1390, ACM, New York.

International Standard Organization (ISO), ISO 9241–11: Ergonomic Requirements for Office Work with Visual Display Terminals (VDTs), Part 11: Guidance on Usability, 1e, International Organization for Standardization, Geneva, CH, 1998–03–15 (1998).

Kumar, Vinod and Anandkumar, Victor (2012). Inclusive Banking: A study on the visually challenged customers' perception of banking services in India, *Proceedings of the SIBR-Thammasat Conference on Interdisciplinary Business and Economics Research*, Vol. 1, Issue 1.

Kumar, Vinod, Maniraja and Anandkumar, Victor (2012). An empirical study on visually challenged customers' preference for mobile banking, *Proceedings of the SIBR-Thammasat Conference on Interdisciplinary Business and Economics Research*, Vol. 1, Issue 1.

Leporini, B. and Paternò, F. (2008). Applying web usability criteria for vision-impaired users: does it really improve task performance? *International Journal of Human-Computer Interaction (IJHCI)* 24(1), pp. 17–47.

Sekaran, U. (2003). *Research methods for business: A skill-building approach*, John Wiley and Sons, Singapore.

Takagi, H., Asakawa, C., Fukuda, K. and Maeda, J. (2004). Accessibility designer: Visualizing usability for the blind. In: *6th International ACM SIGACCESS Conference on Computers and Accessibility*, pp. 177–184.

Theofanos, M.F. and Redish, G. (2003). Bridging the gap: between accessibility and usability, Interaction 10(6), pp. 36–51.

Times of India (2007). "India has largest blind population". Retrieved on August 11, 2012 from: http://articles.timesofindia.indiatimes.com/2007-10-11/india/27977420_1_avoidable-blindness-ophthalmologists-eye-diseases

Wave (2012). "Index of WAVE Icons". Retrieved on August 10, 2012 from: http://wave.webaim.org/icons

Wikipedia. "Financial inclusion". Retrieved on August 12, 2012 from: http://en.wikipedia.org/wiki/Financial_inclusion

Wikipedia. "Web Accessibility". Retrieved on August 10, 2012 from: http://en.wikipedia.org/wiki/Web_accessibility

Shift from CRM to CMR for Performance Enhancement in Banking Sector

S.S. Bhushanam

Vignan's Nirula Institute, Vijayawada

ABSTRACT: *Executing Customer Relationship Management (CRM) for the banking industry involves many issues, including the use of unique processes and solutions. To be successful with CRM, banking organizations must define and develop business strategy as well as a supporting infrastructure for that strategy. Banking industry business has to learn how to segment, cross-sell, up-sell, and retain customers. Additionally, the users can monitor customer life-cycle trends to aid customer portfolio management with a customer equity assets management focus. This paper deals with the role of CRM in banking sector and the need for CRM to increase customer value. This paper explores the approaches to implementing CRM processes in the banking industry. It also highlights the major issues facing the industry in implementing such solutions and how these solutions can be used to increase effectiveness of CRM and to provide a better understanding of an organization's customer base. A shift is recommended from CMR to intelligent businesses thinking about the Customer Managed Relationship (CMR). It is about moving the mindset to the mentality that the customer knows what they want and you need to supply it on their terms.*

Keywords: Analytics, CRM, Business Strategy, Customer Centric, Value Addition.

INTRODUCTION

CRM is a business model that aligns product and sales strategies with customer requirements and preferences. Services are then provided in a timely manner using the channels that are preferred by the customers. Effective CRM starts by focusing on the development of business strategies and by aligning an organization to serve customers. These business strategies are then executed using CRM technology solutions. The most successful business strategies are developed only after an organization learns about customers' behavior patterns and attitudes. Behavior studies show what products or services have been purchased in the past and what products or services are currently being bought. Attitudes studies show what customers are thinking and feeling about future buying decisions. The importance of CRM and its potential is to help to acquire new customers retain existing ones and maximize their lifetime value. At this point, close relationship with customers will require a strong coordination between IT and marketing departments to provide a long-term retention of selected customers.

Uncovers Customers' Behavior Patterns

Uncovering customers' behavior patterns and attitudes involve collecting relevant transactional and survey data, placing the data into a data repository, and then applying analytical techniques. After the information is collected from the data, an actionable business plan can be developed to create the multi-channel customer contact strategies that offer the optimal products or services.

Sound Business Strategy

CRM is a sound business strategy to identify the bank's most profitable customers and prospects, and devotes time and attention to expanding account relationships with those customers. This can be achieved through individualized marketing, re-pricing, discretionary decision making, and customized service-by extracting valid, previously unknown and ultimately comprehensible and actionable knowledge from large databases. It is important that the client not the product is in the center, having the right offer for the right client, at the right time via the right channel. That will lead to improve the subsequent processes and support it with systems.

CUSTOMER RELATIONSHIP MANAGEMENT

CRM can be described from technological and relationship aspects. From marketing perspective emphasis is technological side of CRM while the others consider IT perspective of CRM. Consequently, IT and marketing departments must work closely to implement CRM efficiently. For implementation of CRM in banking sector, focus is on the evaluation of the critical satisfaction dimensions and the determination of customer groups with distinctive preferences and expectations Customer relationships of new technology-based firms, managing relationships with their customers is critical to the firm's long-term success. Customer relationship management based on social exchange significantly assists the firm in developing collaborative, cooperative and profitable long-term relationships. Customized learning approach helps better understanding of customers and the clues for improving customer relationships based on different sources of web customer data. Three main issues can enable the development of CRM in banking sector. They are:

- organizational issues of culture and communication;
- management metrics;
- cross-functional integration between marketing and IT.

CRM OBJECTIVES IN BANKING SECTOR

The objectives of CRM are to helps business to use technology and human resources gain insight into the behavior of customers and the value of those customers. A business can: provide better customer service, make call centers more efficient, cross sell products more effectively, help sales staff close deals faster, simplify marketing and sales processes, discover new customers, and increase customer revenues. It doesn't happen by simply buying software and installing it. For CRM to be truly effective an organization must first decide what kind of customer information it is looking for and it must decide what it intends to do with that information. Next, the organization must look into all of the different ways information about customers comes into a business, where and how this data is stored and how it is currently used.

Importance of CRM for Banking

Benefits for banks by deploying CRM solutions depend on the positioning and focus of a bank. If operational excellence is your key-focus and not customer intimacy, the choices you make in terms of investments in CRM will be completely different. In strategic terms, ABN AMRO has a strong ambition to create value for clients by offering high-quality financial solutions that best meet their current needs and long-term goals. Customer relationship management is a broad approach for creating, maintaining and expanding customer relationships. The concept of product life cycle is giving way to the concept of customer life cycle focusing on the development of products and services that anticipate the future need of the existing customers and creating additional services that extend existing customer relationships beyond transactions.

Customer Centric Banking

Further, customer centric banking means a new way of thinking. Banks need to focus on relationship banking rather than traditional transaction banking. In the world of margin pressure, being a product specialist is hard, so banks need to make advice rather than product price as the basis of the added value in banking. In this situation, CRM is a key because the value of retail banking lies in distribution. Knowing the client is the first requirement of a retailer. It protects business, helps penetrate growth markets.

CRM for Value Addition

It is a strategy integrated in the business model of the banks and clearly oriented to value generation. CRM is a key element of differentiation that lets the bank develops its customer base and sales capacity. A well thought out CRM strategy lets them improve the sales experience of the customer; develop the potential value for customers; increase sales, productivity and efficiency, and create personalized one-to-one service.

C—from Customer to Collaborative

CRM is about enterprises collaborating across the customer value chain to develop and implement solutions that better meet the evolving preferences of individual customer groups. The C in CRM therefore has now evolved from 'Customer' to "Collaborative". The core of CRM requires various entities in a bank to work collaboratively to define and realize a series of business principles which are essential to establish customer-centric organizations. Essentially this means collaboration across those entities that deal with Acquisition (sales and marketing/distribution), Transactions (fulfillment) and servicing (customer service). Using the collaborative approach, leading banks are today trying to achieve a state where the customers become less aware of marketing and selling and feel a constant level of personalized, consistent, high quality service

Technology Maturity, Impact on Banks

Technology has been the nucleus of CRM strategies. Now technology is evolving to a commodity piece within CRM strategies. Having active multi-channel customers is not in "the future" anymore, it is a fact of life today. Investing in multi-channel capabilities is not a choice anymore, it's a must. The benefits of real time are there, but the costs are high to attain these benefits. Huge amounts of data are being gathered by banks, the intelligent deployment in customer related processes is where a lot of banks are struggling. The technology solutions available to banks will continue to improve with a noticeable shift towards integrated, broad technology solutions designed to ease enterprise integration requirements.

CRM COMPONENTS

There is an evolutionary approach to CRM. This approach begins with business strategy development. Next, a data infrastructure is created that supports customer interactions. Then, a technology infrastructure is designed to produce CRM results. Finally, customer communication channel strategies are created, and strategy execution technology is used to create an on-going dialog with the customers.

STRATEGY

CRM is a business strategy than anything else—not just technology, not just analytics, major banks have invested heavily in technology and infrastructure in this area, but hardly any of them have been successful in actually getting it effective. Neither has the customer felt a real difference nor has it contributed to higher ROI. Optimizing every customer contact by effectively creating value for both clients and one's business, using customer knowledge, is the main differentiator compared to non-CRM focused companies.

Business Strategy Development

Customer-focused organizations develop business strategies that use CRM to identify the needs and the "hurt points" of existing customers. Managing customer relationships promote growth by selling products and services to those customers who are most likely to buy, while wasting less time and resources trying to sell to those customers who are less likely to buy. Customers will pay more for a product or service if they have a long-standing relationship with a provider that they believe is responsive to their needs. Successful customer initiatives often include one or more of the following characteristics: they are affordable, they help companies generate Return on Investment through higher profit margins, and they improve operational and administrative efficiency.

Product versus Customer-Centric Business Strategy

Traditionally, banking sector is organized around product-centered and function-centered models rather than a customer-centered model. By becoming truly customer-centered, a bank can achieve the following benefits:

- higher returns on invested capital;
- more profitable customers
- lower capital costs
- larger investment opportunities.

CRM CHALLENGES TO BANKING

The major challenges in designing and implementing CRM strategies in banking sector and their interpretations leading to possible solutions are presented below.

Knowledge about the Clients

Knowing the client and acting on that information in every contact is essential in achieving the benefits. It means, aim to be "personal in every channel" and use CRM to create more and more clients that consider us to be their primary bank. Banks must achieve to improve knowledge about the clients, improve active customer contact, improve the satisfaction of the clients and improve the return per client.

Customer's Demands and Consequences

The main points that describe impact on CRM are: customer demand for sophistication and multichannel approach and orientation. Consequently there are some steps that banks should take to benefit from CRM:

- change their commercial product vision to a customer centric vision;
- effectively integrate different channels;
- ensure data quality and deploy complex marketing strategies.

Focus on Advisory Services

With increasing focus on advisory services, the role of CRM in banks is now more critical and pivotal than ever before. The benefits that banks hope to achieve through deploying CRM solutions will be to arrive at satisfactory, measurable answers to questions such as 'how profitable is the customer, 'which products/services does the customer require; when, where and through which channel and 'what risks does the customer present to the bank.

CRM is Critical in Banking

CRM is not technology, it is business. CRM has to improve the requirement that client is with the bank making the contact more efficient and more satisfactory. So banks have to improve the relationship skills of the advisors. Few years ago, banks thought, CRM should be managed within the technology and systems departments. Now it is a critical part of the agenda of business managers. Since banks pursue high growth strategies, expanding their franchises into growth segments, and are aware of the winning concept of the multi-channel and multi-price approach, CRM becomes key and critical.

Key Aspects for Deploying CRM Solutions

Whether CRM only adds to costs or generates revenues is not a technological but a commercial issue. If, marketing and sales do not adopt the CRM challenge, CRM will not succeed. It requires intense training, a dialogue between marketing, technology departments and all channels; it requires a proactive approach towards using customer intelligence on a continuous basis. Business requirements and targets have to be defined; technology has to make the solution, not the other way round. CRM does not solve all the problems a bank has, so first analyze the problems, and the possible impact of CRM, and then prioritize.

NEW SYSTEMS FOR FURTHER ENHANCEMENT

Fairly recent new systems that are considered that can make better value additions for CRM practices are: (A) Customer Managed Relations (CMR); (B) Customer Life Cycle Management; (C) Analytical CRM. They are presented here.

(A) Customer Managed Relations (CMR)

CRM strategy is called for to both buy time before new product offerings could be sourced and offered and to move significantly ahead of the competition. What is needed is a strategy involving all aspects of the company, including database structure, creative work and staff training that would reduce potential defections, increase pace and build a database for future activity. The aim is to reward those customers and to react swiftly to customer needs. To turn Customer Relationship Management (CRM) into Customer Managed Relations (CMR) is about power of what customers want. A shift is recommended from CRM to CMR, an intelligent businesses thinking. It is about moving the mindset to the condition that the customer knows what they want and you need to supply, on their terms. CMR is a relationship in which a business uses a methodology, to encourage the customer to control access to information and ordering. CMR can be viewed as an alternative to or as a possible approach to include in CRM.

Three Aspects of CMR

According to industry view, there are three aspects of CMR. The first is that customers should own their own information including their profile, transaction history, and any inferred information and even behavior. The second aspect is that customers should have access to this information across all departments. The third aspect is that the entire system should be designed with the customer's needs and feelings having priority. CMR allows a customer to define how they communicate with the company, what services or products they will purchase, and how they will pay for them. CMR is an attempt by enterprises to change with the times by addressing customer demand for more control.

Benefits that CMR Generates

Approaches of creating CMR have the objectives as:

- Discover the customer;
- Incentives and Reward the customer;
- Find more best customers through new customer acquisition;
- Data mine the customer case to make relevant product offerings;
- Utilize the technology to create customer value against rising competition in the market.

CMR generates major benefits as:

- It is easier to implement because the customer is doing the complex stuff;
- It creates a lock—in since customers having invested their data with you will not move easily;
- It allows you to move faster than your competitor since you are in a trusted relationship with your customer.

Belief in Customer's Expectations

Belief should be that customer's expectations must be met or exceeded in order for their experience to be positive. For that to happen, one must investigate all angles of customer's potential needs and plan responses accordingly. This extra planning ensures positive customer interaction, and the experience shapes customer behavior, transforms expectations into successful interactions and above all, CMR enhances one's competitive advantage.

(B) Customer Life Cycle Management (CLM)

CLM is the measurement of multiple customer related metrics, which, when analyzed for a period of time, indicate performance of a business. The overall scope of the CLM implementation process encompasses all domains or departments of an organization, which generally brings all sources of static and dynamic data, marketing processes, and value added services to a unified decision supporting platform through iterative phases of customer acquisition, retention, cross and up-selling, and lapsed customer win-back CLM provides insights and tools to help companies increase the satisfaction—and value—of their customers. CLM can enable powerful customer interaction strategies that create significant business growth and profitability. It focuses on four primary activities:

1. Driving customer lifetime value through deep analytics.
2. Optimizing loyalty program.
3. Implementing front-line transformational change.
4. Improving the customer experience.

(C) Analytical CRM for Integrated Strength

Analytical customer relationship is a decision support system that is targeted to better understanding and capitalize upon their customer needs, the company's interactions with the customer, and the customer buying cycle. Each bank has to build its own definition of Analytical CRM, based upon the prioritized needs of the users. This helps in evaluating systems, architectures, and tools in a timely and cost effective fashion.

Analytical CRM deals with all the operations and processes that do not directly deal with customers. Unlike from operational CRM, where automation of marketing, sales-force and services are done, Analytical CRM is designed to analyze deeply the customer's information and data and disclose the essential intension of customers' behavior on which capitalization can be done by the organization. Primary goal of analytical CRM is to develop, support and enhance the decision making capability of an organization by determining strong patterns and predictions in customer data and information which are gathered from different operational CRM systems.

Key Features of Analytical CRM

Seizing all the relevant and essential information of customers:

- Collaboratively integrating and inheriting all this data into a central repository knowledge base;
- Determining inclusive set of rules and analytical methods to optimize relationship with customers;
- Implementing the results to enhance the efficiency of CRM system and processes;
- Combine and integrate the values of customers with strategic business management of organization.

Advantages of Analytical CRM

Leads in making more profitable customer base by providing high value services:

- Helps in retaining profitable customers through sophisticated analysis and making new customers;
- Helps in addressing individual customer's needs and efficiently improving the relationships;
- Improves customer satisfaction and loyalty.

Components of Analytical CRM

The essential results produced by Analytical CRM system could diversely help the organization to tackle customers' based on values; helps in determining prioritize which customer is best tò invest in. The components are:

- *Customer Analytics:* To analyze customer knowledge base;
- *Marketing Analytics:* To discover new market opportunities and seeks their potential values;
- *Sales Analytics:* Provides environment to plan, simulate and predict sales volumes;
- *Service Analytics:* Enhances the services of customer satisfaction, quality and cost;
- *Channel Analytics:* To determine customer behavior on channel preferences, like web channel.

FUTURE OF CRM IN BANKING

Huge growth of customer relationship management is predicted in the banking sector over the next few years. Banks are aiming to increase customer profitability with customer retention.

CRM for Sound Business Strategy

It is about identifying the profitable customers, prospects, expanding account relationships. It is through individualized marketing, pricing, discretionary decision making; having and acting upon deeper knowledge about the customer, ensure that the customer gets what he wishes from service provider and understand when they are not satisfied.

Create Trust

CRM in banking industry entirely different from other sectors, because banking industry purely related to financial services, which needs to create the trust among the people. Establishing customer care support during on and off official hours, making timely information about all components, products, services and transactions to keep regular relationship with customers.

Shift from Bank Centric to Customer Centric Activities

There is a shift from bank centric activities to customer centric activities that are being opted. Much innovative strategies have to be deployed; it is the time for taking ideas from customers to enrich its service.

Steps to Follow

The steps to minimize the work regarding adoption of CRM strategy are:

- Identification of proper CRM initiatives;
- Implementing adequate technologies in order to assist CRM initiative;
- Setting standards, targets for each initiative and each person involved in that circle;
- Evaluating actual performance with the standard or benchmark;
- Taking corrective actions to improve deviations.

CONCLUSION

Effective CRM requires more than just a software application. It requires a business strategy. That business strategy should enable organizational structures to support a customer-centered business model as well as a product centered and function-centered model. It has to provide a mechanism to develop data that supports the customer-centered model and incorporate a technology infrastructure that optimizes customer relationships. CRM goes beyond the transactional exchange and enables the marketer to estimate the customer's sentiments and buying intentions so that the customers can be provided with products and services before they starts demanding. A section of the industry has an apprehension that

CRM model may not be generating desired level of results. It may be that customers don't want to be managed; Customers want to manage themselves. In this context the recommendations of Customer Relationship Management (CRM) can be considered to generate value addition.

REFERENCES

Berry, M.J.A. and Linoff, G.S. (2000). Mastering Data Mining: The Art and Science of Customer Relationship Management, John Wiley and Sons, Inc.

Chaudhry, Aslam, SAS Institute Inc., Cary, NC CRM: Making it Simple for the Banking Industry.

Colvin, Geoffrey and Selden, Larry (2003). Angel Customers and Demon Customers, Portfolio NY.

*Customer Relationship Management for Performance Enhancement in Banking Sector (*Semih OnutIbrahim ErdemYildiz, Technical University Department of Industrial Engineering Yildiz, 80750, Istanbul, Turkey @yildiz.edu.tr, erdem@yildiz.edu.tr, *Bora Hosver Garanti Bank Customer Relationship and Marketing Department No. 63, Maslak, 80670, Istanbul, Turkey borah@garanti.com.tr)

Customer Satisfaction Measurement in the Private Bank Sector, *European Journal of Operational Research*, 347–360.

Griffin, Jill and Lowenstein, Michael W. (2001). Customer Win back—How to Recapture Lost Customers and Keep Them Loyal JOSSY-BASS. San Francisco, CA.

Industry Round Table Finacle (2009). Infosys Technologies Limited, Electronics City, Bangalore (*Radi Badidi Vice President Marketing Intelligence/CRM ABN AMRO Bank, Netherlands; *Jose Olalla Hevia Director of Commercial Development, Retail Banking Spain and Portugal, Banco Bilbao; *Michael Otto Head of CRM at Erste Bank, Austria; *Gopal Sondur Group Head, Products and Strategy, Finacle, Infosys tech Ltd.).

Peppers and Rogers Group (2003). Peppers and Rogers Group white paper. CRM in a Down Economy Re-visited-Weathering the Economic Storm through Customer Relationship Strategies.

Smith, Sylvana (2003). SAS Institute white paper. SAS® Banking Intelligence Solutions for Customer Relationship Management.

Author Index